Building English Skills

Orange Level
Revised Edition

Building English Skills

Purple Level

Yellow Level

Blue Level

ORANGE LEVEL

Green Level

Red Level

Gold Level

Silver Level

Aqua Level

Brown Level

Plum Level

Pink Level

Cherry Level (K)

THE McDOUGAL, LITTELL ENGLISH PROGRAM

Building English Skills

Orange Level
Revised Edition

Joy Littell, EDITORIAL DIRECTOR

McDougal, Littell & Company
Evanston, Illinois
Sacramento, California

Prepared by the Staff of
THE WRITING IMPROVEMENT PROJECT

Joy Littell, Editorial Director, McDougal, Littell & Company

J. A. Christensen, East High School, Salt Lake City, Utah

Stephen G. Ham, New Trier Township High School East, Winnetka, Illinois

Patricia Phelan, Chairperson, English Department, Hale Jr. High School, San Diego, California

Marcia Baldwin Whipps, East High School, Salt Lake City, Utah

The Staff wishes to thank the more than 1500 students who contributed samples of their writing for analysis.

Acknowledgments: See page 536.

ISBN: 0–88343–874–7

Copyright © 1981 by McDougal, Littell & Company
Box 1667, Evanston, Illinois 60204
All rights reserved. Printed in the United States of America

Chapters 1 and 3 contain, in revised form, some materials that appeared originally in *English Arts and Skills, Grade 9,* by Ronald J. Wilkins et al, copyright © 1965, 1961 by The Macmillan Company. Used by arrangement.

Contents

Chapter 1 Building Your Vocabulary   1

Part 1   **Learning Word Meanings from Context**   2

Definition or Restatement   2
Example   4
Comparison, Contrast   5

Part 2   **Inferring Word Meanings**   9

Inference Based on the Main Idea   9
Inference Based on Stated Details   10
Inference Based on Cause and Effect   11
Inference Based on Implied Comparison   11
Inference Based on Implied Contrast   11

Part 3   **The Multiple Meanings of Words**   13

Part 4   **Gaining Precision in the Use of Words**   16

Using Synonyms   16
Using Antonyms   19

Chapter 2 Using the Senses in Writing   27

Part 1   **The Sense of Sight**   28

Part 2   **The Sense of Hearing**   36

Part 3   **The Sense of Touch**   40

Part 4   **The Sense of Taste**   44

Part 5   **The Sense of Smell**   47

Part 6   **All of the Senses Working Together**   50

Chapter 3 Improving Your Sentences   53

Part 1   **Avoiding Empty Sentences**   54

Sentences That Repeat an Idea   54
Unsupported Statements   56

| Part 2 | **Avoiding Padded Sentences** | 58 |

Taking Out the Padding   58
Reducing Clauses to Phrases   59

| Part 3 | **Avoiding Overloaded Sentences** | 62 |

| Part 4 | **Writing Sentences That Make Sense** | 64 |

Making Sure That the Verb Has a Subject   64
Avoiding a Prepositional Phrase as Subject   65
Avoiding Faulty Comparisons   65
Making Sure Necessary Words Are Included   66

| Part 5 | **Varying Your Sentence Beginnings** | 68 |

Chapter 4 The Process of Writing 75

| Part 1 | **Pre-Writing** | 76 |

| Part 2 | **Writing the First Draft** | 78 |

| Part 3 | **Rewriting, or Revising** | 78 |

GUIDELINES FOR THE PROCESS OF WRITING   81

Chapter 5 Writing Effective Paragraphs 83

| Part 1 | **What Is a Paragraph?** | 83 |

| Part 2 | **Paragraph Unity** | 89 |

| Part 3 | **The Topic Sentence** | 93 |

| Part 4 | **Developing the Paragraph** | 100 |

Using Facts or Statistics   100
Using Specific Examples   103
Using an Incident or an Anecdote   105
Using Comparisons or Contrasts   106

Chapter 6 Types of Paragraphs 111

| Part 1 | **The Descriptive Paragraph** | 111 |

Selecting Details   112
Organizing a Descriptive Paragraph   112

Using Space Words and Phrases   112
Ways of Organizing a Descriptive Paragraph   113
Describing a Person   115
Appealing to the Senses   117

Part 2   **The Explanatory Paragraph**   **121**

Giving Instructions   121
Developing an Explanatory Paragraph   122

Part 3   **The Narrative Paragraph**   **126**

Chronological Order   127
Using Time Words and Phrases   127
The Topic Sentence   128

CHECKLIST FOR WRITING PARAGRAPHS   131

Chapter 7   Writing a Composition   **133**

Part 1   **Defining a Composition**   **133**

Part 2   **Deciding on a Subject**   **136**

Subjects Based on First-Hand Experiences   136
Subjects Based on Learned Information   138
Subjects Based on Imagination   139

Part 3   **Narrowing the Subject**   **142**

Part 4   **Deciding on the Audience and the Purpose**   **144**

Part 5   **Planning the Composition**   **146**

Putting Down Ideas   146
Organizing the Ideas   147
Developing a Working Outline   150
Making a Final Outline   151

Part 6   **Writing the Composition**   **152**

The Body   155
Achieving Unity   157
The Conclusion   162
Rewriting, or Revising   163
Proofreading   164

CHECKLIST FOR WRITING COMPOSITIONS   165

Chapter 8 Types of Compositions 167

Part 1 The Descriptive Composition 167

Point of View 168
Unity 169
Coherence 169
Emphasis 170
Studying a Descriptive Composition 170

Part 2 The Explanatory Composition 172

Part 3 The Narrative Composition 176

Chapter 9 Writing Letters 181

Part 1 Addressing the Envelope 182

Part 2 Writing Informal Notes 186

Part 3 Writing Friendly Letters 189

Part 4 Writing Business Letters 193

Using the Proper Form 193
Being Brief and Specific 199
Types of Business Letters 201
Knowing Where and to Whom To Write 205

Chapter 10 Using the Library 209

Part 1 How Books Are Classified and Arranged 210

The Classification of Books 210
Arrangement of Books on the Shelves 212

Part 2 Using the Card Catalog 213

Card Information 215
Cross Reference Cards 216
Guide Cards 217

Part 3 Using Reference Works 219

Chapter 11 Giving a Talk 229

Part 1 **Giving Informal Talks** 229

Preparing Your Talk 230
Presenting Your Talk 230
Types of Informal Talks 231

Part 2 **Giving Formal Talks** 235

Selecting a Topic 236
Defining Your Purpose 237
Determining Your Thesis 238
Gathering Your Material 239
Organizing Your Material 240
Delivering Your Talk 243

Grammar, Usage, and Mechanics

Section 1 The Sentence and Its Parts 247

Part 1 **The Complete Sentence** 248

Part 2 **The Subject and the Predicate** 249

Part 3 **Simple Subjects and Verbs** 251

Part 4 **The Parts of a Verb** 254

Part 5 **Subjects in Unusual Positions** 255

Sentences Beginning with *There* 256
Other Sentences with Unusual Order 257
Sentences Giving Commands 258

Part 6 **Objects of Verbs** 260

Direct Objects 260
Transitive or Intransitive? 261
Indirect Objects 262

Part 7 **Linking Verbs and Predicate Words** 264

Part 8 **Compound Parts in a Sentence** 268

Part 9 **Kinds of Sentences** 271

Part 10 **Basic Sentence Patterns** 272

Additional Exercises 275

Section 2 **Using Complete Sentences** 279

Part 1 **What Is a Sentence Fragment?** 280

Part 2 **What Is a Run-on Sentence?** 282

Additional Exercises 284

Section 3 **Using Nouns** 286

Part 1 **What Are Nouns?** 287

Part 2 **How Are Nouns Used?** 289

Nouns Used as Subjects 289
Nouns Used as Direct Objects 290
Nouns Used as Indirect Objects 291
Nouns Used as Predicate Words 293

Part 3 **The Plurals of Nouns** 294

Part 4 **The Possessives of Nouns** 296

Additional Exercises 298

Section 4 **Using Pronouns** 301

Part 1 **Personal Pronouns** 302

Part 2 **The Forms of Pronouns** 303

The Subject Form of Pronouns 305
The Object Form of Pronouns 306
The Possessive Form of Pronouns 307

Part 3 **Pronouns in Compound Constructions** 309

Part 4 **Pronouns and Antecedents** 310

Part 5 **Compound Personal Pronouns** 312

Part 6 **Demonstrative Pronouns** 313

Part 7 **Interrogative Pronouns** 314

Part 8 **Indefinite Pronouns** 315

Part 9 **Special Problems with Pronouns** 317

Contractions and Possessive Pronouns 317
Who and *Whom* 319
We and *Us* with Nouns 320
Them and *Those* 320

Additional Exercises 322

Section 5 Using Verbs 325

Part 1 **What Is a Verb?** 326

Action Verbs 326
Linking Verbs 326
Transitive and Intransitive Verbs 327

Part 2 **The Parts of a Verb** 329

Part 3 **Verb Tenses** 330

Part 4 **The Principal Parts of a Verb** 333

Part 5 **Irregular Verbs** 334

Part 6 **Active and Passive Verbs** 341

Additional Exercises 343

Section 6 Using Modifiers 346

Part 1 **Using Adjectives** 347

Proper Adjectives 347
Predicate Adjectives 348
Articles 348

Part 2 **Adjectives in Comparisons** 350

The Comparative 351
The Superlative 351
Irregular Comparisons 353

Part 3   **Using Adverbs**   **354**

    Using Adverbs with Verbs   354
    Using Adverbs with Adjectives and Other Verbs   355
    Forming Adverbs   355

Part 4   **Adverbs in Comparisons**   **358**

    The Comparative   358
    The Superlative   359
    Irregular Comparisons   359

Part 5   **Adjective or Adverb?**   **360**

Part 6   **Troublesome Modifiers**   **364**

    Them and *Those*   364
    Here and *There*   364
    Kind and *Sort*   364
    Good and *Well*   365
    The Double Negative   365

Additional Exercises   368

Section 7   **Using Prepositions and Conjunctions**   **372**

Part 1   **What Are Prepositions?**   **373**

    Words Often Used as Prepositions   374
    Preposition or Adverb?   375

Part 2   **Prepositional Phrases as Modifiers**   **376**

Part 3   **Conjunctions**   **379**

    Coordinating Conjunctions   380
    Correlative Conjunctions   381

Additional Exercises   383

Section 8   **Review of Parts of Speech**   **385**

Part 1   **The Parts of Speech**   **385**

    What Is an Interjection?   386

Part 2 **Using Words as Different Parts of Speech** 387

Additional Exercises 390

Section 9 **Using Verbals** 392

Part 1 **Gerunds** 393

The Gerund Phrase 393

Part 2 **Participles** 396

The Participial Phrase 397
Gerund or Participle? 399

Part 3 **Infinitives** 400

The Infinitive Phrase 401
Uses of the Infinitive Phrase 401
The Split Infinitive 402

Part 4 **A Review of Verbals** 404

Additional Exercises 407

Section 10 **Making Subjects and Verbs Agree** 409

Part 1 **Making Subjects and Verbs Agree in Number** 409

Part 2 **Compound Subjects** 412

Part 3 **Indefinite Pronouns** 413

Part 4 **Other Problems of Agreement** 415

Doesn't and Don't Used with Pronouns 415
Sentences Beginning with There 415

Additional Exercises 417

Section 11 **Using Compound and Complex Sentences** 420

Part 1 **Review of the Sentence** 421

Compound Parts in a Sentence 421
The Simple Sentence 422

Part 2   **The Compound Sentence**   **423**

Compound Sentence or Compound Predicate?   426
Punctuating Compound Sentences   428

Part 3   **The Complex Sentence**   **431**

Clause or Phrase?   432
Subordinate Clauses   432
Definition of the Complex Sentence   434

Part 4   **Adverb Clauses**   **435**

Part 5   **Adjective Clauses**   **437**

Relative Pronouns   438

Part 6   **Noun Clauses**   **441**

Uses of Noun Clauses   441

Part 7   **A Review of Subordinate Clauses**   **443**

Part 8   **Clauses as Sentence Fragments**   **445**

Part 9   **Compound-Complex Sentences**   **446**

Part 10   **A Review of Sentences**   **448**

Additional Exercises   451

Section 12   **The Right Word**   **455**

Part 1   **Standard and Nonstandard English**   **455**

Part 2   **Formal and Informal English**   **456**

Part 3   **Other Types of Language**   **457**

Part 4   **Words Often Confused**   **457**

Part 5   **Troublesome Verbs**   **461**

Bring and *Take, Learn* and *Teach*   461
Let and *Leave, Lie* and *Lay, May* and *Can*   462
Rise and *Raise, Sit* and *Set*   463

Part 6   **Usage Problems**   **464**

Additional Exercises   469

Section 13 Capitalization 471

Proper Nouns and Adjectives 471

Names of People 472
Family Relationships 473
The Pronoun *I* 473
The Supreme Being and Sacred Writings 473
Geographical Names 474
Directions and Sections 475
Names of Organizations and Institutions 477
Events, Documents, and Periods of Time 477
Months, Days, and Holidays 478
Races, Languages, Nationalities, Religions 478
School Subjects 478
Ships, Trains, Airplanes, Automobiles 478
B.C., A.D. 479

First Words 480

Sentences and Poetry 480
Quotations 480
Letter Parts 481
Outlines 481
Titles 481

Additional Exercises 484

Section 14 Punctuation 486

End Marks 486

The Period 487
The Question Mark 488
The Exclamation Point 488

The Comma 490

Using Commas in a Series 490
Using Commas with Introductory Words 492
Using Commas with Interrupters 492
Using Commas with Nouns of Direct Address 494
Using Commas with Appositives 494
Using Commas with Quotations 495
Using Commas in Compound Sentences 495
Using Commas in Dates 497
Using Commas in Place Names 497

Using Commas in Letters   498
Using Commas with Nonrestrictive Clauses   498
Using Commas To Avoid Confusion   499

The Semicolon   **501**

The Colon   **502**

The Dash   **504**

The Hyphen   **505**

The Apostrophe   **507**

Quotation Marks   **509**

Additional Exercises   515

Section 15   Spelling   518

How To Improve Your Spelling   **519**

How To Spell a Particular Word Correctly   **519**

Spelling Rules   **520**

Adding Prefixes   520
Suffixes with Silent *e*   520
Suffixes and Final *y*   521
Adding the Suffixes -*ness* and -*ly*   522
Doubling the Final Consonant   522
Words with the "Seed" Sound   523
Words with *ie* and *ei*   524

Additional Exercises   525

A List of Commonly Misspelled Words   527

Section 16   The Correct Form for Writing   529

Guidelines for Clear Writing   **530**

Acceptable Form   **531**

Writing Numbers   **532**

Using Abbreviations   **534**

The Composition Chapters (First half of text)

Vocabulary Development. Chapter 1 emphasizes *learning word meanings from context, inferring word meanings, multiple meanings,* and *the precise use of words.* An adequate vocabulary, and the ability to use synonyms precisely, are prerequisites to good writing.

Using the Senses. Chapter 2 creates an awareness of the five senses as a way of enriching writing.

Sentence Improvement. Chapter 3 provides an intensive program for sentence improvement based on a study of over 3000 student themes. This program is based on the belief that *the important problems of writing begin at the level of the sentence.* Some of these problems involve errors in grammar, but many of them are problems of meaning and sense. In each book, a chapter is devoted to those sentences which, though grammatically correct, are nonetheless unsatisfactory. In this book, for example, Chapter 3 deals with empty sentences, the circular sentences that say nothing (pages 54–58); it also deals with overloaded sentences, the sentences that contain too many ideas (pages 62–63).

The Process of Writing. Chapter 4 analyzes the three major steps in writing: *pre-writing; writing the first draft;* and *rewriting, or revising,* which includes proofreading.

The Paragraph. Chapters 5 and 6 comprise an intensive study of the paragraph. Chapter 5 provides guided opportunities to write expository paragraphs developed by various methods: using facts or statistics, using specific examples, using an incident or an anecdote, and using comparison or contrast. Chapter 6 treats in detail the descriptive paragraph, the explanatory paragraph, and the narrative paragraph. Both chapters provide a wealth of first-rate models, along with helpful analysis.

The Composition. Chapter 7 provides a clear, workable blueprint for an expository composition. Chapter 8 deals with descriptive, explanatory, and narrative compositions.

Writing Letters. Chapter 9 provides help in writing informal letters. It also presents the proper forms for business letters and discusses various types of letters such as requests for information, letters of order, and letters of complaint.

Grammar, Usage, and Mechanics (Second half of text)

The second half of the text consists of 16 numbered Sections dealing with grammar, usage, and the mechanics of writing (capitalization, punctuation, spelling, and the correct form of writing).

The text explains each topic or concept fully, then follows with examples, and where appropriate, with the definition or generalization printed in boldface type. There are abundant exercises on each topic, and pages of additional exercises at the end of each Section.

Chapter 1

Building Your Vocabulary

Why does this English book begin with a chapter on building your vocabulary? It begins this way because your success in school and work will depend to a great extent on your knowledge of words. Words are tools that you use in reading, writing, speaking, and listening. They are the tools that you will use in mastering other subjects—history, science, foreign languages, and so on.

Studies have shown that the larger your vocabulary is, the greater your chances are for success in school and in later life. If you study this chapter seriously, you will indeed enlarge your vocabulary. More importantly, you will acquire the *power* to add to your supply of words.

This chapter will show you how to unlock the meanings of unfamiliar words by seeing how they are used. It will also show you how to use a dictionary to find the exact word you are looking for.

With a large vocabulary at your command, you will be able to master your school subjects more quickly and easily. You will also be able to express your thoughts and feelings more precisely.

Part 1 Learning Word Meanings from Context

During your study of this chapter, you will learn several ways to find out the meanings of unfamiliar words. The meaning of a word is determined by the *context* in which it is used. The **context** of a word is the sentence or group of sentences in which the word appears. Often the context of an unfamiliar word will help you determine meaning.

From books or television programs, you know that a detective who is called to the scene of a crime examines the surrounding territory for evidence that might help to solve the crime. In much the same way, you can often learn the meaning of an unfamiliar word by examining the "surrounding territory"—the *context* in which the word is used. This examination will frequently give you some clue to help you unlock the meaning of the unknown word.

Several types of context clues can help you discover the meaning of an unfamiliar word. The most common types are these:

1. Definition or restatement
2. Example
3. Comparison
4. Contrast

Once you have learned to use these clues, you can unlock the meanings of many unfamiliar words.

Definition or Restatement

Sometimes a writer will reveal the meaning of a word by defining it for you. This type of clue is the easiest to detect. Study the following example.

> The long climb up the steep cliff was a *grueling* experience— one that left us utterly exhausted.

According to the dictionary, *grueling* means "very tiring, exhausting." Notice that the phrase following the dash is nearly the same as the dictionary definition.

Here is another example.

> Howard Hughes spent the last few years of his life *secluded* in hotel suites, shut off from personal contact with even his closest associates.

Even if you do not know the word *secluded*, the context of the passage points to the words "shut off from." One dictionary definition for this word is "barred or shut off from the view of or relations with others." Thus the context provides a definition of the word *secluded*.

The most obvious context clue in this category is the **appositive,** a restatement of the same idea in other words. Here is an example of this type of restatement.

> The directors of the Bay City Zoo have announced the purchase of a pair of *quetsals*, crested birds native to Central America.

Without the appositive phrase "crested birds native to Central America," you might not know whether quetsals were animals or vending machines.

Here is another example of an appositive.

> Uncle Ivan is very fond of *kohlrabi*, a vegetable related to the cabbage.

For people unfamiliar with kohlrabi, the appositive phrase "a vegetable related to the cabbage" provides a context clue essential to unlocking the meaning of the word.

By skillful use of the context clue of Definition or Restatement, you will be able to unlock the meanings of many unfamiliar words quickly and easily.

Example

Context can also help to unlock the meaning of an unfamiliar word by giving one or more examples. When several examples are cited, they achieve a "snowball" effect; that is, they pile up so that, with a little thought, you can make a guess at the meaning of the word. In this type of clue, watch for certain "key" words that will help you unlock the meaning of the unfamiliar word.

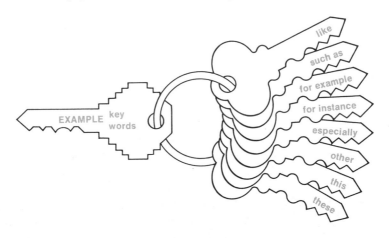

Be alert for key words in the following example.

> A small museum near Vicksburg, Mississippi, contains some excellent examples of Civil War *memorabilia*, such as flags, cannonballs, maps, guns, photographs, and Union and Confederate uniforms.

In this example, several clues help you determine the meaning of *memorabilia*. The word *examples*, the key words *such as*, and the list of examples all help you understand the meaning of *memorabilia*—"a collection of things worth remembering."

Here is another example.

> The reading teacher must be prepared to deal with *dyslexia* and other reading problems.

The skillful reader can use the key word *other* to help unlock the meaning of *dyslexia*—"a type of reading problem."

Comparison

A third very effective type of context clue is comparison. In this type of clue, the writer compares the unfamiliar word with other, more familiar, words. By paying close attention to these comparisons, you can unlock the meanings of many unfamiliar words.

Certain key words can help you determine the meaning of an unfamiliar word when you use the comparison context clue.

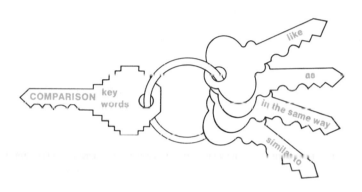

Note how the use of a key word in the following example helps you understand the meaning of the word *dromedary*.

> The *dromedary*, like all other desert animals, can go for long periods of time without drinking water.

Even though the context does not fully reveal that the dromedary is a type of camel, the word *like* helps to point out the dromedary as a type of desert animal. By comparing the unfamiliar word to something more familiar, the writer gives you a key to help unlock the meaning of the unfamiliar word.

Contrast

By contrasting an unfamiliar word with something familiar, the writer of a passage gives you a valuable type of context clue.

Here again, certain key words will help you determine the meaning of the unknown word.

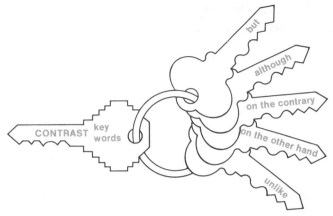

The contrast in the following example helps to make clearer the meaning of the word *archaeologist*.

The *archaeologist*, unlike many other students of ancient history, actually digs in the earth to uncover remains left by former civilizations.

Two context clues help you understand the word *archaeologist* in the example above. The word *unlike* tells you that the archaeologist is being contrasted with someone else. The word *other* tells you that the archaeologist is one student of ancient history. The rest of the sentence tells you that the archaeologist's methods are different from those of the other students of ancient history. Sometimes more than one context clue will be given in a particular sentence.

Exercises Learning Word Meanings from Context

A. The sentences on the next pages contain words with which you may be unfamiliar. Using the context clues that you have just studied, select the *best* meaning for the italicized word in each passage. Write down the letter that you think represents the correct response. After the letter, tell which context clue (or clues) you used to determine the meaning of the italicized word.

1. Several *lustrous* objects added to the brightness of the room, especially the glimmering chrome sculpture, the gleaming crystal chandelier, and the sparkling silver doorknobs.

    A. stolen   B. expensive   C. shining   D. handmade

2. I was simply *petrified* from fright; I couldn't move a muscle.

    A. panicked   B. paralyzed   C. thrilled   D. scared

3. Some nations have unwisely *exploited* their colonies, taking as much wealth out of them as they could.

    A. taken advantage of   C. destroyed
    B. enslaved   D. bought and sold

4. Of course this narrative is *fictitious*; it has no basis in fact.

    A. colorful   C. important
    B. changeable   D. imaginary

5. The story was too *somber*; I prefer something with a more cheerful setting.

    A. sleepy   B. sad   C. lengthy   D. noisy

6. Paul's *scrupulous* attention to detail, such as dotting every *i*, crossing every *t*, and forming every letter perfectly, makes his handwriting a pleasure to read.

    A. careless   C. very careful
    B. left-handed   D. occasional

7. SALT, for Strategic Arms Limitation Talks, and NATO, for North Atlantic Treaty Organization, are examples of *acronyms*.

    A. governmental agencies
    B. important business organizations
    C. words formed from the first letter of other words
    D. words borrowed from foreign languages

8. Although the cheerleaders maintained their customary *exuberance*, the spectators silently mourned the team's tenth consecutive loss.

    A. high spirits   C. appearance
    B. embarrassment   D. routine

9. The works of two *prolific* authors, Agatha Christie and William Shakespeare, fill several shelves in most libraries.

A. poor
B. producing many works
C. internationally famous
D. lucky

10. The sign beside the beautiful fountain in Rome contained the warning AQUA NON POTABLE. Those who failed to heed this *admonition* became sick from drinking the water.

A. invitation   B. information   C. sign   D. warning

B. Read the following passage very carefully. Copy the underlined words on a sheet of paper. After each word, write your idea of the meaning of the word. Check your meaning with a dictionary. (You may want to review the types of context clues before you begin this exercise.)

Shortly after the *Golden Clipper* left Pago Pago, several of the crew members became ill with enterocolitis. Since everyone who suffered from this intestinal disorder had eaten at the same cafe, the ship's doctor surmised that the crew members had contracted this disease by eating tainted fish.

The government of the Philippines, however, fearing the spread of a contagion, refused to let the ship dock in Manila Bay. Instead, the entire crew was transferred to a lazaretto floating three miles offshore. A staff of doctors and nurses cared for those who were ill and carefully observed the other crew members for any signs of the malady. When no new cases developed after three days, the Philippine doctors ruled out any possibility of a contagion. The ailing crew members were then transferred to a hospital in Manila, and the others were permitted to return to the *Golden Clipper* and dock in Manila Bay.

C. Choose a feature article from a newspaper or a magazine. The article can be about fashion, sports, or any other subject. Read the article carefully. When you come across an unfamiliar word, copy the sentence in which it appears. Using the skills you have learned for unlocking the meanings of new words, write the definition you have determined from the context clue. Be prepared to share with the class the context clue that helped you unlock the meaning of the word.

Part 2   Inferring Word Meanings

The context in which an unfamiliar word appears does not always provide clues as obvious as the ones in the examples you have just seen. Instead of directly stating the meaning of the word, the writer may just imply certain things. The reader must read between the lines to pick up clues. This process of reading between the lines to reach some conclusion is called **inference.**

Most of the context clues you used in Part 1 were found in the same sentence with the unfamiliar word. When you are trying to **infer** the meaning of a word, you will frequently have to look elsewhere in the paragraph, or at the whole paragraph, for information that will help you. Among the various types of inference you may use when trying to infer the meaning of an unknown word are the following:

1. Inference based on the main idea
2. Inference based on stated details
3. Inference based on cause and effect relationship
4. Inference based on implied comparison
5. Inference based on implied contrast

Study the following examples carefully. Try to use the suggested inference technique to determine the meaning of the italicized words.

Inference Based on the Main Idea

The main idea of the paragraph at the top of the next page concerns the meaning of *planned obsolescence*. No doubt, you know the meaning of *planned*, but you may not know the meaning of *obsolescence*.

Much of the American economy is based on the principle of planned *obsolescence*. Recently, consumer groups have criticized manufacturers for turning out products that are designed to wear out in a short time, although the technology exists to make longer-lasting products. Criticism has also been directed at the automobile industry for "brainwashing" the consumer into believing that a year-old car is outdated as soon as the new models go on sale.

From the main idea of this paragraph, you can infer that *obsolescence* means one of the following:

A. investment   C. high prices
B. uselessness or outdatedness   D. patriotism

Inference Based on Stated Details

The various details in the following paragraph help you infer the meaning of *impromptu*.

It was an intensely hot summer Sunday. Most of the neighbors were indoors with air conditioners and color TVs going full blast. Suddenly, there was a power failure. After about a half hour, most houses had lost their pleasing coolness, and people began to drift outdoors in search of a gentle breeze. Before long, everyone was sharing soda, lemonade, and iced tea. Food began to appear, someone fetched picnic tables, and an *impromptu* block party developed. All around me, people were getting acquainted, and no one seemed to care that the power was still off. Nor did the spirit of the party die with the end of the evening. We have since organized a block softball team and a number of charity projects. Ever since that power failure, our neighborhood has been a more pleasant place to live.—PETER PAGE

From the details stated in this paragraph, you can infer that *impromptu* means one of the following:

A. done without previous preparation   C. exciting
B. carefully planned and organized   D. wooden

Inference Based on Cause and Effect Relationship

You read the following passage earlier to determine by context the meaning of *admonition*. As you read the passage this time, note that the effect, or outcome, of an action is stated. See if you can correctly infer the meaning of the phrase AQUA NON POTABLE.

The sign beside the beautiful fountain in Rome carried the warning AQUA NON POTABLE. Those who failed to heed this admonition became sick from drinking the water.

The cause and effect relationship in this passage leads you to infer that the Italian phrase means one of the following:

A. keep off the grass C. water for horses only
B. no swimming D. undrinkable water

Inference Based on Implied Comparison

From the implied comparisons in the following passage, try to infer the meaning of *amalgam*.

Sonia's pleasing personality is an *amalgam* of the most desirable traits of the other members of her family. She has her father's cheerfulness, her mother's sense of humor, and her sister's calmness.

From the comparisons in this passage, you can infer that *amalgam* means one of the following:

A. combination C. mockery
B. denial D. delight

Inference Based on Implied Contrast

The contrasts in the following passage should enable you to infer the meaning of *transformation*.

Sophia took a hard look at him; an astounding *transformation* had taken place. No longer did he appear lackluster or even middle-aged. His expression sparkled, his clean-shaven face was flooded with color; he had shifted his shoulders about until his coat fitted him the way the tailor had meant it to; he bristled with a youthful zest and energy. . . . But most important for her were his eyes, now bright, clear, knowledgeable, the lids opened wide to let in all the sights the world had to bestow upon an eager and penetrating mind.—IRVING STONE

What is the best meaning for *transformation* in this passage?

A. accident C. movement
B. change D. sin

Exercise Inferring Word Meanings

Read each of the following passages in its entirety. Then reread each passage, paying particular attention to the italicized word or words. Based on your understanding of the passage, try to infer the meaning of each of the italicized words. Write your inference and check it with a dictionary.

1 Many politicians are masters at the art of *circumlocution*. This fact is often best illustrated in press conferences. In response to a controversial question posed by a reporter, some politicians can talk for several minutes without ever really answering the question.

2 Most Americans would find it difficult to adapt to the *ascetic* lifestyle of a monk. Garage door openers, dishwashers, garbage disposers, stereos, and color televisions—the luxuries that many pampered Americans consider necessities—are missing from the life of a Franciscan monk.

3 The sudden collapse of the Brennan Dam sent a *torrent* of devastation into the St. Thomas Valley. Within a matter of hours, however, numerous organizations and individuals met the *exigency* of the situation with food, clothing, shelter, and medical help.

4   A true *gastronome*, like Julia Child, is probably unimpressed by the billions of hamburgers sold by fast food, carry-out restaurants. Better known as "The French Chef," Mrs. Child is the author of a number of books on French cooking. For her, the measure of cooking rests more in the quality than in the quantity of the final product.

5   The immediate destruction caused by the earthquake was much less than the destruction caused by the *ensuing holocaust*. The earthquake ruptured gas and water lines throughout the city. Without a water supply the fire fighters were unable to combat the fires fueled by the broken gas lines.

6   The Better Business Bureau is investigating a new product that claims to cure practically every type of human ailment. It claims to bring immediate relief for arthritis, headaches, colds, vitamin deficiency, low vitality, backache, and sleeplessness. Because of the *preposterous* claims of the new medicine, the suspicions of the medical profession have been aroused.

Part 3 The Multiple Meanings of Words

Most of your vocabulary development in school thus far has probably involved learning the meaning and spelling of each new word. For many words, this plan is acceptable, but for many other words it does not go far enough. Assigning one meaning to a word often ignores the additional meanings of that word.

Before you read the next section, write a definition for the word *court*. Now compare your definition with the uses of that word in the following sentences.

1. Helen and Alice are going to the tennis *court* for a game this afternoon at three.

2. The strolling players set up their stage in the inner *court* of the castle.

3. The Queen and her *court* attended the New Year's Ball.

4. The judge asked the *court* to consider the evidence carefully.

5. Some politicians do everything in their power to *court* the favor of those whose patronage they desire.

6. The reigning king usually held *court* on the first day of the month, to receive the petitions of his subjects.

7. Did you hear the story of the man who was too shy to *court* the woman he loved?

8. Some persons are foolish enough to *court* danger.

9. Our home is on a very short street known as Canterbury *Court*.

Did your definition of *court* fit any of the sentences? If not, share with the class a sentence using *court* to fit your definition. From these examples, you will see the necessity of being aware of the multiple meanings of a word.

Webster's New World Dictionary lists thirteen different meanings for the word *court*. The multiple meanings of words need not pose a problem for you if you remember what was said in Part 1 of this chapter: The context of a word determines its meaning.

Dictionary Entry for *court*

word used as a noun	**court** (kort) **n.** [OFr. < LL. < L. *cohors:* see COHORT] **1.** an uncovered space wholly or partly surrounded by buildings or walls **2.** a short street, often closed at one end **3.** *a*) an area for playing any of several ball games [a tennis *court*] *b*) a part of such an area ☆**4.** a motel: in full, **motor court 5.** *a*) the palace of a soverign *b*) the family, advisers, etc. of a sovereign, as a group *c*) a sovereign and his councilors as a governing body *d*) any formal gathering held by a sovereign **6.** attention paid to someone in order to get something **7.** courtship; wooing **8.** *a*) a person or persons appointed to examine and decide law cases, make investigations, etc.; judge or judges *b*) a place where trials are held, investigations made, etc. *c*) an assembly or meeting of the judge or judges, the lawyers, and the jury in a law court **—vt. 1.** to pay attention to (a person) in order to get something **2.** to try to get the love of; woo **3.** to try to get; seek [to *court* favor] **4.** to make oneself open to [to *court* insults] **—vi.** to woo **—adj.** of or fit for a court **—out of court** without a trial **—pay court to** to court, as for favor or love **—court'er n.**

- word used as a noun — **court** (kort) **n.**
- word used as a verb (transitive) — **vt.**
- word used as a verb (intransitive) — **vi.**
- word used as an adjective — **adj.**

8 meanings of *court,* used as a noun.

4 meanings of *court,* used as a verb.

1 meaning of *court,* used as an adjective.

14

Exercises Words with Multiple Meanings

A. Just as the word *court* has multiple meanings, each of the words in the following list can be used in several different ways. Write at least five sentences for each of the following words, making sure that each sentence illustrates a different meaning for the word.

note   light   round   ring

B. The word *key* may be used correctly by the persons indicated below. Look up the different meanings in a dictionary and show the use of each in an original sentence.

1. a locksmith
2. a typist
3. a singing teacher
4. a person solving a puzzle
5. a piano tuner
6. a composer of songs
7. a student of the geography of Florida
8. a student studying pronunciations in a dictionary
9. a mathematics teacher

C. Give the meaning of the word *square* in the following sentences. Check with a dictionary in cases where you are not quite sure.

1. A concert will be held in the village *square* tonight.
2. On Monday we can *square* our accounts.
3. Carpenters use *squares* to test right angles.
4. We are going to learn to find the *square root* of numbers.
5. He *squared* the surface with a straightedge.
6. The sergeant told the recruits to *square* their shoulders.
7. What is the formula for the area of a *square*?

D. The following sentences contain phrases using forms of the word *book*. Explain the meaning of each italicized phrase.

1. Even though her team had lost the final game, the coach admitted that the referees had called the fouls *by the book*.
2. Ms. Carr has *kept books* for this company for many years.
3. The officer *booked* the man for suspicion of burglary.
4. The candidate said he wanted to make *an open book* of his family finances.

Part 4 Gaining Precision in the Use of Words

Precision is one of the marks of power. The concert singer who is exactly on pitch, the archer who hits the bull's-eye, the sky diver who lands directly on target—all display a precision that marks superior skill.

Precision in the use of words is essential to achieving word power. Precise use of synonyms and antonyms distinguishes the person with a powerful vocabulary from the person with an ordinary vocabulary.

Using Synonyms

Synonyms are words that have similar meanings. They do not usually mean *exactly* the same thing. Each one has a meaning slightly different from the others. You should have as many synonyms as possible in your vocabulary so that you can say exactly what you want to say and understand exactly what you read and hear.

Let's see how synonyms work. If a neighbor asked you if you were a *pupil* in East High School, would you say "Yes"? If she suggested that your ten-year-old brother was a *student* at Jefferson Elementary School, would she be right? If she called you a *scholar*, would she be using the correct word?

Note how one dictionary sets you right about these three words.

1. The word *pupil* applies to a child in school, or to someone studying privately with a teacher.

EXAMPLES:

Ruthmarie is a *pupil* of the famous singer, Carlo Amato.
Bobby is a *pupil* at Jefferson Elementary School.

2. The word *student* applies to someone attending a high school, a college, or university.

EXAMPLES:

Several hundred high school *students* attended the rally.
I am a first-year *student* at East High.

3. The word *scholar* is reserved for a learned person who is an authority in some field, or to a student who has a scholarship.

EXAMPLES:

Uncle Andrew is a Biblical *scholar.*
Charlotte is a Fulbright *scholar.*

You can see from these examples that you might feel somewhat insulted if someone said you were a *pupil* at East High. You would probably prefer to be called a *student.* At the same time, you will realize that you probably should not be called a *scholar.* This is exactly what is meant by precision in the use of words. The more careful you are in the choice of synonyms, the more effective your use of the language will be.

A good dictionary is a valuable tool for developing precision in the use of synonyms. Most dictionaries contain **synonymies,** listings of synonyms explaining their differences or shades of meaning. Careful use of the synonymy sections of your dictionary is important, especially since there are few absolute synonyms in English.

Examine the synonymy entered in *Webster's New World Dictionary* following the word *brave.*

Dictionary Entry for *brave*

brave (brav) **adj.** [Fr. < It. *bravo*, brave, fine, orig., wild, savage < L. *barbarus*, BARBAROUS] **1.** not afraid; having courage; valiant **2.** fine; splendid [a *brave* new world] —**n.** **1.** any brave man **2.** a N. American Indian warrior —**vt. braved, brav'ing 1.** to face with courage [they *braved* the storm] **2.** to defy; dare —**brave'ly adv. —brave'ness n.**

synonymy

SYN.—**brave** is the general term that implies fearlessness in meeting danger or difficulty; **courageous** suggests readiness to deal firmly with any dangerous situation because of self-discipline and strong convictions; **bold** stresses a daring nature, whether shown by courage, insolence, or defiance; **audacious** suggests reckless boldness; **valiant** emphasizes a heroic quality in the courage shown; **intrepid** implies absolute fearlessness in facing something new or unknown; **plucky** is usually used of someone who continues fighting even though at a disadvantage —**ANT. craven, cowardly**

To the casual user of the language, the words *brave, courageous, bold, audacious, valiant, intrepid,* and *plucky* are interchangeable. To the precise user of the language, they are not. Each synonym carries a meaning not present in the other six words.

A precise user of the language might speak of a *brave* warrior, a *courageous* pioneer, a *bold* robber, an *audacious* plan, a *valiant* knight, an *intrepid* explorer, and a *plucky* youngster.

Synonyms add variety and color to our language. The use of the same words over and over is the mark of a poor writer or speaker. You may overuse some words in your vocabulary. Certain words, particularly colloquial expressions, are overused to such an extent in daily conversation that they lose much of their impact. In your speaking and writing, make a conscious effort to avoid such repetition.

The Thesaurus. A thesaurus is a reference book that can be an invaluable help to the writer. It is a storehouse of synonyms and word usage. Clarity and effectiveness in writing are dependent upon accurate word choice, and a thesaurus can help you find the exact word you need.

Here is an entry from *Roget's Thesaurus.*

DANGER.—I. *Nouns.* **danger,** chance, hazard, insecurity, jeopardy, peril, unsafety, risk, pitfall, endangerment; storm brewing, clouds gathering, clouds on the horizon; crisis.
dangerousness, riskiness, touch and go, unsafety, treachery; venturousness, etc. (see *Adjectives*).
[*dangerous person*] **menace,** threat, serpent, viper; dangerous woman, *femme fatale (F.).*
II. *Verbs.* **endanger,** expose to danger, hazard, jeopardize, peril, imperil, risk, speculate with, venture, compromise.
[*accept danger*] **risk,** hazard, venture, adventure, dare, stake, set at hazard, speculate.
III. *Adjectives.* **dangerous,** chancy, risky, ticklish, touch-and-go, venturous, venturesome, adventurous, adventuresome, speculative; hazardous, perilous, parlous, precarious, insecure, jeopardous, critical, queasy, unsafe, ugly, treacherous, serpentine, viperous.
See also CHANCE, FEAR, THREAT, WARNING.
Antonyms—See PROTECTION.

Using Antonyms

Antonyms are words with meanings that are the opposite of each other. *Summer—winter, night—day, near—far, happy—sad* are examples of antonyms. Knowing how to use antonyms well will make your speech and writing more colorful and more precise. Antonyms will also aid you when you need to present a contrast.

Exercises Gaining Precision in the Use of Words

A. Note the monotonous effect of the overuse of the word *fantastic*.

The Homecoming dance was a *fantastic* affair. The decorations committee did a *fantastic* job. The band, James and Company, was really *fantastic*. The students consumed all of the *fantastic* refreshments. Everyone agreed that this was the most *fantastic* dance ever held at Jefferson High School.

Rewrite this paragraph, substituting other words for the overused word *fantastic*. The rewritten paragraph should be more colorful than the one printed above and should give the reader a more precise picture of what the dance was actually like. After you have rewritten the paragraph, check your words in a dictionary or thesaurus.

B. Study the following synonymy from *Webster's New World Dictionary* given after the word *estimate*. Write a sentence for each of these four words—*estimate, appraise, evaluate,* and *rate*—to illustrate the different shades of meaning of each word.

---

es·ti·mate (es′tə mat′; *for n.* -mit) **vt. -mat′ed, -mat′ing** [< L. pp. of *aestimare:* see ESTEEM] **1.** to form an opinion about [to *estimate* the merits of a movie] **2.** to make a general but careful guess about (size, value, cost, etc.) [he *estimated* the size of the crowd to be 300] —**vi.** to make an estimate —**n. 1.** a general calculation of size, value, etc.; esp., an approximate figuring of the probable cost of a piece of work made by a person undertaking to do the work **2.** an opinion or judgment [this is a good book in my *estimate*] —**es′ti·ma′tive adj.** —**es′ti·ma·tor n.**

SYN.—**estimate** refers generally to the forming of a personal opinion or judgment; **appraise** implies the intention of giving an accurate or expert judgment, as of value or worth [to *appraise* a new house]; **evaluate** also connotes an attempt at an exact judgment, but rarely with reference to value in terms of money [let us *evaluate* the evidence]; **rate** implies the comparing of one person or thing with another or others as to value, quality, etc. [he is *rated* the best in his field]—see also **SYN.** at CALCULATE

---

c. Answer the following. Use your dictionary if necessary.

1. Could the same person be *uninterested* and *disinterested* in the same project at the same time?

2. Could a person be *healthy* in an *unhealthful* climate? Explain.

3. If someone said you were a *bore*, would you be happy about it? If the same person said you were a *boor*, would you feel better or worse?

4. Explain the difference between *flash*, *glitter*, and *sparkle*. Use each in an original sentence.

5. A person with an *irritable* disposition is easily annoyed. A person with an *irascible* disposition has what trouble?

6. Can you be *happy* without being *cheerful*? Could you be *cheerful* without being *happy*?

7. *Neat*, *tidy*, and *trim* are often used interchangeably, but each word implies something different from the others. Use each in an original sentence that will make the distinctions clear.

8. Could you be *eager* without being *anxious*? Explain.

9. You would not object to being told you were *curious*. How would you feel if someone told you you were *inquisitive*?

10. If certain facts were *obvious*, would they also be *apparent*? Under what circumstances would you use *evident*?

D. Answer the following. Use your dictionary if necessary.

1. Would you deal with a person who is *unscrupulous*? What word would you use to designate the opposite trait?

2. *Niggardly* persons have few friends. What quality would they have to cultivate to change the situation?

3. Would an *illiterate* person necessarily have to be *uncultured*? Explain. Give two words opposite in meaning.

4. You attend a student rally; nothing much is accomplished. A classmate says the meeting was *unorganized*; another says it was *disorganized*. Which term is correct? Explain.

5. You find the word *abridged* on the cover of a novel you are about to read. Would you expect a complete telling of the story as the author wrote it?

6. If you found a classroom door marked "Atypical," what type of student would you expect to find entering it?

7. If you were told that doing a certain thing would be a *disservice* to the school, would you persist in doing it? Give a reason for your answer.

8. What type of person is a *malcontent*? What word would you use to indicate someone of opposite disposition?

9. What is the difference between being *asocial* and *antisocial*?

10. What is the difference in meaning between the following: *indecipherable* and *illegible*. Use each in a sentence.

E. Write down two synonyms for each of the words given below. (Use a dictionary or thesaurus if necessary.) Use each synonym in an original sentence that clearly shows the difference in meaning.

1. fear	6. hesitate	11. oblivious
2. lazy	7. spite	12. deplore
3. guard	8. injure	13. observe
4. scoff	9. scanty	14. noticeable
5. scold	10. hateful	15. error

F. Think of an antonym for each of the following words and use the antonym you choose in a sentence. As you discuss the sentences in class, you will notice that different students have chosen different antonyms for the same word. This illustrates that the antonym of one word may have several of its own synonyms.

1. overpass	6. extraordinary
2. arrival	7. lenient
3. immovable	8. huge
4. difficult	9. poverty
5. defective	10. vivid

G. Find in your local newspaper or your favorite magazine five pairs of synonyms and five pairs of antonyms. Be prepared to tell the class why these words have been used correctly.

Summary

In this chapter you have learned and practiced four ways of building your vocabulary.

Sometimes the *context* of a passage will help reveal the meaning of a word:

a. by defining the word for you,
b. by giving one or more examples,
c. by comparing the word with other more familiar words, or
d. by contrasting the word with something with which you are familiar.

A second way to determine the meaning of a word is to make an *inference* based on the general sense of the passage. This requires "reading between the lines."

A third way to build your vocabulary is to learn the multiple meanings and uses of words you already know.

A fourth way to build your vocabulary is to increase your knowledge of synonyms and antonyms and to use them precisely.

Review Exercises

A. Using the techniques of context clues or inference that you studied in Parts 1 and 2 of this chapter, try to determine the meaning of each italicized word in the following sentences. Write down your understanding of the word. Consult a dictionary to see if your definition fits one of the dictionary definitions.

1. One of the pitiful characters of Greek legend is Cassandra. She possessed the ability to foretell future events, but her *fatidic* statements were never believed.

2. Spring *freshets* often wash out many bridges in mountainous regions.

3. Even a brief conversation with Professor MacAllister reveals the extent of her *erudition.* Her *voracious* reading over a period of more

than sixty years has enabled her to speak knowledgeably on topics ranging from Shakespeare's sonnets to nuclear power.

4. After nearly two generations of bloodshed and death, the war-weary residents welcomed the peace treaty and looked forward to *halcyon* days.

5. Among the *witticisms* of the late Senator Everett Dirksen is his often-quoted comment about the *mushrooming* federal budget: "A billion here and a billion there and the first thing you know, it adds up to real money."

6. Joy thought that a modeling career would offer more glamor and excitement than her *mundane* job at the grocery store.

7. Most doctors object to spending time with *hypochondriacs* when they could be devoting more time to patients who really are sick.

8. His writings are much too *verbose;* he fills a whole page with what could better be said in a single sentence.

9. Palm trees are *indigenous* to tropical and subtropical climates.

10. Dr. Haverford was pleased with the progress her patient made following his surgery. Soon he was able to resume his normal activities. Both Dr. Haverford and her patient were amazed and disappointed when a *recrudescence* of the ailment forced his return to the hospital.

B. Each of the following passages contains several words that may be unfamiliar to you. Read each passage in its entirety. Then reread the passage, paying particular attention to the italicized words. Based on your understanding of each word as it is used in the passage, write your own definition for that word. Check your definitions with a dictionary.

1   Dressed in *funereal* attire, friends and relatives gathered at the mortuary to *commiserate* with the *bereaved* young widow. The minister's *eulogy* praised the heroism of her husband, who died after rescuing three children from their burning apartment. Over 100 of his fellow firefighters joined the *cortege* to the cemetery.

2   The winner of the Olympic *decathlon* is often *dubbed* "The World's Greatest Athlete." The *recipient* of the gold medal not only must possess the *dexterity* that enables him to perform well

in each event, but he must also have the *stamina* to endure all ten events.

3   Most people are familiar with the *diurnal* animals of the forests, such as squirrels, chipmunks, and most birds. An afternoon walk on a *sylvan* path will reveal many of these animals engaged in their normal, daily activities. The *nocturnal* creatures, such as owls, bats, and opossums, are much less familiar since most people do not *frequent* their *habitats* at night.

C. Give the meaning of the word *keep* in each of the following sentences. Check with a dictionary in cases where you are not quite sure.

1. Can you *keep* a secret?
2. A little water in the pan will *keep* the carrots from burning.
3. I *keep* the accounts for a small manufacturing company.
4. I'll give you half and *keep* half for myself.
5. The cake will *keep* for a week.
6. I was too tired to *keep* running.
7. Do you *keep* a diary?
8. If you are going to stay here, you will have to earn your *keep*.
9. You gave your word, now you must *keep* it.
10. I'm sure that the gold is in the castle *keep*.

D. Read each sentence and the synonyms below it. Write the synonym that would best fill the blank space in the sentence.

1. When we first saw Rex, he was just a _____ pup.

    tiny   minute   puny

2. The organism was so _____ it could not be seen by the human eye.

    tiny   minute   puny

3. She had a _____ radio on a chain around her neck.

    tiny   minute   puny

4. Without hesitating, the frightened doe _____ across the gully.

   leaped   hopped   vaulted

5. I put both hands on the fence and _____ it before the dog got me.

   leaped   hopped   vaulted

6. Tom _____ around on one foot while he tried to pull his boot on.

   leaped   hopped   vaulted

7. After _____ the arguments, they finally came to a decision.

   investigating   studying   considering   examining

8. I'm going to spend next year _____ medicine in Brazil.

   investigating   studying   considering   examining

9. A team has been _____ the causes of the crash.

   investigating   studying   considering   examining

10. Sylvia was _____ the lock for signs of tampering.

   investigating   studying   considering   examining

Chapter 2

Using the Senses in Writing

Have you ever thought about yourself as a fantastic receiver of information, one who uses sight, hearing, touch, taste, and smell all at one time? Without any conscious effort on your part, all of these senses are operating right now. Your senses bring you knowledge about your world. They enable you to be alive to all the excitement of living today.

When you were a very young child, you experienced the world for the first time. You had a heightened sensitivity to every sensory impression. Your world was newly fresh and exciting every moment. As you grow older, you tend to take your senses for granted because they operate as automatically as breathing. You need to recapture the rich enjoyment of coming alive to your senses. A new awareness will sharpen your perceptions and add new dimensions to your writing.

One of the best ways to collect your sensory data is to record your ideas, observations, and experiences in a journal or diary. This collection of impressions will be a rich treasure house of material from which to draw as you continue to write. The pages that follow will examine your five senses, one at a time, though of course they are always working together.

Part 1 The Sense of Sight

Everything visible in the world can be seen by your eyes. There is a difference, however, between merely looking at a thing and really seeing it. Here is what one writer has discovered.

TO LOOK AT ANY THING

To look at anything,
If you would know that thing,
You must look at it long:
To look at this green and say
"I have seen spring in these
Woods," will not do—you must
Be the thing you see:
You must be the dark snakes of
Stems and ferny plumes of leaves,
You must enter in
To the small silences between
The leaves,
You must take your time
And touch the very peace
They issue from.

JOHN MOFFITT

The writer is telling you that to really see any one thing is to see it with all your senses. You, in fact, must *become* that thing and enter into the core of it. You must experience a new awareness of the thing so that you can transmit its essence to your reader.

Here is a sight question to consider in order to see how observant you are right now. Record the answer in your journal.

What colors were used in painting your classroom? Suppose your classroom is painted yellow. Is it *warm* yellow? *streaked* yellow? *almost* yellow? Is it a *loud* yellow? a *singing* yellow? a *lemon* yellow? Each of these "yellows" creates an entirely different image for your readers, forcing them to bring their own senses into play. A sense of sharing exists between you and your readers as you help them recreate your experience.

Exercise Testing Your Sight Observations

Record your answers to the questions below in your journal. Make your observations as specific and interesting as possible so you can use them later in your writing.

1. What color are your teacher's eyes?
2. What kinds of things are on the walls of your classroom?
3. Are there any clouds in the sky? Describe them.
4. What colors and shapes are the pens and pencils you have with you right now?
5. What color were the clothes your mother or your father was wearing this morning when you left home?
6. Which way does the front door at your house swing when it opens? Describe the door.

Training in Seeing

You are already a kind of expert at observing the world with your eyes. You notice the color when you pick out your favorite shirt. You notice the subtle facial expressions on a person's face that invite a particular response from you. Expert as you are, here are some suggestions for training your sight to be even sharper.

1. On a piece of paper, draw a floor plan of a room at home. Put in all of the major pieces of furniture and the color of each. Share your plan with another person in class. Now take the floor plan home with you and check your sense of sight. Make any necessary corrections or additions to the plan. Be particularly specific about color. Bring it back to class tomorrow and be prepared to tell a group what you discovered.

2. Select a small object near you—something on your desk, on the floor, or on the wall. Study it carefully for a short time. Then move so that you can no longer see it. Write a detailed description of the object, including size, color, shape, texture, and any unusual characteristics. In describing its size, for example, don't be content with saying it's two inches long. Try to bring the other senses into play. Is it the size of a walnut? the size of a matchbox? the size of a toothpick? When you feel you have included all possible details, turn back to see how well your description fits. Share your writing with another person by reading your description of the object without naming it. See if this person can recognize what you are describing.

3. Sit down in a familiar place in a room at home or at school, or outside if you wish. Write down everything you can see without turning or moving your circle of vision. Notice all the things you usually see in this spot; then concentrate on finding something you did not expect to see here. Describe it as specifically as you can, allowing your other senses to affect what you see. Share your experience with someone in class.

4. Stretch your sense of sight by careful observation on your way to or from school. Going your same familiar way, find ten things of interest that you never noticed before. Be prepared to write out this list of new "sights" to share with the rest of the class.

Here is a list of "sight" words to help you make your descriptions more vivid, more exact. Study the words and try to determine in what way each of the related words is different. Add your own words to the list and record them in your journal.

Sight Words

Colors

red

pink
salmon
rose
coral
raspberry
strawberry
tomato
currant
cherry
crimson
cardinal
vermilion
carmine
flame
ruby
garnet
wine
blood
maroon
burgundy

blue

sky
sapphire
azure
delft
porcelain
turquoise
aqua
aquamarine
violet
peacock
cobalt
royal
navy
steel

yellow

beige
buff
straw
peach
apricot
butter
buttercup
lemon
chartreuse
citron
canary
chrome
gold
topaz
ochre
saffron
sulphur
mustard
butterscotch
orange
tangerine
persimmon

green

celery
mint
apple
lime
kelly
emerald
olive
pistachio
chartreuse

white

snow
milky
marble
cream
ivory
oyster
pearl
silver
platinum

purple

lavender
amethyst
lilac
orchid
mauve
plum
mulberry
pansy
fuchsia
magenta

black

jet
ebony
licorice

gray

ashen
dove
steel

brown

sandy
almond
amber
tawny
hazel
cinnamon
nutmeg
chocolate
coffee
copper
rust
ginger
bronze
walnut
mahogany

colorless
rainbow

Movements

fast

hurry
run
scamper
skip
scramble
dart

31

spring
spin
sprint
stride
streak
propel
trot
gallop
drive
dash
bolt
careen
rush
race
zoom
zip
ram
chase
hurl
swat
flick
whisk
rip
shove
swerve
smash
drop
plummet
bounce
swoop
plunge
swing
fly
sail

slow
creep
crawl
plod
slouch
lumber
tiptoe
bend
amble
saunter
loiter
stray
slink
stalk
edge
sneak
stagger
lope
waddle
drag
sway
soar
lift
drift
droop
heave

Shapes

flat
round
domed
curved
wavy

scrolled
globular
rolled
scalloped
ruffled
frilled
crimped
crinkled
flared
oval
conical
cylindrical
tubular
hollow
rotund
chubby
portly
swollen
lumpy
clustered
padded
tufted
pendulous
jutting
irregular
proportioned
angular
triangular
rectangular
hexagonal
octagonal
square
pyramidical
tapering

branching
twiggy
split
broken
spindly
skinny
thin
wiry
shapely
winged
shapeless

Appearance

dotted
freckled
spotted
blotched
wrinkled
patterned
mottled
flowery
striped
bright
clear
shiny
glowing
glossy
shimmering
fluid
sparkling
iridescent
glassy

flashy	formal	frail	elegant
glazed	crisp	fragile	statuesque
sheer	pretty	pale	huge
transparent	heavy	pasty	immense
translucent	flat	sickly	massive
opaque	stout	small	gigantic
muddy	wide	tiny	showy
grimy	rigid	miniature	decorative
young	narrow	timid	distinctive
drab	overloaded	shy	dazzling
dingy	congested	fearful	opulent
dull	cluttered	apprehensive	jeweled
dark	crowded	tearful	lacy
dismal	jammed	nervous	lavish
rotted	packed	frightened	exotic
old	squeezed	terrified	gorgeous
used	bruised	hysterical	radiant
worn	tied	wild	vivid
untidy	stretched	bold	flushed
shabby	tall	dramatic	fiery
messy	erect	tantalizing	blazing
cheap	lean	irresistible	verdant
ugly	slender	exuberant	fresh
ramshackle	supple	energetic	clean
tired	lithe	animated	scrubbed
exhausted	lively	perky	tidy
arid	muscular	attractive	handsome
awkward	sturdy	arrogant	pleasant
crooked	robust	flamboyant	sunny
loose	stolid	expansive	calm
curved	hardy	imposing	serene
straight	strong	regal	unruffled
orderly	healthy	stately	nerveless

Exercises **Using "Sight" Words in Your Writing**

Here is a chance to practice using specific details in order to help your reader "see" as clearly as you do what you are describing.

A. Write a sentence describing each of these nine things. Select sight words that are exactly right to describe what you see.

the sidewalk	a stone	a button
the sky	a dog or cat	a leaf
someone's hair	a slice of bread	a piece of soap

B. Here is a paragraph that recreates a vivid sight impression.

She first saw him that Sunday as he walked down the long steps in clear view from her ledge of rock across the river. Between them was a transparent pool in the mountain pass. Every rock on the bottom shimmered in green-gold helicoid light. Comfortable, conscious of the rock's heat on her stomach through her bathing suit, she watched him down the path, his white shirt flashing through the trees with the motion of his walking. Bronze skin, a tall leanness, eyes blue as the sky, hair brown in the shade and copper in the sun and wavy as the sea. She was sure, thinking of it later, that if there had been the trace of a limp in his walk, she would have noticed it and known who he was. But she watched him walk the entire way, conscious only of his beauty.

—KATIE LETCHER LYLE

Make a list of all the color words in the paragraph. Next, make a list of all the words or phrases that create action or movement. What part of the description does not appeal to the sense of sight?

C. You have stretched your sight experiences and are now ready to write your own paragraph. You may use any of the subjects in Exercise A, any ideas from your journal, or any subjects from the following list. You may also use an entirely new idea.

your room	outside the window	a dream
the kitchen	a puddle of water	a quiet or a busy scene

Part 2 The Sense of Hearing

Have you ever temporarily lost your sense of hearing, perhaps from an ear infection or a bad cold? Only at such times are you likely to be aware of how much you depend on this particular sense as you move through your day, from the alarm clock on waking up, through the sounds of traffic as you cross the street, to the greetings of friends at school, and even your mother's call for dinner in the evening. Here are some hearing questions to help you tune in to this sense. Record your ideas in your journal.

1. Close your eyes and listen for one minute. List the sounds that you were able to hear in the classroom.

2. Right now, pick out a sound that you never heard before in this time and place. Describe it.

3. List the usual sounds at the beginning and end of a period in this class. List the same beginning and ending sounds for another class, to compare them.

4. List all of the sounds that you can remember hearing in the cafeteria or lunch room.

5. List the sounds you are so used to at home that you do not ordinarily notice them.

6. List all of the sounds you like to hear; then list all of the sounds you do not like to hear.

7. Stop up your ears for one minute and concentrate on the kinds of sounds that come to you. Try chewing, humming, shaking your head to see what different kinds of sounds and tones you hear. Describe them.

8. List all of the musical sounds you know.

9. List the sounds you associate with one particular sport.

Training in Listening

In order to increase your sensitivity to sounds, you may sometimes need to close your eyes and concentrate only on listening, without your sense of sight to distract you. It is possible to develop more acute hearing, to notice more with your ears than you did before. Mothers often have unusual hearing where their children are concerned. You probably have better than average ability to detect slight changes in tone of voice that might indicate changes in mood and personality in your parents or friends. Careful listening to sounds can add a rich new dimension to your life and to your writing. Here are some suggestions for training your ears to hear even more. Record your responses in your journal.

1. Take a pad and pencil, or your journal, to bed with you tonight. After you are comfortably settled in the dark room, listen carefully to every sound you can hear. Then turn on the light long enough to write down all of the sounds you were able to hear. Take this list with you to school in the morning so that you can share what you heard with someone else. Did this careful listening have any effect on how easy or difficult it was for you to go to sleep?

2. Listen to three conversations: one at school, one at a store or on the way home, and one at home. Listen particularly for the tone of voice the speakers use and ways in which this tone can affect the meaning of what is being said. Write up your findings from this "hearing" experiment by recreating one of the dialogues as well as you can remember it or by writing a new dialogue of your own. It is easier if you limit the characters in the dialogue to two people. In your writing, indicate changes in tone of voice and the emotion you think each person is feeling. For example:

> *Customer* (loudly and angrily): That item is marked a dollar and nine cents.
>
> *Cashier* (bewildered): Isn't that what I charged you? It's right here on the sales slip.
>
> *Customer* (muttering, trying to save face): I guess you rang it up so fast I didn't see it.
>
> *Cashier* (hurt but well trained): I'm sorry, ma'am.

Now that you are listening more carefully to the sounds in your world, you will want to develop greater skill in describing what you hear. On the next page is a list of "hearing" words to study. As you read each word, try to hear the sound each one conveys. Try to add more words to the list and record them in your journal.

Hearing Words

Loud Sounds

crash	clap	murmur	melody
thud	stomp	whisper	resonance
bump	stamp	whir	harmony
thump	noise	rustle	musical
boom	discord	twitter	
thunder	jangle	patter	**Speech Sounds**
bang	rasp	hum	
smash	clash	mutter	stutter
explode	caterwaul	snap	stammer
roar	clamor	hiss	giggle
scream	tumult	crackle	guffaw
screech	riot	bleat	laugh
shout	racket	peep	sing
yell	brawl	buzz	yell
whistle	bedlam	zing	scream
whine	pandemonium	gurgle	screech
squawk	hubbub	swish	snort
bark	blatant	rush	bellow
bawl	deafening	chime	growl
bray	raucous	tinkle	chatter
bluster	earsplitting	clink	murmur
rage	piercing	hush	whisper
blare	rowdy	still	whimper
rumble	disorderly	speechless	talk
grate		mute	speak
slam	**Soft Sounds**	faint	drawl
	sigh	inaudible	

Exercises **Using "Hearing" Words in Your Writing**

A. Here are fifteen sounds you are familiar with. Spend a few minutes "hearing" the sounds in your mind. Write a sentence about each sound that describes it as vividly as you want your reader to hear it. Record the sentences in your journal.

the wind	a fire
feet walking	rain
a car starting	a door opening
opening a can of soda	turning on a faucet
a police car siren	a lawn mower
sawing a board	a garbage truck
an ice cream wagon	someone roller skating
a train	

B. Here is a paragraph describing the terrifying shift of sounds in these children's world. As you read it, notice the strong contrast between words and phrases that bring to mind loud sounds and strong actions and those that bring to mind quiet sounds and silent images.

It was as if, in the midst of a film concerning an avalanche, a tornado, a hurricane, a volcanic eruption, something had, first, gone wrong with the sound apparatus, thus muffling and finally cutting off all noise, all of the blasts and repercussions and thunders, and then second, ripped the film from the projector and inserted in its place a peaceful tropical slide which did not move or tremor. The world ground to a standstill. The silence was so immense and unbelievable that you felt your ears had been stuffed or you had lost your hearing altogether. The children put their hands to their ears. They stood apart. The door slid back and the smell of the silent, waiting world came in to them.

—RAY BRADBURY

Make two lists, one of the loud sounds and strong actions, and one of the quiet sounds and silent images in the paragraph. What, if anything, is different about the last sentence in the paragraph?

c. Now put all of your hearing experiences and practice together to write a paragraph in which sound plays an important part. Use an idea from your answers to these listening exercises, from the work on listening recorded in your journal, from one of the following starting ideas, or from a new idea.

1. I adjusted the ear plugs to protect my ears, dove into the water, and all of a sudden . . .

2. As I was listening to the radio with my headset on, the strangest thing happened.

3. Without warning, all sound suddenly disappeared. It had become a strange new world in which I did not fit.

4. The elevator dropped swiftly, and the quick descent seemed to plug up my ears.

5. Take an ordinary sound that is familiar to you. Exaggerate this single sound in your writing until it becomes sinister or exciting and takes on a new meaning.

6. Contrast two completely different sounds, or a particular sound and quiet.

7. Describe an event by sound words only. Do not give your reader the final clue as to what you are describing until the last sentence of the paragraph.

8. Go to a place where there is a great deal of activity, such as a store, airport, or carnival. Shut your eyes for a moment and listen. Take notes on what you hear. Now go home and write a paragraph about the place, using as many sound words as possible.

Part 3   The Sense of Touch

With sight and hearing you respond to things around you, objects seen and sounds heard. Your other three senses are much more personal and intimate. Touch is the most intimate of the senses because it brings an immediate sensation. Your brain records a response. Taste requires contact for its functioning. Smell functions when you are close enough to an object for your nose to recognize an odor, or when the odor is overwhelmingly strong. Each of your five senses has an important part to play in your life.

Sudden loss of any sense produces fear and dislocation for most people. If you can remember a time when you were sick, or for some reason temporarily lost the use of one of your senses, you can probably remember how uncomfortable it was, how hard it was to deal with a new and unfamiliar world. The more you use and enjoy all of your senses, the more you fully experience life and the world around you.

The rest of this chapter contains questions and exercises that will help you survey your experiences with touch, taste and smell. Record your responses to these senses in your journal. Your collection of sensory data will furnish you with many good ideas for writing as you go along. Let's begin with the sense of touch.

1. List all of the objects you can touch while you are seated in your chair right now.

2. Describe your physical sensations now. Are you cold, hot, warm, cool, comfortable? How do you know?

3. List any rough objects in the classroom, then any smooth ones.

4. What noticeable physical habits do you have? Do you bite your nails? cross your legs when seated? talk with your hands? run your hand through your hair? If you can't think of any for yourself, list some that you observe in another person in the classroom.

5. List some things that are cold to the touch; hot to the touch; rough; smooth; wet.

6. List some things you do not feel with your hands, such as the wind or the touch of your clothes.

7. Describe the type of ride you get on different forms of transportation. How does a ride in a car, for example, compare to a ride on the subway?

8. Imagine that you are sitting in your classroom on a hot summer day. How do you feel? Now imagine you are in the same

room on a bitter winter day. How do you feel now? Write down your ideas.

Training in Touching

1. While in a car or on a bus, tune in to your sense of touch. Apply all of your nerves to reporting how your body responds to the ride and write up your experience. Here are some questions to consider: Am I comfortable? How do my stomach, my arms, my legs feel? How fast are we going and how can I tell? What is the temperature like? Is there a window open? Is anyone sitting near enough to touch me? Which of my senses is least able to operate fully in this situation?

2. Search around the room, in your pockets or purse for any two objects that have very different textures. Have these near you so that you can write a description that contrasts the way they feel to your touch.

Following is a list of touch words. Study it and write down an object that you think belongs with each word. Add more words and objects to the list and record them in your journal.

Touch Words			
cool	slippery	silky	gritty
cold	spongy	satiny	sandy
icy	mushy	velvety	rough
lukewarm	oily	smooth	sharp
tepid	waxy	soft	thick
warm	fleshy	wooly	pulpy
hot	rubbery	furry	dry
steamy	tough	feathery	dull
sticky	crisp	fuzzy	thin
damp	elastic	hairy	fragile
wet	leathery	prickly	tender

Exercises **Using "Touch" Words in Your Writing**

A. Write sentences describing how each of these things feels. Record your sentences in your journal.

a piece of cotton	an ice cube	the bark of a tree
an apple	a warm bath	roller skating
a dry leaf	a sunburn	a toothache

Would another person know what you were describing if the name of it were left out? Which of the above things requires you to reach out and touch it or pick it up? Which of the things is something you experience as a sensation happening to you?

B. In the following paragraph notice words that are related to feeling, both inner feeling and outer sensations.

> As he tried to make his inept way, the pain was with him, because every time he tried to inhale, the night air hit the holes in his teeth and attacked the open nerves. The street was hard and filled with sharp dark things and he didn't have shoes on to protect him. He was still in his pajamas, a helpless creep just like the stoop gang always said, staggering along with a cripple closing the gap behind him. Something jammed into his foot then, something that hurt enough to penetrate into his brain deeper than the air against the nerves. Babe hoped it wasn't the broken glass but only maybe a rock that would hurt like crazy but not lay his foot open to even more serious pain.—WILLIAM GOLDMAN

All of the sentences in the paragraph contribute to the image of a person desperate to get away, experiencing pain, stumbling on something sharp. Phrases like "pain was with him" and "attacked the open nerves" express his inner state. "Jammed into his foot," "hurt like crazy," "lay his foot open," "more serious pain" are specific descriptions that enable you to feel Babe's hurt with him as he struggles. Helpless images increase the sense of suspense: "a helpless creep," "staggering," "a cripple closing the gap." If you have ever had unpleasant trips to the dentist, you cringe with Babe when the air hits the open nerves in his teeth. If you have ever stepped on something sharp while going barefoot, you have experienced the jabbing thrust of pain.

C. Here is a paragraph that will give you an entirely new feeling about rain.

> There were things that crawled on his skin. Things grew upon him in layers. Drops fell and touched other drops and they became streams that trickled over his body, and while these moved down his flesh, the small growths of the forest took root in his clothing. He felt the ivy cling and make a second garment over him; he felt the small flowers bud and open and petal away, and still the rain pattered on his body and on his head. In the luminous night—for the vegetation glowed in the darkness—he could see the other two men outlined, like logs that had fallen and taken upon themselves velvet coverings of grass and flowers. The rain hit his face. He covered his face with his hands. The rain hit his neck. He turned over on his stomach in the mud, on the rubbery plants, and the rain hit his back and hit his legs.—RAY BRADBURY

Pick out the words in the paragraph that are related to the sense of touch. Instead of a soft and gentle spring rain, something pleasant, this rain is a menace from which the men cannot escape. In every sentence of the paragraph you can "feel" the heavy, never-ceasing rain coming down on your body as you read.

D. Touch is the most intimate of the senses, bringing sensations of pleasure or pain. It is an immediate experience. Having sharpened this sense in practice and experience, write a paragraph emphasizing touch. Look over your notes and what you have recorded in your journal. Choose an object or experience to write about from this material or use one of the following suggestions. You may also develop a new idea.

diving into the water of a lake or pool	trudging through the snow on a cold day
walking along a beach or a road on a hot day	feeling mud or sand between your toes

Part 4 The Sense of Taste

1. List the things you like the taste of; then list the things you dislike the taste of.

2. Think of one taste you like or don't like. Describe what happened when you last experienced this taste.

3. Make a list of some things you have tasted and what quality of taste goes with each thing. For example: lemons—sour, candy —sweet.

4. Survey your family at home or some of your friends to see what tastes they like and don't like. Bring your results to school and compare them with those of a classmate.

Training in Tasting

Record the following experiences in your journal.

1. At dinner tonight plan to concentrate on your sense of taste. Sort out the flavor of each of the different things you eat. After dinner make a list of the foods you had. Beside each food write a short phrase that describes the flavor. Make some notes about your tastes in general. Do you like strong or mild flavors? Are there some foods you would eat hot but not cold, and vice versa?

2. Think for a minute about a taste you like very much and one you strongly dislike. Describe each taste, telling when you tasted it and what it was like.

Here is a list of taste words. As you think about each taste, try to recall your own taste experience with it. What things would you relate to each taste? Try to add more words of your own and record them in your journal.

	Taste Words		
oily	sugary	tangy	gingery
buttery	crisp	unripe	hot
salty	ripe	raw	burnt
bitter	bland	alkaline	overripe
bittersweet	tasteless	medicinal	spoiled
sweet	sour	fishy	rotten
hearty	vinegary	spicy	
mellow	fruity	peppery	

Exercises Using "Taste" Words in Your Writing

A. The sense of taste differs in each person. Here are some things you may have tasted. Write a sentence for each one, trying to use exact words to describe how it tastes to you. Record the sentences in your journal.

a lemon drop	gum
a piece of toast	an egg
a blade of grass	a pencil
ice cream	medicine
an orange	cola

Reread your sentences. Would every member of your family agree with your descriptions? Compare your sentences with those of someone sitting next to you. Where do you agree and disagree?

B. Read the following passage and notice all of the words that appeal to the sense of taste, especially the different kinds of foods included here.

On Sunday mornings Momma served a breakfast that was geared to hold us quiet from 9:30 A.M. to 3 P.M. She fried thick pink slabs of home-cured ham and poured the grease over sliced red tomatoes. Eggs over easy, fried potatoes and onions, yellow hominy, and crisp perch fried so hard we would pop them into our mouths and chew bones, fins, and all. Her cathead biscuits were at least three inches in diameter and two inches thick. The trick to eating catheads was to get the butter on them before they got cold—then they were delicious. When, unluckily, they were allowed to get cold, they tended to a gooeyness not unlike a wad of tired gum.—MAYA ANGELOU

Notice specific words that describe the food.

> ham—thick pink slabs, home-cured
> tomatoes—sliced red
> eggs—over easy
> potatoes—fried, and onions
> hominy—yellow
> perch—crisp, fried so hard. . . .
> biscuits—cathead, three inches in diameter, two inches thick,
> delicious; when cold, gooey like a wad of tired gum

In addition, the writer speaks not just of "eating" the perch; but says, "we would *pop* them into our mouths." She contrasts eating biscuits hot and cold, two different experiences.

c. Do you think your tastes change with time? Are there some things you like now that you didn't like before? After concentrating on tastes, you are ready to write a paragraph of your own in which you appeal to the sense of taste. Look over the ideas in your journal or try some of the following ideas.

1. Ask someone at home to give you something that is all right to eat, but not to tell you what it is. Close your eyes so that you can concentrate only on the taste. In a paragraph, describe the experience and the taste. Keep the events in this experience in the order they happen.

2. What is your favorite taste? Can you remember the first time you tasted it? What was happening at the time? Where were you? Who was with you? In a paragraph, recreate the moment or create a brand new situation in which you would like to be tasting the same thing right now.

Part 5 The Sense of Smell

1. List your favorite smells; then list the smells you dislike.

2. Starting when you leave this room, begin to list everything you can smell. Be aware of how the smells change with place, time of day, temperature, or other variables.

3. Choose a room at home or at school and describe all the different smells that are there when you walk in.

4. Think of an outdoor place where you like to be. List all the smells you can remember that are there. If this is a place you can go to on your way home today, check to see how well your nose "remembers."

5. Think of a past experience you have had that has a particular smell connected with it. List what you can remember about the place, such as the time of day, what happened, and the smells you remember.

Training in Smelling

1. It is difficult to train your sense of smell because you usually react only to strong odors, either pleasant or unpleasant. However, a change of surroundings can often help you develop this sense. Take a note pad or your journal with you and go through your house immediately after you come in from outside. Go into two or three different rooms and take notes about all of the smells you encounter. Do these smells change in intensity with the temperature in the room? Bring your notes to class to discuss with someone else.

2. Make a "nose trip" to a store in your area—a drugstore, supermarket, department store, hardware or automobile supply store, greenhouse, or florist. List all of the different odors you can smell there. Describe each odor carefully enough so that another person who was not there would be able to know what you are talking about. While you are in the store, make a list of the things you can recognize by their odor without using your

eyes or hands to identify them. Compare your results with someone else's. It might be more interesting if you and another person did this in the same store and compared your findings.

Here is a list of smell words. As you study each word, try to recall your experience with the smell. Add your own words to the list and record them in your journal.

Smell Words

sweet	minty	acidy	sickly
scented	odorous	acrid	stagnant
fragrant	pungent	burnt	mouldy
aromatic	tempting	gaseous	musty
perfumed	spicy	reeking	mildewed
heady	savory	putrid	damp
fresh	sharp	rotten	dank
balmy	gamy	spoiled	stench
earthy	fishy	sour	
piney	briny	rancid	

Exercises Using "Smell" Words in Your Writing

A. Write a sentence describing the smell of each of the things listed below. Be sure to identify the kind of flower or food or perfume. Record your sentences in your journal.

a fire	perfume
a flower	toothpaste
food cooking	cookies
wet coats	chalk
rain	popcorn

If the thing you are talking about were not named in the sentence, would your reader still know what you were describing?

B. Read the following paragraph that describes the smells of a small town. Notice all of the words related specifically to this sense. Can you find the two other words that are synonyms for smell?

In my memory, Stamps is a place of light, shadow, sounds, and entrancing odors. The earth smell was pungent, spiced with the odor of cattle manure, the yellowish acid of the ponds and rivers, the deep pots of greens and beans cooking for hours with smoked or cured pork. Flowers added their heavy aroma. And above all, the atmosphere was pressed down with the smell of old fears, and hates, and guilt.—MAYA ANGELOU

Did you notice the following:

odors—entrancing

earth smell—pungent

cattle manure—spiced

ponds and rivers—yellowish acid

greens and beans—with smoked or cured pork

flowers—heavy aroma

The writer also talks about "the smell of old fears, and hates, and guilt." These are experiences not usually related to smells. What do you think she is saying?

C. Concentrating especially on the sense of smell, write a paragraph using smell as a central idea. Use something from your notes in your journal, from the suggestions below, or a new idea of your own.

1. Write the first paragraph of a story that opens with a particular smell. It could be any kind of story, even a mystery in which the smell plays an important part.

2. In the paragraph by Ray Bradbury on page 38, the last line reads: "The door slid back and the smell of the silent, waiting world came in to them." Using this as your first sentence, write a paragraph describing the smells of that world.

Part 6 All of the Senses Working Together

You have spent a lot of time practicing the use of your five senses, concentrating on one at a time and sharpening each one. Now it's time for you to pull together all you have learned. Look over the work you have done thus far on your senses—your lists, notes, and all of the material in your journal. Find the writing that you most enjoyed doing, or the activities that were most satisfying to you. Before you write, study this example of sensory writing in which all of the senses are working together.

> The evening is lovely.
>
> True, it is not raining but still it is lovely. The puriri stands at the window motionless and shadowy, the forest mysterious and still, and between them the clearing, without the foxgloves which have died down in the winter. Water voices drift up from the river, the tui lets fall an occasional note, his signature to the evening, while from the forest emanates an odor made up of all the winter decomposition and all the summer blooming; exotic, pungent . . . heady.
>
> It is the enchanted moment when day faces night, a magic time which holds in itself a capacity for improbability unlikely in the daytime. The fire is still going in the stove with one over-long arm of wood beckoning from the firebox, while moths and other night-winged creatures make a freeway of the window.
>
> —Sylvia Ashton-Warner

List the senses used here, with the words and phrases related to them. What one sense is missing? The writer speaks of enchantment, "magic," "improbability." What senses are involved here? What kind of mood does this passage create in the reader?

In the following paragraph, the effect is quite different. Notice, again, the senses to which the writer appeals.

The Family came for the wedding. In a great autumnal avalanche of maple, sycamore, oak, elm leaf they hissed and rustled, fell into a shower of horse chestnut, thumped like winter apples on the earth, with an overall scent of farewell-summer on the wind they made in their rushing.—RAY BRADBURY

All of the senses are involved here. You see and feel autumn leaves, taste the winter apples, smell autumn, hear the hissing and rustling. Notice the vivid action words: "avalanche, hissed and rustled, fell, shower, thumped, wind, rushing." If you read the paragraph aloud, the words themselves have a crackling, autumnal quality to them.

Exercise All of the Senses Working Together

You are now ready to write about all of the senses working together. Reread John Moffitt's poem "To Look at Any Thing" on page 28. To experience any thing fully, the poet says, you must "Be the thing." If you are a fish, for example, you live in a watery world. Light and dark are shadowy; color is muted. You are cold blooded. You have scales, fins, a tail. Your eyes are on the sides of your head. You have to search for food. Dangers are of a different order. Time doesn't exist as humans know it.

Write a short composition in which you are something other than yourself. Put all your senses to work in your particular world. *Be the thing.*

Here are some suggestions to stir your imagination, but you can be anything else you wish.

a motorcycle	a pillow
a snake	a bird
a bee	an animal
a stone	a window
a rug	a fence
a tooth	a weed

Chapter 3

Improving Your Sentences

You may already know how to write sentences that are grammatically correct. You may know how to express a complete thought by means of a subject, a verb, and modifiers. Is there anything more you should learn about writing sentences? Frequently, there is.

Your sentences may be correct grammatically, yet fail to do the job. *The job of a sentence is to say something—to convey facts, ideas, and feelings.* Some of your sentences may say too little. Others may say too much. Still others may be unsatisfactory because their meaning is not clear.

This chapter will help you improve your sentences. It gives examples of unsatisfactory sentences and shows you how to go about revising them. It then supplies additional sentences for you to revise on your own.

Almost all of the sentences you will work with in this chapter were written by high school students. They did not have a chance to revise what they had written. You will be doing the revising for them.

This chapter is a challenge to you to think clearly and to write clearly.

Part 1   Avoiding Empty Sentences

The purpose of a sentence is to say something. Unfortunately, words may be put into sentence form and still not say anything. Such a sentence is called an **empty sentence.**

There are two kinds of empty sentences.

1. Sentences that merely repeat an idea and end up where they started.

2. Sentences that make statements but fail to support them with a fact, a reason, or an example.

Sentences That Repeat an Idea

Notice the repetition of an idea in the following sentences.

FAULTY   He had no friends, and because of this he was always alone.

  (Omit the second clause. It merely repeats the idea *He had no friends*.)

REVISED   He had no friends.

FAULTY   I have a minor *crisis* in my life, and to me it presents a *problem*.

  (Since *crisis* and *problem* are similar, use only one. Omit the second clause entirely.)

REVISED   I have a minor crisis in my life.

Sometimes a whole sentence is repeated. This repetitious style is boring and monotonous to read.

FAULTY   My father *complains* that I'm always on the phone, no matter what the time of day. His *complaint* is that I don't give anyone else a chance to use it.

REVISED   My father complains that no one else has a chance to
           use the phone because I'm on it all day.
           (Expressing the idea of *complaint* once is sufficient.
           The father's complaint has two parts: (1) *I'm always
           on the phone*, and (2) *I don't give anyone else a
           chance to use it.* Combine these two ideas as in the
           revision above.)

FAULTY   From my earliest days I have been an avid reader. I
           suppose I inherited this love of books from my mother.
           She also loves to read.

REVISED   From my earliest days I have been an avid reader. I
           suppose I inherited this love of books from my mother.
           (The second sentence indicates the mother's love of
           reading in her love of books. *She also loves to read* is
           unnecessary repetition.)

FAULTY   I asked Tom to stop at my house *for a Coke* and *to
           meet my mother.* After he *met my mother,* we went into
           the kitchen and *had a Coke.*

REVISED   Tom accepted my invitation to stop at my house for
           a Coke and to meet my mother.

Two suggestions will help you avoid this writing fault: (1)
read aloud what you have written, and (2) revise.

Exercise **Revising Sentences That Repeat an Idea**

Revise the sentences on the next page.

Suggestions

1. Look for repeated words in the same sentence.
2. Look for repeated ideas in the same sentence.
3. Look for sentences that repeat an idea already expressed.
4. Omit the repetitions wherever possible.
5. Combine two sentences into one, if necessary.
6. Realize that there is more than one way to revise these
   sentences.

1. Many people are interested in chess because it is a very interesting game.

2. The movie was boring, and I found it very dull.

3. Of course, you can't go on a hike without food. Who would ever dream of going on a hike without food?

4. Dad can't understand why I have to call my friends when I get home from school. He claims that I see my friends all day long in school, so I don't have to phone them as soon as I reach home.

5. At this point I usually burst into a torrent of tears. Mom and Dad usually know the right words to comfort me, however, for I soon feel better and begin to be a little more cheerful.

6. Have you ever watched television in a crowd? If you haven't watched it in a crowd, you can't imagine what it is like to watch television with three hundred people.

7. On Sunday we are going on a trip for the day. I am sure we will have a good time if the weather permits. There are seven of us going on the trip, and everyone is praying that we will have a wonderful day for our trip.

8. When I was small, I was rather spoiled. It wasn't because I was an only child, because I had two brothers. I think it was because I was the only girl and the only granddaughter. You see, all my cousins were boys.

9. In our high school, at every lunch period, there is a long cafeteria line. In the cafeteria we can purchase ice cream, candy, pretzels, hot food, and so on. To purchase these items, we must stand in a line.

10. If you have ever been to the zoo, you know what a great time you can have there. The zoo is a place to visit again and again. At the zoo there is always something new, wonderful, and educational to see.

Sentences That Contain Unsupported Statements

A kind of emptiness in writing results from statements that are not supported by reasons, facts, or examples. The question "Why?" is left in the reader's mind.

Try to find the unsupported statement in this group:

Chess is becoming popular with people of all ages. Even young children play it. I think it would be good for everyone to learn the game.

The unsupported statement is not difficult to find. Look for the sentence that involves an opinion. *Why* would it be good for everyone to learn chess?

Exercise Revising Unsupported Statements

Revise the following selections.

Suggestions

1. Locate the statement that needs support.
2. Ask "Why?" Then add whatever reasons or facts you think are necessary.

1. You can get a good laugh from practical jokes played in school. They can relieve the monotony of lessons. However, school is not the place for practical jokes.

2. There are more good job opportunities for minorities now because more good jobs are opening up.

3. Detroit is making a lot of small cars now. I think that is very good. I like these small cars and hope to own one in a few years.

4. Some people are talking about making the school year longer. This would be a mistake. The school year is long enough as it is.

5. I want to get a part-time job this year. I could work at least two hours after school each day. My parents do not approve of the idea.

6. For a long time American cars got bigger and bigger. Then foreign cars came into the picture. Now American companies are making little cars. I think these cars will soon drive the big cars off the market.

7. According to the state law, you have to be eighteen before you can get a decent job. I think this is very bad. I think the law should be changed.

8. Every year a million Americans go to Europe. How many of those people have traveled around this country? People should see their own country before going to Europe.

9. I always cheer for the Steelers (or Bears or Jets) because they are my favorite team.

10. The movie rating system ought to be changed because it isn't effective the way it is.

Part 2   Avoiding Padded Sentences

Some sentences contain padding like *the fact that* and *the reason is*. Others contain clauses that could be reduced to phrases without any damage to the thought. Although such padding may not always be considered incorrect, it often clutters the sentences and prevents writers from expressing their ideas clearly and concisely.

Taking Out the Padding

Phrases that puff up a sentence with unnecessary words get in the way of the meaning of the sentence. Trying to get to the meaning can be like trying to find a path that is overgrown with weeds.

Following are some of the expressions it is better to avoid.

"FACT" EXPRESSIONS	"WHAT" EXPRESSIONS
because of the fact that	what I mean is
owing to the fact that	what I believe is
due to the fact that	what I want is
on account of the fact that	

OTHER EXPRESSIONS TO AVOID

the point is   the reason is   the thing is

Sentences are smoother and simpler when unnecessary words are omitted.

PADDED   My family did not go to the shore *on account of the fact that* there was a storm.

REVISED   My family did not go to the shore *because* there was a storm.

PADDED   *What I mean is* that his ideas of summer camp are not realistic.

REVISED   His ideas of summer camp are not realistic.

PADDED   *The reason* I washed my father's car *was* that he hinted that it was dirty.

REVISED   I washed my father's car *because* he hinted that it was dirty.

PADDED   *What I want* is to go to Baltimore to see my grandparents if I don't get a job.

REVISED   I want to go to Baltimore to see my grandparents if I don't get a job.

PADDED   I know *that* if I study hard *that* I can get a scholarship.

REVISED   I know that if I study hard I can get a scholarship.
         Or, I know that I can get a scholarship if I study hard.

Reducing Clauses to Phrases

Clauses that begin with *who is* and *which is* can sometimes be simplified to phrases or to words in apposition. If these clauses are nonrestrictive (see Section 14, "Using Commas with Nonrestrictive Clauses"), they can be reduced to phrases or appositives or, in some cases, compound verbs.

LENGTHY   We admired the lights at the airport, *which is across the bay.*

REVISED   We admired the lights at the airport *across the bay.*
         (A clause has been reduced to a phrase.)

LENGTHY   Her latest movie, *which is a modern Western,* has been nominated for an Oscar.

REVISED Her latest movie, *a modern Western*, has been nominated for an Oscar.

(A clause has been reduced to an appositive.)

LENGTHY The swimming meet, *which was the most exciting event of the year*, attracted crowds of students.

REVISED The swimming meet, *the most exciting event of the year*, attracted crowds of students.

(A clause has been reduced to an appositive.) *Or,*

The swimming meet was the most exciting event of the year and attracted crowds of students.

(A clause has been reduced to a compound verb.)

Exercises Revising Padded Sentences

A. Revise these sentences by reducing and simplifying them.

Suggestions

1. Look for "fact" expressions, "what" expressions, and other padding.
2. Look for *who* or *which* clauses that can be simplified.
3. Eliminate as many unnecessary words as possible.
4. Realize that there is more than one way to revise these sentences.

1. What Sarah wants is to be a baseball coach.

2. The thing that nobody could understand was Ann's fear.

3. You must admit that even if you don't admire him that he plays well.

4. The Eiffel Tower, which is located in Paris, is a symbol of France.

5. On account of the fact that she had learned to bowl during the summer, Debbie wanted to join the school team.

6. We immediately called Mrs. Vincent, who is our lawyer, to ask for advice.

7. Due to the fact that the fog was dense, the two huge tankers collided.

8. What I believe is that you succeed largely because of your own efforts.

9. The point is that the study of French has many values.

10. Howie, who will do anything for a laugh, wore a T-shirt that had a formal black tie and ruffles printed on it.

B. Revise these sentences.

1. The reason that we took the car through the car wash was that it was covered with tree spray.

2. The rocks that extend out into the bay are dangerous at low tide.

3. The reason that Venice is fascinating is that many of its streets are all water.

4. Whenever it happens to rain hard, our cellar fills up with water and becomes a lake.

5. Many ruins in Rome are visible to tourists on account of the fact that much excavating has been done.

6. What I couldn't help hearing all night was the drone of the planes.

7. I knew that if I had to change the typewriter ribbon that I would create a hopeless tangle.

8. The fountain of Trevi, which is in Rome, is connected with a legend about coins.

9. What we finally did about our rehearsals was hold them in Mr. Steiner's garage.

10. I bought this ring in Harper's novelty store, which is on Walnut Street.

Part 3 Avoiding Overloaded Sentences

Long sentences containing a number of ideas, usually connected loosely by *and*'s, are confusing and ineffective. They give the reader a whole series of ideas to sort out without any clue to their relationship. Such sentences violate the principle that a sentence usually contains *one* central thought. It is better to break them into shorter sentences.

LENGTHY I went into the building, *and* I waited for the elevator in the lobby, *and* when it didn't come I had to walk up eight flights of stairs.

REVISED I went into the lobby of the building and waited for the elevator. When it didn't come, I had to walk up eight flights of stairs.

LENGTHY Horrible faces glared at me from the shelves in the costume shop. All of them were contorted, *and* most of them were scarred, *and* they were a deathly gray with a greenish cast, *and* their eyes looked like black holes.

REVISED Horrible faces glared at me from the shelves in the costume shop. All of them were contorted, and most of them were scarred. The faces were a deathly gray with a greenish cast. Their eyes looked like black holes.

Exercise Revising Overloaded Sentences

Revise the sentences on the next page.

Suggestions

1. Separate each sentence into two or three shorter ones.
2. Reduce the number of *and*'s.

1. Debbie got a white bike for her birthday, and it is a ten-speed model and it has a suede saddle.

2. Dad lost his wallet last Saturday with all his credit cards in it, but, luckily for him, it was returned yesterday by a neighbor who found it in the street outside our house.

3. For the Halloween party Luis dressed as Wolfman Jack, and Anna dressed as the Cookie Monster, and several people came as Evel Knievel, but the Wizard of Oz won the costume contest.

4. My family picked apples at an orchard, and we learned how to tell which apples were ripe and how to keep from bruising the fruit and how to climb ladders to reach the top branches, and the biggest bonus was the juicy apple pies we made.

5. Some children learn to read at age three or four, and others learn in school, and experts disagree about the value of very early training in reading.

6. Different styles of furniture change the mood of a room. Early American furniture has a colonial look, and contemporary furniture has a sleek look, and traditional furniture has a formal look, and there are also ethnic styles, like Mediterranean, Oriental, French, and Scandinavian.

7. One tree in our town is six hundred years old, and it has a hole in the trunk, and twenty people can stand inside it, and Indians used the tree long ago as a meeting place.

8. The art department offers classes in ceramics and photography, and this year there will be a printmaking class, and many students are eager to learn about etching and lithography.

9. Hurricanes are tropical cyclones, and they start over oceans, especially near the equator, and the winds can reach 150 miles per hour, and the most destructive hurricane occurred in 1972.

10. The Olympic Games are patterned after an ancient Greek festival, and the first modern games were held in 1896, and since then the number of sports and participants has greatly increased.

Part 4 Writing Sentences That Make Sense

Sometimes students write sentences that do not make complete sense because they shift from what they started to say to something else. In between, the main idea has become confused or lost. They may also write quickly and carelessly and fail to check what they have written. The result is a hodgepodge, and situations like these occur:

1. A verb has no subject.
2. A prepositional phrase is used as a subject.
3. A faulty comparison is made.
4. Single words, necessary to complete the meaning, are left out.

Making Sure That the Verb Has a Subject

Study the following examples.

FAULTY   If you constantly practice is a help in becoming a better dancer.

    (There is no subject for the verb *is*.)

REVISED   Constant practice helps you to become a better dancer.

FAULTY   His character was very weak and never did the right thing.

    (There is no subject for the verb *did*.)

REVISED   His character was very weak, and *he* never did the right thing.

By rereading and revising what you have written, you can frequently eliminate this problem.

Avoiding the Use of a Prepositional Phrase as the Subject

Study the following examples.

FAULTY   By setting up observation posts near volcanoes and detecting eruptions early can save many lives.

(A prepositional phrase is used incorrectly as the subject of *can save*.)

REVISED   *Setting* up observation posts near volcanoes and *detecting* eruptions early can save many lives.

(The italicized words are acceptable subjects for *can save*.)

Avoiding Faulty Comparisons

A special kind of senseless sentence is one in which there is a faulty comparison or one in which two things not equal are made equal.

FAULTY   *Studying biology* in high school is very different from *college.*

(*Studying biology* should not be compared with *college.*)

REVISED   *Studying biology* in high school is very different from *studying it* in college.

FAULTY   The requirements for the job are an engineer and at least one year of experience.

(An *engineer* is a person and does not equal the word *requirements.*)

REVISED   The requirements for the job call for an engineer with at least one year of experience.

Sentences that have pieces missing are like puzzles that do not form a complete picture because an important part is left out. Rereading and revising can straighten out the confusion.

Making Sure That Necessary Words Are Included

The omission of a single word can make a sentence meaningless. This kind of carelessness can be avoided by rereading and revising your work.

FAULTY   The little Swiss family find themselves comfortably situated as conditions will permit.

(The word *as* has been left out.)

REVISED   The little Swiss family find themselves *as* comfortably situated as conditions will permit.

FAULTY   Elizabeth Barrett, an invalid for many years, knew what she wanted to do but was afraid of her father to attempt it.

REVISED   Elizabeth Barrett, an invalid for many years, knew what she wanted to do but was *too* afraid of her father to attempt it.

Exercises Revising Sentences That Do Not Make Sense

A. Revise the ten sentences on the next page.

Suggestions

1. Make sure that every verb has a subject.
2. Make sure that a prepositional phrase is not used as a subject.
3. Correct the faulty comparisons.
4. Make sure that necessary words have been included.

1. The cost of running a small car is less than a big car.

2. The real test of Donna's personality was her older sister.

3. The easier a subject is and the higher marks you can get with little work does not mean you should choose it.

4. To anyone who observes life and the game of football will soon detect many similarities.

5. The only real problem I find I wear out the rug by dancing.

6. Paula's fever has broken and is now feeling much better.

7. You could tell by my expression the anguish I was through.

8. Andy's explanation of scuba diving is clearer than high-diving.

9. By applying for a summer job early is the best way for a student to be hired.

10. The faster the car goes is not the best reason for buying it.

B. Revise the following sentences.

1. Playing football in college is much different from high school.

2. The way I check a person is how he or she acts.

3. The more you have to do and the less time makes you work harder.

4. Some hobbies are so that you can make money out of them.

5. Going to college or a job is a question every student must face before he or she graduates.

6. I burned the hamburgers is why we finally went to McDonald's.

7. Because it's a white dog with black spots all over it is why I'm sure it's a Dalmatian.

8. Any fad that Jerry hears about, he follows it.

9. Radio commercials don't bother me as much as TV.

10. You tell a good friend what he or she wants to hear is not always the kindest thing to do.

Part 5 Varying Your Sentence Beginnings

This is the usual order of the sentence in English.

$$\text{SUBJECT} + \text{VERB} + \begin{cases} \text{OBJECT (AND MODIFIERS)} \\ \text{or} \\ \text{PREDICATE WORD (AND MODIFIERS)} \end{cases}$$

You are interested in making your writing lively and effective. You want people to *want* to read what you have to say. One way to achieve this effectiveness is to vary the beginnings of your sentences, to give them a new look by inverting the order of their parts. You must be careful not to overwork this plan because inverted order often has a dramatic quality that could be out of place in certain kinds of writing. Use it to intensify a situation or an idea, or momentarily to slow down the pace of your writing.

Ways To Vary Your Sentence Beginnings

1. **Put an adverb before the subject.**

   USUAL ORDER Butch inched his way *cautiously* to the deserted house.

   (adverb)

   INVERTED *Cautiously*, Butch inched his way to the deserted house.

   USUAL ORDER She stopped *abruptly* and stared at him.

   (adverb)

   INVERTED *Abruptly*, she stopped and stared at him.

2. **Put the verb or direct object before the subject.**

   USUAL ORDER The *torrents* of rain *poured* down.

   (verb)   **(subject)**

   INVERTED Down *poured* the *torrents* of rain.

USUAL ORDER	*Anchorage was* twenty miles ahead of us.
	(verb) (subject)
INVERTED	Twenty miles ahead of us *was Anchorage.*

USUAL ORDER	*I* could not tolerate an *insult* like that.
	(object) (subject)
INVERTED	An *insult* like that *I* could not tolerate.

USUAL ORDER	*I* can recall certain *songs* without difficulty.
	(object) (subject)
INVERTED	Certain *songs I* can recall without difficulty.

3. **Begin the sentence with a prepositional phrase, a participial phrase, or an infinitive phrase.** Be sure the phrase modifies the proper word.

USUAL ORDER	Nothing is more beautiful *to me* than a snowstorm.
	(prepositional phrase)
INVERTED	*To me,* nothing is more beautiful than a snowstorm.

USUAL ORDER	I waited alone *for ten minutes.*
	(prepositional phrase)
INVERTED	*For ten minutes* I waited alone.

USUAL ORDER	James led her into the hall, *taking her gently by the hand.*
	(participial phrase)
INVERTED	*Taking her gently by the hand,* James led her into the hall.

USUAL ORDER	We headed for the dude ranch, *excited about our unusual vacation.*
	(participial phrase)
INVERTED	*Excited about our unusual vacation,* we headed for the dude ranch.

USUAL ORDER	Sharon went to the library *to get information about satellites.*

(infinitive phrase)

INVERTED	*To get information about satellites,* Sharon went to the library.

USUAL ORDER	Dick must pass a physical examination *to be eligible for the team.*

(infinitive phrase)

INVERTED	*To be eligible for the team,* Dick must pass a physical examination.

4. Begin the sentence with a subordinate clause.

USUAL ORDER	Paula's mother was at the airport to meet the girls *when they got off the plane.*

(subordinate clause)

INVERTED	*When the girls got off the plane,* Paula's mother was there to meet them.

USUAL ORDER	I felt like a millionaire *as I boarded the ship for France.*

(subordinate clause)

INVERTED	*As I boarded the ship for France,* I felt like a millionaire.

Exercises Varying Your Sentence Beginnings

A. Rewrite the following sentences, varying the positions of the words or word groups in italics.

You may have more than one effective arrangement. Say the sentences out loud to help you decide which arrangement sounds better.

1. We tried not to show our excitement *as we sat on the stage listening to the speaker.*

2. The clock *finally* struck ten.

3. It is spring *once more.*

4. The combo settled down and played good music *after the audience left.*

5. He looked uncomfortable and unhappy, *dressed in his best suit.*

6. The plow was tossing up huge mounds of snow *in the corners of the parking lot.*

7. Nothing will happen *unless I make the first move.*

8. The driver was *suddenly* blinded by a flash of light.

9. I picked up a Super 8 movie camera *at a garage sale.*

10. The frightened people hurried *out into the rain.*

11. I went to the rink *every day* and finally learned to skate.

12. I lost my interest in snowmobiling *after the accident.*

13. Paul buried himself in his work *to fight against his fear.*

14. We sold everything from fish tanks to skis *at our garage sale.*

15. *The tenor sax* is one of the instruments Leona plays.

B. Rewrite each sentence below. Change the positions of words so that you have an effective variation of the sentence. Be careful to punctuate correctly.

1. My pen ran dry in the middle of the test.

2. The swirling, muddy torrent came down, dragging tents and equipment with it.

3. Still we had no coach for the team.

4. Peter sold his stamp collection reluctantly.

5. A young woman sat in one corner, clutching her small baby.

6. My dad gave me my first driving lesson after I reminded him that the car was insured.

7. She went off to the fitting room, carrying three new dresses.

8. Joe's problem grew heavier as he shuffled down Main Street.

9. The police questioned the suspect for eight hours.

10. The treasure, strangely beautiful, was all mine.

11. Diana hurried to the locker room as soon as the game was over.

12. I cannot tell how long it took me to reach home.

13. Andy kept on eating pizza even though he knew he was gaining too much weight.

14. Greta's face lit up like a candle when she smiled.

15. Dad climbs the walls when our kitten climbs the curtains.

Revising Sentences with Various Problems

A. Revise the following sentences. They contain various problems you have dealt with in this chapter.

1. I know that if I try that I can get into college.
2. The pen that has the red felt tip leaks.
3. Each time, I went through a routine that was different.
4. The reception on my parents' stereo is better than my radio.
5. My speech did not go over well due to the fact that I was nervous.
6. What I sometimes really wish is people wouldn't behave like sheep.
7. Mr. Russo is completely bald is probably the reason he always wears a cap.
8. The photos of the surface of Mars look just like the Painted Desert of Arizona.
9. I got sick on account of the fact that I ate too many tacos.
10. Make my bed, clean up my room, but put away my barbell is the only thing I forget to do.

B. Revise the following.

1. Television lets you sit back and let a machine think for you. You don't do any of the thinking yourself.
2. When you think about it, you realize that death is something that happens to everyone, but most of the time you think it will happen only to other people and that it will never happen to you.
3. In Switzerland, skiing is a popular sport. Many Swiss ski regularly.
4. Bill has his CB license, and he is talking all the time with everybody under the sun, and in case you want to talk to him yourself, his handle is "Cookie Monster."
5. Disc jockeys at many radio stations are given a "play list" of songs that have been selected by a computer, and these songs are either popular now or expected to be popular soon, and the disc jockey has to play the songs on the list.

6. A girl from our high school has just been admitted to West Point, and to be admitted she had to be nominated by a U.S. Congressman and, of course, to have good grades and a good all-round record.

7. Last weekend a car smashed into the back of our camper and shook us up, and fortunately nothing was damaged except our bike carrier which was at the back.

8. How to load an Instamatic camera is the thing I have trouble doing.

9. The little chestnut foal, which was born yesterday morning and is still a bit unsteady on her legs, has beautiful soft eyes and is never more than a step away from her mother, who is very protective.

10. My brother says that microcomputers are going to be the hottest home entertainment industry since television, and he says people are just starting to see how much fun these little gadgets can be, and he predicts that people will soon be bored by television.

Chapter 4

The Process of Writing

Learning to write is a continuing process. Once you have learned the basic elements of writing, you can begin to refine your writing. Writing as often as you can becomes increasingly important. You learn to use a more precise vocabulary. You learn to tighten your sentence structure. You begin to find your own "voice" in writing, which enables you to develop a style. You gain a sense of audience for the different kinds of writing you will be doing.

Whenever you write, however, there will always be something that remains the same: the process of writing. There are steps you can follow: pre-writing, writing a first draft, and rewriting, or revising. These steps are critical to the process of writing. They help you decide what to write about, how to organize what you write, and how to rewrite, or revise, what you have written.

Pre-Writing	1. *Possible Topics*
	   my first time skating
	   the Renaissance Fair
	   our school car wash
	
	2. *Selected Topic*
	   the Renaissance Fair

Writing the First Draft	~~*Every summer*~~ ~~*Each year,*~~ *the English Renaissance* *is revived in* ~~*comes to Gurnee, Illinois., Gurnee is*~~ *the site of* ~~*the*~~ *annual King Richard's* *Fair. Visitors to the Ffaire can*
Rewriting, or Revising	*Every summer, the English Renaissance is revived in Gurnee, Illinois, the site of King Richard's Faire. Visitors to the Faire can*

Part 1   Pre-Writing

Sometimes you write in response to an assignment. Sometimes you write in order to communicate something important to you. Whatever you write, and whenever you write, you will find the beginning steps, called pre-writing, very important.

Before you write, you need to focus on your subject. Take your time at this point in the process of writing. Choose a subject that interests you. Use all of your senses to bring your subject clearly into focus. Make a list of possible topics. Select one topic and narrow it so that you can handle it in a given length.

Next, make a list of interesting details that you could use to develop your topic. List as many as you can think of. You can always eliminate those that do not work.

Finally, jot down any notes or ideas related to your topic. You do not have to use all of them. If you need to learn more about your topic, do that, too.

Here is an example of pre-writing notes.

1. Possible Topics
    my surprise party
    the class dance
    championship baseball game
    trip to the Museum of Art
    renting roller skates

2. Selected Topic
    renting roller skates

3. Specific Details
    new, different skates
    blue canvas, size 7
    rubberized wheels
    Royal Sport skates
    $3.00 for 2 hours
    knee pads, elbow pads
    bumps, falling
    Davis Street--smooth, gliding

4. Notes
    narrative paragraph?
    develop with details
    try to show my feelings

Part 2 Writing the First Draft

At this point in the process of writing, you are ready to write. Do not fuss with the writing. Do not worry about organizing ideas. Do not fret about spelling or punctuation. Do not get trapped by trying to make anything perfect at this stage. Let whatever happens, happen. Just write. This is only your first draft. You will rewrite, or revise, later.

Here is an example of a first draft of a paragraph.

FIRST DRAFT

As I tightened the laces of the sleek, rented roller skates, I felt nervous. I had not been on skates since I was eight years old. Those were made of metal, while these were blue canvas with rubberized wheels. Could I manage to roll along with my friends? Would I fall? Would everyone laugh at me? As I took my first steps, I lost my ballance. I fell backwards. I was so flustered, I felt like an awkward kid. Soon I was able to stand up. Later, the gliding wheels carried me smoothly down Davis Street. I felt happy and free.

Part 3 Rewriting, or Revising

Now read what you have written. At this stage of the process, you will need to work more carefully and thoughtfully. You have to check what you have written.

Did you stick to your topic? Did you include everything you wanted to? Did you leave out unnecessary details? Do you like what you have written? Is it lively and interesting?

Read aloud what you have written. Often your ears will catch what your eyes do not. Listen to the rhythm of your writing. Do your ideas flow smoothly?

Concentrate on every word. Is your idea clearly expressed? Did you *show* your reader what you want to say? Is each word the right word?

Is your writing organized logically? Is there a beginning, a middle, and an end to the development of your idea? Take the time to read your writing and to think about it carefully.

Here is the rewritten, or revised, paragraph. Compare it with the first draft. Think about the changes that were made. Notice how the ideas are expressed in a different way.

REWRITTEN, OR REVISED, PARAGRAPH

As I tightened the laces of the sleek rented roller skates, I felt nervous. I had not been on skates since I was eight years old. Those old skates only were made of a frame rusted metal, while these were blue canvas shoeskates with rubberized wheels. Could I manage to roll along expertly with my friends? Would I fall? Would everyone laugh at me? As I took my first steps, I lost my ballance. I fell backwards but no one laughed. I spent a while struggling to stay on my feet, and I finally was so flustered, I felt like an awkward kid. Soon I was able to stand up improved. Later, I was the gliding wheels carried me smoothly down Davis Street. I felt happy and free.

Proofreading

It is important to make your writing correct, as well as clear and lively. Check your spelling. Check capitalization and punctuation. Use whatever references you have available to check your work.

Finally, when you are satisfied that your writing is clear and correct, write it in its final form. Write carefully. Make your work as neat as possible. Be sure to follow the manuscript form that your teacher requires, including heading and margins.

When you have finished your final copy, proofread your work. Read your writing aloud, to yourself, one final time.

Here is the final copy of the paragraph. Compare it with the two preceding paragraphs.

FINAL COPY

I felt nervous as I tightened the laces of the rented roller skates. I had not been on skates since I was eight years old. Those old skates were only a frame of rusted metal. These were blue canvas shoeskates with rubberized wheels. Could I manage to roll along expertly with my friends, or would I fall? Would everyone laugh at me? As I took my first steps, I lost my balance. I fell backwards, but no one laughed. I spent a while struggling to stay on my feet, and I finally improved. Soon I was able to stand up. Later, I was gliding smoothly down Davis Street.

Guidelines for the Process of Writing

Pre-Writing

1. Choose a subject that interests you.
2. Make a list of possible topics.
3. Select a topic and narrow it.
4. Make a list of interesting details that you could use to develop your topic.
5. Jot down any notes or ideas related to your topic.
6. Learn more about your topic if you need to.

Writing the First Draft

1. Begin to write.
2. Continue to write, without stopping to fuss over or correct anything at this stage. Let your thoughts flow freely.

Rewriting, or Revising

1. Read what you have written.
2. Did you stick to your topic?
3. Did you include everything you wanted to?
4. Did you leave out unnecessary details?
5. Do you like what you have written?
6. Is it interesting and lively?
7. Read aloud what you have written.
8. Do your ideas flow smoothly?
9. Are your ideas clearly expressed?
10. Is each word the right word?
11. Is your writing organized logically, with a beginning, a middle, and an end?
12. Rewrite, or revise, wherever necessary.

Proofreading

1. Read your rewritten, or revised, first draft.
2. Check for correct capitalization.
3. Check spelling. Use a dictionary, if necessary.
4. Check to see that all punctuation is correct.
5. Make a neat, final copy. Follow required manuscript form.
6. Read your final copy aloud, to yourself.

Chapter 5

Writing Effective Paragraphs

In Chapters 1 and 2 you studied the use of words to express ideas. In this chapter you will learn to express your ideas in paragraphs. You will learn to write paragraphs that communicate your ideas clearly and in a variety of ways.

Part 1   What Is a Paragraph?

A paragraph is a group of sentences dealing with a *single topic or idea*. Usually, one sentence, called the **topic sentence,** states the main idea of the paragraph. All the other sentences are related to this topic sentence. They further explain or support the main idea.

Example 1

Study the following paragraph.

>   My father was a master storyteller. He could tell a fine old story that made me hold my sides with rolling laughter and sent happy tears down my cheeks. He could tell a story of stark reality that made me shiver and be grateful for my own warm, secure surroundings. He could tell stories of beauty and grace, stories of gentle dreams, and paint them as vividly as any picture with

splashes of character and dialogue. His memory detailed every event of ten or forty years or more before, just as if it had happened yesterday.—MILDRED D. TAYLOR

This is a well organized, well written paragraph. In the first sentence, the writer states, "My father was a master storyteller." In the remaining sentences, she supports that idea by describing the many kinds of stories that her father told.

Example 2

The following is also a well written paragraph.

The wolverine may well be nature's most fearsome fighter. In battle with an enemy, he is a twisting, slashing blur of sheer fury that bewilders and terrifies an adversary. He has been known to attack a 1,200-pound moose—an animal more than forty times his weight—and is capable of defending himself against an entire pack of wolves.—REED MILLARD

The writer begins with the sentence, "The wolverine may well be nature's most fearsome fighter." In the sentences that follow, he describes the wolverine's fighting abilities. By doing so, he supports the main idea stated in the topic sentence.

In this Example, and also in Example 1, all the sentences in the paragraph relate to one idea. They are tied together, or unified, by that idea.

Example 3

Study the following example.

Native Americans cultivated and developed many plants. Among them were white potatoes, sweet potatoes, corn, beans, tobacco, chocolate, peanuts, cotton, rubber, and gum. The log cabin was an adaptation of the Indian log or longhouse. Plants were used for dyes, medicines, soap, clothes, shelter, and baskets.

The first sentence indicates that the paragraph will be about the cultivation and development of plants by Native Americans. However, sentence 3 is about log cabins. This idea is not related to the main idea of the paragraph. The sentence, therefore, violates the unity of the paragraph.

The problem is easily solved by removing the third sentence:

> Native Americans cultivated and developed many plants. Among them were white potatoes, sweet potatoes, corn, beans, tobacco, chocolate, peanuts, cotton, rubber, and gum. Plants were used for dyes, medicines, soap, clothes, shelter, and baskets.

Example 4

The following example has a different problem.

> A whale, one of the largest animals in the world, is killed by Soviet and Japanese whale hunters every seventeen minutes. This makes some people angry. Someday, whales might be like the dinosaur and disappear forever. People are showing their anger in many ways. One Japanese businessman says, "Many Japanese could not live without whale meat." Some people are writing letters to the Japanese Prime Minister, and others are asking people not to buy Japanese products. If this hurts Japanese business enough, the Japanese government may stop the whale hunting.

At first glance, all the sentences in the paragraph seem to relate to the killing of whales. However, it is hard to tell for sure because the ideas are so disorganized. They must be rearranged so that they relate to each other in a logical way.

If you were asked to revise this paragraph, you might begin by listing all the sentences that refer to whales.

1. A whale, one of the largest animals in the world, is killed by Soviet and Japanese whale hunters every seventeen minutes.

2. Someday, whales might be like the dinosaur and disappear forever.

3. One Japanese businessman says, "Many Japanese could not live without whale meat."

Next, list all the sentences that refer to the attitude of the people.

1. This makes some people angry.

2. People are showing their anger in many ways.

3. Some people are writing letters to the Japanese Prime Minister, and others are asking people not to buy Japanese products.

4. If this hurts Japanese business enough, the Japanese government may stop the whale hunting.

The first two sentences about whales are closely related. Sentence 1 is about the killing of whales. Sentence 2 suggests that if the killings continue, whales might someday disappear. The two sentences could be tied together even more closely with the addition of the phrase "if this killing continues" to sentence 2. The first part of the paragraph would then read like this:

> A whale, one of the largest animals in the world, is killed by Soviet and Japanese whale hunters every seventeen minutes. Someday, if this killing continues, whales might be like the dinosaur and disappear forever.

The third sentence, about the Japanese businessman, does not relate to sentences 1 and 2. That sentence should be removed. Then the four sentences about the attitude of the people should be added, making the following six-sentence paragraph.

> A whale, one of the largest animals in the world, is killed by Soviet and Japanese whale hunters every seventeen minutes. Someday, if this killing continues, whales might be like the dinosaur and disappear forever. This makes some people angry. People are showing their anger in several ways. Some people are writing letters to the Japanese Prime Minister, and others are asking people not to buy Japanese products. If this hurts Japanese business enough, the Japanese government may stop the whale hunting.

All the ideas in the paragraph are now expressed in a logical way. Two sentences, however, contain a weak repetition of ideas.

1. This makes some people angry.
2. People are showing their anger in several ways.

The sentences can be combined.

> This makes some people angry, and they are showing their anger in several ways.

Exercise   Making Groups of Sentences into Paragraphs

Study the following groups of sentences. Some are good paragraphs. Others contain sentences that are unrelated to the others or are disorganized in their presentation. Identify the groups of sentences that are not good paragraphs. Then revise them by dropping sentences, by rearranging sentences, or by making other changes that shape the sentences into good paragraphs.

1. Paula Murphy is known as the fastest woman in the world. She has raced over Ontario Speedway and Bonneville Salt Flats fast enough to leave her competition far behind in the dust. She is slim, soft-spoken, and friendly. She has broken through speed records, broken down sex barriers, and broken her neck for racing. She is a female drag-strip racer.

2. The wind was blowing so hard it lifted the trees right out of the ground. Every bush and tree for miles around had been uprooted. There I was, barebacked on my old horse, Dan. I was surprised that I was still riding my horse. My saddle, bridle, blanket, everything had been blown off. I had nothing on except my jeans. The dust was so thick you couldn't see a thing.

3. I have never known a hotter July. There was a soft, hazy, constant heat that hung over everything and never let up—only seemed to turn dark with evening. In our garden the black earth dried and crumbled brown, shrinking away till the twisted tomato roots showed above the ground. Out in the country the fields were a parched patchwork and only the trees were still green against the dust-yellow roll of the hills.

4. Native Americans of long ago placed a high value on mother earth and nature. Land was not owned by individuals, but was held in common by all the people. There is peace in being close to mother earth. The land, water, and animals—all things of nature—were used sparingly and with great respect. They were always used for a purpose and never wasted. At one time large groups of Native Americans lived along the Atlantic coast.

5   I felt good. I think the park had something to do with it. Trees, grass, bushes—everything appeared in brand-new togs of shining green. The warm yellow sunlight sifted down through the trees, making my face feel alive and healthy and casting shadows on the paved walks and the unpaved walks and the wooden benches. Slight breezes tickled my nostrils, caressed my face, bringing with them a good, clean odor of things new and live and dripping with greenness. Such a good feeling made me uneasy.

6   The road was deserted as she'd been told it would be. The trees made a black arch bending in the rain. The sky was filled with dark, heavy thunderclouds. Suddenly, she saw an old woman and a child standing silently in the rain. The old woman held an end of her shawl around the child's shoulder, but the little girl still shivered in the cold.

7   There lived in the Land of Oz two men who were the best of friends. One was a Scarecrow. That means he was a suit of blue Munchkin clothes, stuffed with straw, on top of which was fastened a round cloth head, filled with bran to hold it in shape. On the head were painted two eyes, two ears, a nose, and a mouth. The Scarecrow had never been much of a success in scaring crows; but he prided himself on being a superior man because he could feel no pain, was never tired, and did not have to eat or drink. His brains were sharp, for the Wizard of Oz had put pins and needles in the Scarecrow's brains. The other man was made all of tin, and his arms and legs and head were cleverly jointed so that he could move them freely. He was known as the Tin Woodman, having at one time been a woodchopper. Everyone loved him because the Wizard had given him an excellent heart of red plush.

8   If parents show an interest in the programs their teenagers watch on TV, useful discussions will often result. Few things are more important to fourteen-year-olds than having their opinions listened to and respected. The types of things teenagers watch on TV will change with age. Values and situations shown on television can be the basis for lively exchanges of ideas.

Part 2 Paragraph Unity

Each sentence in a paragraph must relate to one single idea. The sentences either state the idea or contribute in some way to its development. When this is true, a paragraph is said to have *unity*.

The topic sentence of a paragraph plays a key role in establishing paragraph unity. The sentence is like a contract between writer and reader. The writer is saying, in effect, "Look, I have this idea I want to explain to you." The reader is answering, "All right, explain it to me." For the writer to hold to the contract, he or she must explain the idea stated in the topic sentence.

Let's look at three examples of topic sentences.

1. *The shell in my hand is deserted.*
2. *The King was a quiet man who did not like to speak overmuch.*
3. *Teenagers today are detached from their parents.*

Writer 1 says she is going to explain something about a deserted shell. Writer 2 says she wants to explain something about the king's quietness. Writer 3 says he wants to explain something about the detachment of teenagers from their parents. Let's see how well each has held to the contract implied by the topic sentence.

1   *The shell in my hand is deserted.* It once housed a whelk, a snail-like creature, and then temporarily, after the death of the first occupant, a little hermit crab, who has run away, leaving his tracks behind him like a delicate vine on the sand. He ran away and left me his shell. It was once a protection to him. I turn the shell in my hand, gazing into the wide open door from which he made his exit. Had it become an encumbrance? Why did he run away? Did he hope to find a better home, a better mode of living?

The paragraph does give an explanation of the writer's opening statement, so the contract is complete.

2 *The King was a quiet man who did not like to speak overmuch.* This was partly, no doubt, because he had a serious speech defect. He had inherited the long, heavy, out-of-balance jaw of the Hapsburg line, together with their round high forehead, golden hair, and blue eyes. Due to the configuration of his jaw, the King's teeth did not meet squarely; and when he spoke it was with a curious lisp. Besides, I believe that he was shy and that he had learned, in his years at court, that it was fatal to trust anyone with all your heart.

The remainder of the paragraph explains why the king was a quiet man. Again, the contract is complete.

3 *Teenagers today are detached from their parents.* The house is junky; the car is crummy; parents are "out of it." A kid without money can live off friends. Children used to respect their parents, but not any more. One's heart bleeds for the poor parents.

In this paragraph, the writer has not held to the contract. The sentences that follow the topic sentence do not explain the detachment between teenagers and their parents. They do not, therefore, explain the idea presented in the topic sentence.

Paragraph Length

Sometimes a paragraph is not long enough to develop the idea stated in the topic sentence. The writer, by failing to explain the idea completely, does not complete the contract. The reader does not get all the information needed to understand the idea clearly.

Notice in the following paragraph, for example, how incomplete the information is.

Almost anyone would have treated me better than Uncle Eldon did. From the first day, he worked me like his slave.

If the paragraph ended here, you would be left with the question, "Exactly what did Uncle Eldon do to the writer?" The paragraph needs specific detail, as in the following example.

Almost anyone would have treated me better than Uncle Eldon did. From the first day, he worked me like his slave. I cut down trees. I sawed the fallen trees into logs. I dragged the logs to the house and cut them into kindling. Whenever the kindling pile was high, I was sent to clean the drafty old barn or to do other work in the cold.

By expanding the number of sentences from two to six, the writer has developed the topic into an interesting paragraph that explains the idea in the topic sentence and leaves the reader feeling satisfied.

Exercise Analyzing Paragraphs

Read each paragraph carefully. Then decide whether the writer has kept the contract implied by the topic sentence. Give reasons for your decision.

1   My father has a peculiar habit. He is fond of sitting in the dark, alone. Sometimes I come home very late. The house is dark. I let myself in quietly because I do not want to disturb my mother. She is a light sleeper. I tiptoe into my room and undress in the dark. I go to the kitchen for a drink of water. My bare feet make no noise.

2   The rainy season came to the forest, as it must come every year. At night the water fell with a roar like thunder. In the morning it beat against the branches of the trees and tore their leaves from them. It pounded against the thatched roofs of the villages and rushed about the footpaths. Little girls set pots under the sky to catch the water, and ran back slipping and sliding. The small, friendly rivers became deep and wide, and covered the sides of their banks. During the darkness the people fastened their doors and did not even look outside, for they could hear nothing but rain, rain, rain.

3   Your grandmother could probably tell you what it was like to run a house on coal. Back then, she had a ton or so delivered down a chute into the basement.

4   When my little dog died, I was very sad. It happened on Valentine's Day. My birthday is on February 22, eight days after Valentine's Day. I cried a lot, but it didn't bring my little dog back. My Dad and I buried him in a vacant lot down the street, and we placed a tombstone over the grave. On my birthday, I got some new roller skates.

5   People have trouble identifying my heritage. Indians mistake me for one of their own. In Chinatown they give me a menu written in Chinese, and once a Japanese boy asked me if I was Korean. My ancestors are full-blooded Japanese, but I have had to get used to people thinking I'm something else.

6   The needs of our country have changed since its beginnings. The first settlers had to work very hard. Now the majority of American workers do not do hard physical labor. The Pilgrims were able to increase their food supply and build shelters from the cold. In Japan, too, industry is highly mechanized.

7   The main advantage of the metric system is its simplicity. It uses three units of measurement.

8   I grew up on the island of Puerto Rico in an atmosphere of natural story-tellers. I had a father whose occupation took him all over the island; a grandmother whose stories always ended with a nonsense rhyme or song, setting feet to jump, skip or dance; elder sisters who still remembered tales told by a mother; and finally, a stepmother whose literary taste was universal. I never ever went to bed without a round of stories told. The characters of my favorite ones became part of my everyday life: I traveled to strange lands of shepherds, princesses and princes, Kings and Queens; I laughed at the cunning of the animals and suffered with the punished ones.

Part 3   The Topic Sentence

In Part 1, a topic sentence was defined as the one sentence that states the main idea of a paragraph. A topic sentence is usually the first sentence of a paragraph. As such, it performs two tasks:

1. It makes a general statement about what is to follow.

2. It controls and limits the ideas that can be discussed in the remainder of the paragraph.

There is some overlapping in these two tasks. However, on the following pages, each one will be considered separately.

The Topic Sentence Makes a General Statement About What Is To Follow

A topic sentence makes a general statement that is wider in its scope than the rest of the sentences in the paragraph. A good topic sentence is broad enough to be supported or developed by specific details.

To clarify this point, let's look at two good topic sentences:

1. *The English language spoken in the United States owes much to Spanish importation.*

2. *A person can do something for peace without having to jump into politics.*

These sentences contain very little *specific* information. They are well written and interesting, but the information contained in them is only enough to arouse curiosity. After reading them, you might find yourself saying, "Don't stop there. How did the Spanish language influence English? What can a person do for peace? Tell me more."

A good writer will satisfy your curiosity by giving specific details in the rest of the paragraph. The details will explain the general statement in the topic sentence.

Let's see how the writers of the two topic sentences explained their general statements.

1   *The English language spoken in the United States owes much to Spanish importation.*

The English language spoken in the United States owes much to Spanish importation. Such Spanish words as *desperado, sombrero, mesa, sierra, arroyo, cañon, chaparral, mesquite, adobe, ramada, cabaña, hacienda, patio, plaza, coyote, jaguar, serape, machete, mañana* are used all the time. Also, a long list of Spanish words has become so thoroughly "naturalized" that people have forgotten they were ever Spanish—words like *vigilante, filibuster, barbecue, corral, tobacco, vanilla, hammock, tornado, cigar,* and *banana.* More than two thousand cities and towns in the United States have Spanish names. At least four hundred of them are in California, with two hundred and fifty each in Texas and New Mexico, and more than a hundred in both Colorado and Arizona. Spanish place names can be found all over the West and, in fact, in every state in the Union.

          —JOHN TEBBEL AND RAMÓN EDUARDO RUIZ

The writers first make the general statement, "The English language spoken in the United States owes much to Spanish importation." Then they give three supporting details for their statement: Spanish words are used often; Spanish words have been "naturalized" into English; and the United States has thousands of Spanish place names.

2   *A person can do something for peace without having to jump into politics.*

A person can do something for peace without having to jump into politics. Each person has an inner decency and goodness. If the person listens to it and acts on it, he or she is giving a great deal of what the world needs most. It is not complicated, but it takes courage. It takes courage for a person to listen to goodness and act on it.—PABLO CASALS

This writer also makes a general statement, "A person can do something for peace without having to jump into politics." However, instead of giving supporting details, he develops, or expands, his idea. He explains *what a person can do*: listen and act upon decency and goodness; *why it is important*: the world needs decency and goodness; and *what is involved in doing it*: using courage.

Exercises Working with Topic Sentences

A. In the following paragraphs, the topic sentences have been removed, leaving only the specific details. Read the paragraphs carefully. Study the hint given after each. Then write an interesting topic sentence for each paragraph. Be sure your sentence is a general statement that is broader than the details in the rest of the paragraph.

1   At first his feet slipped but then they took hold. He charged low and hard with mouth opened up like a steam shovel. The lower jaw and the big teeth flashed as he crossed the pit bottom. The wildcat fell back from the heavy charge and rolled under the dog. In that second he raked his claws into the dog's stomach.

Hint: The topic sentence should describe the beginning of the attack.

2   Take a lesson from the cat who so well represents potential energy. As he moves, stretches, relaxes, he looks uninterested and almost lazy. He wastes no energy. Let a mouse run by, though, and the cat pounces upon him with one swift, forceful movement.

Hint: The topic sentence should present the idea that human beings can learn from animals about the conservation of energy.

3   It was already hot, and the grasshoppers began to fill the air. Still, it was early in the morning, and the birds sang out of the shadows. The long, yellow grass on the mountain shone in the bright light, and a scissortail hied above the land.

Hint: The topic sentence might include the idea of a person waking up on a summer morning.

4   One group of Indians caught big Southern catfish by diving into the water with any available red object for bait. They grabbed the fish as it approached and dragged it to shore. Inspired by their example, the explorers in Lewis and Clark's party invented new ways to catch fish. Once, using only bayonets, they caught enough salmon to feed themselves. Another time, an explorer killed a sturgeon with an ax.

Hint: The topic sentence should include the information that long ago, people fished without having what is now called "fishing equipment."

5   The largest complexes, like Vail and Aspen, have plenty of rooms, and also plenty of people to fill them. Christmas week and much of February and March are especially hectic there and at all resorts. Many lodges take reservations for these periods as early as July. Most resorts advise that, no matter the time of year, visitors should call ahead for reservations well in advance of their intended trips.

Hint: The topic sentence should indicate that reservations at ski resorts can be a problem.

6   A presidential commission tells us we are a racist nation. Another presidential commission tells us we are the most violent nation in the world. A historian tells us the streets are less safe now than during the Depression when millions were hungry and jobless.

Hint: The topic sentence should make a general statement about the fact that many aspects of American society are being criticized.

B. Following is a list of topic sentences, each of which makes a general statement. Choose at least two of these sentences. For each, make a list of three or four specific details that support or develop the topic sentence. Then write a paragraph that includes the general statement and the details.

1. Autumn was advancing, and the sky was full of luminous clouds.

2. The Rolling Stones are a successful rock group.

3. Mr. Nolan's grocery store had closed its doors for the last time.

4. The teacher thought I was a troublemaker.

5. A television addict is a person who can't turn off a television set.

6. Today people talk about "the good old days."

7. Television advertisers are masters of persuasion.

8. Why does my tongue always freeze at the wrong time?

9. The car wheezed, coughed, and sputtered, fouling the air with dirty black smoke.

10. In the world of make-believe, I can be anything I wish.

11. Shabbiness and neglect marked the apartment building.

12. Pets-a-Plenty is the noisiest store in the shopping center.

The Topic Sentence Controls and Limits the Ideas That Can Be Discussed in the Remainder of the Paragraph

From your earlier study of the paragraph, particularly your study of the topic sentence as a type of contract, you have learned how the topic sentence controls the remainder of the paragraph. The topic sentence states the main idea, and *all the other sentences must be related to this topic sentence.* Therefore, the topic sentence *controls* the content of the paragraph.

In *limiting* what can be discussed in the paragraph, the topic sentence functions in a slightly different way.

The topic sentence makes a general statement, a statement that is broader in scope than the rest of the paragraph. However, if the topic sentence is *too* general, the remainder of the paragraph will have to be either extremely long in order to give an adequate explanation of the idea, or it will have to contain nothing but more general statements.

The following is an example of a paragraph with a topic sentence that is too general.

> Winter is a cold season, but it is also beautiful. The white, glistening snow on the ground, trees, and houses is an eye-catching scene.

"Winter is a cold season, but it is also beautiful" is much too broad a topic sentence to be adequately supported in a paragraph. You could write an entire composition on that subject. Because it is so broad, all the writer can do is give another general statement about the snow. This statement does not explain why the writer thinks winter is cold but beautiful.

To limit the topic sentence so that the idea can be developed in a paragraph, the writer first had to narrow the subject. She narrowed it to a specific winter's morning and wrote the following topic sentence: "The winter morning was cold and still." Then she added specific details to develop the idea, as follows:

> The winter morning was cold and still. The crust of the snow was like fragile glass and shattered with a loud noise as my feet broke through it. The icy air froze my nostrils and numbed my hands. Except for my footsteps, the world was silent, frozen to attention by winter's command.

The writer now has described a cold, still winter morning, using many specific details that help the reader to visualize the scene.

Exercises Working with Topic Sentences

A. Below is a series of sentence pairs. In each pair, one topic sentence is too general; the other is limited in its scope. Decide which one is too broad and which one has been sufficiently limited to be covered in a paragraph.

1. a. Basketball is an interesting game.
   b. Basketball demands quick thinking and split-second timing.
2. a. James failed history because he spent too much time in dramatics.
   b. Extra-curricular activities are time-consuming.
3. a. Several old buildings on Mason Street should be torn down because of their bad condition.
   b. Old buildings should be torn down.

4. a. Mountains are beautiful.
   b. The Blue Ridge Mountains stretched before us like a scene from a movie.

5. a. Pets can be a nuisance.
   b. My cat, Siggy, is constantly getting into mischief.

6. a. Because he bought the cheapest one he could find, Joe's bicycle didn't last very long.
   b. Economy doesn't always pay.

7. a. Graduation from high school is very important.
   b. Without a high school diploma, it is almost impossible to get a good job.

8. a. People of all ages read comic books.
   b. My grandmother likes to read my *Super Comics*.

9. a. Reckless driving is a serious problem.
   b. Statistics show that most automobile accidents are caused by reckless driving.

10. a. Works of art are difficult to create.
    b. Oil painting takes time, effort, and patience.

B. Following is a list of broad topic sentences. Rewrite each one, limiting its scope.

1. Automobiles are not as safe as they could be.
2. Travel is becoming faster—and noisier—all the time.
3. Pedestrians should be careful.
4. The Presidency of the United States is a difficult job.
5. You couldn't find a more interesting neighborhood than mine.
6. Smoking is dangerous to a person's health.
7. Cats are interesting animals.
8. Growing vegetables is educational.
9. Most television programs are alike.
10. I wear different clothes for different occasions.
11. Teenagers don't like discipline.
12. Vacations are fun.

c. Study the following list of subjects. Write a limited topic sentence for each subject.

1. Things I Fear
2. Radio Shows
3. Human Rights
4. Cities
5. The Future
6. Unpleasant People
7. Photography
8. Television Commentators
9. Popular Dances
10. Lonely Feelings
11. Records
12. The Game of Monopoly
13. Vacations
14. School Sports
15. Unfinished Projects

Part 4 Developing the Paragraph

Once you have decided upon—and limited—your topic sentence, the next step is to develop the idea in that sentence into a well organized paragraph. You do this by adding several more sentences that give additional information. There are four ways of doing this.

1. By using facts or statistics
2. By using specific examples
3. By using an incident or an anecdote
4. By using comparisons or contrasts

Using Facts or Statistics

To understand how topic sentences may be developed by the use of facts or statistics, let's look at the following example.

The abacus, probably the earliest calculating tool, was invented by the Chinese so long ago that no one even knows for certain when it was. It is a framework of wires with beads mounted on them. Each bead on the bottom part of the frame, below the crossbar, represents one unit; each bead above the bar represents five. The beads that touch the bar are counted to make up a number, and by moving the beads on different rows, or places, any number can be recorded. The beads can be manipulated to do addition, subtraction, multiplication, or division. Using an abacus, an expert can do addition or subtraction even faster than an electric calculator can. It was many centuries before any other civilization invented a calculating tool so fast and efficient.

—Linda O'Brien

The writer begins with a topic sentence that identifies the abacus as an early calculating tool. She next gives facts about the abacus, facts related to its construction and use. Then, in her final two sentences, she gives facts about the speed and efficiency of the abacus. She moves from the less important facts to the most important.

This method is the one to follow when organizing facts and statistics within a paragraph. You move from a general topic sentence to a series of specific statements, ending with the most important of these statements. In this way you can build your ideas to a climax, or emphasize a particular point. Let's look at another example.

Italy has contributed more immigrants to the United States than any other country except Germany. Over five million Italians came to this country between 1820 and 1963. Large-scale immigration began in 1880, and almost four million Italian immigrants arrived in the present century.—John F. Kennedy

Here again, you can see the same arrangement. The writer has moved from a general topic sentence concerning Italian immigrants to a specific statement concerning the immigrations between 1820 and 1963, then to the final important statement concerning immigration in the present century.

Exercises Developing a Paragraph by Using Facts or Statistics

A. Following is a series of paragraphs that were developed with facts or statistics. For each paragraph, list the facts or statistics given. Then explain briefly how the writer has organized the information within the paragraph.

1   By 1963, almost 130,000 Czechs had migrated to this country. They had settled on rural homesteads and in farming communities. They also had formed enclaves in cities, principally in Chicago, Cleveland, and New York.

2   There are sixty million homes in the United States and over ninety-five percent of them are equipped with a television set. In the average home, the television set is turned on for five hours and forty-five minutes a day. Average viewers, between their second and sixty-fifth birthdays, each watch television for over 3,000 entire days—roughly nine full years.

3   Oysters provide valuable products. In addition to food, pearls can be induced to grow inside their shells. The process is begun when workers place single grains of sand inside the shells of young oysters. Pearls grow around the grains. After a few years the oysters contain a crop of pearls that can be harvested.

4   During the pioneer days, recreation was a family affair. Families read stories by the fire. They liked to sing and listen to music together. Many of their songs were very old. Square dances were also held, and the whole family went to the dances together.

5   The Great Wall of China is the largest fortification ever built. It meanders for 1,500 miles across northern China's mountains and valleys. At its base, the Great Wall is from 15 to 20 feet thick. At the top, 25 feet above the base, the wall narrows to 15 feet. Every 200 to 300 yards, towers project from 35 to 40 feet into the air. These towers were once an important part of China's defense system against fierce northern tribes.

B. Following is a list of general topics, each one of which lends itself to paragraph development through the use of facts or statistics. Choose two of the topics or make up two of your own. Research the topics; then write a limited topic sentence that can be developed in a paragraph. Finally, write a paragraph that moves from the least important facts to the most important facts.

  1. Television violence
  2. Equal rights for women
  3. Computers

4. The advertising business
5. Solar heating
6. The growth of community colleges
7. The movie rating system
8. The pollution of the Great Lakes
9. Native American cultures
10. Mass transportation
11. Declining school enrollments
12. Microsurgery
13. Cars
14. The fight against seal-hunting
15. Breeds of dogs

Using Specific Examples

Sometimes a topic sentence will be a general idea that is best supported through the use of specific examples. Let's look at the following paragraph.

> Life was hard for young Stevie Wonder. No matter how developed his sense of touch became, there were some things he could never understand through touch. He could never touch the sun, or the horizon. He could never touch a mountain. Some things were too fragile, like snowflakes and live butterflies. It would be too dangerous to try to understand burning or boiling through touch. No matter how developed his ability to measure "sound shadows" became, he would only be able to measure the width and bulk of a large building, not its height. He could learn that the sky is blue and the grass green, but he would never *see* blue or green. He could not *watch* television.—JAMES HASKINS

The writer begins with a general statement: "Life was hard for young Stevie Wonder." He goes on to explain that there were many things the boy couldn't understand through touch. In the next seven sentences he gives specific examples of these things.

The following paragraph uses a similar technique.

> Enterprising inventors have made American life richer, safer, and more comfortable. Gail Borden invented condensed milk, a

healthy, safe product, in a time (1859) when fresh milk was often dangerous. In 1902 Willis Carrier invented something he called "air conditioning." Clarence Birdseye developed frozen foods, and Aaron Montgomery Ward brought the department store to the most isolated farm through the distribution of a mail order catalog.—K. S. KNODT

In this example, the writer also states a general idea: "Enterprising inventors have made American life richer, safer, and more comfortable." He then supports that statement with four examples.

1. Gail Borden's invention of condensed milk
2. Willis Carrier's invention of air conditioning
3. Clarence Birdseye's development of frozen foods
4. Aaron Montgomery Ward's distribution of a mail order catalog

Exercise Developing a Paragraph by Using Specific Examples

Here is a list of general topic sentences. Choose three of them or write sentences of your own. Then develop each topic sentence into a paragraph through the use of specific examples.

1. Yesterday's science fiction is today's reality.
2. Even great leaders can fail in something.
3. Animals are often surprisingly intelligent.
4. Some comic strips are more serious than funny.
5. Winners have sometimes overcome severe handicaps.
6. Some common houseplants are poisonous.
7. Some people are experts at everything.
8. Fast food restaurants line the main street of our town.
9. Disaster movies are popular entertainment.
10. Americans are a generous people.
11. There are dozens of video games on the market today.
12. The minor characters in a book are often the best remembered.

Using an Incident or an Anecdote

The incident or anecdote can add a personal touch to almost any form of writing. In this method the writer draws from first-hand experiences to explain or clarify a general idea. The strength of this type of development lies in the fact that an incident or anecdote, if well chosen, can drive a point home sharply and imprint an idea clearly on the reader's mind, as in the following example.

> Children have taught me much of what I know about love. To them love is nothing fancy, but very real—a feeling to be taken seriously. "If you love somebody," a six-year-old boy named Charlie once told me, "you help him put his boots on when they get stuck."—LESLIE KENTON

The writer could have developed the topic sentence with the addition of several more impersonal statements, but instead she includes a simple personal experience that makes the paragraph "come alive."

Writing a paragraph that uses an incident or anecdote is enjoyable because it focuses upon you, the writer. You are drawing from your own unique store of experiences—from things you have done, heard, and felt—to clarify an idea. Notice how the writer of the following paragraph has used her childhood experience.

> I think that one of the reasons I became a writer was because once, when I was driving home with my parents, they let me keep a date with a rainbow. There had been a heavy summer storm, when suddenly I screamed, "Stop the car! I must write a poem about that beautiful rainbow!" My father pulled up at the side of the road and off I went into the drizzle and the sunshine, while they waited. It was one of those special moments that change you, make you more than you've been. It is an experience in saying "Yes!" to life—and that's really what spontaneity and joy are all about.—EDA LESHAN

Here again, the writer could have explained her topic sentence with facts or examples. Instead, she used one simple anecdote to clarify her reasons for becoming a writer.

Developing a Paragraph by Using an Incident or an Anecdote

Here is a list of topic sentences, each one of which may be developed by an incident or an anecdote. Choose two of the sentences or write sentences of your own. Then, drawing from your own personal experiences, develop each of the sentences into a paragraph.

1. A kind friend can help you forget your troubles.
2. Sometimes a bad experience can turn out to be funny after all.
3. An angry word can ruin your day.
4. It usually pays to be on time.
5. Experience is sometimes a tough teacher.
6. You don't have to travel to find adventure.
7. Sometimes you have to learn to say "No!"
8. Baby-sitting is not the world's easiest job.
9. There are some things you can't learn from books.
10. A good laugh can sometimes be "good medicine."
11. A pet can teach you how to love.
12. You don't have to join a team to learn sportsmanship.
13. Repairing a _____ can teach you patience.
14. Hero-worship sometimes pays off.
15. There are times when you have to forgive.

Using Comparisons or Contrasts

You probably do not realize it, but you are constantly comparing and contrasting. You compare the flavor of the hamburgers at McDonald's with the flavor of the hamburgers in the school cafeteria. You contrast Jean's ability as a basketball player with Lynn's; Joe's personality with David's; Mr. McFarlane's teaching ability with Mr. Becker's.

This same approach can be used to develop a topic sentence into a paragraph. In this type of paragraph, you use facts, examples, and incidents. However, you use these details to explain the similarities or differences between two or more things.

Using Comparisons. A paragraph that *compares* persons, things, or events emphasizes the *similarities* between the subjects. The following paragraph is an example of comparison.

> The deaths of President Lincoln and President Kennedy are alike in several ways. Both Lincoln and Kennedy were attacked suddenly by an assassin on a Friday, and each in the presence of his wife. Each man was shot in the head; in each instance, crowds of people watched the shooting. Lincoln's secretary, named Kennedy, had advised him not to go to the theater where the attack occurred. Kennedy's secretary, named Lincoln, had advised him not to go to Dallas where the attack occurred.

The writer's purpose in this paragraph is clear. She wants to point out the similarities between the death of President Lincoln and the death of President Kennedy. She does so by listing seven specific similarities.

1. Both were attacked by an assassin.
2. Both were attacked on a Friday.
3. Both were with their wives.
4. Both were shot in the head.
5. Crowds of people watched both assassinations.
6. Both presidents' secretaries had advised against making the fatal visit.
7. Each president at the time of his death had a secretary with the same name as the other president.

The following is another example of a comparison.

> A five-speed bike combines the worst of a three-speed and a ten-speed. The typical five-speed is built on the same heavy frame as the three-speed, often has the same wide saddle and upright handlebars, but has the five-speed gear cluster and changer bolted on in back. For two extra gears of questionable value, you pay almost as much as you would for a low-priced ten-speed, but pedal around as much weight as you would on a three-speed.
>
> —S. Marshall

By comparing the five-speed bike with three-speed and ten-speed bikes, the writer is able to bring out the disadvantages of the five-speed. He has noted the similarities that illustrate his purpose, leaving out all irrelevant points of comparison.

Using Contrasts. A paragraph that contrasts persons, things, or events emphasizes the *differences* between the subjects. The following paragraph is an example of contrast.

> Although Henry Chatillon and Tête Rouge were the same age, that is, about thirty, they were very different. Henry was twice as large, and fully six times as strong as Tête Rouge. Henry's face was roughened by winds and storms; Tête Rouge's was softened by idle living. Henry had led a life of hardship and privation; Tête Rouge never had a whim which he would not gratify at the first moment he was able. Henry, moreover, was the most disinterested man I ever saw; while Tête Rouge cared for nobody but himself.—Francis Parkman

The personalities of the two men become much clearer and more vividly alive because of the contrasts that the author has chosen to include.

In the following example, the writer contrasts the Signal Mountain of the late 1950's with the Signal Mountain of the early 1970's.

> When we moved to Signal Mountain fourteen years ago, this was still a fairly woodsy area. Vacant lots were grown up to weeds and sassafras. Possums trundled in the ditches, at night little foxes crossed the road in the headlights of cars, and toads trilled from every direction on summer evenings. In this short time the trees have gone, the vacant lots have been cleared and built upon, the wet-weather springs dug up and blasted out and rechanneled. Foxes and possums come no more; the toads no longer sing; I must travel miles to hear a whippoorwill. It has been two years now since yellow jackets nested in my yard—those bright, harmless, sturdy wasps with their tiny-horned goat-heads, which once gave me so much pleasure. My children's children will likely never see their lovely curving flight against the shrubbery.
> —Mary Q. Steele

Exercises Developing a Paragraph by Using Comparisons or Contrasts

A. Following is a list of topics that may be developed through comparison. Choose two topics or make up topics of your own. Do any necessary research on your topics. Then write a paragraph of comparison on each.

1. A novel and a movie based upon the same novel
2. Two of your close friends
3. A garden and a part of a forest
4. Rock music and jazz
5. A boxer and a dancer
6. Modern dress and dress in the 1940's
7. The singing style of two popular singers
8. Ice-skating and roller-skating
9. Your neighborhood and one in a nearby town or city
10. Two American cities

B. Following is a list of topics that may be developed through contrast. Choose two topics or make up topics of your own. Do any necessary research on your topics. Then write a paragraph of contrast on each.

1. Popular music of the 1940's and the popular music of today
2. Riding a bicycle and riding a motorcycle
3. A street before and after a snowstorm
4. A cat and a dog as pets
5. Advertising on radio and advertising on TV
6. Two of your relatives
7. Bathing suits in the 1920's and the bathing suits of today
8. Eating a banana and eating a peach
9. Automobile travel and bus travel
10. Soccer and rugby

Chapter 6

Types of Paragraphs

You have studied four different ways of developing paragraphs —with facts or statistics, with specific examples, with an incident or anecdote, and with comparisons or contrasts. You are now ready to work with types of paragraphs:

1. Descriptive
2. Explanatory
3. Narrative

Part 1 The Descriptive Paragraph

A descriptive paragraph paints a word picture that appeals to a reader's senses. The clarity of the word picture depends on carefully selected words and precise details. Guiding the selection of words and details is the writer's focus and the impression he or she wants to create.

Selecting Details

In the following example, the writer selects details that appeal to your visual sense.

> The village was a fairly typical one. It consisted of small shacks with walls built out of the jagged off-cuts from the sawmill, and whitewashed. Each stood in its own little patch of ground, surrounded by a bamboo fence. The gardens around the shacks were sometimes filled with a strange variety of old tins, kettles, and broken barrels, each brimming over with flowers. Wide ditches full of muddy water separated these "gardens" from the road. The ditches were spanned at each front gate by a small, rickety bridge of roughly nailed branches.—GERALD DURRELL

When the writer of this paragraph decided to describe the village, he had to decide exactly what he wanted his readers to see. He narrowed his focus to the houses and gardens. Then he selected details that help to create a vivid impression of the houses and gardens. Because of the writer's careful selection of precise details, you can clearly visualize the village that he is describing.

Organizing a Descriptive Paragraph

The details, particularly in visual description, are usually organized in some logical order. These orders include from side to side, from top to bottom (or the reverse), and from near to far (or the reverse). Other methods of organization are possible, provided that the order is clear to the readers.

Using Space Words and Phrases

When a writer needs to clarify order, he or she uses space words and phrases. They help the reader to follow the writer's movement from one place or thing to another.

Space words and phrases fall into three general categories: those indicating direction, those specifying distance, and those identifying area.

left	through	around
right	into	between
above	ahead	among
below	behind	in front of
center	across	in back of
up	toward	forward
down	away from	backward
past	against	parallel

DISTANCE

foreground	on the edge of	close to
background	in the center of	next to
first	approximately	leading to
last	twenty feet	far
halfway	about ten miles	near
beyond	twenty kilometers	long
distant	remote	short

AREA OR SPACE

outside	field	hall
inside	plain	stairway
interior	hillside	stage
exterior	acre	alley
lawn	hut	street
garden	villa	road
courtyard	mansion	narrow
park	closet	wide

Ways of Organizing a Descriptive Paragraph

Following are four descriptive paragraphs. In three of them the writers have used common methods of organization. In the fourth, the writer has followed a unique order. As you read the paragraphs, notice the use of space words that lead you from one place or thing to another.

1. FROM SIDE TO SIDE

The set is magnificent. The left half of the stage depicts a hillside in cherryblossom time with, in the foreground, a garden and thatched entrance gateway. The gateway is free-standing—the fence omitted as superfluous. On the right-hand side is a villa raised off the ground. Both outside and interior are visible.

—Wim Swaan

Notice the use of the space words *left*, *foreground*, and *right*—all of which lead the reader from one side of the stage to the other. Notice also the many space words that indicate area.

2. FROM TOP TO BOTTOM (OR THE REVERSE)

Ruiz had come to our town about a month before from Seville, in Spain. He was tall, and his shoulders were so wide and powerful that they seemed to be armored in steel instead of muscle. His hair, which was gold-colored, grew thick on his head like a helmet. He had blue eyes, so blue and handsome that anyone would have envied them. His face was handsome, too, except that around his mouth there always lurked the shadow of a sneer.

—Scott O'Dell

After introducing the character Ruiz, the writer makes a general statement about his size, with emphasis on the man's powerful shoulders. He then leads you downward from hair, to eyes, to face, to mouth. This writer does not need to use space words, as the order of description is clear without them.

3. FROM NEAR TO FAR (OR THE REVERSE)

We drove past a barbed-wire fence, through a gate, and into an open space. There, trunks and sacks and packages had been dumped from the baggage trucks that drove out ahead of us. I could see a few tents set up, the first rows of black barracks, and beyond them, blurred by sand, rows of barracks that seemed to spread for miles across this plain.—Jeanne Wakatsuki Houston and James D. Houston

The writers begin with a description of the scene nearest them. They then draw your attention to "a few tents," to "the first rows of black barracks," to "rows of barracks that seemed to spread for miles across this plain," using space words such as *past, through, into, first,* and *beyond.*

4. UNIQUE ORDER

Our first camp in Glen Canyon is almost unimaginably beautiful. The site is a sandstone ledge below two arched caves. Clear cliffs soar up behind the caves. Just below the camp is the masked entrance of Hidden Passage Canyon. Its outthrust masking wall throws a strong shadow against the cliffs. Beyond this masking wall is the kind of canyon that is almost commonplace here, but that anywhere else would be a wonder.—Wallace Stegner

The writer first explains that the camp is located below two caves, behind which are cliffs. He next describes the scene below the camp. His description moves back to the cliffs, then down again to the scene below. The writer uses space words and phrases to eliminate any confusion that might result from these changes in direction.

Describing a Person

Describing a person is different from describing a place or a thing. The writer must strive to capture the essence of a person by going beyond physical characteristics.

The writer of the following description, for example, selects words and details that reveal much about the inner reality of the woman being described.

She was a big, awkward woman, with big bones and hard, rubbery flesh. Her short arms ended in ham hands, and her neck was a squat roll of fat that protruded behind her head as a big bump. Her skin was rough and puffy, with plump, molelike freckles down her cheeks. Her eyes glowered from under the mountain of her brow and were circled with expensive mauve shadow. They were nervous and quick when she was flustered and darted about at nothing in particular while she was dressing hair or talking to people.—Alice Walker

With phrases such as "rubbery flesh," "ham hands," and "squat roll," the writer creates an overall impression of ugliness. She notes the woman's "expensive mauve shadow," which hints at vanity. She uses words such as *glowered, nervous, quick,* and *darted* to imply suspicion and insecurity.

The writer makes the woman come alive for the reader. She paints a picture of an interesting human being who is more than a collection of physical characteristics.

Here is another description, this time of a young boy. Try to determine how the writer has made his description so colorful.

> When Wheldon first arrived at our school, he was carrying a natty little briefcase and wore a pink spotted tie and short trousers. His long, thin face was as white as a sheet in a TV ad, and his eyes were so watery behind his huge spectacles that gazing into them was like looking out of the portholes of a sinking ship. He had collapsed shoulders almost meeting under his chin, and his hair looked as if each separate strand had been carefully glued into place, ready for church. He reminded me of a cheerful but undernourished sheep.—PETER JONES

The writer has used descriptive words such as *natty, pink spotted, watery,* and *collapsed.* He has also incorporated several direct and indirect comparisons into the description. For example:

> He compares the color of the boy's face to a sheet in a TV ad.
> He equates gazing into the boy's eyes with looking out of the portholes of a sinking ship.
> He compares the boy to an undernourished sheep.

Like the writer of the previous description, this writer has presented a physical description that reveals inner qualities as well. Can you describe in your own words some of these qualities?

Exercises **Writing Descriptive Paragraphs**

A. Following is a list of topics that may be developed into descriptive paragraphs. Choose one and decide on the best method of organization. Then write a paragraph, using space words and phrases where necessary.

1. An interesting building in your home town
2. The waiting area in an airport or train station
3. A machine shop or car repair garage
4. The street on which you live
5. The check-out counter of a store
6. A doctor's or dentist's office
7. A busy street
8. A mountain

B. Following is a list of topics that may be developed into paragraphs describing people. Choose one. Decide exactly what qualities you wish to reveal about the person. Then write a paragraph that communicates those qualities.

1. An interesting person you have known
2. A character in a movie
3. A grandparent
4. A brother or sister
5. A singer
6. The host on a TV game show
7. A friend
8. A next-door neighbor

Appealing to the Senses

Thus far the examples of description have appealed to the sense of sight. Descriptive paragraphs may also appeal to the other senses, either individually or in combination. Following are five paragraphs, four of which appeal to a single sense and one of which appeals to two senses.

SOUND

Through the window next to her chair she heard the household noises as sounds on a distant stage. There was Father's pipe clacking against the ashtray, and the rustle of his newspaper. There was a small boy throwing books onto a chair, and the cookie jar thudding onto tile.—ROSEMARIE BODENHEIMER

TASTE

Gradually the peat glowed, the water boiled, and an hour later Miyax had a pot of caribou stew. On it floated great chunks of golden grease, more delicious than the butter from the gussak store. She put a savory bite into her mouth, sucked the juices, then chewed a long time before she swallowed.

—JEAN CRAIGHEAD GEORGE

TOUCH

A few months ago, on her sixteenth birthday, Mr. Dale had given Muffin a new, wide suede watchband. Lately, she found herself rubbing the velvety leather, letting her fingers smooth the fine, sleek texture, but then suddenly dragging her fingers backward against the grain, feeling the bits of leather recoil.

—SHARON BELL MATHIS

SMELL

The filthy streets are seldom cleaned. The inaccessible alleys and rear yards are never touched, and in the hot summer months the stench of rotting things will mark these places. Here and there an unwitting newcomer tries the disastrous experiment of keeping a goat, adding thereby to the distinctive flavor of the neighborhood.

COMBINATION

Early morning is a time of magic in Cannery Row. In the gray time after the light has come and before the sun has risen, the Row seems to hang suspended out of time in a silvery light. The street lights go out, and the weeds are a brilliant green. The corrugated iron of the canneries glows with the pearly lucence of platinum or old pewter. No automobiles are running then. The street is silent of progress and business. The rush and drag of the waves can be heard as they splash in among the piles of the canneries. It is a time of great peace, a deserted time, a little era of rest.—JOHN STEINBECK

Exercises Using the Senses in Describing

A. Write a short paragraph in which you describe the *sound* of one of the following:

1. A jet landing
2. A motorcycle in the distance
3. Eating potato chips
4. A cricket
5. A police siren
6. A dog barking
7. A clock ticking in an empty room
8. A baby crying
9. Traffic on a city street
10. A musical group

B. Write a short paragraph in which you describe the *taste* of one of the following:

1. An onion	6. A fresh strawberry
2. Root beer	7. A pickle
3. Raw celery	8. Peanut butter
4. Buttermilk	9. Fresh mushrooms
5. A lemon	10. Vanilla ice cream

C. Write a short paragraph in which you describe the *feeling to the touch* of one of the following:

1. Walking barefoot on a sandy beach
2. Snow down your back
3. Sandpaper
4. A cold shower on a hot day
5. Walking barefoot on wet grass
6. A sidewalk on a hot day
7. Burning your finger
8. Walking in the rain
9. Petting a dog or cat
10. Drinking ice water

D. Write a short paragraph in which you describe the *smell* of one of the following:

1. Frying fish
2. A carnation
3. A dentist's office
4. A stale garbage can
5. Ripe apples
6. Frying hamburgers
7. A school gymnasium
8. A laundromat
9. Stale cigarette smoke in a closed room
10. A city street on a hot day

E. Write a short paragraph in which you use a *combination of senses* to describe one of the following:

1. Chalk scratching on the blackboard
2. A cut finger
3. Eating a raw carrot
4. A rainy afternoon
5. A jet flying overhead
6. A football game
7. A classroom
8. A child crying
9. Riding a bicycle
10. A bouquet of flowers

F. Select one of the following statements as the topic sentence for a paragraph. Write a short description in which you create a single sensory impression.

1. The scene before me was one of total dreariness.
2. Have you ever lain awake at night while everything about you was strange, silent, and still?
3. The room was bright with color.
4. The street was a carnival of activity.
5. The delicious smells made my mouth water.

6. The outfit was as crazy as the wearer.
7. I had never seen him so angry.
8. He was trying to make lunch for the children.
9. He had spent the morning cleaning the kitchen.
10. The room was an absolute mess.

Part 2 The Explanatory Paragraph

A friend who was absent wants you to explain the English assignment. Your mother wants to know why you were late coming home from school. Your history teacher asks you to summarize the events leading to the Civil War. A stranger asks for directions to the airport. In each of these situations, you are being asked to explain something.

Explanations are often oral. However, they can also be written. When a written explanation takes the form of a paragraph, it is called an *explanatory paragraph.*

Giving Instructions

In its simplest and most practical form, the explanatory paragraph is used to give instructions. The following paragraph, for example, explains how to grow bean sprouts.

> Here's a quick and easy way to grow bean sprouts. Put about two tablespoons of bean seeds into a wide-mouthed jar and cover with at least three-quarters of a cup of warm water. Let the seeds soak overnight. In the morning, drain the water off the swollen seeds and rinse them with warm water. Drain well and return to the jar. Cover the jar with two layers of cheesecloth held in place with a rubber band. Keep the jar in a dark place. Rinse the seeds with warm water morning and night. The sprouts will be about one inch long in two to three days. When they are one to two inches long, place them in the refrigerator to stop growth. You can eat the entire sprout—root, seed, and if there are some, the tiny leaves.—BARBARA AND D. X. FENTEN

The paragraph communicates clear, accurate, and well organized instructions to the reader.

Most explanatory paragraphs that give instructions are organized in *chronological order*; that is, first things first. Notice, for example, the clear order of the following two paragraphs.

1   The quickest way to the airport from here is by the freeway. Go three blocks north to 9th Street, then turn left, and go three blocks west. That will take you to Michigan Avenue where you'll see the on-ramp to the Westbound Freeway. Stay on the freeway until you see the "Airport Exit" sign about eight miles west of town.

2   During a fire, opening a hallway door to attempt an escape can be dangerous. To minimize the risks, take these simple precautions. First, touch the door. A hot door means danger. Do not open it. If the door is not hot, brace your foot against the bottom and carefully open the door about an inch. If you feel pressure against the door or an in-rush of heat 'and fire, close the door at once. If there is no pressure or heat, open the door wide enough to look into the hall. An absence of fire and extreme heat means that the hallway is safe. You can proceed rapidly through it to the outside.

In each paragraph, the instructions are presented in the order in which they should be followed.

Developing an Explanatory Paragraph

Explanatory paragraphs, other than those that give instructions, can be developed by using the techniques described in Chapter 5, Developing the Paragraph. These techniques include using facts or statistics, using specific examples, using an incident or an anecdote, and using comparisons or contrasts. Whatever the technique, the writer does the same basic thing—he or she explains the idea presented in the topic sentence.

The following paragraphs illustrate the four methods for developing explanatory paragraphs.

FACTS

Cornbread, cornmeal mush, and succotash may not appear on American dinner tables as frequently as they did in colonial times, but corn reaches us just the same. About eighty-five percent of the American corn crop is used to feed the hogs, cattle, chickens, and other livestock that we eat. The balance of the crop that is used for food appears as fresh, canned, or frozen corn; as cornmeal and hominy; as snacks, confections, and breakfast cereals such as cornflakes; as cornstarch, corn syrup, and corn oil. Industrially, corn oil turns up in paints and soaps; corn proteins in synthetic fibers, adhesives, and explosives; cornstarch in fabrics, leather, and paper. Even the cornstalks are used in building and packing materials—Lila Perl

EXAMPLES

Faced with rising food costs, several of the nation's self-supporting zoos have hit upon a cagey scheme to enlist community assistance in feeding their hungry hoarders. At the Gladys Porter Zoo in Brownsville, Texas, patrons are invited to join the "Take a Lion to Lunch Bunch." As zoo officials are careful to explain, patrons are not required to take one of the big cats to a drive-in for burgers and fries. They are merely asked to pick up the tab for the cost of feeding an animal at the zoo for a day, week, or month. Lunch for a lion comes to $4.72, but you can treat a gorilla for $2.01, and it costs only 17 cents a day to play host to a boa constrictor.—Woman's Day

INCIDENT

To Mary Ann Slovaki, a CB radio is more than an expensive toy; it is a lifeline. One night Mary Ann was driving home about ten o'clock when the radiator hose in her car broke. The mishap occurred on one of Chicago's most crime-ridden streets, but she didn't even have to roll down her window to ask for help. A request over her CB radio brought three immediate responses—one of them from the police.—T. E. Deiker

COMPARISONS OR CONTRASTS

Unlike as Whittier and Franklin were in many respects, they were alike in others. Both had a sympathy for the poor that came from early similar experiences. Both learned a handicraft; Franklin set type and worked a printing press, and Whittier made slippers. To both of them literature was a means, rather than an end in itself. Verse to Whittier and prose to Franklin were weapons to be used in the good fight.

In each of these paragraphs, the writer draws upon a store of knowledge and offers the reader information that explains an idea.

Exercises Writing Explanatory Paragraphs

A. Choose one of the following and write an explanatory paragraph that gives instructions.

1. Explain how to find information in the Yellow Pages of the telephone directory.

2. Explain how to adjust a television set.

3. Explain how to repair a flat bicycle tire.

4. Explain how to sew on a button.

5. Choose a park, a municipal building, a shopping center, or an historical site in your area. Write a paragraph explaining the best way to get there from your house.

6. Find a detailed road map or a street map of your area. Find a town or a street at some distance from you. Pretend that you have a friend who lives there. Write a paragraph explaining the best way to get to your friend's house.

B. Choose one of the following and write an explanatory paragraph.

1. A new wrist watch you have had for only a short time has already stopped running three times. You have decided to send the watch back to the company for a refund. Write a one-paragraph letter to the company, explaining why you are returning the watch.

2. You have just read a help-wanted ad for a job that interests you. Write a one-paragraph letter to the company, explaining why you are qualified for the job.

3. Write a paragraph explaining why you like, or don't like, something.

4. Read the following poem. Write a paragraph explaining what you think the poem means.

FOR POETS

Stay beautiful
but don't stay down underground too long
Dont turn into a mole
or a worm
or a root
or a stone

Come on out into the sunlight
Breathe in trees
Knock out mountains
Commune with snakes
& be the very hero of birds

Dont forget to poke your head up
& blink
Think
Walk all around
Swim upstream

Dont forget to fly

AL YOUNG

C. Choose one of the following topics for an explanatory paragraph. Decide whether the paragraph will give instructions or will be developed by using facts, examples, an incident, or comparison or contrast. Be sure that your topic sentence is narrow enough to develop adequately in a paragraph.

1. The major points of interest in your home town
2. What you look for in a TV show
3. A failure-proof method for making fudge brownies
4. The effect of TV on young children
5. _____ is a good book because _____.

6. Smoking is dangerous to your health.
7. The most unusual animal I have ever seen
8. One way to improve your school
9. Do people really fall for advertising gimmicks?
10. The best way to study for a test
11. What makes a person a unique individual?
12. We don't always see what we think we see.
13. A funny incident at _____
14. How to make a _____
15. Learning to read is important.

Part 3   The Narrative Paragraph

The narrative paragraph is the telling of events. "Once upon a time . . ."; "Last night while I was watching television . . ."; "On the way to school this morning . . ." are just a few examples of the kinds of phrases that signal the beginning of a narrative.

The narrative paragraph is a simple, natural form of writing that includes many variations. It may be based on fact, on the imagination, or on a combination of both. It may recall a personal experience of the writer or an event observed by, or related to, the writer. It may be written in the first person or in the third person as in the following example.

Leaning on his cane, Mr. Mendelsohn stood up and walked out of the kitchen and down the long hallway into the living room. It was empty. He went over to a large armchair by the window. The sun shone through the window, covering the entire armchair and Mr. Mendelsohn. A canary cage was also by the window, and two tiny yellow birds chirped and hopped back and forth energetically. Mr. Mendelsohn felt drowsy; he shut his eyes. So many aches and pains, he thought. It was hard to sleep at night, but here, well . . . the birds began to chirp in unison and the old man opened one eye, glancing at them, and smiled. Then he shut his eyes once more and fell fast asleep.—NICHOLASA MOHR

Chronological Order

The events in a narrative paragraph are usually told in chronological order, the order in which they occurred in time. In some paragraphs, such as the following, the chronological order is clear and direct from beginning to end.

A fisherman walked along a beach on a moonlit night, searching for firewood. Above the reaches of the high tide, he saw a gnarled branch, polished by the rough sand and entwined in seaweed. In the eerie silver light and sudden shadows, the branch seemed almost alive. The fisherman lifted it cautiously and shook off the sand. As he turned it in his hand and the moonlight gleamed on its polished surface, he saw the subtle outline that had caused him to mistake the branch for a living creature. The fisherman took his knife from his pocket and quickly cut away the protruding twigs. Then he carefully cut, shaped, and smoothed the ancient wood. Finally he held in his hand a graceful wood sculpture—the perfect, almost living form of an undersea serpent!

BARBARA BRUNO

Using Time Words and Phrases

Many narrative paragraphs indicate the order of time and the passing of time by words and phrases such as the following:

A POINT IN TIME

one month	next year	at midnight
two days	yesterday	tonight
tomorrow	last week	at this moment

ORDER OF TIME

next	soon	immediately
then	instantly	the next day
later	finally	the following Friday

PERIODS OF TIME

| one moment | during the day | after a long time |
| for an hour | after a week | during the winter |

ACTIONS REPEATED IN TIME

| once | seldom | occasionally |
| twice | sometimes | frequently |

A BREAK IN TIME

at the same time   meanwhile   before this happened

When chronological order is clear and direct, as in the paragraph about the fisherman, time words and phrases merely reinforce the flow of the narrative. However, in paragraphs such as the following, in which the passage of time is uneven, time words are essential to understanding the events described.

> *Soon* the biggest of the boys poised himself, shot down into the water, and did not come up. The others stood about, watching. *After a long time* the boy came up on the other side of a big, dark rock, letting the air out of his lungs in a sputtering gasp and a shout of triumph. *Immediately*, the rest of them dived in. *One moment*, the morning seemed full of chattering boys; *the next*, the air and the surface of the water were empty, but through the heavy blue, dark shapes could be seen moving and groping.
>
> —DORIS LESSING

The Topic Sentence

Because narrative paragraphs are not always constructed like other kinds of paragraphs, they do not always have a topic sentence. In the following paragraph, for example, the writer begins telling her story without making a preliminary controlling statement.

> Paul was cutting trees one morning up in Minnesota. He had to get them to the sawmill which was in New Orleans, and he decided that the best way to do it would be by river—but there was no river. So Paul had a light lunch of 19 pounds of sausage, 6 hams, 8 loaves of bread, and 231 flapjacks, and each flapjack was slathered with a pound of butter and a quart of maple syrup. It

was a skimpy lunch for Paul, but he figured on eating a hearty supper to make up for it. Paul dug his river that afternoon and he called it the Mississippi, which as far as I know, is what it is called to this day.—BARBARA EMBERLEY

For now, however, you should practice writing narrative paragraphs *with* topic sentences, as in the following two examples:

1   *I spent the day wandering aimlessly through the bright streets.* The noisy penny arcades with their gaggle-giggle of sailors and children and the games of chance were tempting. After walking through one of them, though, it was obvious that I could only win more chances and no money. I went to the library and used a part of my day reading science fiction.—MAYA ANGELOU

2   *One day a strange thing happened.* It was spring, and for some reason I had been hot and irritable all morning. It was a beautiful spring. I could feel it as I played barefoot in the backyard. Blossoms hung from the thorny, black locust trees like clusters of fragrant, white grapes. Butterflies flickered in the sunlight above the short, new, new-wet grass. I had gone into the house for bread and butter, and coming out I heard a steady, unfamiliar drone. It was unlike anything I had ever heard before. I tried to place the sound. It was no use. It was like a sensation I had when searching for my father's watch, heard ticking unseen in a room. It made me feel as though I had forgotten to perform some task that my mother had ordered. Then I located it, overhead. In the sky, flying quite low and about a hundred yards off was a plane! It was a little plane, flying no higher than the eaves of our roof. Seeing it come steadily forward, I felt the world grow warm with promise. I would catch the plane as it came over and swing down fast and run into the house before anyone could see me. Then no one could come to claim the plane. It droned nearer. Then, when it hung like a silver cross in the blue directly above me, I stretched out my hand and grabbed. It was like sticking my finger through a soap bubble. The plane flew on, as though I had simply blown my breath after it. I grabbed again, frantically, trying to catch the tail. My fingers clutched the air and disappointment surged tight and hard in my throat. Giving one last desperate

grasp, I strained forward. My fingers ripped from the screen. I was falling. The ground burst hard against me. I drummed the earth with my heels and when my breath returned, I lay there bawling.—RALPH ELLISON

Exercise Writing Narrative Paragraphs

Following is a list of topics, each of which may be developed into a narrative paragraph. Choose two, or make up topics of your own. Then, drawing from your experience or imagination, write two narrative paragraphs based on those topics.

1. I Learn To Swim
2. My First Experience as a Baby-Sitter
3. A Trick That Backfired
4. My First Date
5. The Day My Pet Died
6. How I Learned About Recycling
7. The Night I Cooked Dinner
8. A Frightening Experience
9. The Diary of a Dog
10. Hitchhiking Is Not for Me
11. The Results of My Little White Lie
12. Making a New Friend
13. My First Trip to the City/Country
14. We Lost the Game
15. A Night Alone
16. A Memorable Meal
17. We Moved to a New Neighborhood
18. A Day at the Fair
19. Caught in a Storm
20. I Met a Famous Person

Checklist for Writing Paragraphs

This Checklist will help to remind you of the qualities necessary for good paragraphs. However, your writing procedure should also follow the steps in Guidelines for the Process of Writing on page 81.

1. Is the paragraph a group of sentences dealing with only one main idea?

2. Does the paragraph have a topic sentence that states the main idea?

3. Does the topic sentence make a general statement about what is to follow?

4. Does the topic sentence control and limit the ideas that are discussed in the rest of the paragraph?

5. Does the paragraph have unity? Does each sentence relate to the main idea?

6. Is the paragraph long enough to explain the idea clearly?

7. If the paragraph is developed by facts or statistics, do they move from the least important to the most important?

8. If the paragraph is developed by specific examples, are there enough examples to develop the paragraph fully? Do they all relate to the main idea?

9. If the paragraph is developed by using an incident or an anecdote, is it drawn from first-hand experience?

10. If it is a descriptive paragraph of a place or an object, does it use sensory details? Does it describe in a logical order? Does it use space words and phrases?

11. If it is a descriptive paragraph of a person, does it try to capture the essence of the person? Does it appeal to the senses?

12. If it is an explanatory paragraph, does it give instructions in chronological order? Is it developed by facts or statistics? specific examples? an incident or anecdote? comparisons or contrasts?

13. If it is a narrative paragraph, is it developed in chronological order? Does it use time words and phrases?

Chapter 7

Writing a Composition

From your work in Chapters 5 and 6, you are familiar with the paragraph and with several of the ways in which it may be developed. In this chapter you will build on your knowledge of paragraphs. You will study the ways in which they work together as parts of longer compositions.

Part 1   Defining a Composition

The definition of a composition is only slightly different from that of a paragraph.

A paragraph is a group of sentences dealing with a single topic or idea. Usually, one sentence, called the topic sentence, states the main idea. All the other sentences are related to this topic sentence. They further explain or support the main idea.

A **composition** is a group of paragraphs dealing with a single topic or idea. Usually, one paragraph, called the introductory paragraph, states the main idea of the composition. All the other paragraphs are related to the introductory paragraph. They further explain or support the main idea.

A composition has three main parts: the introductory paragraph, the body, and the conclusion. The introductory paragraph is similar to the topic sentence of a paragraph. It presents the main idea of the composition. The body, or middle, paragraphs explain or support the main idea. The conclusion, or final paragraph restates the main idea, summarizes the information that has been presented in the preceding paragraphs, or makes a final comment on the information that has been given. The paragraphs work together to develop the single topic or idea that is the subject of the composition.

Here is an example of a composition.

TELEVISION

We sometimes find it difficult to think of our television sets as mere pieces of machinery. They greet us with news and music in the morning, baby-sit for our children, entertain us in the evening, and soothe us to sleep at night. They are an integral part of the world in which we live.

Television has had more influence than any other mass communications medium on the political and social philosophy of contemporary Americans. It has affected our feelings about politics by inviting us into the conventions and bringing us face to face with the candidates. It has affected our feelings about violence in our cities and on our campuses by giving us close-up views of the disorders. Finally, it has affected our feelings about war by bringing the ugliness and the pain of the battlefields into our living rooms.

Television has upgraded our general level of education with news coverage, special reports, and talk shows, as well as with programs and series specifically labeled "educational." Educators, acknowledging the import of television presentation, have brought television, both public broadcasting and closed circuit, into many classrooms.

Television has greatly affected the popular arts. Despite some of its poor drama, television has encouraged some good playwrights and produced several good plays. By offering entertainment that competes with movie theatres and by showing movies, television has stimulated the movie industry to produce films that are destined for the home screen. Television has also affected the book publishing industry. By raising the general level of public knowledge, TV encourages people to buy books. On the other hand, it lures some people away from books by providing a competitive source of entertainment and escape.

The inferiority of so many television programs stems from the economic forces that control the industry. Most broadcasting in this country is commercial; it is paid for by advertisers. Programs are selected and retained, not for their quality but for the number of viewers they can reach and convert into customers. This practice of broadcasting to consumers and of programming for immediate financial advantage has, thus far, prevented television from realizing its full educational and cultural potential.

—Rissover and Birch

The introductory paragraph tells you that the composition is going to be about television in our lives. The next three paragraphs explain this idea by giving the following information.

1. The political and social influence of television
2. The impact of television on education
3. The effect of television on the popular arts

The final paragraph comments on the economic factors that have limited television's potential influence on the political, social, educational, and artistic aspects of American life. Each paragraph develops in some way the main idea of the composition.

Notice that the composition has five paragraphs. Although compositions vary in length, those selected as examples for this chapter are all made up of five paragraphs.

Part 2 Deciding on a Subject

The first step in writing a composition is to choose a subject. When doing so, it will help to keep these three guidelines in mind.

1. *Choose a subject that interests you.* This is important because without interest on your part you will have a difficult time creating interest on the part of your readers.
2. *Choose a subject that is familiar to you.* You will then be able to write with confidence about your subject.
3. *Choose a subject that has value for you.* You will then communicate something of value to your readers.

Your best source of subjects that are interesting, familiar, and valuable is you—your feelings, your ideas, your knowledge, your memories. In general, these kinds of subjects fall into three groups.

1. Subjects based on first-hand experiences
2. Subjects based on learned information
3. Subjects based on imagination

Subjects Based on First-Hand Experiences

You are an individual. No one else in the world is exactly like you. No one has lived the same life as you. No one has had the same experiences or the same feelings about the experiences.

Your experiences, therefore, are a good source for unique composition subjects.

Subjects based on things that have happened to you are likely to meet the three guidelines for choosing subjects. They are interesting because they are drawn from your own life. They are familiar because they are part of you. They are valuable because your experiences and feelings help to make you the person you are.

The writer of the following composition has drawn from his experiences to communicate his thoughts and feelings about being a Native American in today's world.

OUR SAD WINTER

You call me Chief and you do well, for so I am. The blood of chieftains flows in my veins. I am a chief, but you may ask where are my warriors, their feathered heads, their painted faces.

I am a chief, but my quiver has no arrows and my bow is slack. My warriors have been lost among the white person's cities. They have melted into the crowds as once they did into the forests, but this time they will not return. Yes, my quiver is empty and my bow is slack.

Yes, I could make new arrows and I could tighten my bow, but what little use it would be. My arrow would not carry far, as once it did. The bow has been reduced to a plaything. What was once a weapon is now a child's toy.

I am a chief but my power to make war is gone, and the only weapon left me is my speech. It is only with tongue and speech that I can fight my people's war.

Today my people are tempted to look into the past and say, "Behold our noble forebears." Perhaps it is pleasant to look to the ages gone by and speak of the virility that once was ours. But my people can never return to campfire and forest. The campfire no longer exists outside of their own dreams. They will wear out many moccasins walking, searching, searching, and they will never return from the journey when what they seek is no longer there.—CHIEF DAN GEORGE

Subjects Based on Learned Information

Every day you broaden your knowledge in some way. You broaden it through observing the world around you; through reading; through listening to teachers and classmates; through talking with friends, relatives, and neighbors. You broaden it through listening to radio programs, through watching television, through seeing movies. Some of the knowledge you gain becomes part of you, as familiar as your own experiences. Other knowledge is stored away in your memory, ready to be retrieved. This vast body of knowledge available to you is a second source for composition subjects.

Subjects based on learned information can meet the three guidelines at the beginning of Part 2. They can be interesting to you and, therefore, to your readers. They can be familiar enough so that you have something to say to your readers. They can be subjects worth writing about both from your viewpoint and from that of your readers. Here is an example of a composition based on learned information.

VENOM

The most valuable product provided by snakes comes from their greatly feared venom. Some collections of poisonous snakes are maintained for the specific purpose of extracting venom. Once removed from the snakes, venom is used in making snakebite serum and also in some surprising other ways.

No machines have been invented that can carry out the dangerous task of extracting venom. To obtain the precious golden fluid, a trained herpetologist carries a venomous snake to a special table to which a sterile collecting vial is fastened. As the herpetologist holds the snake, the serpent sinks its fangs into the fleshlike, rubberized covering of the container. The fluid from the snake's fangs trickles down the inside of the collecting vial until the venom supply is used up. The snake's fangs are then lifted from the collecting glass, and the poison is stored in a freezer.

To produce snakebite serum, small quantities of snake venom are injected into "donor horses." These horses are kept under special care for many months. Eventually the injections of poison cease to have an effect on the horses. As each horse becomes immune to the snake venom, a quantity of its blood is collected. In a medical laboratory the horse blood is processed into snakebite serum, which is distributed to hospitals and doctors. When a person bitten by a poisonous snake is injected with the horse serum, or antivenin, the snake poison in the victim's body is made ineffective.

Medical researchers have developed many drugs from snake venom. One is *cobroxin*, an astonishing, painkilling drug made from cobra venom that does not cause addiction as narcotic painkillers often do. Another is a blood-clotting medication containing venom from the Russell's viper. This drug is administered by dentists to stop bleeding after a tooth has been pulled. Researchers are working on a drug made from the poison of the Egyptian cobra that someday may be used to overcome the body's rejection of transplanted organs and tissues.

Ounce for ounce, venom has a greater dollar value than gold, but its medical value to mankind cannot be measured in terms of money.—J. M. ROEVER

Subjects Based on Imagination

Some subjects are drawn not from personal experience or from learned information, but from the writer's imagination. These subjects often are developed into narrative compositions. However, they can also be developed into other types of compositions, as illustrated in the following description of an imaginary future.

A FABLE FOR TOMORROW

There was once a town in the heart of America where all life seemed to live in harmony with its surroundings. The town lay in the midst of a checkerboard of prosperous farms, with fields of grain and hillsides of orchards where, in spring, white clouds of bloom drifted above the green fields. In autumn, oak and maple and birch set up a blaze of color that flamed and flickered across a backdrop of pines. Foxes barked in the hills and deer silently crossed the fields, half hidden in the mists of the fall mornings.

Then a strange blight crept over the area and everything began to change. Some evil spell had settled on the community: mysterious maladies swept the flocks of chickens; the cattle and sheep sickened and died. Everywhere was a shadow of death. The farmers spoke of much illness among their families. In the town the doctors had become more and more puzzled by new kinds of sickness appearing among their patients. There had been several sudden and unexplained deaths, not only among adults but even among children, who would be stricken suddenly while at play and die within a few hours.

There was a strange stillness. The birds, for example—where had they gone? Many people spoke of them, puzzled and disturbed. The feeding stations in the backyards were deserted. The few birds seen anywhere were moribund. They trembled violently and could not fly. It was a spring without voices. On the mornings that had once throbbed with the dawn chorus of robins, catbirds, doves, jays, wrens, and scores of other bird voices there was now no sound. Only silence lay over the fields and woods and marsh.

On the farms the hens brooded, but no chickens hatched. The farmers complained that they were unable to raise any pigs—the litters were small and the young survived only a few days. The apple trees were coming into bloom, but no bees droned among the blossoms, so there was no pollination and there would be no fruit. The fields browned and withered as though swept by fire. These, too, were silent, deserted by all living things.

No witchcraft, no enemy action had silenced the rebirth of new life in this stricken world. The people had done it themselves.—RACHEL CARSON

Exercises Choosing a Subject

A. The following subjects are meant to stimulate your thinking about possible topics for compositions. Study them. Then draw from your own experiences, knowledge, and imagination to make a list of at least ten subjects. If any of the subjects listed here interest you, add them to your list.

1. I Am Owned by a Cat/Dog
2. Violent Storms
3. Growing Up Bilingual
4. My Dreams
5. A Strange Noise in the Night
6. An Appealing Career
7. The History of My Family
8. Summertime Memories
9. Being a Friend
10. Thank Heaven, No Bones Were Broken
11. Original Ideas
12. Getting in Shape for _____
13. I Shouldn't Have Said It
14. Learning To Play _____
15. Mythological Characters
16. The Day I Grew Up
17. Rural Life
18. The Uniqueness of My Parents
19. Collections
20. I Wish I Were _____
21. The Art of Following Directions
22. How I Have Changed in the Past Year
23. Family Rituals
24. Radio in Your Life

B. Study your list of subjects carefully. Select the one that interests you the most. This is the first step of pre-writing in the Process of Writing.

Part 3   Narrowing the Subject

In your study of the paragraph, you learned that an idea must be narrowed enough to be developed adequately within the limits of the paragraph. The same holds true for the composition. The topic must be narrow enough to be covered in a few paragraphs.

Subjects that are based on first-hand experiences often do not need to be narrowed. That is because a writer usually has a specific incident in mind when selecting the topic.

Subjects based on learned information may need to be narrowed. Consider, for example, the subject "Japanese Culture." It is so broad that to develop it would take an entire book. Even if the subject were narrowed to "Japanese Culture in the Twentieth Century," it would still be too broad for a short composition.

The general topic "Japanese Culture" does, however, contain a number of possible composition topics. For example:

Japanese Family Relationships	A Japanese Garden
The Japanese New Year Celebration	Koto Music of Japan
Residential Architecture in Japan	

Many more topics could be added to the list. Each could be developed adequately in a composition.

Another example of a subject that is too broad for a composition is "The Rodeo: Last Frontier of the Old West." This general subject, though, contains several specific topics.

The Ropers	Steer Wrestling
Bronc Riding	The Bull Ride

By choosing one of these specific topics, you could cover the material in a short composition, as did the writers of the following composition.

BRONC RIDING

A generation ago, the broncbuster was as important to American industry as the bookkeeper and the salesman. Utilizing the skills of a present-day test pilot, auto racer, and automobile master mechanic, the broncbuster supplied ranchers, the U.S. Army

Cavalry, the stage lines, and Wells Fargo wagons with fresh annual supplies of horses. Rodeo's bronc rides developed from this tradition of the professional horse tamer.

Bronc riding, usually the day's "opener" at a rodeo, tingles with action and color. The horse bounds out of the chute, twisting and jumping "as if it had a bellyful of bed springs." Some broncs work silently. Others snort, scream, and put on as frightening a display as an enraged bull. Part of this is good showmanship, but most of it is as sincere as the wild mustang's, cayuse's, or pinto's dislike of having "something alive on its back."

Under the strict rules of professional rodeo, the "bareback bronc ride" really isn't. In the chutes, each animal is rigged out with two belts. Up front, right behind his forelegs, is fastened a "rigging" or "surcingle." A strap that looks like a suitcase handle is attached to the top of the rigging. This handle fits atop the bronc's back and is the contestant's handhold. The second strap, usually padded with wool, fits around the bronc in front of the hind legs. It is called the flank strap. Its only purpose is to make the horse "itchier" to kick and buck.

Both bronc and buster must perform according to a meticulous set of rules. The rider must keep one hand free and away from the horse throughout the ride. The ride is discounted if that hand so much as flickers a hair on the horse's tail or mane during those stiff-legged, writhing jumps, hump ups, and headstands. Also, the rider must spur the horse above the point of the shoulders during the first jump out of the chute. If the rider fails to do this, the judges won't even score the ride.

Most bareback bronc contests are limited to eight seconds. That, say the professionals, is really long enough to "paint the picture," because a bronc's strongest bucks come during the first two or three seconds. Any rider who can sail those out has pretty much got it made.—HOWARD AND ARNOLD

Exercise Narrowing the Subject

In your last assignment, you choose a subject for a composition. Think about that subject and decide whether it is narrow enough to be covered in a five-paragraph composition. If it is not, list several specific topics within the general subject and choose one as the topic for your composition.

Part 4 Deciding on the Audience and the Purpose

Before you begin to develop a plan for your composition, you must answer two questions.

1. For whom are you writing the composition?
2. What is your purpose for writing?

Your Audience. You should know two things about your readers. First, you should know their approximate age. The need for this information is clear. If your readers will be students younger than you, you must use simpler words, present less difficult information, and explain more carefully than if your readers will be your classmates or adults.

Second, you should know the readers' familiarity with your subject. How much they already know will influence the amount and difficulty of the information you can include and the number and types of explanations and definitions that you must give.

Your Purpose. Before developing a plan for your composition, you must decide whether you want to tell a story; to describe an object, place, or person; or to explain something. You must decide whether you want your readers to laugh, to cry, to be moved by the beauty or ugliness of a scene, or to think seriously about an idea.

A one-sentence *statement of purpose* might help you to clarify your goal. This statement is for your own guidance only. It will not be included as such in your composition. Here are three examples of such statements.

1. In my composition I will present three convincing reasons for taking part in extracurricular activities.
2. In my composition I will describe the three most beautiful areas of Yellowstone Park.

3. In my composition I will describe a humorous incident that happened on my first day of high school.

Sample Paragraphs. The two paragraphs that follow are both written on the same general subject, sickness. However, they are written with two entirely different audiences and purposes in mind.

1   Finding the cause of a sore throat calls for some detective work. Your doctor will ask you questions, give you an examination, and maybe do some tests. Doctors do this to get clues. The clues help them to figure out what kind of sore throat you have. The doctor will ask how you feel, how long you have been sick, and if anything else hurts. When you tell the doctor how you feel, you are telling your symptoms. The doctor will examine you to look for other clues, called signs. Some signs that doctors look for are fever, rash, swollen tonsils, and swollen lymph nodes, small lumps under the skin on the sides of the neck.

—DONAHUE AND CAPELLARO

2   Snooks, under a pile of faded quilts, made a small, gravelike mound in the bed. His head was like a ball of black putty wedged between the thin covers and the dingy yellow pillow. His little eyes were partly open, as if he were peeping out of his hard, wasted skull at the chilly room. The forceful pulse of his breathing caused a faint rustling in the sheets near his mouth, like the wind pushing damp papers in a shallow ditch.—ALICE WALKER

Paragraph 1 explains the detective work needed to find the cause of a sore throat. Most of the words are simple; two of the harder words, *symptoms* and *lymph nodes*, are defined within the context of the paragraph. The writer presents simple information that could be easily understood by most young readers.

Paragraph 2 paints a grim picture of a very sick child. In contrast to Paragraph 1, it contains difficult words; longer, more complicated sentences; and complex language. The writer of this paragraph had a much older, more experienced audience in mind than the writer of Paragraph 1.

A. Decide on the audience for your composition.

B. Decide on the purpose for your composition. Then write a one-sentence statement of purpose.

Part 5 Planning the Composition

Developing a plan, an important part of the pre-writing process for writing a composition. involves four separate steps:

1. Putting down ideas
2. Organizing the ideas
3. Developing a working outline
4. Making a final outline

After completing these steps, you will know exactly what you are going to say in your composition and the order in which you are going to say it.

Putting Down Ideas

As you begin to plan your composition, you probably have ideas about what you want to include. Write these ideas on a sheet of paper or on 3" x 5" cards, keeping in mind your audience and your purpose for writing. As you think more about your topic, additional ideas will come to you. Jot them down also. Make no attempt at this time to write the ideas in any particular order.

Either of the two suggested methods for recording ideas is workable. However, having your ideas on cards will make it easier to group and regroup them when organizing and· outlining your composition.

One writer chose the coast of Oregon in the second week of June as the subject for his composition. He made the following list of ideas.

THE COAST OF OREGON

1. Seals and sea lions in the ocean
2. Fir, spruce, hemlock, myrtle, and cedar trees
3. Golden Scotch broom
4. Cliffs and headlands along the coast
5. Fields of daisies
6. *Kalmiopsis leachiania*—blooming for 65 million years
7. Seagulls, cormorants, and murre birds beyond the breakers
8. Salmon fishermen in Newport
9. Bright green meadows
10. *Kalmiopsis leachiania,* a living fossil
11. Timeless beauty of the coast
12. Sand crabs on the beach
13. Sculpins in the tidal pools
14. Azaleas, rhododendron, and wild roses in bloom
15. Inland from the Pistol River
16. The second week of June
17. Otters in the ocean

Each idea is a detail that the writer has decided to include in the composition. Notice that the list has no apparent organization. That is because the purpose of this first step in planning is to get down as many ideas as possible. The sorting and organizing of the ideas comes in the second step.

Exercise Writing Down Ideas

Make a list of ideas related to your composition topic. Keep in mind your audience and your purpose for writing.

Organizing the Ideas

Your next step in planning is to organize your ideas in relation to each other; that is, to group similar ideas together.

The writer of the composition "The Coast of Oregon" studied his list of ideas. He determined that the ideas fell into three general groups.

I. The wilderness area that is not seen from the coast road
II. The vegetation that is to the left of the road
III. The wildlife that is below the cliffs at the edge of the sea

He then listed the related ideas under each heading.

I. The wilderness area that is not seen from the coast road
   Kalmiopsis leachiania—blooming for 65 million years
   Kalmiopsis leachiania, a living fossil

II. The vegetation that is to the left of the road
   Fir, spruce, hemlock, myrtle, and cedar trees
   Golden Scotch broom
   Fields of daisies
   Bright green meadows
   Azaleas, rhododendron, and wild roses in bloom

III. The wildlife that is below the cliffs at the edge of the sea
   Seals and sea lions in the ocean
   Seagulls, cormorants, and murre birds beyond the breakers
   Sand crabs on the beach
   Sculpins in the tidal pools
   Otters in the ocean

After grouping your ideas, you may have a few "extras" that do not seem to fit under any of your headings. The writer of the sample composition had four such ideas.

1. Cliffs and headlands along the coast
2. Salmon fishermen in Newport
3. Timeless beauty of the coast
4. The second week of June

He set these aside for possible use later when writing the introduction and conclusion of his composition.

Exercises Grouping Ideas

A. Following is a list of ideas related to the topic "Camping in a Cabin." They can be grouped under two general headings.

I. Six A.M.
II. Midnight

Write each idea under the appropriate heading.

1. Sounds: a scratching, a rustling, then silence
2. Sights: sunlight in the cabin
3. Sights: stars, blackness
4. Sights: moonlight through the window
5. Smells: coffee, bacon
6. Sounds: friends laughing and talking
7. Sounds: fire crackling, bacon sizzling
8. Smells: lingering trace of smoke

B. Following is a list of ideas. Decide which of these ideas should be general headings. Then group the remaining ideas under the appropriate headings.

1. provide adequate street lighting
2. pedestrians injure themselves
3. they cross streets diagonally
4. they cross streets in the middle of the block
5. they walk with their backs to traffic on the highway
6. pedestrian lives can be saved
7. they step into traffic from parked cars
8. provide traffic lights for pedestrians
9. they step from behind parked cars
10. give traffic tickets to pedestrians
11. they cross against lights
12. they don't watch for traffic

C. Study the ideas for your own composition. Decide on three general headings that seem to cover most of them. Then list each idea under the appropriate heading.

Developing a Working Outline

The third step in planning is to develop a working outline. This step involves three activities.

1. Arranging groups of related ideas into logical order
2. Organizing the ideas within each group
3. Putting the ideas into outline form

Logical Order. Logical order is an order that is appropriate to the content of the composition and is, therefore, easy for a reader to follow. Unfortunately, no one order applies to all compositions. Each composition presents an organizational problem of its own.

Some compositions are organized in *chronological order*; that is, in the order of time. For an example of chronological order, look at Exercise A under "Grouping Ideas." The ideas related to "Camping in a Cabin" are going to be grouped by time. The details that describe the camp at six A.M. will come before those that describe it at midnight.

Some compositions are organized in *order of importance*; that is, from the least important to the most important, according to the writer's way of thinking. When order of importance cannot be established, a writer might arrange groups of ideas in *order of familiarity*, from the most familiar to the least familiar.

Turn your attention to Exercise B under "Grouping Ideas." The ideas in this exercise can be grouped into three career areas: classroom teaching, special education, and administration. The writer of a composition could choose to organize the three groups of ideas in order of importance or in order of familiarity. Whatever the choice, the order would depend completely on the viewpoint of the writer.

A fourth way to organize compositions is in *spatial order*; that is, in the order in which a writer wishes to describe a place, object, or person. For example, if a writer has decided to describe a room from near to far, the group of details that describes the nearest part of the room would be first; the group of details that describes the farthest part of the room would be last.

The writer of the composition "The Coast of Oregon" arranged his three groups of ideas in spatial order.

THE COAST OF OREGON

I. The vegetation that is to the left of the road
   A. Golden Scotch broom
   B. Bright green meadows
   C. Fields of daisies
   D. Fir, spruce, hemlock, myrtle, and cedar trees
   E. Azaleas, rhododendron, and wild roses in bloom

II. The wildlife that is below the cliffs at the edge of the sea
   A. Seals and sea lions in the ocean
   B. Seagulls, cormorants, and murre birds beyond the breakers
   C. Sand crabs on the beach
   D. Sculpins in the tidal pools
   E. Otters in the ocean

III. The wilderness area that is not seen from the coast road
   A. Inland from the Pistol River
   B. *Kalmiopsis leachiania,* a living fossil
   C. *Kalmiopsis leachiania*—blooming for 65 million years

The writer rearranged not only his groups of ideas but also some of the ideas within each group. He then wrote the ideas as an outline, using the standard outline form.

Exercise **Making a Working Outline**

Organize the three groups of ideas for your own composition in a logical order. If necessary, rearrange the ideas within each group. Then make a working outline, using your three general headings as topics I., II., and III. of your outline.

Making a Final Outline

Earlier, you learned that a composition has three main parts: the introductory paragraph, the body, and the conclusion. A working outline is a plan for the body. A final outline includes the information from the working outline. It also includes an introductory paragraph and a conclusion. A final outline follows this pattern.

TITLE   (The topic of the composition)

    I. The introductory paragraph

   II. The body

      A. Topic I. from the working outline

      B. Topic II. from the working outline

      C. Topic III. from the working outline

  III. The conclusion

Your final outline will be your guide when you are writing your composition. It will help you to express your ideas in a logical order that can be easily followed by your readers.

Exercise Making Your Final Outline

Make the final outline for your composition, using your working outline to complete section II.

Part 6   Writing the Composition

Your pre-writing stage is now finished. Your topic has been selected, your audience and purpose identified, and your ideas organized into an outline. You are now ready to write the first draft of your composition.

The Introductory Paragraph

The introductory paragraph of a composition serves two important functions.

1. It gives the main idea of the composition.
2. It catches the reader's attention.

The opening sentence of an introductory paragraph sets the tone for the entire paragraph. A good writer, therefore, avoids dull and uninteresting opening sentences such as these.

1. In this paper, I am going to describe someone who died.

2. Families can be fun.
3. I am going to explain something about being an American.
4. The coast of Oregon is beautiful.

Each of these sentences indicates, in a general way, the main idea of the composition. However, the sentences lack the specific details that would catch the interest of a reader.

Following are four introductory paragraphs that begin with good opening sentences. Each paragraph gives the main idea of a composition in a way that makes you want to read further.

1   Charley Lockjaw died last summer on the reservation. He was very old—a hundred years, he had claimed. He still wore his hair in braids, as only the older men do in his tribe, and the braids were thin and white. His fierce old face was like a withered apple. He was bent and frail and trembling, and his voice was like a wailing of the wind across the prairie grass.—DOROTHY JOHNSON

2   There were seldom fewer than fifteen men, women, and children at our Sunday get-together. On the Sundays when it rained, there would be as many as thirty. It was obvious that no one else in Mount Allegro had as many relatives as I did. It was also true that no one else's relatives seemed to seek one another's company as much as mine did. Sundays or weekdays, they were as gregarious as ants but had a far more pleasant time. There were always relatives and friends present or about to arrive. When they finally left for the night, they occasionally came back for a surprise visit which they called a *sirinata.*—JERRE MANGIONE

3   "We, the people" is an eloquent beginning. However, when the Constitution of the United States was completed on the seventeenth of September in 1787, I was not included in that "We, the people." I felt for many years that somehow George Washington and Alexander Hamilton just left me out by mistake. Through the process of amendment, interpretation, and court decisions I have finally been included in "We, the people."
—BARBARA JORDAN

4   In the second week of June, the coast of Oregon is alive as at no other time of year. I don't mean alive with people, although the weekend salmon fishermen are crowded into the bars and cafés along the bay front in Newport. To see the kind of life I'm talking about, you have to leave town and drive down the magnificent coast along the cliffs and headlands.—CHARLES KURALT

Paragraph 4 is the introductory paragraph to the composition "The Coast of Oregon." Notice that the writer included these three of the "extra" ideas that did not fit into the plan for the body of the composition.

1. The second week of June
2. Salmon fisherman in Newport
3. Cliffs and headlands along the coast

Exercises Writing the Introductory Paragraph

A. Read the following opening sentences for introductory paragraphs. Decide which ones have definite reader appeal. Be ready to explain why the others do not catch your attention.

1. By the time the saber-toothed tiger had slunk into oblivion, and the mastadon was only a memory, the human being had developed two brains.

2. In skiing and skating and riding a bicycle, the beginner is faced with a problem.

3. This composition is about learning to meditate.

4. My horse is an interesting animal.

5. As I rounded the curve of the mountain, I saw the tiny village far below me.

6. I spent a very exciting week at the Mardi Gras in New Orleans.

7. First of all, I want to introduce myself.

8. I'm glad I'm a woman!

9. I'm glad I'm a man!

10. Once we lived in my grandfather's house near Cedar Fort.

11. Well, this young girl I'm going to tell you about was named Angela.

12. At first the boy didn't impress me very favorably.

13. My mother had an unusually happy childhood.

14. Most zoos are old.

15. My teacher has asked me to write a paper about mythology.

16. I was prepared to dislike Max Kelada even before I knew him.

17. Imagine, if you can, a small room, hexagonal in shape, like the cell of a bee.

18. The little fellow was lying on the bare hospital cot, arms rigidly straight and teeth clenched tightly together.

19. I remember my first pet.

20. His name was Frank X. Farrell and I guess the X stood for "Excuse me."

B. Write the introductory paragraph for your composition. Be sure that it gives the main idea of your composition and that it will catch your readers' attention.

The Body

The body is the second major part of a composition. In the body paragraphs, the main idea of the composition, which is presented in the introductory paragraph, is supported or explained.

Let us look again at the introductory paragraph of the sample composition "The Coast of Oregon."

> In the second week of June, the coast of Oregon is alive as at no other time of year. I don't mean alive with people, although the weekend salmon fishermen are crowded into bars and cafés along the bay front in Newport. To see the kind of life I'm talking about, you have to leave town and drive down the magnificent coast along the cliffs and headlands.

The introductory paragraph indicates that the composition will describe the life to be found along the coast of Oregon in the second week of June. The final outline for this composition shows that the body paragraphs will describe three kinds of life: the vegetation to the left of the road, the wildlife at the edge of the sea, and the wilderness area not seen from the coast road. The writer developed these three supporting ideas into the following body paragraphs.

As you travel south on the coast road, the countryside to your left is alive with color. Golden splashes of Scotch broom bank the road, improbably beautiful in the sun. The bright green coastal meadows are carpeted with daisies, and the fragile white flowers contrast with the sturdy, dark trunks of towering Douglas fir, the spruce and hemlock, the myrtle and cedar. Everything that blooms is in bloom in the Oregon June—azaleas and rhododendron and, back at the edge of the forest, wild roses.

You look to the left and up to see all this, but if you do, you will be missing all the life that is to the right and down, below the cliffs at the edge of the sea. There are seals down there, and sea lions emerging from their caves to frolic in the surf. There are seagulls and cormorants, and murre birds, which look like miniature flying penguins, skimming beyond the breakers. The sand crabs scuttle along the beach, the sculpins dart through the tidal pools, and otters roll in the coral sea.

In this season there is too much of life to see it all. To the south, inland from Pistol River, there is a wilderness area where the rarest kind of flower grows, a kind of heath called *Kalmiopsis leachiania*. The *Kalmiopsis* is a living fossil, much studied. The visitor regarding with awe the burst of life and beauty in the second week of June, and wondering how many springs this has been going on, learns that the *Kalmiopsis* has been blooming now for sixty-five million years.

The body of the composition is divided into three paragraphs. Each begins with a topic sentence that gives the main idea of the paragraph. The first body paragraph begins with this topic sentence: "As you travel south on the coast road, the countryside to your left is alive with color." The rest of the paragraph describes the colorful flowers near the road and the dark forest that is beyond the bright flowers.

The second body paragraph begins with this topic sentence: "You look to the left and up to see all this, but if you do, you will be missing all the life that is to the right and down, below the cliffs at the edge of the sea." The sentences that complete the paragraph give details about the wildlife near the sea.

The third paragraph begins with this sentence: "In this season there is too much life to see it all." The main idea of the paragraph is developed with an example of a flower that is not seen from the coast road but is found in the inland wilderness.

The first line of each paragraph is indented. A paragraph indentation signals the reader that a new idea is about to be introduced. Indentations make a composition appealing to the eye of the reader by breaking up the typing or writing on a page. Without indentations, a composition would look long and uninviting. Many readers would not even make an attempt to read it.

Achieving Unity

In a composition, the supporting details in each paragraph are directly related to the topic sentence. Each paragraph is directly related to the introductory paragraph. The composition, therefore, is unified by one main idea that is presented in the opening paragraph.

To reinforce the unity of idea, a writer may repeat key words and phrases throughout a composition. For example, the writer of the sample composition repeated the word *life*, or a form of the word, in the introductory paragraph and in each body paragraph.

A writer may also make use of transitional devices. These words and phrases tie the paragraphs of a composition together by referring both to the idea that precedes and the idea that follows.

There are six basic transitional devices.

1. **Using a Word That Indicates Time.** Such words include the following.

first	before	meanwhile
next	after	until
then	afterwards	later
finally	today	hundreds of years ago

EXAMPLE

A special type of Japanese wrestling is called *sumo*. Sumo is probably Japan's oldest sport. It began hundreds of years ago as part of a Shinto religious ceremony. Some Shinto shrines had special buildings built for sumo matches, held to honor the gods. In the year 858, it is said, the two sons of the emperor wrestled to see who would succeed to the throne.

Today sumo is so popular that tournaments are held every year in the large cities. Thousands go to the huge stadiums to watch the matches. Others view them on television. The sumo wrestlers are tall and heavy, sometimes weighing 300 pounds. Each wrestler wears only a ring about his waist and a loincloth. The place where they perform is a circle that measures fifteen feet across.—Lee W. Farnsworth

2. **Using a Word That Shows the Relationship Between Ideas.** Such words include the following.

and	because	therefore	moreover	unless
also	since	besides	similarly	

EXAMPLE

For the individual American, the main advantage of the metric system is its simplicity. Instead of the fifty-five measurement units of the English system, the metric system has only three: meters, grams, and liters.

Calculations are simpler because all multiples are powers of ten. To multiply, you simply move the decimal point.

3. **Using a Word That Shows an Opposite Point of View.** Such words include the following.

but	while	on the other hand
however	although	in contrast

EXAMPLE

Over the years, oil and natural gas gradually replaced coal as the major fuels for homes and industry. Gas and oil were cheaper. They were also more convenient.

Today, however, America is faced with an energy dilemma. The demand for gas and oil has outstripped domestic supplies. Now, America must rely heavily on foreign imports. Gas and oil are no longer cheap or convenient.

4. Using a Word That Repeats a Word Used Earlier.

EXAMPLE

Almost everybody daydreams. What do such dreams indicate about a person? How do one person's dreams differ from another person's?

Science is just beginning to probe the deeper meanings of daydreams, yet it has come up with some startling preliminary findings.—DOROTHY BRANT WARWICK

5. Using a Synonym for a Word Used Earlier.

EXAMPLE

A tornado blew through Arcadia, Nebraska, last week, and the next day in a town seventy-five miles east, somebody picked up a canceled check that had been in an Arcadia businessman's desk drawer. Impressed by this news, I turned to Roger Welsch, who teaches folklore at the university and keeps up with which way the Nebraska wind blows, to ask him if storms like that are common here.

Roger said that after one of these Nebraska cyclones, a sleeping man found himself still in bed, but the bed was in the kitchen. The only damage done was that his underclothes were on upside down and buttoned in the back.—CHARLES KURALT

6. Using a Pronoun That Refers to a Word Used Earlier.

EXAMPLE

Along the cool morning dew, along the cool forest floor crept a spider, a shabby little thing of a spider, looking for a place to spin a silken line or two.

Over speckled fishlike skins of leaves he crept, over earth-soft mossy pads, over turtle still adream, earth-anchored in its shell, over bogs of stones and crackling twigs he crept, crept on and on, seeking a place to spin a silken line or two.—GEORGE MENDOZA

Exercises Studying and Writing Body Paragraphs

A. Study the following pairs of paragraphs carefully. Identify the transitional device, or devices, that each writer has used to tie the paragraphs together.

1   The coach, noting Sarah's unusual stamina and fluid motion, had convinced her that long-distance events were her best, and Sarah had trained long and hard for them.

Henry's coach, on the other hand, had permitted Henry to play basketball even though he knew that he lacked peripheral vision.—*Woman's Day*

2   I was standing in the driveway, alone, stock still, but shivering. Someone had given the polyphemus moth his freedom, and he was walking away.

He heaved himself down the asphalt driveway by infinite degrees, unwavering. His hideous, crumpled wings lay glued and rucked on his back, perfectly still now, like a collapsed tent.
—ANNIE DILLARD

3   They came, silently, dark-bellied clouds drifting up from the south, and the wind, increasing, swept in the heavy scent of the approaching storm. Lightning flashed over the low, distant hills, and the clouds closed quietly around the moon. The thunder rumbled and the heavy drops began to fall, slowly at first, then irregularly, then increasing to a rhythmic rush of noise as the gusts of wind forced the rain in vertical waves across the shingled roof.

Much later, when the rain had moved ahead and the water began to drip from the roof and the countless leaves, the boy slipped out of his worn denim pants and took off his shirt and lay down.—DURANGO MENDOZA

4   Paul loved his father "like no one in all the world," although as a young man he would later regret that his childhood was so programmed. "If I had had time . . . that wasn't blocked out and filled in for me, I think my imagination would have been more developed. As it is, I've almost none. All my time was crowded with lessons to learn, games to play, books to read. I never can remember having had hours in which I had nothing to do, and had actually to entertain myself out of my own mind."

Nevertheless, he always looked forward to the summer, when his sister and brothers would come home on vacations. He would play football with Ben, who would show him how to throw a pass, how to block and tackle. Bill, the brain of the family, taught him how to question what he read, how to draw his own conclusions, and how to defend them. Then there was Marion, who intended to become a teacher like her mother. Strong-willed but cheerful, she always brought laughter to the household.

—Dorothy Butler Gilliam

5   We were in the marsh now, moving, on our way to say goodbye to Bald Head Island.

Bald Head sits at the southeastern tip of North Carolina, where the Cape Fear River flows into the Atlantic Ocean, and the best access is by boat, across four miles of relatively tranquil water from the shrimp and fishing village of Southport.

—William McIlwain

6   They circled a square and slipped into a quiet, narrow street overlooking a park, stopping before the tallest of the apartment houses in the single commanding row.

Alighting, Miss Cynthie gave this imposing structure one sidewise, upward glance, and said, "You live like bees in a hive, don't you?"—Rudolph Fisher

7   I walk on past brown unpainted houses, chipped sidewalks. Home is near and I want to get there and feed my hungry stomach. I see a plain brick house and run towards its broken

wooden gate. I smile at the smell of stewing beans. I enter and sit at a table made of Hunt's tomato boxes. My mother silently brings me a plate of cooked beans with sliced onions and chile and a half-dozen tortillas.

She sits next to me and watches me eat. I dip a large spoon into the beans, bring it up to my mouth and, slurping, swallow the stuff on it. A rolled tortilla follows, and munching sounds come from me.—RUDY GALLARDO

B. Write the body of your composition, following section II of your final outline. Make certain that each paragraph is directly related to the introductory paragraph and that the paragraphs are tied together with appropriate transitional devices.

The Conclusion

After you have finished writing the body of your composition, your final step is to write the conclusion. The concluding paragraph indicates to the reader that the composition is finished. It can restate the main idea of the composition, summarize the ideas that have been presented in the body paragraphs, or make a comment about the information that has been given. Because the conclusion is the final idea that your readers will take from your work, it should be as interesting and as important as the introductory paragraph.

The sample composition "The Coast of Oregon" ended with this statement.

"Timeless beauty" is an expression that has meaning in June on the coast of Oregon.

The writer's comment about the beauty of the scene in June on the coast of Oregon restates the main idea of the composition.

The writer of the following conclusion summarizes his feelings toward his subject, mountain rivers.

By such a river it is impossible to believe that one will ever be tired or old. Every sense applauds it. Taste it, feel its chill on the teeth. it is purity absolute. Watch its racing current, its steady renewal of force. It is transient and eternal. Listen again to its symphony of sounds hiss and splash and gurgle, the small talk of side channels, the whisper of blown and scattered spray gathering itself and beginning to flow again, secret and irresistible, among the wet rocks.—WALLACE STEGNER

The following writer ends his composition with a moving statement on the death of his dog.

That afternoon I drove Shamrock's body back to the gorge in the hills and buried him there. The bear cubs will tell the others that the little white lion has come home at last. When winter comes, the deer will step high in the snowdrifts in that green glade, over the place where lies my little friend, the one I can never forget.—FREDERICK A. BIRMINGHAM

Each of these three conclusions signals "The End" to the readers of the compositions.

Exercises Finishing the Composition

A. Write the concluding paragraph of your composition. Be sure that it ties in well with the rest of your paper.

B. Write the title for your composition. You can take the title from your final outline, or you can write a new one.

Rewriting, or Revising

Now that you have completed your first draft, you are ready to rewrite, or revise, the third step in the Process of Writing. Check

Step 3 of the Guidelines on page 81. You may also wish to review the Checklist for Writing Paragraphs on page 131 and the Checklist for Writing Compositions on page 165.

Proofreading

Follow the steps for Proofreading on page 81. Use the sections on grammar, usage, and mechanics at the back of this book, or any other reference necessary.

Checklist for Writing Compositions

As you write a composition, follow the steps in Guidelines for the Process of Writing on page 81. Use this Checklist after you have written your composition.

1. Has the subject been narrowed to a topic that can be covered in a few paragraphs?

2. Does the composition deal with a single topic or idea?

3. Does it have an introduction, a body, and a conclusion?

4. Does the introduction present the main idea? Does it catch the reader's interest?

5. Does the body explain or support the main idea?

6. Does the conclusion restate the main idea, summarize the information, or comment upon it?

7. Do the paragraphs work together to develop a single topic or idea that is the subject of the composition?

8. Is the composition appropriate for the audience for which it is intended? Is the purpose clear?

9. Are the ideas presented in a clear, logical order?

10. Does the composition have unity? Are the supporting ideas in each paragraph related to the topic sentence? Is each paragraph directly related to the main idea in the introductory paragraph?

11. Are there transitional devices that tie the paragraphs together?

12. Is the title meaningful and interesting?

Chapter 8

Types of Compositions

Just as there are three basic types of paragraphs, there are three types of compositions: descriptive, explanatory, and narrative. In this chapter, you will apply your knowledge of paragraphs and of compositions to the three types of compositions. In addition, you will study three important characteristics of well written compositions—unity, coherence, and emphasis.

Part 1   The Descriptive Composition

Description is seldom the basis for an entire composition. Rather, it is usually used in conjunction with other types of writing. However, there may be times when you are particularly moved by a place, a scene, or a person and want to communicate your feelings in writing. The descriptive composition is one way of doing so.

Before analyzing or writing a descriptive composition, you need to understand *unity, coherence,* and *emphasis* as they apply to this type of writing. You also need to understand point of view, which influences the other three characteristics. While point of view applies to all types of compositions, it will be explained here only in relation to description.

Point of View

Physical Point of View. In your study of the descriptive paragraph, you learned to organize details into logical order. You learned to describe things from side to side, from top to bottom (or the reverse), and from near to far (or the reverse). You learned to use other methods of organization, along with key words that indicate a change in direction.

What you learned about organizing paragraphs also applies to compositions. You can arrange the details in a composition in any order, as long as it is logical and consistent. No matter what organizational plan you choose, though, you must have a *physical point of view*. This is the place from which you choose to view the object of your description.

Selecting Details. Once you have established a physical point of view, your description should include only those details that can be sensed from that given point. For example, if you choose a high cliff overlooking a mountain valley as your physical point of view, you will describe only the things that you can hear, see, touch, taste, and smell from that vantage point.

Mental Point of View. Point of view is also mental. In a description, mental point of view varies according to mood and the individual. If, for example, as you look at a mountain valley, the sky is dark; heavy, black clouds are forming on the horizon; the wind is moaning faintly through the pines; and thunder crashes over the distant peaks, you may feel sad and depressed. This is your mental point of view at the moment and will be reflected in your composition.

If, on the other hand, the morning sun is shining; the sky is a cloudless blue; a woodpecker is clattering rhythmically in the distance; and a hint of pine scents the air, you may feel happy, carefree, even excited. This is the mental point of view that will influence what you write.

Unity

When you write a descriptive composition, your purpose is to create a single, unified impression in the mind of the reader. You achieve this by doing the following:

1. Maintain a definite point of view, both physical and mental.
2. Choose details carefully.
3. Make sure that the sentences in each paragraph relate to the topic sentence and that each paragraph relates back to the introductory paragraph.
4. Use transitional devices that tie ideas together.

Choosing Details. Choosing details carefully means selecting those details that contribute to the impression you wish to create. It also means describing the details with precise words that create a clear image for the reader.

For an example of precise writing, contrast the following sentences:

1. The bird sang in the tree.
2. The mourning dove grieved in the old pine.

The first sentence is vague, general, and lacking in precision. The second sentence precisely identifies the bird, the tree, and the action being performed.

Here is another example:

1. The elephant moved down the ramp.
2. The huge elephant lumbered down the wooden ramp.

The second sentence includes specific adjectives and a strong, precise verb; it creates a much clearer image than does the first sentence.

Coherence

Coherence, or clarity, is achieved through the logical arrangement of ideas. Several logical orders were mentioned in the discussion of physical point of view. Another order is chronological, or time, order. It is used occasionally in description, but more often in explanatory and narrative compositions.

Emphasis

Emphasis is achieved (1) by selecting a central idea, then grouping details around that idea; and (2) by stressing those details that are important in relation to the central idea.

In describing a scene, for example, the writer often chooses a center of interest—an unusual mountain, a unique building, an interesting play of light or color—and groups details around it. The central image dominates the scene; all other details are described in relation to it.

Studying a Descriptive Composition

The following composition illustrates the concepts presented thus far in Part 1.

NOVEMBER AFTERNOON

It is not yet 4:30, and the sun is nearing the low ridge to the west. Soon the brightness of the late autumn afternoon will yield to twilight, to dusk, and to dark.

The sun begins to set behind the ridge. The last, long light climbs from the valley's frosted pasture grass up the gray trunks of the naked maples and seems to pause on the hilltops to the east. Then it is gone. Twilight, the glow of November evening, possesses the day.

At first there is the bright, shadowless light, a sunless daylight in which the growing moon, halfway up the eastern sky, is only a ghost. Then the glow comes, a rosy suffusion so subtle it could be a reflection of the maple leaves at the roadside or the bronze-red grass in the neglected meadow. The air seems to thin and brighten, and the chill diminishes distances. The world comes close, the familiar world of this place called home.

The glow fades. Dusk creeps in, unhurried but insistent, and the clarity of vision dims. In its place is a deceptive clarity of hearing. The farm dog barking just down the road sounds no closer than a truck shifting gears on a hill a mile away. The rustle of leathery leaves in an oak not ten feet away seems as far off as the hooting of the barred owl across the valley. And time somehow has lost its dimensions. It is evening and it is autumn, and the moon has begun to glow. The scuffle of leaves at the roadside just ahead could be a noontime cat or a midnight fox or the evening breeze.

Sunset, twilight, dusk, darkness, all by six o'clock on a mid-November evening, is late autumn's summary of serenity.

—*The New York Times*

The physical point of view is a valley. The mental point of view is one of serenity, of peace.

The single, unified impression is one of serenity. Unity is achieved through a stable point of view and the choice of precise details. Carefully chosen words, such as "The last, long light climbs from the valley's frosted pasture grass"; "the growing moon, halfway up the eastern sky, is only a ghost"; "Dusk creeps in, unhurried, but insistent"; and "The rustle of leathery leaves in an oak" reinforce the impression of serenity.

Each paragraph relates to the introductory paragraph by telling something about the late autumn afternoon. The paragraphs, and the ideas within the paragraphs, are tied together by the repetition of the word *light* and by the repeated use of synonyms for light; for example, *brightness*, *glow*, and *rosy suffusion*.

Coherence is achieved through the logical arrangement of ideas into chronological order. The writer describes sunset, twilight, dusk, and darkness in the order in which they happen.

Emphasis is achieved by grouping the details in relation to *light*. The changing light, reflecting the oncoming night, is the dominant or central image in the composition; all other objects are seen and heard through this light.

Exercise **Writing a Description**

Following the techniques described in Chapter 7, Writing a Composition, write a descriptive composition of five paragraphs. Begin by choosing a subject based on personal experience. Then proceed as follows:

1. Narrow your subject.
2. Decide on your audience and your purpose.
3. Jot down your ideas.
4. Group your ideas.
5. Organize your ideas into a working outline.
6. Make a final outline that includes the introductory paragraph, the body paragraphs, and the conclusion.
7. Decide on your point of view, both physical and mental.
8. Write your composition, following your final outline.
9. Check to make sure that all ideas are related to each other and to the introductory paragraphs.
10. Make sure that your composition has unity, coherence, and emphasis.
11. Check to be sure that you have used strong verbs, precise nouns, and vivid descriptive words and phrases.
12. Revise carefully where necessary.

Part 2 The Explanatory Composition

An explanatory composition can give instructions. It can explain an idea, using facts or statistics, specific examples, incidents or anecdotes, and comparison or contrast. Like all compositions, an explanatory composition opens with an introductory paragraph that catches the reader's attention and gives an indication of what will follow. The body paragraphs explain or support the ideas presented in the opening paragraph. A concluding paragraph signals the completion of the composition.

Throughout, the well written explanatory composition is characterized by unity, coherence, and emphasis. These three qualities are achieved in much the same way as they are achieved in descriptive compositions. Unity is created by a structure in which all the parts are interrelated, by precise details, and by transitional devices that tie ideas together. Coherence is created by the logical arrangement of ideas. In some compositions, especially those that give instructions and those that include incidents or anecdotes, logical order means chronological order. In others, logical order fits the unique content of the compositions. The third quality, emphasis, is achieved by selecting a central idea that dominates the other ideas presented in the composition.

Following is an example of an explanatory composition. See if you can identify the specific methods used by the writer to achieve unity, coherence, and emphasis.

HOW TO READ FASTER

When I was a kid in Philadelphia, I must have read every comic book ever published. I zipped through all of them in a couple of days, then reread the good ones until the next issues arrived. As I got older, my eyeballs must have slowed down or something! I mean, comic books started to pile up faster than my brother Russell and I could read them. It wasn't until much later, when I was getting my doctorate, that I realized it wasn't my eyeballs that were to blame. The problem is that there is too much to read these days, and too little time to read every word of it. That's when I started to look around for common-sense, practical ways to help me read faster. I found three that are especially good. And if I can learn them, so can you—and you can put them to use immediately.

The first way is previewing. It is especially useful for getting a general idea of heavy reading like long magazine or newspaper articles and nonfiction books. To preview, read the entire first two paragraphs of whatever you've chosen. Next read only the first sentence of each successive paragraph. Then read the entire last two paragraphs. This will give you a quick, overall view of long, unfamiliar material. It will keep you from spending time on things you don't really want—or need—to read.

The second way to read faster is skimming. It is a good way to get a general idea of light reading like popular magazines or the sports and entertainment sections of the paper. It is also a good way to review material you've read before. To skim, think of your eyes as magnets. Force them to move fast. Sweep them across each and every line of type. Pick up only a few key words in each line. You will end up reading about half the words in *less* than half the time it would take to read every word.

The third way to increase your reading speed is clustering. Clustering trains you to look at groups of words rather than one at a time. For example, instead of reading a line like this: My—brother—Russell—thinks—monsters, you would read it like this:

$$\boxed{\text{My brother Russell}} \quad \boxed{\text{thinks monsters}}$$

For most of us, clustering takes constant practice because it's a totally different way of seeing what we read. To practice clustering, begin with something easy to read. Read it as fast as you can. Concentrate on seeing three to four words at once rather than one word at a time. Then reread the piece at your normal speed to see what you missed the first time. Practice fifteen minutes every day until you can read clusters without missing much the first time.

So now you have three ways to help you read faster: previewing to cut down on unnecessary heavy reading; skimming to get a quick, general idea of light reading; and clustering to increase your speed and comprehension. With enough practice, you'll be able to handle more reading at school and at home in less time. You should even have enough time to read your favorite comic books!—BILL COSBY

The introductory paragraph explains that the composition is about reading, specifically three ways to help you read faster. The three body paragraphs develop this idea. The sentences in each paragraph relate directly to the topic sentence. Following the body is a conclusion, which summarizes the ideas in the composition and which relates back to the introductory paragraph.

The tight, unified structure of the composition is shown clearly by the following outline.

I. Introductory paragraph: three ways to read faster
II. Body
    A. First way: previewing
    B. Second way: skimming
    C. Third way: clustering
III. Conclusion: three ways to read faster

Another way that the composition is unified is by the repetition of the words *read* and *way*. This transitional device is used throughout the five paragraphs.

Coherence is achieved by the logical arrangement of ideas throughout the composition and within each paragraph. The opening paragraph introduces the idea of three ways. The next three paragraphs each explain one way. Each paragraph is structured so that it first names the way, next tells a little more about it, then gives specific directions, in chronological order, for applying the method.

Emphasis is achieved by grouping all the ideas around the central idea of reading faster. Details about why it is important to read faster, about what kinds of materials can and should be read faster, and about the ways to increase reading speed are all related to the central idea.

Exercise Writing an Explanatory Composition

Study the following possible subjects for compositions. If you think of others, add those to your list. Choose one subject and write an explanatory composition, following the steps described in Chapter 7. Be sure that your completed composition has unity, coherence, and emphasis.

1. Secret Places
2. Favorite Movies
3. What Makes a Great Teacher?
4. My Best Quality/My Worst Quality
5. Why Study History?
6. It Is the Best of Times/It Is the Worst of Times
7. Urban Challenges
8. The Advantages of Newspaper News over Television News
9. Earning Money
10. Spectator Sports

Part 3   The Narrative Composition

The narrative paragraph describes an event; so does the narrative composition. However, because the narrative composition is longer, elements such as character, setting, and conflict are more fully developed.

Character refers to the people (or animals) in the narrative. In thinking about the characters in a composition, you might ask questions similar to the following: Who are the characters? What are they like? What do they do? What do they want?

Setting refers to the place or places where the event described in the narrative happens. In thinking about setting, you might ask: What is the setting? What is it like? Does it have any effect on the characters?

Conflict refers to the struggle or the problem in which the characters become involved. Conflict is usually brought about because of something the character, or characters, want. There are four basic types of conflict:

THE INDIVIDUAL AGAINST A SUPERNATURAL FORCE: the struggle against God, or the gods (as in the ancient myths and legends) or against the devil.

THE INDIVIDUAL AGAINST NATURE: the struggle to survive natural catastrophes, such as floods, earthquakes, and hurricanes, that might destroy human life. This would also include the struggle against beasts, reptiles, insects, and other animals and, in some cases, against plants.

THE INDIVIDUAL AGAINST SOCIETY: the struggle against social forces such as injustice, prejudice, and loss of individual freedom. This also includes the struggle of one individual against another.

THE INDIVIDUAL AGAINST SELF: the struggle within the mind or conscience of an individual as he or she attempts to make a personal decision.

Following is an example of a narrative composition. As you read it, keep in mind the definitions of character, setting, and conflict and the methods described previously for achieving unity, coherence, and emphasis.

RASCAL

All raccoons are attracted by shining objects, and Rascal was no exception. He was fascinated by brass doorknobs, glass marbles, my broken watch, and small coins. I gave him three bright, new pennies which he hoarded with the happiness of a little miser. He felt them carefully, smelled them, tasted them, and then hid them in a dark corner with some of his other treasures.

One day Rascal decided to carry one of his pennies to the back porch. Poe-the-Crow was perched on the porch rail teasing the cats, but keeping just beyond their reach. This raucous old bird, who cawed and cussed in crow language, was arching his wings and strutting like a poolroom bully as Rascal pushed open the screen and trundled into the sunlight, his penny chining like newly minted gold.

Poe and Rascal had taken an instant dislike to each other when first they met. Crows, like most other birds, know that raccoons steal birds' eggs and sometimes eat fledglings. In addition Poe was jealous. He had seen me petting and pampering my small raccoon. However, Rascal was large enough now to pull a few tail feathers from the big, black bird during their noisy squabbles. And Poe, who was no fool, was taking few chances.

The penny, however, was so tempting that the crow threw caution to the winds and made a dive for the bright object (for crows are as insatiably attracted by glittering trinkets as are raccoons and in addition are inveterate thieves). Rascal was carrying the penny in his mouth, and when Poe swooped to conquer, his beak closed not only on the penny but upon half a dozen of Rascal's coarse, strong whiskers. When the black thief tried to make his fast getaway he found himself attached to the raccoon, who with a high scream of fury began fighting for his property and his life. Such a tangle of shining, black feathers and furious fur you have seldom seen as Rascal and Poe wrestled and struggled. I arrived to untangle them, and both were angry with me. Rascal nipped me slightly for the first time, and Poe made several ungracious comments.

The penny, meanwhile, had rolled from the porch into the grass below, where the crow promptly spotted it, seized it once again, and took wing. I gave the incident no more thought, pacified Rascal with another penny, and resumed work on my canoe in the living room.—STERLING NORTH

There are three characters in this narrative. The major characters are Rascal, a pet raccoon, and Poe-the-Crow, an ill-tempered old bird. The minor character is the narrator. The setting is the back porch of the narrator's house. It is on the porch that the conflict between Rascal and Poe-the-Crow takes place, a struggle between two individuals over possession of a bright penny.

The writer of the narrative achieves unity by developing the idea presented in the introductory paragraph; he explains what happens because of Rascal's attraction to shining objects. He makes use of two other unifying techniques as well. He uses colorful, interesting details throughout, and he ties together ideas with these transitional devices:

1. Repeating the names *Rascal* and *Poe*
2. Repeating the words *crow, raccoon,* and *penny*
3. Using synonyms for the word *shining*
4. Using the word *however* to show opposite points of view
5. Using the words *and* and *in addition* to show the relationships between ideas
6. Using *one day, now, when,* and *meanwhile* to indicate time

The writer achieves coherence in the narrative by organizing the ideas into chronological order. With the exception of one flashback in which he recalls the dislike between Rascal and Poe, the writer describes the incident as it happened.

The writer achieves emphasis by focusing on one central idea—the fight between Rascal and Poe over the penny. All the details, including those that he gives about Rascal's attraction to shining objects, about Poe's character, and about the animals' dislike for each other, relate to that central idea.

Exercise Writing a Narrative Composition

Consider possible subjects for a narrative composition. They can be based on events in which you participated, on events that were observed by you, or on events that were described to you by someone else. They can be based on fact, on imagination, or on a combination of both.

After you have listed several possible subjects, develop a composition following the steps presented in Chapter 7. When revising your composition, make sure that it is characterized by unity, coherence, and emphasis.

Chapter 9

Writing Letters

Letters! Every day over two hundred million pieces of first-class mail are handled by the United States Postal Service. People are mailing get-well notes, love letters, birthday cards, business letters, and many other kinds of communications. Children are writing letters home from camp. Grandparents are writing to their grandchildren, hoping for a peanut butter-stained response. College students are writing home for money. Families and friends are arguing, apologizing, and "chatting" across many miles.

How about you? Every time you are faced with a letter to write, do you make excuses, find other things you have to do, and finally telephone instead? If so, you are not completely alone. The problem is usually that you do not know what to write, and exactly how to start. You can put the words on paper, but they do not sound right. If your letters seem like recorded messages, if you are uncertain how to write different types of letters, if you would like to get a message to someone without paying a long distance telephone bill, this chapter can help you.

Part 1   Addressing the Envelope

Let's start with the simplest part of letter-writing first—the envelope. Probably the worst thing that could happen to a letter you have painstakingly written is that it is not delivered. Hundreds of thousands of letters end up in the Dead Letter Office in Washington, D.C. The usual problem is an incorrect address, which can be easily avoided. Double-check to be certain you have not transposed any numbers in the address. Do not forget the ZIP code. This is a five-digit code that identifies a small area within a city or state, and enables the post office to sort mail much more efficiently and rapidly. The ZIP should immediately follow the state in addresses. If you do not know the ZIP, and cannot find it in your telephone directory, call your post office. They have a complete ZIP code listing for every community in the United States and will be happy to help you.

Always put your return address on the envelope.

Ms. Betty Sergeant
1429 Oakridge Road
Ft. Worth TX 76135

Mr. Larry Spenser
341 Queen Avenue
Yakima WA 98902

Envelopes come in many different sizes and colors. The two most-used sizes are 9½″ x 4″ and 6½″ x 3½″. When sending a business letter, you should always use a white 9½″ x 4″ envelope.

If you are writing a specific person or department within a large company, you will use four lines for the address.

Ms. Betty Sergeant
1429 Oakridge Road
Ft. Worth TX 76135

Mr. Larry Spenser
A · G Electronics Company
341 Queen Avenue
Yakima WA 98902

When addressing the small, square envelope that is usually included with invitations or note cards, you may put your return address on the flap on the back of the envelope, with the receiver's name and address centered on the front.

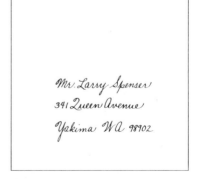

Caution: Be sure to check the back on any envelope before addressing it. You may have it upside down.

Did you notice the abbreviations of the names of states on the examples? These may be used in addressing envelopes, but you *must* use the ZIP code with them. When you use these abbreviations, you do not need to separate the city and state with a comma. However, if you do not use these abbreviations, you must place a comma between the city and state.

Mr. Larry Spenser
341 Queen Avenue
Yakima WA 98902

Mr. Larry Spenser
341 Queen Avenue
Yakima, Washington 98902

Abbreviations of State Names

Alabama	AL	Montana	MT
Alaska	AK	Nebraska	NE
Arizona	AZ	Nevada	NV
Arkansas	AR	New Hampshire	NH
American Samoa	AS	New Jersey	NJ
California	CA	New Mexico	NM
Canal Zone	CZ	New York	NY
Colorado	CO	North Carolina	NC
Connecticut	CT	North Dakota	ND
Delaware	DE	Ohio	OH
District of Columbia	DC	Oklahoma	OK
Florida	FL	Oregon	OR
Georgia	GA	Pennsylvania	PA
Guam	GU	Puerto Rico	PR
Hawaii	HI	Rhode Island	RI
Idaho	ID	South Carolina	SC
Illinois	IL	South Dakota	SD
Indiana	IN	Tennessee	TN
Iowa	IA	Trust Territories	TT
Kansas	KS	Texas	TX
Kentucky	KY	Utah	UT
Louisiana	LA	Vermont	VT
Maine	ME	Virginia	VA
Maryland	MD	Virgin Islands	VI
Massachusetts	MA	Washington	WA
Michigan	MI	West Virginia	WV
Minnesota	MN	Wisconsin	WI
Mississippi	MS	Wyoming	WY
Missouri	MO		

Exercises Addressing Envelopes

A. Put each of the addresses below in proper three or four-line form as it should appear on an envelope. Capitalize, abbreviate, and punctuate correctly.

1. 462 zane avenue philadelphia pennsylvania 19111 mrs. jill erikson

2. washington d c 20013 national geographic society melvin m payne post office box 2895

3. 111 west washington street chicago illinois 60602 chicago title insurance company

4. salt lake city utah 84104 appliance department 1133 glendale drive gibson's discount center

5. mr. john johnson oklahoma city oklahoma 1462 longridge road 73115

B. Draw four "envelopes" on plain paper. Three of the envelopes should measure 9½" × 4", and one 5" × 5". Now pick three of the choices below and with the aid of a telephone directory write the addresses correctly on the envelopes. Address the 5" × 5" envelope to your best friend. Do not forget to include your return address.

1. Anyone whose last name is Smith
2. The service department of an automobile agency
3. Your favorite disc jockey
4. An employment agency
5. The sportswear department of a department store
6. A television station

Now that you are familiar with addressing envelopes, you are ready to study the different types of letters to put inside them. The form for an envelope does not change; it is the same for any letter.

Part 2 Writing Informal Notes

Whenever you have written a short letter thanking a relative for a gift or expressing your appreciation for a weekend visit, you have used a form of letter known as an **informal note.**

These notes all have one thing in common. They are short. They could be referred to as "people-pleasers" because they definitely impress the receiver. You might have been less than completely delighted with the complete dental-care kit your aunt and uncle sent you for Christmas, but they will be pleased to receive your letter of thanks.

Informal notes have a definite form:

Date
August 30, 1981

Salutation

Dear Uncle Fred and Aunt Fran,

You never told me you had ESP—how else could you have known I've been craving that particular album? It's great! I've played it at least twenty times, and Mom says that next time you send an album to me, she'd Body *appreciate your enclosing a pair of earplugs for her.*

Thanks so much for the perfect gift. I hope you can visit sometime and hear it for yourselves—before I wear it out!

Closing *Love,*

Signature *Jennie*

The first part of the form of an informal note is the **date.** Remember to leave a margin between the end of the date and the right side of the paper.

The second item is the **salutation.** This simply addresses the person to whom you are writing. Always use a comma after the salutation. Next is the **body** of the letter, or the message. The **closing** can be one of many, depending on the relationship. *Sincerely, Affectionately, Lovingly, Happily,* or *Good luck* are some of the choices. If the closing is more than one word, capitalize only the first word. Always use a comma after the closing.

As you can see, a casual language style is fine. Write naturally, the way you would normally speak to the person to whom you are writing.

There are other varieties of the informal note. Apologies, congratulations, invitations, and R.S.V.P.'s are the most common. Of these, only the R.S.V.P. might require some explanation.

> *July 27, 1981*
>
> *Dear Jim,*
>   *You are invited to attend my birthday dinner on August 16. It will be held at the Sundance Room of the Hotel Towers at 7:30 p.m.*
>   *I'm looking forward to seeing you.*
>
>   *Sincerely,*
>   *Mary Barnes*
>
> *R.S.V.P.*

R.S.V.P. is an abbreviation for a French phrase meaning "please respond." It is necessary for the sender to have an exact count of the attending guests before the party. Unless you want to appear "uninformed," you must reply. You write a brief note stating your intention to attend or not.

> August 1, 1981
>
> Dear Mary,
>   I would love to attend your birthday dinner, but will be unable to as we are planning a vacation and will be out of town on August 16.
>   Have a very happy birthday!
>
>   Sincerely,
>   Jim Harris

> August 1, 1981
>
> Dear Mary,
>   Thank you so much for the invitation to your birthday dinner. I'd be delighted to attend.
>
>   Sincerely,
>   Jim Harris

Exercise **Writing Informal Notes**

Choose two of the following and write the appropriate notes on plain paper. On the back draw an envelope for each and address it correctly.

1. Write a note thanking a friend for the fantastic party he gave last Saturday.

2. Write to your friend's parents, apologizing for dropping a full bowl of punch on their new white carpet.

3. Write a note of congratulation to a friend who has moved from your neighborhood. You have just learned that he or she has won a cash prize in a contest. You determine the contest.

4. Write a note thanking a relative for something. The only problem is that you have no idea what the item is.

5. Write an invitation to a party, using R.S.V.P. Exchange your invitation with another student and write a reply.

6. Write a note to a friend's mother or father for something very nice the person did for you. You decide the reason.

7. Write a note to a cheerleader at your school, apologizing for tackling her during the last game.

8. Write a note congratulating your dog for passing obedience school.

Part 3 Writing Friendly Letters

These letters seem to be going down in popularity as your long-distance telephone bills go up. Haven't you tearfully said goodbye to a friend, promising to write, and then put it off until you didn't know what to write or where to start? It happens to everyone, and it's too bad. Through this type of letter, friendships endure over many years and more miles. This should be an easy letter to write, as you're communicating with someone you know very well—someone who has shared many experiences with you. Just keep sharing experiences—only now through letters. The language is informal, just as you would speak to the person.

There is a little more involved in the form of a friendly letter than in informal notes. Below is an example. Once you learn the parts of a friendly letter, you'll have to concentrate only on writing the body of the letter itself.

Heading

162 New Road
Raleigh, North Carolina 27608
July 16, 1981

Salutation

Dear Jess,

Body

Love, Closing

Jill Signature

The **heading** is written in three lines. The first line consists of your street address. The second line contains the city, state and ZIP. The third line is the date of the letter. Don't abbreviate on the date line.

The **salutation** can be casual in a friendly letter. The only two rules are to capitalize the first word and any proper nouns, and to use a comma following the salutation.

Dear Sue,   *Hi Slim,*

Howdy Pete,   *Hello Mark,*

The **closing** is usually kept simple: *Love, Sincerely, Always,* etc. The first word is the only one capitalized. You can use your originality and the closeness of the friendship for something more appropriate for the particular person to whom you are writing.

Lovingly yours,   *Still waiting,*

Always here,   *Frustrated,*

The most important part of any letter is the **body.** Let's hope you haven't received or been guilty of sending such an empty letter as the following:

162 New Road
Raleigh NC 27608
July 16, 1981

Dear Jess,

    Your letter arrived yesterday and I'm happy to hear about all the great things you've been doing.

    As usual, things around here aren't very exciting. The weather's been hot for so long I can't remember what "cool" means.

    Everyone here says to say "hi".

    There's not much more to write. Wish you were here so we could have a good talk. Write soon.

Love,

Jill

All that is needed to turn dull paragraphs into interesting ones is detail. If the person to whom you are writing were with you, what would you say? Here are a few points to remember when writing a friendly letter:

1. Make comments on the letter you have received.
2. Avoid the constant use of *I*.
3. Write one or two detailed paragraphs regarding events and people. They will be much more interesting than a series of one-sentence statements.
4. Ask questions. Then the person has something to write to you about.

With a little more time and thought, Jill might have written two opening paragraphs like this:

Maybe this letter should be written in special ink so you can read it underwater—don't you ever get waterlogged? From the sound of things you're either in training for the Olympics or trying to get a role in the next "Jaws." You're way out of my class now—unless they've started giving medals for floating in a tube. Couldn't you manage to compete in a meet around here?

Things here are not too exciting—and that's an understatement! It's been so hot for so long that everyone's dragging. I've been lying around the yard or the house most of the time. But you know my Mom—if I'm not "doing something" I can't possibly be happy. So she keeps finding things for me to "do." Clean out your closet. Water the lawn. Straighten your dresser. Water the lawn! Run to the store. Water the lawn!! I'm beginning to feel as if I've got a hose growing out of my right arm! The lawn's so soaked now we could grow rice! Next summer a job is a necessity —only with my luck it would probably be watering lawns.

Detail, along with conversational writing, can make a letter come to life. Choose one of the statements in Jill's letter on page

191 and rewrite it in a detailed paragraph. Make it interesting. Be prepared to exchange your paragraph with a classmate, or read it aloud to the class.

Exercise Writing Friendly Letters

One of your best friends has moved out of the city. Write a friendly letter detailing three events that have taken place since he or she left. You can use actual events or choose from the list below.

1. Your school team lost a close game for the state basketball championship.

2. A good friend gave you a surprise birthday party.

3. You are certain that someone tried to break into your house when your parents were out.

4. Your new puppy is methodically eating his way through the house—couch, chairs, carpets, shoes.

Part 4 Writing Business Letters

Over ten thousand business letters are processed for each friendly letter or informal note that is written. With odds like that, the business letter has to be an important letter to master. The term *business* means that the letters have a definite purpose to accomplish, not that they are written only by and for business firms.

There are two main skills to master in writing a business letter: (1) Use the proper form. (2) Be brief and specific.

Using the Proper Form

There are two basic forms for business letters: **block form** and **modified block form.**

Heading

416 Paxton Road
Rochester, New York 14617
April 23, 1981

Inside Address

Sales Department
Stereophonics, Inc.
231 Garrison
Boston, Massachusetts 02116

Salutation

Ladies and Gentlemen:

_____
_____
_____   Body
_____
_____
_____

Sincerely,   Closing

José Martinez

José Martinez   Signature

Note: Always use plain white 8½″ x 11″ paper for business letters, whether you handwrite or type them.

416 Paxton Road
Rochester, New York 14617
April 23, 1981

Sales Department
Stereophonics, Inc.
231 Garrison
Boston, Massachusetts 02116

Dear Sir or Madam:

_____
_____
_____
_____ Body
_____
_____
_____

Sincerely,   Closing

José Martinez

José Martinez   Signature

You are already familiar with the heading of a letter. It is the same as that used for writing friendly letters.

The one section that has been added is the **inside address.**
It is important to have the name and address of the person or department to whom you are writing on the face of the letter.
Occasionally a letter is opened by mistake and the envelope misplaced; if this happens, the name and address are still clearly
visible. The inside address is usually four lines on a business letter,
as you will be writing to a specific person or department within a
company. Leave a space between the inside address and the
salutation.

The salutation varies, depending upon the first line of the inside address. If you are writing to a company or department
within a company, use one of the following:

```
Dear Sir or Madam:
Ladies and Gentlemen:
```

If you are writing to a particular person, but do not know his
or her name (such as the Personnel Manager, President, or General Manager), you should use *Dear Sir or Madam:*

The form for writing to someone whose name you know is
quite simple:

```
Dear Mr. Brown:
Dear Ms. Allred:
Dear Miss Allred:
Dear Mrs. Allred:
```

Capitalize only the first word and any proper nouns in the salutation, and always follow the salutation with a colon. Leave a space
between the salutation and the body of the letter and between
the body of the letter and the closing. Capitalize only the first
word of the closing, and always follow the closing with a comma.

```
Sincerely,
Very truly yours,
Respectfully yours,
```

Type or print your name four spaces below the closing, and
write your signature in the space between. Typing or printing

your name makes it legible if you have a fancy but illegible signature.

Make a Carbon Copy. Whenever you write a business letter, make a carbon copy for yourself. Then you will know just what you wrote or ordered in case you do not receive an immediate reply. To use carbon paper, first place a piece of plain paper on your desk. Then place a sheet of carbon paper on top of it. The "shiny" or carbon side of the paper should be face down. Now place another piece of plain paper on top and you are ready to write. To avoid slippage, you can use a paper clip to hold the three pieces together. When you write, be certain you use the type of carbon paper that is made for pen or pencil. Typewriter keys exert much more pressure on the carbon paper than a person's hand.

Fold the Letter Correctly. Folding a business letter correctly is sometimes a problem. You want only two folds in your paper when using a standard 9½″ x 4″ envelope. Starting at the bottom of the paper, fold it into thirds toward the top. Usually you will find that after the first fold is completed, only the inside address and heading will be visible to you. When properly folded, the letter will easily fit into the envelope, and can readily be taken out by the receiver.

First Fold   Second Fold   Complete

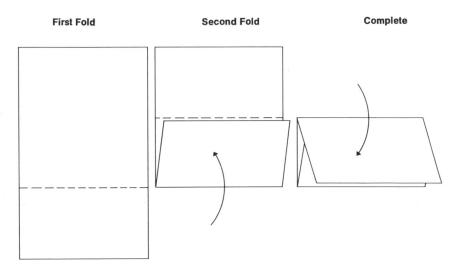

Exercises Using the Proper Form

A. Below is an example of a business letter in modified block form. There are errors in capitalization, punctuation, and spacing. Correct the errors by rewriting the letter on a plain sheet of paper.

Jan. 14, 1981
1452 Balboa Drive
Pensacola Florida, 32506

General supply Company
sales mgr.
462 acacia avenue
Palo Alto Calif. 94306

Dear Sir or Madam,

    Regarding the order I placed with you on December 15, _____

_____

_____

_____

_____

_____

Very Truly Yours

Thomas A. O'Leary

Thomas A. O'Leary

B. Using correct form, write a letter of your own with a local company as the addressee. You do not have to write the body of the letter.

Being Brief and Specific

When you write a business letter you include only what is absolutely necessary. State the purpose of the letter and then stop. Use only those details that are vital to accomplish your purpose.

1942 Griffin Road
Indianapolis, Indiana 46227
June 14, 1981

West Hills Pro Shop
571 Moon Clinton Road
Coraopolis, Pennsylvania 15108

Dear Sir or Madam:

Please send me the following items which appeared in your advertisement in the June issue of <u>Travel</u> and <u>Leisure</u>.

1 pr.	Foot—Joy Golf Shoes	Size 11D	Black	$ 48.00
2	Canvas Sunday Bags		@$19.00	38.00
1	Model M—20 Lynx Putter			25.00
			Total	$111.00

Enclosed is a money order for $111.00. The advertisement states that prices include postage and insurance.

Yours truly,

Scott Andersen

Scott Andersen

Whenever you place an order, be sure you have a complete description or a model number. Include sizes, colors, and the number of items desired. Check the charge for postage. In some instances the buyer will pay for postage and this amount must be included with the order. Also check instructions about sales tax. Any errors on your part will result in a delay in delivery, or in receiving unwanted merchandise. It is much easier to double-check an order than to return merchandise. Keep a carbon copy in case any mix-ups occur.

Exercise **Being Brief and Specific**

Clip an advertisement from a magazine, or choose one of the groups below and write an order letter. Total the order and add any postage that is necessary. On the back of the order draw an envelope and address it correctly.

1. Columbia House, 1400 North Fruitridge Ave., Terre Haute, Indiana 47808

> 1 8-track cartridge No. JCA34860 *Chicago XI* $7.98
> 1 record No. RS-2-4200 *BeeGees Greatest* $6.98
> 1 two-record set No. 2HS3350 *Tusk* $15.98
> Postage $.75

2. Walter Drake & Sons, 4085 Drake Building, Colorado Springs, Colorado 80940—Advertisment in August issue of *Better Homes and Gardens*

> No. S717—two sets of 1,000 name labels @ $1.00 per set
> No. S854—one set of personalized pencils @ $.89 per set
> No. S6066—two full-page magnifiers @ $1.98 each
> Postage and handling—$.40

3. Sea Horses, Box 342096, Coral Gables, Florida 33134—Advertisement in July issue of *Boy's Life*

> 3 live sea horse kits   @ $ 2.98
> 2 custom aquariums @ $ 5.98
> 1 deluxe aquarium $10.95

> Air mail postage paid by advertiser—live delivery guaranteed

Types of Business Letters

The three main types of business letters are these:

1. **Requests for Information.** Perhaps you have been thinking about buying some specialized stereo equipment. You could write a business letter requesting information regarding additional speakers.

2. **Letters of Order.** You would order your stereo equipment through a business letter if you were unable to purchase it locally.

3. **Letters of Complaint.** If your speaker did not operate when you received it, you would write a business letter to complain. The ability to write this type of letter is invaluable.

Requests for Information. Letters that request information must be as specific as possible. Also, since you are really asking the receiver to take time to reply, you must always check for politeness.

1315 Summer Road
Trenton, New Jersey 08618
May 15, 1981

Chamber of Commerce
Zuni
New Mexico 87327

Dear Sir or Madam:

As a class assignment, I am working on a paper dealing with the Indians of New Mexico, and particularly the Zuni tribe. Any information or addresses you could provide would be appreciated.

I am particularly interested in the culture of the Zuni Indians today as compared with the culture of the 1800's.

Very truly yours,
Susan Campbell

Special Note for Typists: If any of your business letters are extremely short you may double-space for the sake of appearance. If you do double-space, be consistent with the prescribed form.

Exercise Writing a Request for Information

1. Write a letter to a chamber of commerce asking for information about their city. Be specific as to why you need this information: you are planning to move to that city; you are interested in vacationing there; or you have been given that particular area to research as a class assignment.

2. Write to a college or university requesting information regarding tuition costs. State your major field of interest: law, medicine, computer science, etc.

3. Write to a company in your area asking for information about summer employment. Let them know your age, qualifications, and previous experience.

4. In groups, plan the "ideal" vacation to an exotic spot. Write the various letters necessary for transportation, hotels, and tours. Then plan the vacation with the information you receive.

Letters of Complaint. Have you ever purchased something that fell apart, did not work, or was a disappointment? Write a letter of complaint. This is not a "gripe" letter; it is written to let a store or company know that there is a problem and you would like to have it taken care of. Most companies are interested in hearing from you. If you are not happy with a purchase you probably will not buy that brand again, or maybe you will shop at a different store. This is of great concern to the seller. After all, he or she wants you to keep buying that particular product or coming to the store. Do not merely sit around and tell your friends how upset you are; let the proper people know you are unhappy. You will be surprised at their response.

Avoid the temptation to be sarcastic, angry, or vulgar. This will not accomplish your purpose; it will merely make you look bad. Let the store or company know when and where you purchased the item and exactly what is wrong with it. Volunteer to mail the item if they would like to inspect it. Manufacturers can rapidly tell if the problem was their fault or yours.

631 Inca Lane
St. Paul, Minnesota 55112
October 6, 1981

Public Relations Department
Woolcraft, Inc.
1300 West Fremont Place
St. Louis, Missouri 63142

Gentlemen:

In September I purchased one of your new "Ski-Sno" sweaters from a local department store. After wearing it twice, I washed it according to the directions on the label. While it is still soft and the colors are as bright as when it was brand-new, it is now several sizes smaller. Needless to say, I am very disappointed.

I would be happy to send the sweater directly to you, as there has obviously been some oversight in your washing instructions. I would appreciate an explanation.

Sincerely,
Elsa Johnson

Perhaps your problem is closer to home than Elsa's. After many futile phone calls to a local company, you might find it easier to state your problem in a letter.

123 La Clede Avenue
Memphis, Tennessee 38126
August 31, 1981

General Manager
Sutton's Department Store
432 Oak Street
Memphis, Tennessee 38142

Dear Sir:

In June I purchased a pair of water skis in your Sporting Goods Department. These skis are model no. 143 and the price was $26.95, on sale. I used my parents' charge account, number 47727, for this purchase. Enclosed is a copy of the sales receipt.

The July statement which we received shows a charge in the amount of $269.50. Upon calling the Billing Department, I was informed that this was a computer error and would be corrected. The August statement has a past-due charge of $2,695.00. Is there some way you can communicate with the computer and correct this error?

Your earliest attention to this problem would be greatly appreciated.

Very truly yours,
Benjamin Erickson

Writing a Letter of Complaint

Write a letter of complaint regarding one of the following problems.

1. The new jeans you purchased fell apart after three wearings. (Write to the manufacturing company.)

2. You ordered a CB antenna through the mail, but received an aquarium. (Write to a hobby shop.)

3. The records you ordered from your club were warped when delivered. (Write to a record club.)

4. The live sea horses you ordered through the mail weren't. (Write to a pet shop.)

5. Four weeks ago you ordered $28.70 in supplies for a science project. You have not received them and it is now too late to complete your project. Explain the problem and ask for a refund. (Write to a hobby shop.)

Knowing Where and to Whom To Write

You can spend a great deal of time writing the "perfect" letter, addressing it correctly, and still not receive a response. It is frustrating, but curable. The usual problem is that you have not directed the letter to a specific person or department. There are many different departments within each large company which have different purposes. A request for employment would go one place and a complaint another. There are special sections to handle orders, service calls, parts, etc. If the address on your letter is simply to the company, it might take a week or more for it to find its way to the person qualified to respond.

Knowing Where and to Whom To Write

A. Using the list provided, where would you send a letter dealing with each of the problems on the next page.

Personnel Department   Sportswear Department
Accounting Department   Service Department
Parts Department

1. Employment information
2. Ordering parts
3. Requesting information regarding the operation of a product
4. Asking if a store carries a specific brand of swimwear
5. Being charged twice for the same item

B. How many different departments does a large store in your area contain? Can you list the different departments within a large corporation such as the telephone company? Write them down; then look in a telephone directory to see how close you are.

If your particular problem is one that originated with the manufacturer and not the store where you made the purchase, you should write directly to the manufacturer. The address is usually on the label attached to the product. If not, you can obtain the necessary information through your local store. There is a special department that will pay particular attention to your letter and is interested in hearing from you. This department is referred to as Public Relations. They would like to hear from you because they want to keep you happy. One important thing to bear in mind is that you do not have to have a complaint to write a business letter. If you have been thoroughly happy with one particular product, let the manufacturer know. After all, we all appreciate a nice comment now and then.

Chapter 10

Using the Library

Learning to use library resources efficiently and quickly will be of great practical value not only for your work in English but for all your studies. In high school you will do research in literature, history, science, and other subjects. You will find the library an indispensable tool.

Before you can make efficient use of the library, however, you will have to know how books are classified and arranged on the shelves. You will have to know how to use the card catalog to find books. You should also be familiar with a wide variety of reference works, so that you will be able to find easily the best available information on any subject.

Suppose, for example, that you were asked to write a brief biographical sketch of Mark Twain. Would you read a short biography, or read entries on Twain in *Twentieth Century Authors* and in a large encyclopedia? What other sources could you use? If you know what resources the library has, you will be able to answer these questions immediately.

This chapter will give you the basic information you need to make the best use of the library.

Part 1 How Books Are Classified and Arranged

It is important for you to understand the classification and arrangement of books in a library. Knowing how and where books are placed will enable you to find any book you need.

The Classification of Books

Fiction. Novels and short-story collections are usually arranged in alphabetical order by author. For example, if you want to read the American classic *The Pearl*, by John Steinbeck, you would first look for the section in the library that has shelves marked FICTION. Then you would look for books that have authors whose last names begin with S and find the book in its alphabetical position. If the book is not there, someone else has borrowed it, or a browser has carelessly returned it to the wrong position. You would be wise to check part of the shelf to see if the book has been returned out of alphabetical order. If you do not find the book and you need it soon, fill out a reserve card (a postcard mailed to you when the book has been returned to the library) that the librarian will give you.

Nonfiction. Most libraries classify nonfiction books according to the Dewey Decimal System. This system, which is named for its originator, the American librarian Melvil Dewey, classifies all books by number in ten major categories:

000–099	**General Works**	(encyclopedias, handbooks, almanacs, etc.)
100–199	**Philosophy**	(includes psychology, ethics, etc.)
200–299	**Religion**	(the Bible, theology, mythology)

300–399	**Social Science**	(sociology, economics, government, education, law, folklore)
400–499	**Language**	(languages, grammars, dictionaries)
500–599	**Science**	(mathematics, chemistry, physics, biology, etc.)
600–699	**Useful Arts**	(farming, cooking, sewing, nursing, engineering, radio, television, gardening, industries, inventions)
700–799	**Fine Arts**	(music, painting, drawing, acting, photography, games, sports, amusements)
800–899	**Literature**	(poetry, plays, essays)
000–999	**History**	(biography, travel, geography)

As you can see from the major categories of the Dewey Decimal System, each discipline has a classification number. For example, all science books have a number between 500 and 599, and all history books have a number between 900 and 999. The system becomes more detailed as each of these major groups is subdivided. The table below shows how the subdividing works in the literature category (800–899).

800–899 Literature	**810–819 Literature Subdivided**
810 American literature	810 American literature
820 English literature	811 Poetry
830 German literature	812 Drama
840 French literature	813 Fiction
850 Italian literature	814 Essays
860 Spanish literature	815 Speeches
870 Latin literature (classic)	816 Letters
880 Greek literature (classic)	817 Satire and Humor
890 Other literatures	818 Miscellany
	819 Canadian-English Literature

Arrangement of Books on the Shelves

You will see at a glance that books are arranged on the shelves numerically in order of classification. Most libraries mark their shelves prominently with the numbers indicating the books to be found in each particular section. Within each classification except biography, books are arranged alphabetically by authors' last names. Biographies are arranged alphabetically by the last name of the person the book is about.

Biography. The Dewey Decimal System division for Biography is 920. However, large libraries will often place biographies in a separate section because of the large number of these books. In this case they will have a "B" or a "920" on the spine of the book and on the catalog card. If you are looking for a particular biography and are unable to find it, ask the librarian for assistance.

Reference Books. Reference books of particular types or on specific subjects are also shelved together, often with the letter R above the classification number.

Exercises How Books Are Classified and Arranged

A. In which major division would the following information be located?

1. Plays for high school productions
2. How to plant a vegetable garden
3. A comparison of Greek and Roman gods
4. "Killer" bees
5. Motocross racing
6. Recessions and depressions in the United States
7. Macramé
8. Rules for playing lacrosse
9. How to say "no" in any country
10. Operating a CB radio

B. Using the Dewey Decimal System listed on pages 210 and 211, assign the correct classification number to each of the following books:

1. *Voices of the Rainbow: Contemporary Poetry by American Indians*, ed. Kenneth Rosen.
2. *Great Religions of the World*, ed. Merle Severy.
3. *America*, by Alistair Cooke.
4. *Metric Power*, by Richard Deming.
5. *A History of American Painting*, by Ian Bennett.
6. *Dolphins*, by Jacques Cousteau and P. Diolé.
7. *Planning the Perfect Garden*, ed. Good Housekeeping.
8. *A Treasury of Afro-American Folklore*, ed. Harold Courlander.
9. *The Art of Printmaking*, by E. Rhein.
10. *Clarence Darrow: A One-Man Play*, by David W. Rintels.

Part 2 Using the Card Catalog

To determine whether the library has a book you want and where to find it, use the **card catalog.** The card catalog is a cabinet of small drawers or file trays containing alphabetically arranged cards. Each card bears the title of a book that the library has on its shelves. The card also carries the classification number, or as librarians say, **call number,** in the upper left-hand corner. (See the illustration on the next page.)

To find your book, write down the call number on a slip of paper. If it is a literature book—for example, *Selected Poems* by Langston Hughes—the call number will be in the 800 range. Specifically, American poetry will be found in 811.

Go to the section of shelves marked 811, and you will find your book alphabetically placed among those authors' last names that begin with *H*. The same call number you originally found on the catalog card will be imprinted on the spine of the book near the bottom.

There are usually three cards for the same book in the card catalog: the *author card*, the *title card*, and the *subject card*.

The Author Card. Perhaps you are writing a paper about a modern-day sports figure, or you are simply interested in reading about sports. Sports conditioning is the topic of a book by Frank O'Neill. You will find the author card in the card catalog, and it will look like this.

613.7   O'Neill, Frank, 1929–

     Sports conditioning: getting in shape, playing your best, and preventing injuries; by Frank O'Neill, with Bill Libby. 1st ed. Garden City, N.Y. Doubleday, 1979.
     194 p., [16] leaves of plates; ill. Includes index.

Author cards for all books by one author will be filed together alphabetically according to title. Notice also that books *about* the author are filed *behind* his or her author cards.

The Title Card. Suppose you do not know the author's name, but do know the title of the book about sports conditioning. Look in the card catalog for a card bearing the title at the top as follows:

613.7   Sports conditioning

     Sports conditioning: getting in shape, playing your best, and preventing injuries; by Frank O'Neill, with Bill Libby. 1st ed. Garden City, N.Y. Doubleday, 1979.
     194 p., [16] leaves of plates; ill. Includes index.

The place of the title card in the catalog is determined by the first letter of the first word in the title. (A, An, and *The* do not count as first words.)

The Subject Card. You may not know whether a book has been written about sports conditioning. However, because it is an important part of sports, you suspect that there may be a book about it. If you look through the cards cataloged under the subject Sports, you will find the following:

613.7   **SPORTS**

      Sports conditioning: getting in shape, playing your best, and preventing injuries, by Frank O'Neill, with Bill Libby. 1st ed. Garden City, N.Y. Doubleday, 1979.

      194 p., [16] leaves of plates; ill. Includes index.

Subject cards are most useful when you want information on a specific topic from a variety of sources. Cards for all books on a particular subject are cataloged together. The subject card may also indicate whether a book has chapters on a single aspect of the topic you are interested in. The publication date on the card will help you find the most up-to-date book on your subject. Note that the heading is printed in capital letters. This will help you distinguish a subject card from an author or title card.

Card Information

Notice that all three types of catalog cards (author, title, subject) give the same information. This information includes the following:

1. The call number.
2. The title, author, publisher, and date of publication.

3. The number of pages, and a notation on whether the book has illustrations, maps, tables, or other features.

Often the catalog card will provide more information.

4. A brief description of the nature and scope of the book. (This will help you decide whether the book will be useful to you.)
5. A listing of other catalog cards for the book.

Cross Reference Cards

Occasionally, in looking up a subject, you will find a card that reads *See* or *See also*. The "See" card refers you to another subject heading in the catalog that will give you the information you want. Let's say you want a book on television commercials, and you find a card that reads as follows:

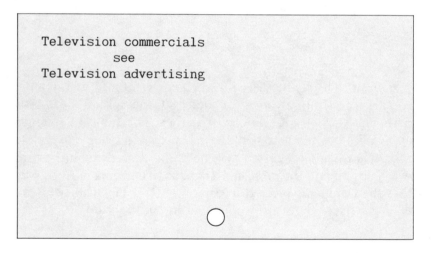

It means that the library catalogs all books on television commercials under the heading of television advertising.

The "See also" card refers you to other subjects closely related to the one you are interested in. This card may be helpful to you in making sure that your research on a particular topic is complete. A "See also" card appears on the next page.

```
Biology

    see also
Natural history
Physiology
Psychobiology
Variation (Biology)
Vitalism
Zoology

    See also headings beginning
with the word Biological

        ◯
```

Guide Cards

Besides the catalog cards, you will find guide cards in the cabinet trays. These are blank except for the guide word on a tab that projects above the other cards. Guide cards aid you in finding other catalog cards quickly. For example, if you want books on cartooning, you will find them easily by means of alphabetically arranged guide cards such as the following:

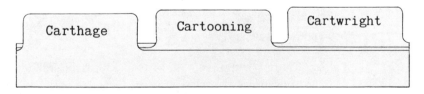

Exercises Using the Card Catalog

A. The drawing at the top of the next page represents the first six trays of a card catalog. The items at the right name authors, titles, and subjects that would be filed in these trays. Copy the list at the right on a separate sheet of paper, and write 1, 2, 3, 4, 5, or 6 in the blanks to show in which trays you would find the items listed.

1—	A—Boat
2—	Bog—Cist
3—	City—Deep
4—	Den—Ebony
5—	Eco—Fed
6—	Fil—From

___*A Doll's House*

___Charles Dickens

___*The Call of the Wild*

___*The Art of Walt Disney*

___Backgammon

___E. E. Cummings

___Frisbees

___*The Bermuda Triangle Mystery—Solved*

___Backpacking

___*A Christmas Carol*

B. Use the card catalog in your public library to find the title, author, call number, and publication date of the following books. Number your paper from 1 to 10 and write the answers.

1. A book by Ray Bradbury
2. A book about Harry S. Truman
3. A book on consumerism
4. A book on Renaissance art
5. A book by Agatha Christie
6. An anthology containing poems by Robert Frost, Emily Dickinson, and Carl Sandburg
7. A book with information on immigration to the U.S.
8. A book with plays by Eugene O'Neill and Thornton Wilder
9. A book by Harper Lee
10. A book about cross-country skiing

C. What subject cards would direct you to books about the following topics? Discuss your answers in class.

1. "Peanuts" cartoons
2. Repairing minibikes
3. Developing photographs
4. Stamp collecting
5. How films are made
6. The origin of the Olympics
7. The first astronauts
8. Popular music
9. Fashions of today's youth
10. The first television program

D. Using the card catalog, list the title, author, call number, and publication date of all books about two of the following people:

1. Eleanor Roosevelt
2. Henry Kissinger
3. Mark Twain
4. Gwendolyn Brooks
5. Pablo Picasso
6. Billie Jean King
7. James Baldwin
8. Walt Whitman
9. Beverly Sills
10. Ernest Hemingway

Part 3   Using Reference Works

One of the best ways to get information is to consult a reference work. Suppose your teacher asked you to write a brief biographical sketch of the American writer John Steinbeck. One good source would be *Twentieth Century Authors*, by Kunitz and Haycraft. It may be found in the reference room of most libraries. Know the various types of reference works and where they are kept in your school and public library.

Reference works are tools, and like tools, should be used in definite ways. Information may be arranged in any of various ways within a reference work. It may be alphabetical, chronological, or under major subject headings. Most reference works have prefaces that describe how information is arranged, show sample entries, and explain the symbols and abbreviations used in the book. Before using any reference work for the first time, you would be wise to skim the preface.

Nine basic types of reference works are described in this part.

1. Dictionaries. The most widely used reference books in the library are the general dictionaries. They may be classified in three major types. The first is the unabridged (complete) dictionary containing more than 500,000 words. Second, there are abridged (shorter) editions, commonly called "desk" or "collegiate" dictionaries. The third group are pocket-sized; they are convenient for checking the spelling of ordinary words, but too limited for high school and college use.

Here is a list of reliable dictionaries for your use.

The American Heritage Dictionary of the English Language
The Macmillan Dictionary
The Random House Dictionary of the English Language
Thorndike-Barnhart Dictionary
Webster's New World Dictionary of the American Language
Webster's Third New International Dictionary of the English Language

Another group of dictionaries are those dealing with certain aspects of the English language: synonyms and antonyms, rhymes, slang, Americanisms, etymology, and so forth. Finally, there are special-purpose dictionaries that deal exclusively with music, medicine, biography, and many other subjects. The list below is by no means complete, but it provides good source material for you. You may check your school and community library as to the availability of specific-subject dictionaries.

DICTIONARIES ON SPECIFIC SUBJECTS

Abbreviations Dictionary (Abbreviations, Acronyms, Contractions, Signs, and Symbols Defined)
Acronyms, Initialisms, and Abbreviations Dictionary
Brewer's Dictionary of Phrase and Fable
Comprehensive Dictionary of Psychological and Psychoanalytical Terms: A Guide to Usage
Compton's Illustrated Science Dictionary
Dictionary of Biology
Dictionary of Economics
Dictionary of Literary Terms
Dictionary of Science and Technology
A Dictionary of Slang and Unconventional English
A Dictionary of Word and Phrase Origins (3 volumes)
Gregg Shorthand Dictionary
Grove's Dictionary of Music and Musicians (10 volumes)
Harper's Dictionary of Contemporary Usage
Harvard Dictionary of Music

Mathews' Dictionary of Americanisms
The New Roget's Thesaurus in Dictionary Form
The Oxford Dictionary of English Etymology
Roget's International Thesaurus
Webster's Biographical Dictionary
Wood's Unabridged Rhyming Dictionary

2. Encyclopedias. These are collections of articles, alphabetically arranged, on nearly every known subject. Guide letters on the spine of each volume and guide words at the top of the pages aid you in finding information. It is best, however, to check the general index first when looking for information. It may list several good sources. For up-to-date information on a topic, check the yearbook that many encyclopedias issue. (A word of caution: When you write essays and reports, you must put all material taken verbatim from encyclopedias and all other sources in quotation marks.) The following are some of the most reliable encyclopedias:

GENERAL ENCYCLOPEDIAS

Collier's Encyclopedia (24 volumes)
Compton's Encyclopedia (26 volumes)
Encyclopaedia Britannica (30 volumes)
Encyclopedia Americana (30 volumes)
World Book Encyclopedia (22 volumes)

The library has many special-purpose encyclopedias dealing with a wide variety of subjects. These encyclopedias are located in the library's reference room or area.

ENCYCLOPEDIAS ON SPECIFIC SUBJECTS

The Baseball Encyclopedia
The Concise Encyclopedia of Archaeology
The Concise Encyclopedia of English and American Poets and Poetry
The Concise Encyclopedia of Modern Drama
Encyclopaedia of Occultism
Encyclopaedia of Religion
The Encyclopedia of American Facts and Dates

Encyclopedia of Animal Care
Encyclopedia of Auto Racing Greats
Encyclopedia of Careers and Vocational Guidance
The Encyclopedia of Chemistry
Encyclopedia of Gardening
Encyclopedia of World Art (15 volumes)
Grzimek's Animal Life Encyclopedia (13 volumes)
The Illustrated Encyclopedia of Aviation and Space
The Illustrated Encyclopedia of World Coins
The International Encyclopedia of Cooking
International Encyclopedia of Social Sciences (17 volumes)
LaRousse Encyclopedia of Mythology
McGraw-Hill Encyclopedia of World Biography (12 volumes)
McGraw-Hill Encyclopedia of World Drama (4 volumes)
The Mammals of America
The New Columbia Encyclopedia
The Pictorial Encyclopedia of Birds
Universal Encyclopedia of Mathematics

3. Almanacs and Yearbooks. Published annually, almanacs and yearbooks are the most useful sources of facts and statistics on current events, as well as matters of historical record in government, economics, population, sports, and other fields.

Guinness Book of World Records
Information Please Almanac, Atlas and Yearbook
Statesman's Yearbook
Statistical Abstract of the United States
Women's Rights Almanac
World Almanac and Book of Facts

4. Biographical References. There are brief biographical notations in dictionaries and longer biographical articles in encyclopedias. Ofter, however, a better source is one of these specialized works.

American Men and Women of Science
The Book of Presidents
Current Biography

Dictionary of American Biography
Dictionary of National Biography
The International Who's Who
Twentieth Century Authors
Who's Who
Who's Who in America
Who's Who in the East (*and Eastern Canada*)
Who's Who in the Midwest
Who's Who in the South and Southwest
Who's Who in the West
Who's Who in American Women

5. Books About Authors. Six good reference works are the following:

American Authors 1600–1900
British Authors of the Nineteenth Century
Contemporary Authors
Twentieth Century Authors
Twentieth Century Authors: First Supplement
Writers at Work

6. Literary Reference Books. The following are valuable reference books on the history of literature, on quotations and proverbs, for locating poems and stories, and for finding information about writers.

Bartlett's Familiar Quotations
Contemporary Poets
Cyclopedia of Literary Characters
A Dictionary of Literature in the English Language
Encyclopedia of World Drama
Granger's Index to Poetry
A Literary History of England
A Literary History of the United States
Mencken's *A New Dictionary of Quotations*
The Oxford Companion to American Literature
The Oxford Companion to English Literature
The Oxford Companion to the Theater

Poetry Handbook
Twentieth Century Authors
World Authors

7. Pamphlets, Handbooks, and Catalogs. Many libraries have pamphlets, handbooks, booklets, and clippings on a variety of subjects, including vocations, travel, census data, and program schedules. They also have a collection of college catalogs. All of these are kept in a set of file cabinets called the **vertical file.** This file can be an invaluable source to you when writing a report or looking for information on careers.

8. Atlases. We usually think of an atlas mainly as a book of maps, but it contains interesting data on a number of subjects. The excellent *National Geographic Atlas of the World*, for example, lists some of the following topics in its table of contents: "Great Moments in Geography," "Global Statistics," and sections on population, temperatures, oceans, and place names. Following is a list of other widely used atlases.

> *Atlas of World History*
> *Atlas of World Wildlife*
> *The Britannica Atlas*
> *Collier's World Atlas and Gazetteer*
> *Goode's World Atlas*
> *Grosset World Atlas*
> *The International World Atlas from Rand McNally*
> *The Times Atlas of the World*
> *Webster's Atlas with Zip Code Directory*

9. Magazines. The *Readers' Guide to Periodical Literature* lists the titles of articles, stories, and poems published during the preceding month in more than 100 leading magazines. It is issued twice a month from September through June and once a month in July and August. An entire year's issues are bound in one hardcover volume at the end of the year. Articles are listed alphabetically under *subject* and *author* (and *titles* when necessary). You will find the *Readers' Guide* invaluable when looking for articles on a subject for a composition.

The following excerpt from the *Readers' Guide* illustrates how articles are listed:

Excerpt from the *Readers' Guide*

PARISH management. See Church management — *"see" cross reference*
PARK CITY, Utah
Park City Utah. C. Pepper. Trav/Holiday 151:31 F '79
PARKER, Ann, and Neal, Avon
Molas: dazzling folk art of the Cuna Indians. il Horizon — *title of article*
22:60-4 Mr '79
PARKER, Dave
Loudmouth and his loud bat. R. Blount. il por Sports Illus — *name of magazine*
50:42-5 Ap 9 '79 *
PARKER, David M.
Thoughts on wind wanes; excerpt from Ocean voyaging.
Motor B & S 143:60+ Ap '79
PARKER, Olivia — *volume number*
Clear Yankee eye. O. Edwards. il Sat R 6:46-7 Mr 3 '79 *
PARKER, Sanford S. and others — *page reference*
Business roundup. See issues of Fortune
PARKER, Stewart
Spokesong. Reviews
N Y 12:85 Ap 2 '79 •
New Yorker 55:53 Mr 26 '79 •
— *date of magazine*
PARKER, Thomas Wendell
Topographical and marine paintings in the Bostonian Society.
il Antiques 115:522-33 Mr '79
PARKER, Tracey
She sets sights on the Olympics. il pors Ebony 34:47-8+ F '79 * — *illustrated article*
PARKER-SPARROW, Bradley
Public monies a solution to this musician's job needs. por
Down Beat 46:10 Mr 22 '79
PARKER Pen Company. See Pens—Manufacture
PARKES, Joseph P.
Ireland after England leaves. America 140:210-12 Mr 17 '79
PARKING meters
Is it such a sin to put another nickel in? P. Carlyle-Gordge. — *subject entry*
il Macleans 92:4 Ja 15 '79
PARKINSON, C. Northcote
To the tables down at Guernsey. Sat R 6:57-8 Mr 31 '79 — *author entry*
PARKINSON'S disease
Parkinson's disease: search for better therapies. J. L. Marx.
il Science 203:737-8 F 23 '79
PARKS, Lillian (Rogers)
Her tales of White House life head for TV. G. Clifford. il
pors People 11:26-7 Ja 29 '79 *
PARKS
See also
National parks and reserves
Playgrounds
— *"see also" cross reference*

Exercises Using Reference Works

A. Find information on one of the following subjects by using the general index of three different encyclopedias available in your school or public libraries. You may need to look under more than one subject heading. Write a brief report on the topic. At the end of your report tell which encyclopedia was most useful and why.

The Middle Ages	Greek Mythology
The Globe Theatre	Aberdeen Angus Cattle
Ellis Island	The Metric System
The Roaring Twenties	The Structure of a Cell
The Opera	Great American Humorists

B. Using the dictionaries available in your library, write answers to the following questions. After each answer, write the title of the dictionary used. Do not use the same dictionary twice.

1. Define the word *crepuscular* and use it in a sentence.
2. What is the origin of the American word *gerrymander?*
3. List four synonyms for the word *product.*
4. List three antonyms for the word *delightful.*
5. List fifteen words that rhyme with *kind.*
6. Define the word *antediluvian.* Discuss its origin and use it in a sentence.
7. List three synonyms for the word *devote.* Define each one.
8. Define the word *nepotism* and use it in a sentence.

C. Use the current issue of the *World Almanac* to answer the following questions.

1. When was the Smithsonian Institution established?
2. What is the principal form of religion in Japan?
3. What happened on the evening of May 4, 1886, in Chicago?
4. What team won the Stanley Cup in hockey last year?
5. Where are the following national parks located?

Bryce Canyon	Rocky Mountain
Everglades	Mammoth Cave
Yosemite	Acadia

D. Use the *Readers' Guide* to answer the following:

1. Turn to the "Key to Abbreviations" and write the meaning of the following symbols used in the *Readers' Guide:*

bibliog	v	Je	Mr	pub	abr	Jl
O	il	rev	no	bi-m	ed	ja

2. List the titles of three articles on each of three subjects of current international importance. (List titles, authors, magazines, page numbers, and dates.)

3. Following the directions above, make a list of articles about a prominent person who interests you.

E. Using the special-purpose dictionaries, encyclopedias, and biographical and literary reference works noted in this chapter, find answers to the following questions. Write the name of the reference work you used after each answer.

1. Who are the authors of the following passages and from what works are they taken?

"Hog butcher for the world, Tool maker, stacker of wheat, Player with railroads and the nation's freighthandler; . . ."

"I'm Nobody! Who are you? Are you—Nobody—Too?"

2. What reference works contain information on the following:

Susan B. Anthony	William Shakespeare
Carl Sandburg	Gerald R. Ford
Helen Keller	Clarence Darrow

3. What literary reference work includes a discussion of *Tom Sawyer?*

4. What are pelagic animals?

5. Name four works by the conductor-composer Leonard Bernstein.

6. In what year did the Russian author, Alexander I. Solzhenitsyn, win the Nobel Prize?

7. Who was Crispus Attucks, and what did he do?

8. What great American president lived at Monticello, and where is it located?

Chapter 11

Giving a Talk

There is one assignment that seems to strike fear into the heart of most students and turns the biggest and bravest into a mass of quivering bones and quavering voices. That assignment is, "Next week you will present an oral report to the class." However, the problem can be overcome by acquiring a few skills involved in delivering an effective talk. Once you have mastered these skills, you will not only be able to speak effectively and knowledgeably, you may even enjoy speaking to a group. Some of you will always shake inside, but with a little practice no one else will even notice.

Part 1 Giving Informal Talks

Let's deal first with those instances that come up quite often in your school years and require some oral presentation, but are not formal talks. At this point it is doubtful that you will be asked to stand up and tell the class what you did on your vacation, but there are other types of oral presentations in which you will be involved.

Preparing Your Talk

While the amount of preparation involved for an informal talk is not lengthy, you must do some background work. In most instances you will not be speaking for more than a minute or two, so it is easy to write out the talk. For brief announcements you will find that notes are adequate, but make sure you do some amount of preparation. You must know what you are going to say and how you are going to say it. *Always* practice reading your material aloud. What looks good on paper is sometimes difficult to read orally.

Presenting Your Talk

There are some strategies you can employ to overcome your fears. First, until you feel comfortable speaking before a group, do not try to make eye contact. That is, do not look directly at anyone in the audience. Instead, choose a spot just above their heads and move your eyes slowly around the group. It will seem to your audience that you are looking directly at each of them.

Good posture is another strategy. You must appear relaxed, even though you feel as if every one of your joints is welded together. Do not pose; just stand easily. Putting one foot slightly ahead of the other, or adopting a little wider stance than usual, will help you maintain your balance. Do not be afraid to move. If your teacher permits, make your first few presentations from the safety of a lectern or desk. As you gain self-confidence—and you will—you can dispense with these aids. Try to speak without notes in your hand unless you really feel you need them.

The most important principle of presentation is to be well prepared. If you know exactly what you are going to say, it will be much easier. Practicing with a tape recorder can be helpful, as you seldom actually "hear" yourself. Hearing yourself can help you overcome repetition, vary the pitch of your voice, and slow your delivery. For some reason, everyone is inclined to speed up when giving a talk.

Mainly, relax and try to enjoy yourself.

Types of Informal Talks

Making Announcements

The simplest informal talk is the announcement, but no matter how short or how simple it seems, you must remember the following points:

What is happening?
Where is it happening?
When is it happening?
Why should the listeners be interested?

Always repeat *where* and *when*. There are those who do not listen to the beginning of an announcement but become interested about halfway through. They need to hear *where* and *when* repeated at the conclusion. Speak distinctly and clearly. Do not rush. Emphasize the important points.

There are times when you will be asked to make an announcement concerning something that has already taken place, much like a newscast. This talk will be a little longer and will require a little more preparation. Again, you must tell your audience *what* happened, *where* it happened and *when* it happened. In this newscast you may also need to deal with *why* it happened or *how* it happened. Make some notes so that you will not leave out an important fact, and so that you can keep your presentation flowing smoothly without long pauses.

Exercises Making Announcements

A. Make an announcement to the class regarding one of the events below, or announce something else that is going on at your school or in your community. After three or four announcements have been given, see how many *what's*, *where's*, *when's*, and *why's* the class can remember. Listening is as important a skill as speaking.

an athletic event	an Honor Awards assembly
a school-sponsored movie	tryouts for cheerleaders
a club meeting	a skateboard competition
school elections	a procrastinators' party

B. Prepare and present a sixty-second newscast regarding something that has happened recently at school, or a fictitious happening. It could also be a sportscast, reporting on an athletic event. Keep your audience's attention with your voice. Again, do not face the audience, but deliver your newscast from the back of the classroom or behind a screen.

Giving Directions

Have you ever stopped someone on the first day of school to ask the location of a classroom? Isn't it amazing how few people can really help you? The reply is usually as follows:

> Just go down this hall and then turn by the water fountain (there are three) and then keep going past the type room (you have no idea where the type room is) and then turn at the next corner (which way?) and you'll find it.

When giving directions, use accurate details, be as clear as possible, and never back up to correct yourself. Instead, start over again and be sure you are being understood.

> Go down this hall toward the front of the building. Turn right at the second water fountain. At the next corner turn left and the room will be the third one on your left.

This is still complicated for a new student, but at least you have a chance of being in the right part of the building. Of course, if you ask for directions you have to be a good listener.

Exercises Giving Directions

A. Choose a specific place with which the other students are familiar. It can be in the school building, close to the grounds, or in your community. Without identifying the place, give students specific directions for getting there. When you have finished, see how many know the exact place.

B. Each student is to give directions on how to draw a certain figure. It could be a stick figure, or a geometric figure of some kind using squares, triangles, rectangles, or circles, such as a house or barn. This is a difficult assignment because you have to go over the figure time and again yourself while planning this talk, so keep it simple.

The other students can try to follow the directions as you are speaking, but they cannot ask questions. You will know if they understand by the expressions on their faces. When you have finished, see how many students actually drew the figure. Was the problem in the directions? Was it that those who did not draw the correct figure were not listening closely? Try to analyze the problem.

Giving a Demonstration Talk

Have you ever tried to tell someone how to tie his or her shoes without demonstrating the procedure with your hands? It seems impossible to do. Try sitting on your hands and telling a friend how to swing a baseball bat or how to do a simple exercise. There are some instances when it is absolutely necessary to demonstrate what you mean. Of course, as you are demonstrating you are also giving oral instructions. This type of direction-giving sounds easy, but your thinking must be extremely well organized. What seems easy and uncomplicated to you can be sheer frustration to someone else.

Exercise Giving a Demonstration Talk

Give a demonstration talk to the class. You might show how to do one of the following:

swing a golf club	bake a cake or pie
repot a plant	groom a dog
work with macramé	change a bicycle tire
plant a terrarium	build a bird house
prepare a Caesar salad	handle a rod and reel
hook a rug	arrange flowers
make a candle	throw a frisbee
make a collage	

Doing Commercials

Does a future as a salesperson appeal to you? How would you like to perform in a commercial on television? Being able to sell a product to the public may be valuable; after all, you sometimes have to "sell" yourselves to teachers, friends, and employers. You might want to convince your parents that a backpack family vacation trip would be better than visiting relatives in a big city, or to try to promote a band trip to the summer Olympics to the school administration. Selling can involve more than products; it can also involve ideas. The specific criteria are that you must be sincere, persuasive, and above all, enthusiastic. The salesperson who starts with, "I don't suppose you'd be interested in . . ." will not get too far.

Exercises Doing Commercials

A. Make a list of the television and radio commercials you like best, and those you like least. Decide what makes the good ones effective and the poor ones unconvincing. Then share your ideas with the rest of the class.

B. Sell a fictitious product to the class in a one-minute commercial. Do not use any product that is currently on the market; devise your own. It might be a breath freshener that solves the problem by completely sealing your mouth, or a wrinkle cream for those who want to look older. Be original!

Making Introductions

The chances are good that at some time you will be asked to introduce someone. It might be to a class, a club, an organization, or some other group with which you are involved. This will require more than, "This is Anita Rivera, president of the ninth grade." First, you must get some background information on the person to give to the audience. Who is she? What has she done? Why is she here? Try to find some interesting or amusing incident to lighten your introduction. Be careful, though. While everyone should be amused; *no one* must ever be embarrassed.

Exercises Making Introductions

A. Choose a well known person and write an introduction that could have been used at some time in his or her life, or could be used today. You decide the occasion and the circumstances.

B. Choose a character from a book, movie, or television series and introduce him or her to the class.

C. Introduce one of your classmates.

Part 2 Giving Formal Talks

Formal talks are delivered to a specific group for a specific purpose, and on a specific topic. They are lengthier than informal talks and require more thought, time, and preparation. You will first have to organize them completely on paper, and then spend some time rehearsing out loud for the best possible effect. This sounds complicated, but taken one step at a time it becomes a routine process at which you will be adept in no time.

What is the reason for discussing formal talks rather than oral reports? It does seem that you are asked to give many oral reports in school, and few formal talks. Oral reports and talks do differ in some respects, but an oral report can always be turned into a formal talk. Reports often tend to be dry and dull, simply because you prepared them as written reports and gave little thought to the fact that they were to be presented orally. Being able to turn your report into an informative formal talk can bring instant results in the form of audience interest.

Preparation. Every talk will require six steps.

1. Select your topic.
2. Define your purpose.
3. Select your theme.
4. Gather your material.
5. Organize your material.
6. Deliver your talk.

Selecting a Topic

There are times when you will be given a specific topic to speak on. This makes it easier, as you can proceed with the next step immediately. However, more often than not you will simply be asked to talk to a certain group about ecology, current events, today's school, or some other general subject. You will have to make the decision as to the final topic. Do not hesitate to choose a topic you know little about if you have time to research it. Your new interest will add enthusiasm and liveliness to your talk.

Choose a topic you are sure will interest your audience. Here are a few things to be aware of.

The unusual appeals to everyone.

The familiar has value; but be sure to furnish some new side-lights on any familiar topic, or it will be dull.

The factual is sometimes useful, but it can also be dull. Avoid using facts already known to your audience.

Remember one thing: There are no uninteresting subjects. There are just uninterested people. If you are really interested in the topic, that interest will be contagious to your audience.

Exercises Selecting a Topic

A. Choose three of the following occasions and decide on a topic for each.

1. You are a class officer and must prepare a talk for the opening assembly.

2. Your scout troop has asked you to deliver a talk for the awards banquet.

3. Your class has decided that you are the one to deliver a talk to a group of Senior Citizens.

4. You are to give a talk to the PTA or PTSA concerning an issue of importance to the students.

5. You are to give a talk to your geography class regarding some section of the United States.

6. It is getting close to a particular holiday, and you have been asked to talk about a custom.

7. You are the captain of the team and have to give a talk after the final game.

8. A sixth-grade teacher has asked you to give a talk to his or her class.

Before you can even begin to deal with the actual talk, however, you must be aware of the one vital concern to any speaker: the audience. Consider their age, background, economic level, and education. Be aware of what brings them into this one setting to listen to a talk. Know that they must be able to relate to what you are saying on an individual level. For example, a talk given to a group of elementary children would differ considerably from a talk given to the faculty of your school. You might change your topic somewhat if you were giving it before a group of parents rather than to the football team.

Plan your talk so you will get the attention of your audience. Make it interesting, so they will listen and respond. Speak to them knowledgeably and give them something to think about. By the time you deliver your talk you will have as much information on the topic as anyone in the room, so you are the expert.

B. What would you title each of the following talks if you were asked to present it to (1) a sixth-grade class, (2) a group of parents, (3) your class, and (4) a club or organization to which you belong?

| voting | drug addiction | vandalism |
| teenage drivers | school drop-outs | |

Defining Your Purpose

There are three major purposes that cover almost any talk you will be asked to give: to inform, to persuade, to entertain. You must decide which of these three your talk involves.

TO INFORM

This is the type of talk you are asked to give more than any other. Most class reports are supposed to be informative. You simply want your audience to understand or appreciate what you are telling them. Talks to inform might describe the advantages of belonging to a school club, explain the brake system of a car, or report on a book.

TO PERSUADE

To be successful, this kind of talk should lead to some change in the listener's point of view, attitude, or course of action. Talks to persuade, for example, may appeal for the election of a candidate, try to enlist support for some school or charitable activity, or try to prevent a course of action that you think unwise.

TO ENTERTAIN

In this kind of talk you simply want your audience to enjoy what you say. A talk to entertain might be an after-dinner speech, an account of a humorous or embarrassing experience, or a between-the-acts speech by a master of ceremonies.

Of course, any one of these talks does not exclude aspects of the others. An informative talk, for example, should contain something entertaining. A talk aiming to persuade should contain information to support its points.

Exercise Defining Your Purpose

How many formal talks have you listened to in the past month? Write down the occasions, the topics, the audience, and the purposes of the talks. Were they effective? If not, briefly state why you think the speaker failed in his purpose. Limit yourself to five different talks.

Determining Your Thesis

Your thesis is the main idea you want to get across to your audience. At first you should write it down in full sentence form:

Violent crimes are increasing rapidly in our community.
Strip mining will destroy the natural environment.
We should organize a procrastinators club.

Your thesis sentence is the key to your entire talk. Everything you say should support this thesis in some way. You may wish to use your thesis sentence in your talk, either early in the talk, or at the end, or both. It should not be used as a title.

Exercise Determining Your Thesis

Using your class as an audience, select a topic for a talk you will prepare and give. Decide the purpose and state the thesis. Do no more on it at the present time.

Gathering Your Material

In gathering material for your talk, look for ideas, details, illustrations, facts, figures, and quotations. Some of your material will come from firsthand experience; some you will obtain from the experience of others. Try to deal with personal experience whenever possible. It is much more interesting to listen to someone who has actually been on a survival trip speak about survival than to someone who has merely researched it. You can expand on your personal experience through reading and talking to others, but your talk will bear more weight if you can actually speak with the authority of one who has been there.

This does not mean you must deal exclusively with personal experiences. You must also rely on reading for more information. Here are some guidelines.

1. **Read for specific purposes.** For a talk, your purposes will be to gather facts, details, and illustrations to develop your thesis.

2. **Read for the main points.** Do not get lost in the forest of words.

3. **Evaluate the material you read.** Do not accept all ideas just because they are in print. Is the material useful to you? Is it up-to-date? Is it authoritative?

4. **Make the material your own.** Except for direct quotations, summarize and condense what you want to use. Remember one important point: Put it into your own words. Word-for-word copying is plagiarism, for which you could be severely penalized.

Your library will be an indispensible asset in gathering your material. Unless you are contrasting ancient practices with modern ones, you will be dealing mainly with the vertical files and the *Readers' Guide to Periodical Literature*. This guide is an alphabetical index of contemporary magazine articles, so your information can be as current as possible.

Take notes on any reading you do. If you interview someone in the field, be sure to take notes during the interview. Notes are the backbone of any good talk, so take more than you need. You can always discard the surplus.

Exercise Gathering Your Material

Using 4" x 6" cards, take notes on everything you might include in a talk on the topic you have chosen.

Organizing Your Material

At this point you have much more material than you can possibly use. You must now organize it so you will end up with a coherent, logical talk. The only way to achieve this purpose is to divide your material into three parts: *the introduction, the body,* and *the conclusion.*

The Introduction

The introduction is used to gain interest and attention. You might use an anecdote to relax an audience and gain their co-operation. You might use the introduction to explain the title of your talk or to state your thesis. You could also use it to refer to any background information. Your introduction should be forceful. It must set the tone of the speech and be appropriate for the occasion.

Here is the introduction to a talk given by Carl Sandburg to the House of Representatives. He was invited to address a Joint Session of the House and Senate on the one hundred-and-fiftieth anniversary of Lincoln's birth.

> Not often in the story of humankind does a man arrive on earth who is both steel and velvet, who is as hard as rock and soft as drifting fog, who holds in his heart and mind the paradox of terrible storm and peace unspeakable and perfect. Here and there across centuries come reports of individuals alleged to have these contrasts. The incomparable Abraham Lincoln, born one hundred and fifty years ago this day, is an approach if not a perfect realization of this character.

The Body

The body of the talk is the most important. This is the part of the talk that must inform, entertain, or persuade your audience. After drawing them in with your introduction, you now give them the facts and information to support your thesis. You should be aware of the amount of time your total talk will take. The body of the talk should take at least twice as much time as the total of the introduction and conclusion. Here are some guidelines for organizing the body of your talk:

1. **Determine your major points.** The amount of time you have allotted for your talk will determine how many major points you wish to cover. You would be wise to outline your talk so you can be sure that your points are actually major ones and that they are in a logical, coherent order. Use your notes to sort out your major points.

2. **Develop your major points.** After you have decided exactly what major points you are going to cover, use the information from your notes to develop those points. You will develop each point in exactly the same way you develop each paragraph in a composition. The theme of your talk, along with the purpose, will determine your use of facts, statistics, details, illustrations, descriptions, anecdotes, personal experience, or a combination of these.

3. **Build your talk toward a climax.** To build your talk toward a climax, you will want to present your ideas in order of their importance. In some cases you will have to present your ideas in a logical time sequence. An outline will help you see immediately if your ideas are well ordered, if each of them is specifically related to your theme, and if each of them is fully developed.

The Conclusion

The conclusion is a summary of the main points of your talk. When preparing a persuasive talk, you might want to appeal to or challenge the audience in the conclusion. In an informative talk, a quotation or illustration could appropriately conclude your talk. This is a good place to repeat your thesis, bearing in mind the purpose of your talk. The purpose of Carl Sandburg's talk was to pay tribute to a great and enduring man. Here is the conclusion of that talk.

> Perhaps we may say that the well assured and most enduring memorial to Lincoln is invisibly present, today, tomorrow, and for a long time yet to come in the hearts of lovers of liberty, men and women who understand that wherever there is freedom there have been those who fought, toiled, and sacrificed for it.

A successful talk should conform to the rules for good speechmaking. The introduction attracts attention; the body holds that attention and gains consideration; the conclusion summarizes briefly. Sufficient detail, and reference to authority, make the talk compelling. Ideas are presented in a logical manner so that any listener can follow them and understand the talk.

Exercise Organizing Your Material

Using the material you have gathered, organize it in outline form into the three divisions: introduction, body, and conclusion. Then write your talk.

Delivering Your Talk

The effective presentation of a formal talk is no easy task. The ideal speaker would stand easily and comfortably, words flowing from his or her mouth in beautifully modulated tones. Unfortunately, most people are not that professional. However, it is not impossible to give the same impression if you work at it. Here are some guidelines.

1. **Rehearse your talk aloud many times.** You will finally get to the point where it does flow easily.

2. **Take advantage of a tape recorder to listen to your delivery.** Be critical. If something does not sound right, try it again with emphasis on a different word or phrase. If it still does not sound right, rework your ideas into smoother sentences. Perhaps your sentences do not seem to flow smoothly from one idea to another. If they do not, revise your sentences so they say exactly what you want them to say. Check also to see if each idea actually does flow out of the one preceding it. Maybe an idea is in the wrong place.

3. **Choose a method of delivery that is comfortable for you.** If you prefer to memorize the entire talk, do it. If you would feel more comfortable referring to notes, have them in an inconspicuous place. Do not merely read the talk. You will be so engrossed in the paper that any personal contact with the audience will be lost, and they will feel left out. You want an audience involved, not isolated. For your first experience use a lectern; it promotes feelings of security and authority, and makes it easier not to worry about the lower half of your body. Do not lean on the lectern or drape yourself over it. You want your audience to focus on your talk, not on your posture.

Exercise Delivering Your Talk

Deliver your talk to the class.

Grammar and Usage

Section 1. **The Sentence and Its Parts** 247

Section 2. **Using Complete Sentences** 279

Section 3. **Using Nouns** 286

Section 4. **Using Pronouns** 301

Section 5. **Using Verbs** 325

Section 6. **Using Modifiers** 346

Section 7. **Using Prepositions and Conjunctions** 372

Section 8. **Review of Parts of Speech** 385

Section 9. **Using Verbals** 392

Section 10. **Making Subjects and Verbs Agree** 409

Section 11. **Using Compound and Complex Sentences** 420

Section 12. **The Right Word** 455

The Mechanics of Writing

Section 13. **Capitalization** 471

Section 14. **Punctuation** 486

Section 15. **Spelling** 518

Section 16. **The Correct Form for Writing** 529

A detailed Table of Contents appears in the front of this book.

Grammar, Usage, and Mechanics

The following sixteen Sections of this text deal with grammar, usage, and the mechanics of writing (capitalization, punctuation, spelling, and the correct form for writing).

Each of the Sections is divided into Parts. Each Part explains a topic or concept fully and gives specific examples. Definitions appear in boldface type. There are numerous exercises in each Part to test your understanding of the concepts explained. There are also pages of additional exercises at the end of each Section.

As you study each Section, try to apply what you have learned to your own writing and speaking.

Section 1

The Sentence and Its Parts

You may not think of yourself as a mechanic. However, speaking and writing English is somewhat like building an engine. Like a mechanic working on an engine, you combine parts to build the driving force of English, the sentence.

An engine is composed of pistons, shafts, and cylinders. In a similar way, a sentence is made from its separate parts—subjects, verbs, modifiers, objects, and more. When the parts of a motor are put together properly, it runs smoothly. A well put-together sentence also is smooth and efficient.

In this section you will learn about the parts of a sentence and how they are put into working order.

Part 1 The Complete Sentence

Sometimes in conversation, you use only parts of sentences. For example, you might reply to a question with a word or two:

Not now.   That one.   Yes.

In writing, however, complete sentences are important. With them, your ideas are clear and understandable. **A sentence is a group of words that expresses a complete thought.** A sentence makes sense because it is a whole idea, not just part of one.

These groups of words are sentences:

Sean skated down the sidewalk.
That red car is blocking the alley.
The alarm sounded late last night.

Sometimes part of an idea is missing from a sentence. Then the group of words is a sentence fragment. A **sentence fragment** is a group of words that does not express a complete thought. For example, these are sentence fragments:

Skated down the sidewalk. (Who skated?)
That red car. (What about the car?)
Late last night. (What happened?)

Exercise A   Number your paper from 1 to 10. For each group of words that is a sentence, write **S.** For each sentence fragment, write **F.**

1. Lost fifteen pounds.
2. The boxers entered the ring.
3. The final score.
4. Opened the top drawer.
5. A photo of the family.
6. This gas station is open.

7. Val planned the route.
8. Vendors at the ballpark.
9. Where was the wedding held?
10. Elston works at a hospital.

Exercise B Follow the directions for Exercise A.

1. Dave Kingman hit a homer.
2. Who is this disc jockey?
3. Dialed the wrong number.
4. A downpour stalled the game.
5. Needs a lot of help.
6. A group of close friends.
7. Smoke from the blaze.
8. A new source of energy.
9. Kim noticed the want ad.
10. The cashier made a mistake.

Part 2   The Subject and the Predicate

Every sentence is made up of two basic parts: the subject and the predicate. The **subject** tells *whom* or *what* the sentence is about. The **predicate** tells something about the subject.

Subject	Predicate
(*Who or what*)	(*What is said about the subject*)
The volcano	erupted again.
A reporter from the paper	relayed the news.
The subway riders	raced for the doors.

Each of these sentences expresses a complete thought. Each of them tells something about a person, place, or thing.

There is an easy way to remember the parts of a sentence. Think of the sentence as telling who did something or what happened. The subject tells *who* or *what*. The predicate tells *did* or *happened*.

Who or What	Did or Happened
The soft mud under my feet	cushioned my toes.
Our lead-off hitter	got a stand-up double.
All four tires	need air.

The subject of the sentence tells *who* or *what* did something, or what the sentence is about.

The predicate of the sentence tells what is done or what happens.

Exercise A Head two columns *Subject* and *Predicate*. Write the proper words from each sentence in the columns.

Example: My cousin needs a part-time job.

Subject	Predicate
My cousin	needs a part-time job.

1. A line of motorcycles zoomed down the freeway.
2. The blaze roared through the forest.
3. Ronald carries his radio with him.
4. Those small cars get good gas mileage.
5. Our career counselor has information on interviews.
6. The new P.E. wing contains two gyms.
7. This year's harvest included soybeans.
8. Those jeans have been washed many times.
9. I need new glasses.
10. Tickets for the Wings concert sold fast.

Exercise B Follow the directions for Exercise A.

1. Cara's friends waited at the corner.
2. The cheapest seats are in the bleachers.

3. Few people remember all of their dreams.
4. The projection booth overlooks the theater.
5. Dancers at the disco rocked with the music.
6. The second semester begins in January.
7. Two friends of mine cut an album.
8. The other people at the party didn't notice Les at first.
9. Frozen yogurt pie is a good dessert.
10. A local woman had quintuplets.

Part 3 Simple Subjects and Verbs

In every sentence a few words are more important than the others. These essential words are the basic framework of the sentence. Look at these examples:

Subject	Predicate
The **volcano**	**erupted** again.
A **reporter** from the paper	**relayed** the news.
The subway **riders**	**raced** for the doors.

All the words in the subject part of the sentence are called the **complete subject**. Within the complete subject is a key word, the **simple subject**. In the last example above, *the subway riders* is the complete subject. *Riders* is the simple subject.

The **complete predicate** is all the words that tell something about the subject. The key word within the complete predicate is the **simple predicate** or **verb**.

In the sentence about the subway riders, the complete predicate is *raced for the doors*. The key word is *raced*.

The key word in the subject of a sentence is called the simple subject. We refer to it as the *subject*.

The key word in the predicate is the simple predicate. The simple predicate is the **verb**. Hereafter we will refer to the simple predicate as the *verb*.

Finding the Verb and the Subject

In any sentence, the verb and the subject are the most important words. The other words only tell more about these key words. To find these key words in any sentence, first find the verb. It shows action or a state of being. Then ask *who* or *what* before the verb. That answer will give you the subject of the verb.

> An attendant at the station checked the oil.
> *Verb:* checked
> *Who checked?* attendant
> The subject is *attendant.*

> The plane glided down the runway.
> *Verb:* glided
> *What glided?* plane
> The subject is *plane.*

Diagraming Subjects and Verbs

A sentence diagram is a drawing of the parts of a sentence. It shows how the parts fit together.

A sentence diagram shows the importance of the subject and the verb. These key parts are placed on a horizontal main line. They are separated by a vertical line that crosses the main line. The subject appears before the verb. Later you will learn how every other word in the sentence has its own place in the diagram, too.

In diagraming, only words capitalized in the sentence are capitalized in the diagram. No punctuation is used.

> Adam spoke quietly.

Adam	spoke

Janelle writes poetry.

Janelle	writes

Exercise A Label two columns *Verb* and *Subject*. Number your paper from 1 to 10. For each sentence, write the verb and its subject.

1. That nursery needs aides.
2. Ten students volunteered.
3. This map of the city indicates bus routes.
4. The eager drivers revved their engines.
5. The network canceled that show.
6. Dana's sister sets high goals for herself.
7. Six different ingredients topped the pizza.
8. A professional stuntman performed the fall.
9. The annual carnival attracted large crowds.
10. Daytime television features soap operas.

Exercise B Follow the directions for Exercise A.

1. Many popular songs are old folk melodies.
2. Clint Eastwood's new film played downtown.
3. A violent tornado destroyed several homes.
4. The radio by my bed wakens me each morning.
5. The crew worked overtime on the highway project.
6. A package arrived in the morning mail.
7. All lockers in the south wing have mirrors.
8. The bridge to Canada crosses the St. Lawrence Seaway.
9. The theater across the street has a sneak preview.
10. Some fans of silent films adore Charlie Chaplin.

Part 4   The Parts of a Verb

A verb may consist of one word, or of several words. The verb may be composed of a **main verb** and one or more **helping verbs.**

Helping Verbs	+	Main Verb	=	Verb
will		return		will return
would		expect		would expect
is		leaving		is leaving
must have		shown		must have shown

To name the verb in any sentence, you must name all the words that make up the verb.

These words are frequently used as helping verbs:

am	are	have	will	may
is	be	do	would	might
was	has	does	can	shall
were	had	did	could	should

Separated Parts of a Verb

At times you will find words inserted between the parts of a verb. These words are not included in the verb. Look at the following sentences. The parts of the verb are in bold print.

> Cassie **had** never **driven** a tractor.
> My friends **could** not **offer** any advice.
> The artist **will** gladly **show** you her work.

Some verbs are joined with other words to make contractions. In naming verbs that appear in contractions, pick out only the verb. The word *not* and its contraction *n't* are adverbs. They are never verb parts.

> Vernon **did**n't **notice** the car. (*Did notice* is the verb.)
> The carpenter **had**n't **measured** exactly. (*Had measured* is the verb.)

Exercise A Number your paper from 1 to 10. List the verbs in the following sentences.

1. Bluegrass musicians were gathering for a festival.
2. You haven't ever needed any help before.
3. We could often read his mood.
4. David has never seen an ice hockey game.
5. Yolanda will surely return next week.
6. The umpire didn't respond to the catcalls.
7. That bill hasn't been passed yet.
8. This year I will probably get a paper route.
9. The price does not include delivery.
10. We have never called ourselves experts.

Exercise B Follow the directions for Exercise A.

1. Summer vacation doesn't begin until Tuesday.
2. A relief pitcher will sometimes finish the game.
3. Sue has already taken her driver's test.
4. A good job will usually require two coats of paint.
5. The birth rate has recently dropped.
6. They are always complaining about homework.
7. Your ideas will certainly help.
8. McDonald's doesn't open until 7:00 A.M.
9. The new clinic on Long Street will soon open.
10. Most players have already signed contracts.

Part 5 Subjects in Unusual Positions

The subject of a sentence usually comes before the verb. In some sentences, however, part or all of the verb comes before the subject.

To find the subject in any sentence, first find the verb. Then ask *who* or *what* before it. The answer will be the subject.

Sentences Beginning with *There*

In sentences beginning with *there*, the verb often comes before the subject.

There is used in two different ways. It may be used to explain the verb. It tells where something is or happens.

> There are your gloves. (*Gloves* is the subject; *are* is the verb. *There* tells where your gloves are.)
> There is the exit. (*Exit* is the subject; *is* is the verb. *There* tells where the exit is.)

Sometimes *there* is used simply as an introductory word to help get the sentence started.

> There is a shortage of fuel in this country. (*Shortage* is the subject; *is* is the verb.)
> There are jobs available. (*Jobs* is the subject; *are* is the verb.)

To diagram sentences beginning with *there*, you must know if *there* tells *where* or is an introductory word. If *there* tells *where*, it belongs on a slanted line below the verb. If *there* is an introductory word, it belongs on a horizontal line above the subject.

There stood the manager of the store.

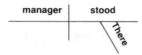

There has been a mistake.

There
mistake | has been

Exercise A Write the subject and the verb in each sentence. Tell whether *there* is used to tell *where* or as an introductory word.

1. There is the joggers' path.
2. There will be a press conference.
3. There were some questions about the new schedule.
4. There is no excuse.
5. There is the new deadbolt lock.
6. There has been a change of plans.
7. There is the city's civic center.
8. There are the applications.
9. There is the toll booth.
10. There have been many recent medical advances.

Exercise B Follow the directions for Exercise A.

1. There is our canoe.
2. There is a simple solution.
3. There is the factory.
4. There is the pay phone.
5. There are your X-rays.
6. There will be special concerts.
7. There was a junior high reunion.
8. There are two new courses this year.
9. There is the dance floor.
10. There might be another election.

Other Sentences with Unusual Word Order

Sentences beginning with *there* are just one kind of sentence with unusual word order. Here are some others.

1. Sentences beginning with *here*

Here comes the parade. (*Parade* is the subject; *comes* is the verb.)

Here is your wallet. (*Wallet* is the subject; *is* is the verb.)

Unlike *there*, the word *here* always tells *where* about the verb.

2. Questions

Have you finished? (*You* is the subject; *have finished* is the verb.)

Will Kate be joining us? (*Kate* is the subject; *will be joining* is the verb.)

3. Sentences starting with phrases or other words

Slowly came her reply. (*Reply* is the subject; *came* is the verb.)

Around the curve raced the runners. (*Runners* is the subject; *raced* is the verb.)

To find the subject in a sentence with unusual word order, first find the verb. Then ask *who* or *what*.

Here are the scripts.
Verb: are
Who or what are? scripts
Subject: scripts

Unusual word order in a sentence does not change the sentence diagram. The verb and the subject are still placed on the horizontal main line with the subject first and then the verb.

Under the rock slithered the snake.

Sentences Giving Commands

In sentences that give commands, the subject is usually not stated. Since commands are always given to the person spoken to, the subject is *you*. Because *you* is not stated, we say that it is *understood*.

Repeat the question. (*You* is the subject of *repeat.*)
Draw a straight line. (*You* is the subject of *draw.*)

To diagram a sentence giving a command, place the subject *you* in parentheses.

Try again.

(you)	Try

Exercise A Label two columns *Subject* and *Verb*. Number your paper from 1 to 10. Write the subject and verb for each sentence.

1. Tell another joke.
2. Here is a good book.
3. Have the plants been watered?
4. Here come the paramedics.
5. Give me that wrench.
6. Will you save a seat for me?
7. Enter through the side door.
8. Into the spotlight danced Marisa.
9. There are too many rules in this game.
10. Underneath my foot lay a dollar bill.

Exercise B Follow the directions for Exercise A.

1. In the distance swam a shark.
2. Have you seen Rod Stewart in concert?
3. Quickly came the answer.
4. Here are my old boots.
5. Here is a quick sketch.
6. Steadily came the drumbeat.
7. Eat a balanced diet.
8. Have you repaid your debt?
9. Do you need glasses?
10. Drive carefully.

Part 6 Objects of Verbs

Some verbs do not need other words to complete their meaning in a sentence. The action they describe is complete.

The players *rested.* The rain finally *stopped.*
Nathan *was worrying.* The T-shirt *will fade.*

Some verbs, though, do not express a complete meaning by themselves. They need other words to complete the meaning of a sentence.

Tony reserved _____. (Reserved what?)
The campers brought _____. (Brought what?)

Direct Objects

Tony reserved a *space.*
The campers brought *firewood.*

One kind of word that completes the action of a verb is called the **direct object**. A direct object receives the action of the verb. In the sentences above, *space* receives the action of *reserved. Firewood* receives the action of *brought.*

Sometimes the direct object tells the *result* of an action.

We drew *pictures.*
Keats composed a *poem.*

To find the direct object, first find the verb. Then ask *whom* or *what* after it.

Steve invited six friends.
   Verb: invited
   Invited whom: friends
   Direct object: friends

Ann repaired the motorcycle.
   Verb: repaired
   Repaired what: motorcycle
   Direct object: motorcycle

A verb that has a direct object is called a **transitive verb.** A verb that does not have a direct object is called an **intransitive verb.** Notice the difference in these sentences:

> The sun *was shining.* (*Was shining* is intransitive. It has no direct object.)
> Our teacher *gave* a lecture. (*Gave* is transitive. It has a direct object, *lecture.*)

A verb may be transitive in one sentence and intransitive in another.

> Intransitive: Your sister called.
> Transitive: Your sister called a taxi.

Transitive or Intransitive?

Look at the following sentences. Are the verbs transitive or intransitive?

> Louise *left* early.
> Louise *left* in the afternoon.
> Louise *left* the room.

In the first two examples, the verb *left* has no direct object. In those sentences, *left* is intransitive. However, in the third sentence, if you ask *whom* or *what* after the verb, you find that *room* is the direct object. In that sentence, *left* is a transitive verb.

> Louise left the room.
> *Verb:* left
> *Left what:* room
> *Direct object:* room

Exercise A Number your paper from 1 to 10. For each sentence, write the direct object of the verb.

1. The actors studied their lines.
2. Mr. Mendez has opened a new business.

3. The sailors finally reached land.
4. In the morning, the workers will finish the project.
5. Please return my notebook.
6. I enjoyed the performance.
7. The attendant checked the carburetor.
8. Sara quickly smothered the flames.
9. The bus driver had nearly missed the exit.
10. On Saturdays, Keith washes cars.

Exercise B Number your paper from 1 to 10. Decide whether the verb in each sentence is *transitive* or *intransitive*.

1. My cousins visited yesterday.
2. She visited her friends.
3. Amy led an expedition.
4. The general led courageously.
5. Some hedges grow quickly.
6. Miles grows herbs.
7. Some members joined late.
8. A new worker joined the crew.
9. The foreman gives orders.
10. This blood donor gives frequently.

Indirect Objects

In addition to direct objects, some sentences also have **indirect objects** of the verb. Indirect objects sometimes tell *to whom* or *to what* about the verb. At other times they tell *for whom* or *for what* about the verb.

> Jeff told **Marla** the *news*. (told *to* Marla)
> The clerk sold **us** the wrong *battery*. (sold *to* us)
> Carlos made **us** a Mexican *dinner*. (made *for* us)

In the sentences above, the words in bold type are the indirect objects. The words in italics are the direct objects. Indirect objects appear only in sentences with direct objects.

Indirect objects are found between the verb and direct object. Never use the words *to* and *for* with an indirect object.

> Andrew handed the *teller* his deposit. (*Teller* is the indirect object of *handed*.)
> Andrew handed his deposit to the *teller*. (*Teller* is not an indirect object.)

In a diagram, place a direct object on the main line after the verb. The vertical line between the verb and object does not go below the main line.

Lana bought a hat.

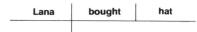

The indirect object belongs on a horizontal line attached below the verb.

Lana bought her brother a hat

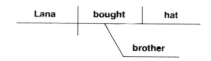

Exercise A Number your paper from 1 to 10. Label three columns *Verb*, *Indirect Object*, and *Direct Object*. For each sentence below, write down those parts. Not all sentences will have all three parts.

Example: We brought Wendy a gift.

Verb	Indirect Object	Direct Object
brought	Wendy	gift

1. Jonah handed Sarah her ticket.
2. The florist arranged the roses.
3. Diana Nyad told the reporters her story.
4. This store gives customers a discount.

5. Someone asked the boss a question.
6. The neighbors are repairing their porch.
7. Joe left the waitress a tip.
8. Many waitresses earn generous tips.
9. This restaurant has terrific chili.
10. The cook taught me his secret.

Exercise B   Follow the directions for Exercise A.

1. Some restaurants serve children smaller portions.
2. The President announced his new policy.
3. The photographer used floodlights.
4. Ms. Orlando gave us more time for the test.
5. We repair engines in the machine shop.
6. The director gave the crew a signal.
7. Tom put sprouts on his salad.
8. The cafeteria serves pancakes for breakfast.
9. We poured syrup on our waffles.
10. That cartoonist drew us some funny portraits.

Part 7   Linking Verbs and Predicate Words

Some verbs do not express action. Instead, they tell of a state of being. These verbs link the subject of a sentence with a word or group of words in the predicate. Because they link the subject with some other word or words, they are often called **linking verbs.**

> Jessica *is* a soprano.   Thomas *must be* angry.
> We *are* the winners.   The typists *were* busy.

The verb *to be* is the most commonly used linking verb. *To be* can have many forms. This list will help you to become familiar with them:

be	been	is	was
being	am	are	were

The verbs *be*, *being*, and *been* can also be used with helping verbs. These are examples:

should be	were being	had been
may be	was being	could have been
will be	is being	might have been

The words linked to the subject by linking verbs like *to be* are called **predicate words**. The three kinds of predicate words are **predicate nouns, predicate pronouns,** and **predicate adjectives.** All of them tell something about the subject.

Brad is a *plumber*. (predicate noun)

That was *he*. (predicate pronoun)

Carlotta was *happy*. (predicate adjective)

In the above sentences, the subjects and predicate words are joined by the linking verbs *is* and *was*.

Here are some other common linking verbs.

appear	seem	sound	grow
feel	look	taste	become

Like *be*, these linking verbs have various forms (*grew, looked,* or *tastes*). They can be used with helping verbs, as in *will become, can seem,* or *might have sounded*.

The chair *looked* comfortable.

The varnish *felt* sticky.

Bruce *has become* an excellent gymnast.

In a sentence diagram, place a predicate word on the main line after the verb. A slanted line above the main line separates the verb from the predicate word. That line, like the predicate word, points back toward the subject.

Ms. Freeman is the new advisor.

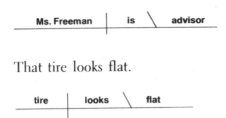

That tire looks flat.

| tire | looks \ flat |

Direct Object or Predicate Word?

A verb may be completed in one of two ways. It may have a direct object. Or it may have a predicate word. How can you tell the difference between a predicate word and a direct object?

The verb is the key word. Decide if the verb is an action verb. If so, the word following it that tells *whom* or *what* is a direct object.

> The nurse comforted the patient. (*Comforted* is an action verb. *Patient* is its direct object.)
> The ambulance rounded the *corner*. (*Rounded* is an action verb. *Corner* is its direct object.)

Is the verb a linking verb? If so, the word following it that tells about the subject is a predicate word.

> David Brenner is a *comedian*. (*Is* is a linking verb. *Comedian* is a predicate word.)

> These French fries seem *soggy*. (*Seem* is a linking verb. *Soggy* is a predicate word.)

Look at the following sentences:

> Phil Rogers is a *welder*.
> Phil Rogers hired a *welder*.

The first sentence has a linking verb, *is*. The word *welder* follows the linking verb and tells about the subject. It is a predicate word. In the second sentence, *hired* is an action verb. In this sentence, *welder* tells *whom* about the action verb. It is a direct object.

Exercise A   Label three columns *Subject, Linking Verb*, and *Predicate Word*. Find these parts in the sentences below and place them in the proper columns.

1. Those headlights are dim.
2. The band sounded great.
3. Students were the performers.
4. The skits were hilarious.
5. Curry tastes hot.
6. The sky appeared pink.
7. Kim must feel miserable.
8. The guide is she.
9. Tracy will become president.
10. Roller skates have become popular.

Exercise B   Make four columns on your paper. Head the columns *Subject, Verb, Direct Object*, and *Predicate Word*. Find these parts in the sentences below and place them in the right columns. Remember, no sentence can contain both a direct object *and* a predicate word.

1. Janet Gregory is a Congresswoman.
2. Her home is Alaska.
3. First, she was a Congressional aide.
4. That job gave her experience.
5. She ran several unsuccessful campaigns.
6. Finally, she became a legislator.
7. She seems fair.
8. She makes wise decisions.
9. She favors changes in the tax laws.
10. Her district supports her strongly.

Part 8 Compound Parts in a Sentence

The word *compound* means "having two or more parts."

Each of the sentence parts described so far in this section can be compound—subjects, verbs, direct objects, indirect objects, and predicate words.

Two parts in a compound form are joined by a conjunction (*and, or, but*). In a compound form of three or more parts, the conjunction usually comes between the last two parts.

Diagraming Compound Subjects

To diagram compound subjects, split the subject line. Place the conjunction on a dotted line connecting the subjects.

Marshmallows, nuts, and cherries covered the sundae.

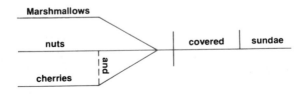

Diagraming Compound Verbs

To diagram compound verbs, split the verb line in the same way.

The crowd booed, hissed, and whistled.

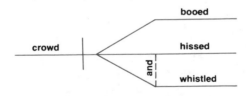

Diagraming Compound Objects

To diagram compound direct objects or indirect objects, split the object line.

Gonzales hit a homer and two singles. (compound direct object)

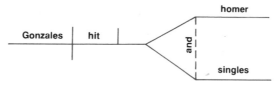

The director gave Brendon and Sandra lead roles. (compound indirect object)

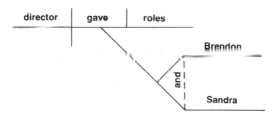

Diagraming Compound Predicate Words

To diagram compound predicate words, split the predicate word line.

The new coaches are Brock and Rudolph. (compound predicate word)

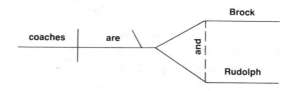

Exercise A As your teacher directs, show the compound parts in the following sentences. Tell whether they are compound subjects, verbs, objects, or predicate words.

1. The Soviet Union and the United States produce the most coal.
2. Coal is plentiful and inexpensive.
3. In strip mines, machines remove earth and rock.
4. In other mines, workers and equipment dig coal underground.
5. Miners cut, drill, and blast.
6. Cars or belts take the coal to the surface.
7. Machines wash and sort the coal at a plant.
8. Two mining problems are ventilation and support.
9. Sometimes walls weaken and collapse.
10. Gases and dust in coal mines may be explosive.

Exercise B For each of the following sentences, make the part noted in parentheses compound. Write the new sentences.

Example: The baby scooted across the floor. (*verb*)
The baby scooted and wriggled across the floor.

1. Sharon wrote several plays. (*direct object*)
2. The audience watched carefully. (*verb*)
3. The chairs were broken. (*subject*)
4. The Coast Guard patrols the lakes. (*direct object*)
5. The owner made a good profit. (*subject*)
6. Our car sputtered down the driveway. (*verb*)
7. Their creative Halloween costumes were colorful. (*predicate word*)
8. The music told a story. (*subject*)
9. The teacher told the parents her goals for the coming year. (*indirect object*)
10. The picnickers brought a grill. (*direct object*)

Part 9   Kinds of Sentences

There are several different reasons for using sentences. Sometimes you want to state something. Sometimes you want to ask a question. At other times, you want to give a command. There are also times when you want to express strong feeling. In each case, you use a different kind of sentence.

A **declarative sentence** is used to make a statement. It ends with a period (.).

> The young woman waited patiently.
> We watched the game on TV.

An **interrogative sentence** asks a question. It ends with a question mark (?).

> Has the wrestling meet begun?   What time is it?

An **imperative sentence** gives a command. It ends with a period.

> Wait for the signal.   Save me a seat, please.

An **exclamatory sentence** expresses strong emotion. It ends with an exclamation point (!).

> You ruined everything!   What a day this has been!

Exercise A   For each of the following sentences, write *Declarative, Interrogative, Imperative,* or *Exclamatory* to show what kind each is. Add the proper punctuation mark.

1. Are you going to a trade school
2. Turn off the lights
3. I live on the thirteenth floor
4. Do the elevators work
5. What a long climb that would be
6. Don't leave the windows open

7. This door has four locks
8. Where is the fire escape
9. Pick a card
10. The subway runs on electricity

Exercise B   Follow the directions for Exercise A.

1. When is the next game
2. Sheila plays the drums
3. I enjoy club activities
4. Are you avoiding me
5. What a view this is
6. Use the dictionary
7. Where do you go to school
8. What a blaze that was
9. Who is your employer
10. Brian's application was accepted

Part 10   Basic Sentence Patterns

Words can be organized into sentences in an endless number of ways. However, most sentences follow certain basic **sentence patterns.** The five patterns that follow are the most common ones.

Study each sentence pattern carefully. Try to think of an example of your own for each pattern.

Pattern One

This is the basic type of sentence. It has a subject and a verb. The subject is usually a noun or pronoun. In this chart, N stands for the noun (or pronoun) in the complete subject. V stands for the verb in the complete predicate.

N	V
Fashions	change.
We	worked hard.
The weekend	goes quickly.
The young man	danced gracefully.

Pattern Two

In this pattern, the noun (or pronoun) that follows the verb is a direct object.

N	V	N
The manager	opened	the store.
Marian	found	her old mitt.
Police	named	a suspect.
The coach	helped	us.

Pattern Three

Two nouns follow the verb in this pattern. The first is an *indirect object*. The second is a *direct object*.

N	V	N	N
Steve	slipped	me	a note.
Nobody	could give	us	directions.
The mayor	told	the reporters	his plans.

Pattern Four

The verb in this pattern is a *linking verb* (LV). The noun that follows it is a *predicate noun* (or predicate pronoun).

N	LV	N
The experiment	was	a success.
Carpentry	is	a trade.
This cap	is	mine.

Pattern Five

In this sentence pattern, a linking verb is followed by a *predicate adjective* (Adj).

N	LV	Adj
Ice hockey	is	rough.
The gears	seem	stiff.
This route	should be	direct.

Exercise A Tell which sentence pattern is used in each sentence.

1. Lopez was the victor.
2. The workers called a strike.
3. Jobs were scarce.
4. The fish are fresh.
5. David works hard.
6. Rhoda gave Leslie a hint.
7. Eric photographed the skyline.
8. K-Mart is a discount store.
9. That request seems unfair.
10. A tornado hit.

Exercise B Follow the directions for Exercise A.

1. The game ended early.
2. That dessert looks rich.
3. We handed the usher our tickets.
4. Meredith delivers pizzas.
5. Beth told Jim her worries.
6. Computers have become necessary.
7. This check is a forgery.
8. Erica slept late.
9. Dense fog is a hazard.
10. The doctor taped Jason's ankle.

Additional Exercises

The Sentence and Its Parts

A. Identify sentences and sentence fragments. On your paper, tell whether each group of words is a *Sentence* or a *Fragment*.

1. Musicians entered the studio
2. Whistling in the dark
3. The next game is on Saturday
4. Dan wants a cheeseburger
5. Arranged them in alphabetical order
6. A jigsaw puzzle with hundreds of pieces
7. Sent postcards to her friends
8. The director gave the signal
9. The top album on the stack
10. Worked out on the parallel bars

B. Find the complete subjects and complete predicates. Head two columns *Complete Subject* and *Complete Predicate*. Write the proper words from each sentence in the columns.

1. The stunt man leaped from the horse.
2. Some gardeners grow plants in water.
3. The helicopter hovered over the small field.
4. The downhill skiers zipped through the course.
5. A large yellow van pulled into the driveway.
6. Citrus fruit grows in warm climates.
7. Truckers from all over gathered at Mel's.
8. Jeffrey led the scavenger hunt.
9. Two debaters from our school won awards.
10. Many celebrities appear in commercials.

C. Find the verb and its simple subject. Label two columns *Subject* and *Verb*. Write the proper words from each sentence in the columns.

1. Paxton scored the first goal.
2. The nervous actors prepared for the first act of the play.
3. Bright banners decorated the floats.
4. Beth's cousin appeared on TV.
5. Students from the drama club make the stage sets for our shows.
6. Donna asked for a sundae with hot fudge and bananas.
7. Few stations play music all night.
8. A local store sponsors the contest.
9. The music at the concert was excellent.
10. Each new student sees a counselor.

D. Find the verb parts. Number your paper from 1 to 10. Write all parts of the verb in each sentence. Then write the simple subject. Watch for unusual kinds of sentences.

1. This bus is seldom late in the morning.
2. The pilot has already radioed the central tower for instructions.
3. There is a special on TV tonight.
4. The cafeteria usually doesn't open until 11:00 A.M.
5. Here is a secret compartment.
6. On the sidelines stood a man in a chicken costume.
7. We should have reported the incident to one of the officers.
8. Some streets have not been plowed yet.
9. Boil the eggs for five minutes.
10. Does Randi write for the school newspaper?

E. Recognize objects. Number your paper from 1 to 10. Label three columns *Verb, Indirect Object,* and *Direct Object.* For each sentence, write the words in the proper columns. Not every sentence will have an indirect object.

1. Last night Eric saw a ballet.
2. Linda showed Jamie her new radio.
3. The union finally settled its contract.
4. Every spring the theatre department produces a musical.
5. Barry scheduled another appointment with the dentist.
6. The doctor gave her patient a prescription.
7. Neil composes songs on his guitar.
8. Nicole showed Pat the violin.
9. The bank teller handed Lyle his money.
10. The audience gave the singer a standing ovation.

F. Find predicate words and objects. Label four columns *Subject, Verb, Direct Object,* and *Predicate Word.* When these parts appear in the sentences below, write them in the columns. Remember, no sentence can contain both a direct object *and* a predicate word.

1. The first ten rows are full.
2. Kim entered an exciting contest.
3. The English department added new courses.
4. These brownies seem very chewy.
5. Tony recently sold his trombone to Lisa.
6. Chocolate cake is my favorite dessert.
7. Mindy read a newspaper on microfilm.
8. Terry is a volunteer at the hospital.
9. The musicians were playing jazz.
10. Roseann is Aaron's cousin.

G. Find compound parts in a sentence. Write the compound parts in the following sentences. Tell whether they are compound subjects, verbs, objects, or predicate words.

1. Ted and Wendy smiled at each other.
2. Roald Dahl has written many novels, plays, and stories.
3. We washed and dried clothes at the laundromat.
4. Down jackets look soft and warm.
5. The parachutist waited and then jumped.
6. The trainers reward and punish the animals in these circus acts.
7. This gum is sweet but sugarless.
8. Vicky and her friends threw a farewell party for Roger.
9. Diane and Jay were the lifeguards.
10. The rowboat bounced and splashed through the waves.

H. Identify kinds of sentences. Decide whether the following sentences are *Declarative, Interrogative, Imperative,* or *Exclamatory.* Write your answer on your paper. Also write what punctuation mark should be used.

1. Smile at the camera
2. Did you get a haircut
3. Elena couldn't face her friends
4. How cheerful she seems
5. Who won the tournament
6. Please fill this order
7. What does this code mean
8. Look out
9. Clap your hands with the music
10. Mom writes articles for the local newspaper

Section 2

Using Complete Sentences

Sentences communicate ideas and feelings. When they are well composed, sentences get your ideas across clearly and completely.

Sometimes, however, people put words together in a confusing way. Then the message gets jumbled or lost.

One cause of confusion is leaving out part of a sentence. The remaining group of words is a **sentence fragment.** Another problem is created when two or more sentences are written as one. This group of words is called a **run-on sentence.**

Both of these writing errors weaken communication. In this section you will learn how to avoid them.

Part 1   What Is a Sentence Fragment?

A group of words that is only part of a sentence is a **sentence fragment**. A sentence fragment does not express a complete thought.

A fragment is confusing because something is missing from the sentence. Sometimes the subject is left out. Then the reader wonders *who* or *what* the sentence is about. At other times the verb is left out. Then the reader wonders *what happened?* or *what about it?*

Fragment: Shifted into fourth gear. (Who shifted? The subject is missing.)

Sentence: The speeding trucker shifted into fourth gear.

Fragment: The quarterback near the ten-yard line. (What happened? The verb is missing.)

Sentence: The quarterback fumbled near the ten-yard line.

Fragments Due to Incomplete Thoughts

Sometimes a writer is in a hurry. He or she jots down only bits of ideas. These ideas are incomplete. The writer's pen doesn't keep up with his or her flow of thoughts.

Maybe the writer understands these pieces of ideas. However, to a reader they will probably seem unclear.

Here is an example of a series of fragments:

Cars in line for gasoline. On some days are not open. Price of a gallon of gas up sharply.

These complete sentences show what the writer meant:

Cars wait in line for gasoline at many service stations. On some days no stations are open. The price of a gallon of gas has risen sharply.

Fragments Due to Incorrect Punctuation

All sentences end with punctuation marks. The mark may be a period, a question mark, or an exclamation point. Sometimes a writer uses one of these punctuation marks too soon. The idea is incomplete. A sentence fragment results.

Fragment: Cars with brake problems. Were recalled by General Motors.

Sentence: Cars with brake problems were recalled by General Motors.

Fragment: On a hot July afternoon. Crowds jammed the beaches.

Sentence: On a hot July afternoon crowds jammed the beaches.

Fragment: A diver freed a baby whale. From a fishing net.

Sentence: A diver freed a baby whale from a fishing net.

Exercise A For each group of words that is a sentence, write *S* on your paper. For each sentence fragment, write *F*. Be ready to add words to change the fragments into sentences.

1. A TV show about police work
2. A new series will begin this season
3. Several young actors
4. The director offers advice
5. Scenery, props, and sound effects
6. Will be seen on Monday evenings at 7 P.M.
7. Each episode has a chase scene
8. A stunt person jumps from a building
9. Each scene is filmed several times
10. Usually ends with an arrest

Exercise B Follow the directions for Exercise A.

1. Greg ordered a root beer float
2. His sister worked behind the counter

3. Forty-two flavors of ice cream
4. The movie begins at eight o'clock
5. Teenagers gathered outside
6. Endless rows of bright street lights
7. The police car raced after a speeder
8. Sitting on the porch in the cool evening
9. Potholes in the road
10. Carly Simon writes the lyrics for some of her songs

Part 2   What Is a Run-on Sentence?

A **run-on sentence** is two or more sentences written incorrectly as one.

A run-on confuses the reader. It does not show where the first idea ends and the second one begins. The reader needs a period or other punctuation mark to signal the end of each complete thought. Here are some examples:

Run-on: A motorcycle turned into the alley it skidded on the gravel.
Correct: A motorcycle turned into the alley. It skidded on the gravel.

Run-on: Tom likes disco music Carla likes a Latin beat.
Correct: Tom likes disco music. Carla likes a Latin beat.

Sometimes writers make the mistake of using a comma instead of a period. Again, the result is a run-on.

Run-on: The rookie running back carried the ball, he made a touchdown.
Correct: The rookie running back carried the ball. He made a touchdown.

Run-on: The floats were ready, the parade could begin.
Correct: The floats were ready. The parade could begin.

Exercise A Correct the following run-on sentences.

1. Some radio stations have powerful signals, they can be heard in nearby states.

2. One disc jockey reads letters from listeners he also jokes with callers.

3. Several stations hold contests, prizes are often albums.

4. Tanya won one contest she named a song correctly.

5. The sound equipment is complex, few people could operate it.

6. The Reds won the pennant they will play in the World Series.

7. Rod Carew hit a line drive, the centerfielder caught it.

8. Tony has a set of barbells he lifts weights every day.

9. We saw an old Hitchcock film, it was a classic thriller.

10. Megan hung another poster she has nearly covered her walls.

Exercise B Follow the directions for Exercise A.

1. Lou painted his car, first he sanded it.

2. The racecar driver pulled off the track the pit crew went into action.

3. The expressway is being repaired all lanes are closed.

4. Heavy machinery is blocking the street a worker is directing traffic.

5. Owen works at this station he works four days a week.

6. Gail attached brackets to the wall, she used toggle bolts.

7. The picnic is scheduled for Saturday, sunny weather is predicted.

8. Steve comes from a very large family he has three brothers and four sisters.

9. The hospital staff works on shifts, there are three shifts of eight hours each.

10. A loud noise startled the hikers, a dead tree had fallen.

Additional Exercises

Using Complete Sentences

A. Recognize sentences and sentence fragments. Tell whether each group of words is a *Sentence* or a *Fragment*.

1. Ms. Ross repairs furniture in her spare time
2. A nationally known cartoonist
3. The opening game of the football season
4. The horoscope in the daily paper
5. A subway train sped past
6. The overturned truck blocked traffic
7. Led the group in exercises
8. The cook grilled two hamburgers
9. Steve types at a fast pace
10. Draws with charcoal

B. Recognize sentences and run-on sentences. For each group of words that is a sentence, write *S*. For each run-on sentence, write *R*.

1. Ray was a back-up singer now he sings lead.
2. Tony tried to skate, he ended up with a sprained arm.
3. They live on the fourth floor, let's take the elevator.
4. Before the game we went to a pep rally.
5. The German neighborhood celebrated Oktoberfest.
6. Larry was trained as a carpenter he learned quickly.
7. A pipe burst water flooded the basement.
8. My sister has a part-time job at the grocery store.
9. The school sponsors adult classes, many people attend.
10. The lights went out everybody lit candles.

C. Correct sentence fragments and run-on sentences. Correct each fragment by adding words to complete the thought. Correct each run-on by adding the proper punctuation and capitalization.

1. A photographer from the local newspaper.
2. A large pothole in the middle of the street.
3. A boy dashed past he was chasing a large collie.
4. Had operated the television cameras.
5. Ramon was at bat the bases were loaded.
6. Dad glanced at the headline, he was shocked to see his name.
7. A dolphin trainer at the city zoo.
8. Kara waved to us then she ran toward the canyon.
9. Rode their bicycles down the hallway.
10. At a birthday celebration last week.
11. Toss me the ball, I'll serve next.
12. Tanya is visiting relatives she'll be back next week.
13. Keeps his pet rabbit in a cage in the back yard.
14. The girl in the center of the picture.
15. Brian sat down he seemed unusually quiet.

Section 3

Using Nouns

Good, clear sentences are not accidents. They result from understanding how words work.

The words used in sentences fall into certain groups or classes. You can talk and write without knowing these labels. However, skilled speakers and writers understand the different classes of words.

In this section you will learn about one important group of words: nouns.

Part 1   What Are Nouns?

You use words to name the people, places, and things around you. Words that name are called **nouns.**

A noun is a word used to name a person, place, or thing.

Nouns name things that can be seen, like cities, streets, furniture, and books. They name things you cannot see, such as feelings, ideas, and beliefs.

Persons: landlord, Greg, Anne Murray, actor
Places: Wyoming, kitchen, Savannah, hotel
Things: blanket, mirror, energy, concern

Exercise   Make three columns on a sheet of paper. Label them *Names of Persons, Names of Places,* and *Names of Things.* Find the nouns in the following paragraph. List each one in the proper column.

Thirty years ago Frisbees began as tin plates from pies. The plates came from the Frisbee Baking Company in Connecticut. People played with the plates. Now the game is not just play. Frisbee has become a sport. The championships are held in Pasadena. Entrants compete in five events. Players even come from other countries.

Proper Nouns and Common Nouns

How do these two italicized nouns differ?

One *sailor*, *George Ruiz*, jumped from the ship.

The word *sailor* is a general term. It refers to many people. It is a common noun. A common noun is a general name.

The noun *George Ruiz*, on the other hand, refers to only one person. It is a **proper noun.** A proper noun is a specific name.

A common noun is the name of a whole group of persons, places, or things. It is a name that is common to the group.

A proper noun is the name of a particular person, place, or thing. It is capitalized.

Look at the following examples of common nouns and proper nouns. As you can see, some nouns are made up of more than one word.

Common Nouns	Proper Nouns
magazine	*Sports Illustrated*
mountain	Mount Everest
cartoonist	Gary Trudeau
game	Super Bowl
city	Burlington
senator	Senator Hayakawa

Exercise A Make two columns on your paper. Label one column *Common Nouns* and the other *Proper Nouns*. Place each of the following nouns in the correct column. Capitalize all proper nouns.

1. holiday inn, motel, seabreeze motel, shores hotel
2. restaurant, diner, burger king, cafeteria
3. singer, lou rawls, album, willie nelson, ballad
4. allentown, town, village, ridgeville, asheville
5. court, judge, judge ellen rodriguez, jury
6. nation, new zealand, spain, country, canada
7. airlines, trans world airlines, united airlines, airport
8. evanston hospital, hospital, clinic, sheridan dental clinic
9. first national bank, bank, banker, robert abboud, continental bank
10. team, dallas cowboys, manager, cheerleader

Exercise B Write five sentences of your own, using at least one proper noun in each sentence.

Part 2 How Are Nouns Used?

Nouns Used as Subjects

As you learned in **Section 1,** the subject of a sentence tells who or what is being talked about. Nouns are frequently used as subjects.

> *Scientists* can predict earthquakes. (The noun *scientists* is the subject of the verb *can predict.*)

> *Ace Hardware* in Bellwood sponsors our bowling team. (The noun *Ace Hardware* is the subject of the verb *sponsors.* Notice that in this sentence, the subject is not next to the verb.)

Two or more nouns may form a compound subject.

> The *divers* and *crew* planned the voyage carefully. (The nouns *divers* and *crew* are the subject of the verb *planned.*)

> The *bus* and the *truck* collided in the intersection. (The nouns *bus* and *truck* are the subject of the verb *collided.*)

Exercise A Number your paper from 1 to 10. Write the nouns used as the subjects of these sentences.

1. A factory dumps wastes into this river.
2. The comedian told terrible jokes.
3. The workers organized a car pool.
4. That legend has been told for centuries.
5. The networks and newspapers cover sports events.
6. Many businesses need computers.
7. Vanessa and Nicole have applied for jobs.
8. Sara's wages have gone up each year.
9. Jon has been saving money for a motorcycle.
10. Many families are cutting their expenses.

1. The cost of movie tickets has risen.
2. Sharon tape-records her friends' albums.
3. Many employees eat in the cafeteria.
4. Shoppers looked for bargains at the sale.
5. The photographer printed her film.
6. A group of soldiers patrolled the shore.
7. The explorers plunged into the wilderness.
8. Ansel Adams is a fine photographer.
9. Lynn and Rice are powerful sluggers.
10. The Russian spacelab returned to earth.

Nouns Used as Direct Objects

A direct object completes the action of a verb. It answers *whom* or *what* about the verb. Nouns are frequently used as direct objects.

> The magician fooled the *audience*. (The noun *audience* tells *whom* about the verb *fooled*.)
>
> In the shop class the students wear *goggles*. (The noun *goggles* tells *what* about the verb *wear*.)
>
> Roger shaped *mugs* and a *pitcher* out of clay. (Both the nouns *mugs* and *pitcher* are direct objects. They tell *what* about the verb *shaped*.

Exercise A As your teacher directs, write the nouns used as direct objects in the following sentences.

1. Danielle pounded the ball for a home run.
2. Jim has a short, flat swing.
3. Weight-training built Reed's strength.
4. City folks wear boots, too.
5. Todd reads *Time* every week.

6. That apartment has no heat.
7. Josh piled blankets onto the bed.
8. Will made his own drums.
9. The truckers load crates at the warehouse.
10. Carrie plays softball and basketball.

Exercise B   Follow the directions for Exercise A.

1. Britt took a trip to San Francisco.
2. The judge instructed the jury.
3. The company hired a lawyer.
4. Our family has medical insurance.
5. Customers must pay the cashier.
6. That used car has a radio and whitewalls.
7. Kim put radial tires on her car.
8. Bryant tackled the quarterback.
9. The lifeguard rescued two young children.
10. Woods line the coast of Maine.

Nouns Used as Indirect Objects

Another use of the noun is as an **indirect object**. The indirect object tells *to whom* or *for whom* or *to what* or *for what* about the verb.

> The coach showed the *quarterback* a new play. (The noun *quarterback* is the indirect object. It tells *to whom* about the verb *showed*.)

> Sarah gave the *bookcase* and the *shelves* another coat of varnish. (The nouns *bookcase* and *shelves* are the compound indirect object, telling *to what* about the verb *gave*.)

An indirect object is used only with a direct object. The indirect object appears before the direct object in the sentence.

Subject	Verb	Indirect Object(s)	Direct Object
Gail	showed	the cabbie	the route.
Leslie	fed	the dog	its food.
Dairy Queen	offered	Jim and Alice	jobs.

As you have seen, the word *to* or *for* is never used with an indirect object.

Exercise A Find the nouns used as indirect objects in the following sentences.

1. Mr. Scott gave Bonita her paycheck.
2. Police read the suspect his rights.
3. Kent gave the operator the number.
4. The store sent Ms. Alvarez a bill.
5. Sheila handed the teller her deposit.
6. The catcher gave the pitcher a signal.
7. Mark showed Michelle the rabbit's nest.
8. Suzanne gave Les and Maureen her new address.
9. The waiter handed each diner a menu.
10. Andy Kaufman told the audience a joke.

Exercise B Follow the directions for Exercise A.

1. The manager gave Kim a promotion.
2. The coach gave her team a workout.
3. Carolyn handed the conductor her ticket.
4. Debbie made her sister a club sandwich.
5. Cal owes Steve six dollars.
6. Jenny loaned Erin a dress for the dance.
7. Don gives his brother his old clothes.
8. The commander gave Phil his orders.
9. The doctor gave her patient some advice.
10. The interviewer asked the President a tough question about inflation.

Nouns Used as Predicate Words

Sometimes a noun in the predicate part of a sentence is linked to the subject. That noun is called a **predicate noun**. It always follows a linking verb. It means the same thing as the subject.

Carlos was a carpenter's *assistant*.

The counselors were former *teachers*.

Two early autos were the *Model* T and the *Model* A.

The nouns *assistant, teachers, Model T,* and *Model* A are predicate nouns.

Exercise A Find the nouns used as predicate nouns in the following sentences.

1. Canada is the birthplace of ice hockey.
2. The Freeport team is our strongest rival.
3. Saturday is the best day for a party.
4. British coins are shillings and pence.
5. Tyrone's last game was a no-hitter.
6. Pauline is an Olympic contender.
7. Mr. Johnson became the varsity coach.
8. Carl's sister is a bus driver in the city.
9. Gary's construction job is hard work.
10. The running backs were Earl Campbell and Walter Payton.

Exercise B Follow the directions for Exercise A.

1. Many young people will someday become parents.
2. Richard Pryor was the host of the talk show.
3. The Loop is the central area of downtown Chicago.
4. The stars of the movie were Bo Derek, Dudley Moore, and Julie Andrews.

5. Two parts of a brake are the drum and the shoe.
6. Cornelia Street is the subway's last stop.
7. The Marx brothers were comic actors.
8. "Satchmo" was Louis Armstong's nickname.
9. The Steelers are tough defensive players.
10. *The High and the Mighty* was the late movie last night.

Part 3 The Plurals of Nouns

When a noun names one thing, it is singular. When a noun names more than one thing, it is plural.

Here are some rules for forming the plurals of nouns.

1. To form the plural of most nouns, just add *s*:

prizes   dreams   circles   stations

2. When the singular noun ends in *s, sh, ch, x,* or *z,* add *es*:

waitresses   brushes   ditches   axes   buzzes

3. When the singular noun ends in *o,* add *s*:

solos   halos   studios   photos   pianos

For a few words ending in *o*, add *es*:

heroes   tomatoes   potatoes   echoes   cargoes

4. When a singular noun ends in *y* with a consonant before it, change the *y* to *i* and add *es*:

army—armies   candy—candies   baby—babies

When a vowel (*a, e, i, o, u*) comes before the *y*, do not change the *y* to *i*. Just add *s*:

boy—boys   way—ways   jockey—jockeys

5. For some nouns ending in *f*, add *s* to make the plural:

roofs   chiefs   reefs   beliefs

For many nouns ending in *f* or *fe*, change the *f* to *v* and add *s* or *es*. Since there is no rule to follow, you will have to memorize such words. Here are some examples:

life—lives   calf—calves   knife—knives
thief—thieves   shelf—shelves   loaf—loaves

6. Some nouns have the same form for both singular and plural. They must be memorized.

deer   sheep   moose   salmon   trout

7. Some nouns form their plurals in special ways. They, too, must be memorized.

man—men   tooth—teeth   ox—oxen
woman—women   mouse—mice   foot—feet
goose—geese   child—children   louse—lice

Dictionaries show the plural of a word if it is formed in an unusual way. Here is a dictionary entry for the noun *duty.* The entry shows the plural, *duties.*

du·ty (dōōt′ē, dyōōt′ē) *n., pl.* **-ties** [< Anglo-Fr. *dueté*, what is due: see DUE & -TY[1]] **1.** obedience or respect that is due to parents, older people, etc. **2.** something that one ought to do because it is thought to be morally right or necessary [the *duty* of a citizen to vote] **3.** any action required by one's occupation or position [her *duties* include writing the reports] **4.** a sense of obligation [*duty* calls] **5.** service, esp. military service **6.** a payment due to the government, esp. a tax on imports, exports, etc. **7.** service or use: see HEAVY-DUTY —**on** (or **off**) **duty** at (or having time off from) one's work or duty

Use the dictionary if you have a question about plurals.

Exercise A Write the plural of each of these nouns. Then use your dictionary to see if you are right.

1. leaf	6. sky	11. echo	16. spy
2. year	7. knife	12. tomato	17. goose
3. deer	8. tooth	13. bunch	18. hoof
4. holiday	9. radio	14. window	19. wish
5. coach	10. fox	15. moose	20. copy

Exercise B Write each sentence. Correct the errors in plural forms of nouns.

1. The childs were told not to play ball in the alleys.
2. The donkeys carried pouchs of gold.
3. Several tooths from sharkes were found on the beachs.
4. These forkes and knifes are scratched.
5. Basketball hoops are ten foots from the floor.
6. Basketes measure eighteen inchs across.
7. Both halfs of the court have basketes.
8. There are many types of passs and shots in the game.
9. Many large citys have pro teames.
10. Bill Russell and Wilt Chamberlain are my heros.

Part 4 The Possessives of Nouns

Nouns can indicate possession or ownership.

Mr. Lowe's car   a farmer's land   Betty's keys

Nouns can show that something is part of a person.

Meg's sense of humor   Harold's concern

The 's makes the above nouns show ownership. Words like *farmer's*, *Meg's*, and *Harold's* are called **possessive nouns.**

Usually, people and animals possess things. Sometimes, however, things are also used in the possessive. We speak of a *week's wages*, *a day's work*, or *a city's growth*.

Forming Possessives

There are three rules for forming the possessive of nouns.

1. If the noun is singular, add an apostrophe (') and s.

Amanda—Amanda's arm
Ross—Ross's desk

2. If the noun is plural and ends in s, add just the apostrophe.

artists—artists' studios   Spencers—Spencers' home

3. If the noun is plural but does not end in s, add an apostrophe and s.

women—women's discussion   people—people's choice

Exercise A   Write the possessive form of each of these nouns.

1. mayor	6. ranch	11. car	16. admiral
2. Meg	7. child	12. Charles	17. Jenny
3. country	8. player	13. runner	18. salesperson
4. senator	9. Penny	14. store	19. boss
5. today	10. host	15. secretary	20. Linda

Exercise B   Follow the directions for Exercise A.

1. people	6. guests	11. mice	16. families
2. fans	7. friends	12. wives	17. men
3. brothers	8. women	13. workers	18. clerks
4. hours	9. doctors	14. sheep	19. islands
5. experts	10. teachers	15. Jacksons	20. bodies

Exercise C   Write the possessive form for each italicized word.

1. The *Bears* lineup looks strong.
2. *Jerry* car needs new shock absorbers.
3. *Tuesday* game features the Steelers and the Cowboys.
4. The *voters* choice is Ms. Marie Tonelli.
5. Reynolds beat the other *racers* times.
6. *Louis* pass landed in the end zone.
7. The assistant *state* attorney met with the reporters.
8. The *children* zoo has baby animals.
9. Everyone watched the *astronauts* splashdown.
10. *Donna* neighborhood has a softball league.

Additional Exercises

Using Nouns

A. Distinguish common and proper nouns. Head two columns *Common Nouns* and *Proper Nouns*. Place each noun in the proper column. Capitalize the proper nouns.

1. actress, jodi foster, meryl streep, movie, *grease*
2. walden pond, ohio river, lake, stream, crater lake
3. city, suburb, portland, town, glenview
4. dan rather, anchorperson, newscaster, jane pauley
5. network, television, american broadcasting system
6. prince albert, duke, duchess of windsor, prince
7. boston red sox, team, pitcher, tom seaver, league
8. beach, oahu, island, jamaica, sicily
9. planet, comet, jupiter, satellite, kohoutek
10. acadia national park, forest, park

B. Find common and proper nouns. List the nouns in each of the following sentences. Be sure to capitalize each proper noun.

1. A strong wind blew the lamppost to the ground.
2. A ferry takes passengers to nantucket.
3. Charlene brought sandwiches and chips.
4. The art institute in chicago has paintings by renoir.
5. On tuesday our class visited the lincoln memorial.
6. The hurricane tore through cuba and haiti.
7. After we toured lake michigan, our ship docked in milwaukee.
8. Mr. rodriguez identified the thief from a photograph.
9. During vacation lee polished her bicycle.
10. The firefighters and police went on strike last august.

C. Recognize nouns used in sentences. Decide how each italicized noun is used in these sentences. Write the word and label it *Subject, Direct Object, Indirect Object*, or *Predicate Noun*.

1. The first *day* of school seemed strange.
2. Last month Evan visited *New Mexico*.
3. The difficult climb was a *challenge* to even the experienced campers.
4. Did Erin give *Elliot* my message?
5. *Kara* bought three boxes of Girl Scout cookies from her sister.
6. The decorators painted the *ceiling* first.
7. The end of the movie was a *surprise*.
8. Jessica showed *Kate* the shortcut.
9. The president assigned each *person* on the committee a task.
10. The whole *team* celebrated after the victory.

D. Form the plurals of nouns. Write the plural form of each noun. Use a dictionary to check the plurals of any words you are not sure of.

1. scarf		14. woman
2. life		15. potato
3. rodeo		16. freshman
4. coach		17. class
5. spy		18. sheep
6. piano		19. ax
7. tax		20. county
8. hobby		21. thief
9. tooth		22. fox
10. alley		23. beach
11. hero		24. folio
12. moose		25. ox
13. dish		26. convoy

E. Form the possessives of nouns. Write the possessive form for each italicized noun.

1. *Nicholas* shirt doesn't match his pants.
2. *Jenny* family left for Cape Cod.
3. Someone misplaced the *painters* ladder.
4. Sarah carried *Josh* backpack.
5. The emcee asked for the *contestant* answer.
6. *James* heroic act brought him much attention.
7. The *Student Council* funds come from special projects.
8. The *Johnsons* dog is a collie.
9. *Ms. Marsh* trip was a disaster.
10. The *children* theater produced a lively musical.
11. We heard the *gulls* cries as they whirled above us.
12. Jack Nicklaus followed his *caddy* suggestion.
13. *Men* clothing styles don't change much.
14. The newspapers printed the *President* speech.
15. *Ross* baseball mitt is five years old.

Section 4

Using Pronouns

If you only had nouns to refer to people, places, and things, you would have to express an idea like this:

> Andy strummed Andy's guitar and sang the lyrics that Andy had written.

Luckily, you can avoid such awkward sentences. Instead of nouns, you can use **pronouns.** Then you can say:

> Andy strummed *his* guitar and sang the lyrics that *he* had written.

Notice how the words *his* and *he* take the place of the noun *Andy*. These pronouns convey the same meaning in a direct way.

Part 1 Personal Pronouns

A pronoun is a word used in place of a noun. Pronouns are very helpful words. They may be used in three situations:

1. They may refer to the person speaking.

    I pole-vault.   *We* played cards.

2. They may refer to the person spoken to.

    You tune *your* own car, don't *you?*

3. They may refer to other people, places, or things.

    She asked *him* a question.   *They* opened *their* mail.

The examples above show that a pronoun often refers to a person. For that reason, the largest group of pronouns is called **personal pronouns.**

There are many variations of personal pronouns. Like nouns, personal pronouns may be singular or plural. In the following chart, see how personal pronouns change from singular to plural.

Singular:	I	me	my, mine
	you	you	your, yours
	he, she, it	him, her, it	his, her, hers, its
Plural:	we	us	our, ours
	you	you	your, yours
	they	them	their, theirs

As the chart shows, most plural pronouns are totally different from their singular forms. Notice these examples:

Singular	Plural
I escaped.	*We* escaped.
Stop *her!*	Stop *them!*
It fell.	*They* fell.

Exercise A Number your paper from 1 to 10. Write the pronouns used in place of nouns in these sentences. After each pronoun, write the noun or nouns it stands for.

1. A crane lifted the boulder and loaded it onto a truck.
2. Beth and George parked their motorcycles.
3. The hailstones bounced as they landed.
4. The politician repeated his promises.
5. "I have hay fever," complained Jason.
6. Marietta uses her hands when she talks.
7. The dancers rehearsed for their performance.
8. The paramedics arrived. They took charge.
9. The mirror shattered when it dropped.
10. Susan, did you get a checking account?

Exercise B Follow the directions for Exercise A.

1. Joel and Christina held a garage sale in their driveway.
2. The doctor made her rounds.
3. Barry took the wreck and made it run.
4. Kate met Steve and walked home with him.
5. The little girl stuck out her tongue.
6. The passengers had their luggage searched.
7. Sonia and Brett brought popcorn with them to the movies.
8. An usher directed Ellen to her seat.
9. "Have you ever tasted anchovies?" Laurel asked Richard.
10. Alison bought a Pepsi and drank it with her lunch.

Part 2 The Forms of Pronouns

Pronouns can be used in all the ways that nouns are used. Personal pronouns can be subjects, objects, predicate words, and possessives.

However, a personal pronoun changes forms as its use in a sentence changes. Look at these sentences:

He pitched. (*He* is the subject.)
Riley tagged *him*. (*Him* is the direct object.)
His pitch was wild. (*His* shows possession.)

The three pronouns in these examples all refer to the same person. The forms, though, are different.

The three forms of a personal pronoun are **subject form**, **object form,** and **possessive form.** Here are the forms for all the personal pronouns:

	Subject	Object	Possessive
Singular:	I	me	my, mine
	you	you	your, yours
	he, she, it	her, him, it	his, her, hers, its
Plural:	we	us	our, ours
	you	you	your, yours
	they	them	their, theirs

Exercise The following sentences use different forms of pronouns correctly. Read each sentence aloud.

1. *We* reported the accident.
2. A blizzard halted *us*.
3. Did *you* endorse *your* check?
4. Wendy and *she* showed *their* identification.
5. The editorial convinced *me*.
6. That was *he*.
7. *They* served on a jury.
8. The camera is *his*.
9. *I* went fishing with Joe and *her*.
10. The dog gnawed *its* bone.
11. *Our* car bumped *her* bike.
12. Sandy makes candles and sells *them*.

13. The next dance is *yours*.
14. The pleasure was *mine*.
15. The car dealer sold *him* a Fiesta.

The Subject Form of Pronouns

Subject Pronouns

I	we
you	you
he, she, it	they

For the subject of a sentence, the subject form of the personal pronoun is used. These sentences use the subject form for the subject:

> *They* laughed and sang.   *He* punted the ball.
> *She* carried the boxes.   *I* drew a map.

Using pronouns as subjects usually causes few problems. A more troublesome use, though, is the predicate pronoun. A predicate pronoun is a pronoun that is linked with the subject. It follows a linking verb, just as a predicate noun does.

Look at these examples of predicate pronouns:

> That must be *she*. (*She* is a predicate pronoun used after the linking verb *must be*.)
> The caller was *he*. (*He* is a predicate pronoun used after the linking verb *was*.)

As you see, the subject forms of pronouns are used for predicate pronouns. That form may not sound natural at first. If you are in doubt about which form to use, try reversing the subject and the predicate pronoun. The sentence should still sound correct.

> The singer was *she*.
> *She* was the singer.

Here are more examples of the correct use of the subject form for predicate pronouns:

That was *he* on the phone.
Was it *she* at the door?
The winner was *she*.

Always use the subject form for subjects and predicate pronouns.

The Object Form of Pronouns

Object Pronouns

me	us
you	you
him, her, it	them

When personal pronouns are used as objects, the object form is correct. Any pronoun that is not a subject or a predicate pronoun is an object.

There are three kinds of objects: direct objects, indirect objects, and objects of prepositions.

In these sentences the object form of the pronoun is used for direct objects.

Dennis knows *them*.   The manager trained *me*.
Carla followed *us*.   The visitors surprised *her*.

These sentences use the object form for indirect objects:

Terry loaned *me* his pen.   Carol sent *them* gifts.
The school finds *us* jobs.   Mr. Lyle gave *her* some advice.

The third kind of object is the object of a preposition. Prepositions are short connecting words like *to, for,* and *with.* The pronouns that follow such words are the objects. For more explanation of prepositions, see Section 7.

These sentences use the object form for objects of prepositions:

We practiced with *him*.
My friends threw a party for *me*.
Ben sketched a portrait of *her*.
The stagehands prepared the set for *us*.

The Possessive Form of Pronouns

Possessive Pronouns

my, mine	our, ours
your, yours	your, yours
his, her, hers, its	their, theirs

Possessive pronouns show belonging or ownership. Many times, possessive pronouns are used by themselves. Then, like a noun, a possessive pronoun has one of these uses: subject, object, or predicate word. Look at these examples:

That suitcase is *his*. (predicate pronoun)
H*ers* is much heavier. (subject)
Paul and Maria are carrying *theirs*. (direct object)
Steve gave *his* a shove. (indirect object)
This suitcase looks like *mine*. (object of preposition)

At other times, possessive pronouns are not used alone. Instead, they are used to tell about nouns. Look at these sentences:

Phil trained *his* German shepherd.
Each ethnic group has *its* customs.
The team celebrated *their* victory.
Will you read *your* lines?

Exercise A Choose the correct pronoun from the two given in parentheses. Write it. Read the sentence to yourself.

1. The news shocked (he, him).
2. The waiter spilled spaghetti on (I, me).
3. (They, Them) moved to our neighborhood.

4. The cashier gave (she, her) incorrect change.
5. Was that (he, him)?
6. All of (we, us) are taller than our parents.
7. The idea was (my, mine).
8. The artist sold (her, hers) work at a fair.
9. Joy sent (he, him) a funny birthday card.
10. The security guards stopped (we, us).

Exercise B Follow the directions for Exercise A.

1. A pro team drafted (he, him).
2. Is this makeup (your, yours)?
3. The caller is (she, her).
4. During the summer (I, me) work at a day-care center.
5. Next year, (we, us) will be able to vote.
6. Wasn't it (he, him) at the door?
7. Garbage surrounded (they, them).
8. Aaron handed the earphones to (I, me).
9. Rebecca brought (her, hers) favorite album.
10. All of those drawings are by (he, him).

Exercise C The personal pronouns in the following sentences are in italics. Write each pronoun and label it *Subject Form, Object Form,* or *Possessive Form.*

1. Laura rehearsed the scene with *him.*
2. *She* loaded the film into the camera.
3. The movie bored *us.*
4. It's *they!*
5. Curt's older sister gave *him* a haircut.
6. Last week *I* got my first paycheck.
7. Wendy painted pinstripes on *her* car.
8. The best artwork is *his.*
9. *We* ate all of the tacos.
10. Beth loaned *me* a sweatshirt.

Part 3 Pronouns in Compound Constructions

Compound sentence parts, or **compound constructions,** in a sentence have more than one part. The parts are joined by *and, or,* or *nor,* as in *Ben and me.* A pronoun may be one or both of these parts.

You may wonder which pronoun form to use in a compound construction. Here are sentences with pronouns used correctly as compound parts:

> *Laura* and *I* learned a form of self-defense. (*Laura* and *I* are both subjects. The subject form *I* is used.)
>
> Mr. Kim taught *her* and *me* judo. (*Her* and *me* are both indirect objects. The object forms are used.)
>
> Just between *you* and *me,* I'm tired. (*You* and *me* are objects of the preposition *between.* The object forms are used.)

You can avoid problems with compound parts if you think of each part separately. For instance, in the first example above, omit the words *Laura and.* Should the sentence read *I learned a form of self-defense* or *Me learned a form of self-defense?* The pronoun *I* is correct.

Here is another example:

> Gail gave Dennis and (I, me) more coffee.
> Gail gave *me* more coffee.

Exercise A Choose the right pronoun from the two given.

1. Rick and (she, her) are going to the show.
2. Save seats for Lori and (I, me).
3. Ann invited (we, us) for supper.
4. Soap operas don't appeal to Janet and (I, me).
5. The argument was between Jamie and (they, them).
6. The judge fined Pam and (she, her).
7. Scott's best friends are Chris and (he, him).

8. My uncle and (he, him) are business partners.
9. My boss relies on (she, her) and (I, me).
10. Just between you and (I, me), I'm nervous.

Exercise B   Follow the directions for Exercise A.

1. The shopkeeper ignored Meg and (she, her).
2. Katy and (he, him) met on a bus.
3. That speeding car headed toward John and (I, me).
4. The clerk gave Phil and (she, her) their money back.
5. A child with a water pistol squirted Britt and (he, him).
6. Someone yelled at (they, them) and (we, us).
7. Bogan and (we, us) both have good teams.
8. Tony and (I, me) may join the Navy.
9. The best dancers are Marshall and (she, her).
10. Leave some chili for Marla and (he, him).

Part 4   Pronouns and Antecedents

A pronoun is defined as a word used in place of a noun. This noun is called the pronoun's **antecedent**. A pronoun refers to its antecedent.

> Anna never answers *her* phone.
> (*Her* takes the place of the noun *Anna*. *Anna* is the antecedent.)

> The shop closed *its* doors.
> (*Its* refers to the noun *shop*. *Shop* is the antecedent.)

The antecedent usually appears before the pronoun. The antecedent may appear in the same sentence or in the preceding sentence, as in this example:

> The tractor pushed the stones and bricks. It cleared a path.
> (*It* stands for the antecedent *tractor*.)

Pronouns may be the antecedents of other pronouns:

You missed *your* bus.
(*You* is the antecedent of *your*.)

A pronoun must be like its antecedent in one important way. A pronoun must have the same number as its antecedent. If the antecedent is singular, the pronoun must be singular. If the antecedent is plural, then the pronoun must be plural.

A pronoun must agree with its antecedent in number.

The photographers grabbed *their* cameras.
(*Photographers* is plural; *their* is plural.)

The typist erased *his* error.
(*Typist* is singular; *his* is singular.)

TV fans have *their* favorite shows.
(*Fans* is plural; *their* is plural.)

Exercise A In these sentences the personal pronouns are italicized. Write each pronoun and its antecedent.

1. The window washers saw the street far below *them*.
2. The girl carried a radio on *her* shoulder.
3. Jim looked at the gift and knew *it* was an album.
4. Don't wear those shoes if *they* hurt.
5. Tony made a pizza and topped *it* with salami.
6. Mrs. Barclay quit *her* job.
7. Lee gave the boys *their* dinner.
8. Frieda and I studied *our* menus.
9. Ali regained *his* balance.
10. Erik Estrada had an accident during the filming of *his* TV show.

Exercise B Follow the directions for Exercise A.

1. Some people hide *their* feelings.
2. The ship veered from *its* course.

3. I have lost *my* voice.
4. Mr. Monroe moved to *his* new apartment.
5. Gayle opened the battery and filled *it* with water.
6. Some gas caps have locks on *them*.
7. Linda planned the route for *her* next trip.
8. Rod and I split the cheesecake between the two of *us*.
9. Do you need *your* pen back?
10. Adam didn't see the car behind *him*.

Part 5   Compound Personal Pronouns

A **compound personal pronoun** is a pronoun with *-self* or *-selves* added.

myself	ourselves
yourself	yourselves
himself, herself, itself	themselves

Notice how compound personal pronouns are used for emphasis:

Maggie *herself* opened the vault.
The manager *himself* handled the sale.
I planned the reunion *myself*.
They called the police *themselves*.

Exercise A Number your paper from 1 to 10. Beside each number write the correct compound personal pronoun for each of the following sentences. After it, write its antecedent.

Example: The actor thinks of (pronoun) as a star.
himself, actor

1. Dana and I wrote the lyrics (pronoun).
2. Amy gave (pronoun) a permanent.

3. The workers (pronoun) choose their hours.

4. The governor (pronoun) pardoned the prisoner.

5. The members (pronoun) set the club rules.

6. I cooked this meal by (pronoun).

7. The cheerleaders yelled (pronoun) hoarse.

8. The special effects were good, but the movie (pronoun) was dull.

9. Make (pronoun) comfortable, Elliot.

10. We watched (pronoun) on TV.

Exercise B Follow the directions for Exercise A.

1. The general (pronoun) issued the orders.

2. Brian and Bob found (pronoun) in trouble.

3. The doctor (pronoun) became very sick.

4. Sarah drove (pronoun) to the hospital.

5. Give (pronoun) enough time, Debbie.

6. JoAnn tuned the engine (pronoun).

7. Carlos went camping by (pronoun).

8. The problem will work (pronoun) out.

9. Chris wanted the engine but not the car (pronoun).

10. Vic and I made (pronoun) sick by eating too much candy.

Part 6 Demonstrative Pronouns

The pronouns *this*, *that*, *these*, and *those* point out people or things. They are called **demonstrative pronouns.**

This and *these* point to people or things that are near in space or time. *That* or *those* point to people or things that are farther away in space or time.

This makes a good dessert.	*These* are leather boots.
That was our first date.	*Those* were great times.

Exercise Number your paper from 1 to 10. Write the correct demonstrative pronoun for the blank space in each sentence.

1. _____ are your gloves, not these.
2. _____ are terrific tacos we're eating.
3. _____ is better than that.
4. _____ was a good concert last night.
5. _____ is my bike beside me.
6. _____ must be our bus over there.
7. _____ is my counselor in the principal's office.
8. _____ is beautiful weather today.
9. _____ is the canyon out there.
10. _____ were our happiest years.

Part 7 Interrogative Pronouns

Certain pronouns are used to ask questions. They are called **interrogative pronouns.** The interrogative pronouns are *who, whom, whose, which,* and *what.*

> *Who* won an Emmy award?   *Which* is your favorite?
> *Whom* did Gloria call?   *What* started the fire?
> *Whose* is this parka?

Exercise Number your paper from 1 to 10. Write all the pronouns in these sentences. After each pronoun, write *Demonstrative* or *Interrogative* to show what kind it is.

> Example: Is that the law?
> *That*—demonstrative pronoun

1. Who knows the old man's age?
2. That makes sense.
3. Which is Carlos's suitcase?
4. These are strange lights.
5. Is that Rob's handwriting?
6. Whom does Cal trust with the money?

314

7. These are the latest fashions.
8. Are those the house keys?
9. What makes Ramona so lucky?
10. Whose are these?

Part 8 Indefinite Pronouns

Some pronouns do not refer to a definite person or thing. Such pronouns are called **indefinite pronouns.**

The following are indefinite pronouns. They are singular.

another	each	everything	one
anybody	either	neither	somebody
anyone	everybody	nobody	someone
anything	everyone	no one	

Because they are singular, the above pronouns are used with the singular possessive pronouns *his, her,* and *its.*

Each of the stores has *its* own hours.
Somebody forgot *his* ski cap.
Somebody forgot *his or her* ski cap.

The final example uses the phrase *his or her* instead of simply *his.* That phrase shows that the indefinite pronoun may refer to a male or female. Many people prefer such a phrase.

Although most indefinite pronouns are singular, some are plural. They refer to more than one person or thing. The following indefinite pronouns are plural. They are used with the plural possessive *their.* Study these examples.

both   many   few   several

Both of the swimmers timed *their* sprints.
Few of the passengers left *their* seats.
Many of our neighbors grow *their* own vegetables.
Several of the racers overturned *their* cars.

A few indefinite pronouns can be either singular or plural, depending on their meaning in a sentence. Read these examples:

> all   none   some
>
> *All* of the water has chemicals in *it*.
> *All* of the drivers loaded *their* trucks.
>
> *None* of the medicine has lost *its* strength.
> *None* of these comedians use *their* own material.
>
> *Some* of the fire burned *itself* out.
> *Some* of the workers took *their* breaks.

Exercise A   Number your paper from 1 to 10. For each sentence write the indefinite pronoun.

1. None of us caught a fish.
2. Did someone call me?
3. Anyone can win the sweepstakes.
4. What is everybody waiting for?
5. Only one of the headlights works.
6. Several of the players signed contracts.
7. Many of the starting players fouled out.
8. Kelly made both of the free throws.
9. Why is everyone cheering?
10. Brady got all of the rebounds.

Exercise B   Choose the right pronoun from the two given.

1. One of the actresses missed (her, their) cue.
2. Many of the stores have lowered (its, their) prices.
3. Somebody left (his or her, their) checkbook here.
4. Everyone listed (his or her, their) address.
5. If anyone calls, tell (him or her, them) I'll be right back.
6. Neither of our wrestlers pinned (his, their) opponent.
7. Some of the runners wore out (her, their) shoes.

8. Each of these sundaes has (its, their) own special sauce.

9. All of the passengers in the boat wore (his or her, their) lifejackets.

10. Did anybody go out of (his or her, their) way to help?

Exercise C Number your paper from 1-10. For each sentence write the indefinite pronoun and the correct word from the two in parentheses.

1. Nobody has received (his or her, their) tickets yet.
2. Has everyone checked (his, their) equipment?
3. Few of the actors needed (his or her, their) scripts.
4. Neither of the girls remembered (her, their) music.
5. One of the trees lost all of (its, their) leaves.
6. All of the candidates approved (his or her, their) staffs.
7. Each of the horses had (its, their) mane braided.
8. Some of the artists displayed (his or her, their) work.
9. Many of the winners wrote (his or her, their) own speeches.
10. Some of the food has lost (its, their) flavor.

Part 9 Special Problems with Pronouns

Contractions and Possessive Pronouns

Certain contractions are sometimes confused with possessive pronouns.

Contractions are formed by joining two words and omitting one or more letters. An apostrophe shows where letters are left out.

it's = it + is   they're = they + are
you're = you + are   who's = who + is

The above contractions are sometimes confused with the possessive pronouns *its, your, their,* and *whose.* The words sound alike but are spelled differently.

Incorrect: The plant lost it's leaves.
Correct: The plant lost its leaves.

If you can't decide which word is correct, substitute the words the contraction stands for. If the sentence sounds right, then the contraction is correct.

Incorrect: Their enjoying they're trip.
Correct: They're (They are) enjoying their trip.

Exercise A Choose the right word from the two in parentheses.

1. The movers parked (their, they're) van in front of the building.
2. (Your, You're) expecting a call, aren't you?
3. Wax gives the car (its, it's) shine.
4. (Whose, Who's) signature is this?
5. Is that (your, you're) camera?
6. (Their, They're) trapped in the mine.
7. (Whose, Who's) taking the ball out of bounds?
8. (Its, It's) half time now.
9. (Whose, Who's) the woman with the microphone?
10. (Your, You're) friends are waiting at the station.

Exercise B Write the words each contraction below stands for.

1. They're appealing to a higher court.
2. I'd like to ride the rapids.
3. Soon we'll be on our own.
4. You're spilling your tea!
5. She's ready for a change.
6. They've scouted all the teams.
7. Who's offered you a job?

8. What's wrong with the picture tube?
9. I'm playing third base.
10. We'd like longer weekends.

Who and Whom

Many people have problems with the pronouns *who* and *whom*.

Who sounds natural in most questions. Use *who* as the subject of a sentence.

> *Who* tuned the piano?   *Who* is there?

Whom is harder to get used to. *Whom* is used as an object.

> *Whom* did the Regans adopt?
> (direct object of the verb *did adopt*)
>
> To *whom* are tax forms sent?
> (object of the preposition *to*)

Exercise A Choose the right pronoun from the two given in parentheses.

1. (Who, Whom) can predict weather?
2. (Who, Whom) insulted your friend?
3. (Who, Whom) did you tape record?
4. (Who, Whom) were you watching on TV?
5. (Who, Whom) is the sportscaster?
6. (Who, Whom) towed your car?
7. (Who, Whom) runs the drill press?
8. (Who, Whom) will you stay with?
9. (Who, Whom) do these running shorts belong to?
10. (Who, Whom) did you visit in St. Louis?

Exercise B Follow the directions for Exercise A.

1. (Who, Whom) works the switchboard?
2. (Who, Whom) did the lifeguard rescue?

3. (Who, Whom) did the noise awaken?
4. To (who, whom) is the telegram addressed?
5. (Who, Whom) did your mother hire?
6. (Who, Whom) showered in the locker room?
7. For (who, whom) was the school named?
8. (Who, Whom) polluted the canal?
9. (Who, Whom) do you compete with?
10. (Who, Whom) needs a yearly physical exam?

We and *Us* with Nouns

The pronouns *we* and *us* are often used with nouns, as in the phrases *we boys* or *us students*. Sometimes such phrases cause problems.

To decide whether to use *we* or *us*, omit the noun. Say the sentence with *we* and then with *us*. You will then probably be able to choose the correct pronoun.

Problem: (We, Us) linemen do the blocking.
Correct: We do the blocking.
Correct: We linemen do the blocking.

Problem: Nothing stops (we, us) campers.
Correct: Nothing stops us.
Correct: Nothing stops us campers.

Them and *Those*

Them and *those* are sometimes confused. To use the words correctly, remember that *them* is always a pronoun. It takes the place of a noun.

A search party found *them*. (In this sentence, *them* is used as the direct object.)

Them is never used to tell about or describe a noun. *Those* should be used.

320

Incorrect: Have you ever worn them clogs?
Correct: Have you ever worn those clogs?

Exercise A Choose the correct pronoun from the two given in parentheses.

1. (We, Us) girls hooked up the antenna.
2. (We, Us) officers have special quarters.
3. Did you see (them, those) state troopers?
4. Can you take advantage of (them, those) new airfares?
5. (Them, Those) greeting cards are funny.
6. The flag signaled (we, us) drivers.
7. (We, Us) athletes are often tense before games.
8. Micki King tried one of (them, those) back dives.
9. When will (we, us) Americans host the Olympics?
10. The ball nearly hit (we, us) spectators.

Exercise B Follow the directions for Exercise A.

1. The Army Reserve wants to talk to (we, us) students.
2. Will (them, those) additives improve gas mileage?
3. (We, Us) boys pushed the stalled car.
4. Can any of (them, those) computers translate languages?
5. Braille is used by (we, us) blind people.
6. There is a lounge for (we, us) employees.
7. Did you eat all of (them, those) strawberries?
8. Yesterday (we, us) campers hiked up a mountain.
9. The hospital treats (we, us) patients well.
10. (Them, Those) stakes hold the tent in place.

Additional Exercises

Using Pronouns

A. Find the pronouns. Number your paper from 1 to 10. Write the pronouns you find in each of the following sentences.

1. We sped down the toboggan slide.
2. She held her breath for seventy seconds.
3. I sent him a get-well card.
4. He waters his plants once a week.
5. Ms. Duncan gave them an unusual project.
6. They turned off their TV for a month.
7. The dog retrieved your Frisbee from the lake, didn't he?
8. My uncle restored a Victorian house.
9. Jeff saved her a seat next to him.
10. Do you have an allergy?

B. Use subject, object, and possessive forms of pronouns. Choose the correct pronoun from the two given in parentheses.

1. (She, Her) took the photos during the ceremony.
2. The Yankees beat (they, them) in the World Series.
3. The coach asked Suzanne and (I, me) for help.
4. Todd and (she, her) work in a sporting goods shop.
5. A chunk of plaster landed on (him, his) head.
6. Greg and (he, him) learned a new dive.
7. It was (he, him) who suggested the place.
8. Alec took Nancy and (I, me) to a roller derby.
9. Did Jill and (she, her) take archery in gym class?
10. Bill showed (I, me) his winning raffle ticket.

C. Find the antecedents of pronouns. Write each pronoun and its antecedent.

1. Cheryl rode her horse into its stall.
2. Jon keeps his bike in the rack outside of school.
3. Alison and Kate had their lunch at the lake in Thornwood Park.
4. The sky divers released their parachutes.
5. Laura had just hung up the phone when it rang again.
6. Yolanda is usually a guard, but today she is playing forward.
7. Nicole and Tom are good friends, but sometimes they argue over nothing.
8. Mike, have you and Lee finished your tennis game?
9. The band got new uniforms. They are red and blue.
10. Will you sing the solo, Stephanie?

D. Recognize different kinds of pronouns. Number your paper from 1 to 10. Write the pronouns in these sentences. After each pronoun, write *Demonstrative, Interrogative,* or *Indefinite* to tell what kind it is.

1. A computer could do this in a second.
2. Which of the cars finished the race?
3. This is Uncle Dan's customized van.
4. Are these Sue's mittens?
5. Anyone can learn to play a recorder.
6. Whom did the President call?
7. What was the rumor?
8. Nora had never heard that before.
9. Everyone filed into the stadium.
10. Many of the witnesses refused to answer.

E. Use indefinite pronouns correctly. Choose the correct pronoun from the two given.

1. Neither of the runners slowed (her, their) pace.
2. Only one of the gymnasts has done (his, their) routine.
3. All of the teams brought (its, their) mascots to the state meet.
4. Both of the boys wore (his, their) hockey skates to the ice rink.
5. All of the money is in (its, their) proper place.
6. Most of the stores advertise (its, their) sales a week ahead of time.
7. Some of the candidates gave (his or her, their) speeches.
8. Has anyone had (his or her, their) fortune told?
9. Some of the players have (her, their) own warm-up exercises.
10. Each of the parking lots has (its, their) own rates.

F. Solve special pronoun problems. Choose the correct word from the two in parentheses.

1. Have (your, you're) friends been waiting all this time?
2. (Who, Whom) did you consult?
3. The president thanked (we, us) committee members.
4. (Who, Whom) brought the FM radio?
5. (Who, Whom) did she sign her new recording contract with?
6. (We, Us) city dwellers are used to noise.
7. (Whose, Who's) starring in that new comedy?
8. Have you tried one of (them, those) egg rolls?
9. The guide was very polite to (we, us) tourists.
10. The bikers loaded (their, they're) backpacks with food for the trip.

Section 5

Using
Verbs

The verb is the key part of a sentence. It brings a sentence to life. Without a verb, there would be no sentence.

You have already learned to recognize this special class of word. In this section you will find out more about verbs and how they are used.

Part 1   What Is a Verb?

A verb tells of an action or a state of being.

Action Verbs

One kind of verb may indicate action, even if the action is unseen.

Sarah *smiled*.   Bill *expects* a raise.
A plane *landed*.   Sue *has* many new friends.

An **action verb** tells that something is happening, has happened, or will happen.

Linking Verbs

Some verbs simply tell that something exists. Such verbs express a state of being rather than action.

The election *is* Tuesday.   Spencer *was* ready.
Rita *seems* happy.   The cake *tastes* moist.

These verbs are called **linking verbs.** They link the subject with some other word or words in the sentence.

Here are the most common linking verbs:

be (am, are, is, was,	look	smell	seem
were, been, being)	appear	taste	sound
become	feel	grow	

Some linking verbs can also be used as action verbs.

Linking Verb	Action Verb
The T-shirt *looked* dirty.	Kim *looked* at the painting.
The meal *grew* cold.	The gardener *grew* zinnias.

When you look at the verb in a sentence, see how it is used. Decide whether it expresses action or simply links the subject with a word in the predicate.

Transitive and Intransitive Verbs

In many sentences an action verb expresses an idea by itself. In other sentences a direct object completes the action of the verb. The direct object, as you have learned, answers *whom* or *what* about the verb.

Verbs that have direct objects are **transitive verbs.**

> Dave *met* the mayor.
> > (The direct object *mayor* completes the meaning of the verb *met*.)
>
> The officer *wore* several medals.
> > (The direct object *medals* completes the meaning of the verb *wore*.)

Verbs that do not have direct objects are another kind of verb. They are called **intransitive verbs.**

> The winners *rejoiced*.
> > (The verb *rejoiced* has no direct object.)
>
> Steve *rested* under a tree.
> > (The verb *rested* has no object.)

Some action verbs are always transitive or always intransitive. Other verbs change. The same verb may be transitive in one sentence and intransitive in another. Compare these examples.

Transitive Verb	Intransitive Verb
The artist *sketched* the model.	The artist *sketched* by the sea.
The girls *swam* a mile.	The girls *swam* in the pool.
Keith *drove* a taxi.	Keith *drove* slowly.

Exercise A Write the verb in each sentence. After each verb write *Action* or *Linking* to show what kind it is.

1. The Congress cut taxes.
2. Our nation's supply of oil is low.

3. The Senator campaigned for reelection.
4. That old building is dangerous.
5. Diane programmed the computer.
6. The flight seemed very smooth.
7. The ranch was high in the Rockies.
8. Water became scarce during the summer.
9. We saw an old-fashioned rodeo.
10. The company drills for oil.

Exercise B Follow the directions for Exercise A.

1. The state government operates several large parks.
2. A hurricane swept the island.
3. Everyone ran for shelter.
4. Many people were homeless.
5. This armchair feels comfortable.
6. Do those big cars guzzle gas?
7. The Omni is a front-wheel drive car.
8. Meyers was an All-American from U.C.L.A.
9. Reporters uncovered a scandal.
10. A special task force studied crime.

Exercise C Write the action verb in each sentence. After it write *Transitive* or *Intransitive* to show what kind it is.

1. Those trucks have diesel engines.
2. Each fall, many new TV series begin.
3. The networks show recent movies.
4. The spacecraft explored Saturn.
5. Joggers ran by the lake.
6. The train from Washington finally arrived.
7. Tom often cooks dinner.
8. During the storm the airport closed.
9. Sarah reads *Time* and *Newsweek*.
10. All night, the stereo blared.

Part 2 The Parts of a Verb

Many verbs are made up of a **main verb** plus one or more **helping verbs.**

The most common helping verbs are forms of *be, have,* and *do.* They may also be used as main verbs. Here are their forms:

> be—am, is, are, was, were, been, be
> have—has, have, had
> do—does, do, did

Used as Main Verb	Used as Helping Verb
I *was* lucky.	I *was eating* lunch.
Jill *has* a cold.	Jill *has finished* her report.
We *did* our chores.	We *did like* the movie.

Here are other frequently used helping verbs:

can	will	shall	may	must
could	would	should	might	

Helping verbs combine with the main verb to become parts of the verb.

Helping Verb(s) + Main Verb = Verb		
will	stay	will stay
had	stayed	had stayed
should have	stayed	should have stayed
must	join	must join
has	joined	has joined

Sometimes the parts of the verb are separated. The words that come between them are not part of the verb. Study these examples.

> Chinese food *has* always *seemed* tasty.
> The team *was* barely *paying* attention.
> When *will* the President *hold* a press conference?
> *Did* the press secretary *speak*?

Exercise A Make two columns. Label them *Helping Verb* and *Main Verb*. Find the parts of the verb in each sentence. Write them in the proper columns.

1. The glider was soaring.
2. A new snack shop has opened.
3. This train does not stop at Webster Avenue.
4. A computer will prepare the payroll.
5. Has the movie been banned?
6. No fuel should be wasted.
7. Do you use sugar in your coffee?
8. No one had ever climbed that mountain.
9. Construction workers on a job site must often wear hardhats.
10. A smoke alarm could have alerted us to the fire.

Exercise B Follow the directions for Exercise A.

1. The ice rink has been closed for repairs.
2. Greg is expecting a call.
3. The guard had warned us several times.
4. Will the Buckeyes receive the kickoff?
5. Jonas should have tried these barbells.
6. Did Melissa run for office?
7. The temperature has already climbed to 98°.
8. Have you ever worked in a boiler room?
9. Diaz will surely pitch in Thursday's game.
10. The flight attendants must often reassure passengers.

Part 3 Verb Tenses

Verbs indicate time. They tell when an action or state of being occurs. Verbs can indicate past time, present time, or future time by changing form.

These changes in form to show time are called **tenses.** The changes are usually made these ways:

1. Change in spelling
   ran→run   try→tried   close→closed
2. Use of helping verbs
   had eaten   will survive   has fallen

This list shows examples of the six main tenses for the verbs *paint* and *watch.*

Present Tense	I paint.	She watches.
Past Tense	I painted.	She watched.
Future Tense	I will paint.	She will watch.
Present Perfect Tense	I have painted.	She has watched.
Past Perfect Tense	I had painted.	She had watched.
Future Perfect Tense	I will have painted.	She will have watched.

Simple Tenses

The **present tense** shows time in the present. The present tense form is usually the same as the name of the verb. For verbs used with most singular subjects, an -s is added to the verb.

I *know.*   Cathy *knows.*   My mother *knows.*

The **past tense** shows past time. Most verbs form the past tense by adding -d or -ed.

Ben raced.   Yvonne called.   I laughed.

Some verbs form the past tense in different ways.

They rode.   Sue went to the game.   Adam swam.

The **future tense** shows time in the future. In this tense, use *shall* or *will* with the verb.

Keith will start.   Donna will guess.   I shall return.

The three tenses just described are called the **simple tenses.**

Perfect Tenses

The **perfect tenses** are used when we have to speak of two different times, one earlier than the other. The perfect tenses are formed by using the helping verbs *has*, *have*, and *had*.

The **present perfect tense** tells of an action or state of being in some indefinite time before the present. The helping verb *has* or *have* is used.

> Dean *has practiced* often.   Maggie *has chosen.*
> They *have arrived.*

The **past perfect tense** tells of a time before another time in the past. The helping verb *had* is used.

> They *had been* lonely until we *came.*
> Marie *had waited* for the bus for hours, but it never *arrived.*
> We *had* just *gone* into the house when the storm *hit.*

The **future perfect tense** tells of a time in the future *before* some other time in the future.

> By this time tomorrow, *you will have met* the Governor.
> When the hike is over, *we will have walked* ten miles.

Exercise A Find the verbs in the following sentences. Tell the tense of each.

1. Keith spotted a dog in the alley.
2. A self-serve gas station has opened nearby.
3. The Packers have accepted the penalty.
4. Bernstein kicks most of the field goals.
5. An overtime will decide the game.
6. Each suspect will take a lie detector test.
7. Helmets protect motorcycle riders.
8. By 1990 the birth rate will have risen.
9. Police searched the hideout.
10. The mobsters had already fled.

Exercise B Write a sentence for each of the verbs below. Use the tense indicated.

1. judge (past)
2. try (present perfect)
3. notice (past perfect)
4. live (present)
5. pile (past)
6. drive (present)
7. show (future)
8. prepare (future perfect)
9. work (present perfect)
10. jump (future)

Part 4 The Principal Parts of a Verb

The **principal parts** of a verb are its basic forms. By combining these forms with helping verbs, you can make all tenses.

The principal parts of a verb are the **present tense**, the **past tense**, and the **past participle.** They are usually written in that order.

Most verbs form the past tense and past participle by adding -d or -ed to present form. These verbs are called **regular verbs.** They are called regular verbs because they form the past tense and past participle in regular ways.

Present	Past	Past Participle
trust	trusted	(have) trusted
want	wanted	(have) wanted
move	moved	(have) moved
change	changed	(have) changed

Some regular verbs change their spelling when the -d or -ed is added. Study the examples on the next page.

Present	Past	Past Participle
try	tried	(have) tried
trot	trotted	(have) trotted
say	said	(have) said
slip	slipped	(have) slipped

The past participle is used for perfect tenses. It must have a helping verb.

They have changed.	We had tried.
Mark must have known.	Beth has slipped.

Exercise Make three columns on your paper. Label them *Present, Past,* and *Past Participle.* List the principal parts of these verbs in the proper columns.

1. cook	6. copy	11. follow
2. marry	7. happen	12. open
3. seem	8. lift	13. claim
4. belong	9. act	14. trip
5. pull	10. toss	15. drag

Part 5 Irregular Verbs

You have learned the principal parts for regular verbs. Many verbs, though, do not follow the regular pattern. They do not add -*d* or -*ed* to form the past tense and past participle. They are called irregular verbs. Here are some examples:

Present	Past	Past Participle
throw	threw	(have) thrown
feel	felt	(have) felt
spring	sprang	(have) sprung
tell	told	(have) told
cut	cut	(have) cut

You will notice that some of the verbs have one or two different forms. Others have three different forms.

If you do not know the principal parts of a verb, look up the verb in a dictionary. If no parts are listed, the verb is regular. If the verb is irregular, the dictionary will list the irregular forms. It will give two forms if both the past and past participle are the same, as in *catch, caught,* for example. It will give three forms if all principal parts are different, as in *ring, rang, rung,* for example.

Using Irregular Verbs

There are two ways to be sure of the forms of irregular verbs. One way is to look up the verbs in the dictionary. The other way is to learn the principal parts of commonly used irregular verbs.

Once you know the principal parts, keep these ideas in mind. Use the past participle with *have* and *be* helping verbs. The past participle is used for present perfect and past perfect tenses. The past form is not used with helping verbs.

The principal parts of irregular verbs can be confusing. They may seem simpler if you learn the following five patterns.

Group 1 Some irregular verbs keep the same form for all three principal parts. These are easy to remember.

Present	Past	Past Participle
burst	burst	(have) burst
cost	cost	(have) cost
cut	cut	(have) cut
let	let	(have) let
put	put	(have) put
set	set	(have) set

Here are some sentences using verbs from this group:

Some license plates *cost* twenty dollars. (present)
I *put* my signature on the contract. (past)
Matt *has set* up the scenery. (past participle)

Group 2 Another group of irregular verbs changes form only once. The past and the past participle are the same.

Present	Past	Past Participle
bring	brought	(have) brought
catch	caught	(have) caught
lead	led	(have) led
lend	lent	(have) lent
lose	lost	(have) lost
say	said	(have) said
sit	sat	(have) sat

These sentences use irregular verbs from Group 2:

I *sit* in the lifeguard station. (present)
Tyrone *led* the league in R.B.I.'s. (past)
Garrett and Lynn *have caught* three salmon. (past participle)

Exercise A Choose the correct form of the verb.

1. The convention (brang, brought) out-of-towners to Chicago.
2. The infielder has (catched, caught) the foul ball.
3. Rent (costed, cost) half of Tim's pay.
4. Estelle (put, putted) a tape deck in the car.
5. Lauren (lent, lended) me a special wrench.
6. The stage crew (set, setted) up the props and scenery.
7. No one has ever (sayed, said) that before.
8. A hose in the engine (burst, bursted).
9. Duncan has (sat, sitted) on the bench all season.
10. Kris (leaded, led) in scoring for the Wildcats.

Exercise B Follow the directions for Exercise A.

1. All the workers (lost, losed) track of the time.
2. The reward was (setted, set) at $1,000.
3. Suddenly, Jane (burst, bursted) into the room.
4. Jim has (put, putted) a coffeepot on the camping stove.

5. Deena (caught, catched) the flu.
6. The fishermen have not (brang, brought) enough bait.
7. In 1978 gas (cost, costed) less than a dollar a gallon.
8. The soldiers (sat, sitted) in their barracks.
9. Porter (led, leaded) in the primary election.
10. The lawyer has (said, sayed) little about the case.

Group 3 Verbs in this group add -n or -en to the past tense to form the past participle.

Present	Past	Past Participle
break	broke	(have) broken
choose	chose	(have) chosen
freeze	froze	(have) frozen
speak	spoke	(have) spoken
steal	stole	(have) stolen
wear	wore	(have) worn

Here are three sentences using Group 3 verbs:

Speak into the microphone. (present)
Everyone *wore* strange costumes. (past)
Joan and Bill *have chosen* their teams. (past participle)

Exercise A Choose the correct form of the verb from the two forms given.

1. Ms. Gomez has (chose, chosen) a blue interior for her car.
2. The group has (spoke, spoken) of a plot.
3. Money had been (stole, stolen) from the cash register.
4. The rock group (wore, worn) gold and glitter.
5. Evans (broke, broken) a land-speed record.
6. Tires squealed as the cars (tore, torn) around the track.
7. The side of beef was (froze, frozen).
8. A rock (broke, broken) the display window.
9. The country has (chose, chosen) a new leader.
10. The astronauts (wore, worn) special suits.

Exercise B   Follow the directions for Exercise A.

1. A pickpocket (stole, stolen) Ken's wallet.
2. The sign read, "Spanish is (spoke, spoken) here."
3. The sailors (wore, worn) their dress uniforms.
4. The lawyers have (chose, chosen) a jury.
5. Rain (froze, frozen) on the windshield.
6. Lori accidentally (tore, torn) up a dollar bill.
7. The relay team has (broke, broken) a world record.
8. The mourners have (wore, worn) black clothing.
9. Some top-secret papers have been (stole, stolen).
10. The social worker (spoke, spoken) about conflicts.

Group 4   The irregular verbs in this group change their final vowels. The vowel changes from *i* in the present tense to *a* in the past tense and *u* in the past participle.

Present	Past	Past Participle
begin	began	(have) begun
drink	drank	(have) drunk
ring	rang	(have) rung
sing	sang	(have) sung
swim	swam	(have) swum

Here are examples of irregular verbs from Group 4:

I *sing* off-key. (present)
The chimes *rang* softly. (past)
The police *have begun* a crackdown. (past participle)

Exercise A   Choose the correct verb form.

1. Ellie (began, begun) a new job.
2. Someone must have (drank, drunk) my Pepsi.
3. Bill (rang, rung) for the flight attendant.
4. Donna Summer (sang, sung) "Last Dance."
5. The telephone had (rang, rung) all day.
6. The church choir (sang, sung) hymns.

7. Construction work on the highway has (began, begun).
8. The hikers (drank, drunk) from canteens.
9. The hospital has (began, begun) a blood drive.
10. Stevie Wonder (sang, sung) his latest hit single.

Exercise B   Follow the directions for Exercise A.

1. The loud noises (rang, rung) in my ears.
2. Leslie (swam, swum) in the icy water.
3. The team (began, begun) to rally in the fourth quarter.
4. The boys have (drank, drunk) all of the coffee.
5. Tropical fish (swam, swum) in the huge tank.
6. The candidates have (began, begun) to campaign.
7. After the wedding, bells (rang, rung).
8. Some soups may be (drank, drunk).
9. Many operas are (sang, sung) in Italian.
10. Diana Nyad has (swam, swum) great distances.

Group 5   For some Irregular verbs the past participle is formed from the present tense. The past participle looks more like the present tense than the past tense.

Present	Past	Past Participle
come	came	(have) come
do	did	(have) done
eat	ate	(have) eaten
fall	fell	(have) fallen
give	gave	(have) given
go	went	(have) gone
grow	grew	(have) grown
know	knew	(have) known
ride	rode	(have) ridden
run	ran	(have) run
see	saw	(have) seen
take	took	(have) taken
throw	threw	(have) thrown
write	wrote	(have) written

Here are sentences using Group 5 verbs:

I *eat* only vegetables and grains. (present)
Marcy *knew* a shortcut to the station. (past)
Suzanne *has taken* inventory of the stock. (past participle)

Exercise A   Choose the correct verb form from the two given.

1. The jogger (ran, run) along a lakefront path.
2. Cary (threw, thrown) a terrific party.
3. A passenger has (fell, fallen) overboard!
4. Vera (ate, eaten) raw fish at a Japanese restaurant.
5. Ken (grew, grown) a beard and a moustache.
6. Charles Kuralt has (went, gone) to all corners of America.
7. Jory had (saw, seen) hundreds of horror films.
8. Chicago is (knew, known) for its pizza.
9. Sterling and Darrell (took, taken) a Greyhound bus to Arizona.
10. Samantha has (rode, ridden) a bike across the state.

Exercise B   Follow the directions for Exercise A.

1. The dictator has (fell, fallen) from power.
2. The job had (came, come) along just in time.
3. A gymnast (did, done) handsprings across the mat.
4. George Gallup has (took, taken) polls of public opinion.
5. Dennis (saw, seen) a strange object flying in the night sky.
6. Has everyone (gave, given) up on this project?
7. Anne (went, gone) to City Hall to see the mayor.
8. The candidate has (ran, run) her campaign honestly.
9. *The Outsiders* was (wrote, written) by S. E. Hinton.
10. The escaped prisoners were last (saw, seen) in an Oklahoma town.

Part 6 Active and Passive Verbs

You have seen how the tenses of verbs indicate *time*. There is another way that verbs help you say exactly what you mean.

Suppose that a window has been broken. If you know who broke it, you can say:

My brother broke the window yesterday.

However, suppose you don't know who broke the window. Then you might say:

The window was broken yesterday.

In the first sentence, the subject tells who performed the action. When the subject performs the action, the verb is said to be **active.**

In the second sentence, the subject tells what received the action. When the subject tells the receiver or the result of the action, the verb is said to be **passive.** The word *passive* means "acted upon."

Forming the Passive

The passive form of the verb is made with the past participle. A form of *be* is the helping verb.

Active	Passive
Meg *has finished* the project.	The project *has been finished* by Meg.
Chris *has shown* the slides.	The slides *have been shown* by Chris.
The store *will add* the tax.	The tax *will be added* by the store.
Max *washed* the floor.	The floor *was washed* by Max.

Find the direct objects in the sentences in the first column above. In the sentences in the second column, the direct

341

objects have become the subjects. Only verbs that have objects (transitive verbs) can be changed from active to passive.

A verb is active when its subject performs the action stated by the verb.

A verb is passive when its subject names the receiver or result of the action stated by the verb.

Exercise A Write the verb in each sentence. After each, write *Active* or *Passive* to tell what kind it is.

1. One of the boys baked bread.
2. The weather service predicted a record snowfall.
3. A citizens' group patrolled the streets.
4. The local merchants held a street fair.
5. Ms. O'Brien read the class an interesting article.
6. A meeting had been planned by the workers' union.
7. Several sites were considered by the builder.
8. The Potter's Wheel also sells ceramic supplies.
9. The S.W.A.T. unit was called to the scene.
10. Liz's plans were affected by inflation.

Exercise B Change the verbs in the following sentences from passive to active. Rewrite the sentences.

1. The rug was cleaned by Mr. Harvey.
2. The scores are given by the sportscaster.
3. A new comedian was introduced by Johnny Carson.
4. Paintings are sold to the museum by the Art Club.
5. The trophy had been won by our team once before.
6. Five buildings were destroyed by the fire.
7. Mr. Walters is known by everybody.
8. The error has been found by Bret.
9. The judge's decision will be appealed by the lawyer.
10. Letters had been sent to the President by our class.

Additional Exercises

Using Verbs

A. Identify action and linking verbs. Write the verb in each sentence. After it, write *Action* or *Linking* to tell what kind it is.

1. Mike painted a mural for the lounge.
2. The sky appeared pale yellow.
3. The lineman ran out for the pass.
4. That photo of the Grand Canyon is beautiful.
5. Some sports are more dangerous than others.
6. As a library aide, Susan shelves books.
7. Ms. Wright seems happy in her new job.
8. Was Amy Russell the pinch hitter?
9. Leslie rested her head on her arms.
10. In the lobby, I looked for a phone booth.

B. Recognize transitive and intransitive verbs. Write the verb in each sentence. After it, write *Transitive* or *Intransitive* to show what kind it is.

1. Nicole pounded the last nail into the bookcase.
2. Some company employees organized a volleyball team.
3. The band practices every day after school.
4. Keith's Frisbee landed on the telephone wires.
5. The timekeeper reset the clock for the next race.
6. Lee calls Jessica almost every night.
7. Students gather after school in the courtyard.
8. Doug tightened the brakes on his bike.
9. Which candidate won in that primary election?
10. The Mosses traveled in New Mexico and Arizona.

C. Recognize verbs. Find the parts of the verb in each sentence. Put them in two columns labeled *Helping Verb* and *Main Verb*.

1. Everyone was crowding against the door.
2. Those books must be rare volumes.
3. My jeans have finally faded.
4. The troop leader wouldn't give Amy the compass or his canteen.
5. We will organize a softball league.
6. Bart has often lent Rick his bike.
7. The passenger train will be passing through the tunnel in a few minutes.
8. These rapids seem dangerous.
9. The helicopter was not flying smoothly in those high winds.
10. Nancy should be practicing for the play.

D. Identify verb tenses. Write the verb in each sentence. Tell its tense: present, past, future, present perfect, past perfect, or future perfect tense.

1. Lana is our camp counselor.
2. The actors' makeup will look strange.
3. Tony has spotted the Big Dipper.
4. We climbed into the rowboat.
5. Are mouthpieces a necessary part of the football uniform?
6. The countdown will soon begin.
7. Poisonous gases from that chemical factory had leaked into the air.
8. By tomorrow the fog will have cleared.
9. The divers have thoroughly searched the river.
10. Mary rides her bicycle to school each day.

E. Use irregular verbs correctly. Write the correct verb form from the two given.

1. Jon had (put, putted) the maps into the car.
2. Medical care has never (costed, cost) more.
3. The raft (brang, brought) us to safety.
4. The Celtics (lost, losed) by one point.
5. Someone (tore, torn) down the notice.
6. Has anyone (spoke, spoken) to the career counselor?
7. Stephanie has (broke, broken) her glasses.
8. The actress had (began, begun) with only bit parts.
9. The hikers (drank, drunk) from the cool brook.
10. Eliza (saw, seen) the filming of a movie.

F. Recognize active and passive verb forms. Find the verb in each of the following sentences. Then tell whether it is *active* or *passive*.

1. The Coast Guard patrols the shore.
2. Lyle was removed from the game.
3. The Bears received a penalty.
4. Residents have been informed of the danger.
5. The flight to Miami has been canceled.
6. The cast is holding its dress rehearsal.
7. Katie has searched the classroom carefully.
8. Lunch was provided by the camp.
9. The lost boy was found late last night.
10. The pilot should have informed the crew.

Section 6

Using Modifiers

Try to tell someone about your best friend, your favorite song, or your new shirt. You'll need more than nouns, verbs, and pronouns.

Nouns and pronouns name. Verbs show action or state-of-being. You also need words, though, to describe the sights, sounds, and smells around you.

Look at these two sentences:

> Water seeped into the room.
> *Brown, murky* water seeped into the room.

The **modifiers** make the difference. **Modifiers are words that modify, or change, other words.**

Besides describing, modifiers can also help you explain and express feeling. Read these two sentences.

Rod Stewart sings.
Rod Stewart *always* sings *powerfully*.

Without modifiers, your writing would seem incomplete and dull. Modifiers help you to express precise ideas. In this section you will learn to identify and use modifiers.

Part 1   Using Adjectives

One kind of modifier is an **adjective.**

An adjective is a word that modifies a noun or pronoun.

Adjectives can tell three different kinds of things about nouns or pronouns.

Which one or ones?

this step, *that* hall, *these* bills, *those* glasses

What kind?

yellow line, *shiny* boots, *happy* mood, *ugly* alley

How many or how much?

three months, *several* visitors, *less* pain, *little* snow

Proper Adjectives

One special kind of adjective is the proper adjective.

A **proper adjective** is formed from a proper noun. Therefore, it refers to a specific person, place, or thing. This kind of adjective is always capitalized. Here are some examples:

Italian food	an Olympic medal
a British accent	a Pacific island
a Japanese car	an American outpost

Predicate Adjectives

Another special kind of adjective is the predicate adjective. Most adjectives come before the words they modify:

The cars collided with a *dull, solid* thud.
(*Dull* and *solid* modify *thud*.)

The predicate adjective, though, comes after the word it modifies. A **predicate adjective** follows a linking verb and modifies the subject of the sentence.

Nothing seemed *clear* anymore.
(*Clear* modifies the subject, *nothing*.)

The fight was *brutal*.
(*Brutal* modifies the subject, *fight*.)

As you can see, *clear* and *brutal* are predicate adjectives. They follow linking verbs, *seemed* and *was*. Each one also modifies the subject of the sentence.

Articles

The adjectives *a*, *an*, and *the* are called **articles.**
The is the **definite article.** It points out a specific person, place, or thing.

Keep *the* ball in play. (a particular ball)

A and *an* are **indefinite articles.**

Did you find *a* ball? (any ball)
I would like *an* ice-cream cone. (any ice-cream cone)

Notice that *a* is used before a consonant sound (*a* rest, *a* school, *a* trip). *An* is used before a vowel sound (*an* elbow, *an* oboe, *an* urge).

Pay attention to the sound, not the spelling. We say *a* helper, but *an* honor, for instance.

Diagraming Adjectives

In a sentence diagram, an adjective appears below the word it modifies. It is placed on a slanted line.

This team has a quick backfield.

Predicate adjectives are diagramed differently. Like predicate nouns and pronouns, they are placed on the main line. A slanted line goes between the verb and the predicate adjective.

These opponents are tough.

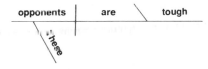

A compound predicate adjective appears on a split line.

The stereo sounds rich and full.

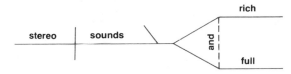

Exercise A   Number your paper from 1 to 10. Write the adjectives in each sentence. After each adjective, write the word it modifies. Do not include articles.

1. The tiny shop sells old books, unusual games, and strange costumes.

2. Two small jeeps rumbled down the steep road to the wide beach.

3. Ellie spilled purple paint on that new yellow shirt.

4. Chuck wears flashy clothes and drives a red Camaro.

5. Several foreign leaders had a private meeting with the President.

6. Many experts stress the need for solar heat.

7. Ten people rode in the back of the dirty, rusty truck.

8. Most workers at that site wear yellow helmets.

9. Janice drank more water with the salty fish and tangy peppers.

10. In a sudden surge, the red car inched in front of the other twelve cars.

Exercise B Number your paper from 1 to 10. Write the predicate adjectives in these sentences.

1. The new President seems forceful.

2. Small cars are becoming popular.

3. The team feels confident about the game.

4. The jury felt sure of the decision.

5. The gash looked deep.

6. Safety precautions are necessary.

7. My supervisor is young and bright.

8. Nearly half of the work force is female.

9. How many people are happy with their work?

10. The unemployment rate is high.

Part 2   Adjectives in Comparisons

You often learn about new things by making comparisons. You compare new things with things you already know. You might describe a restaurant's food, for example, as "*better* than homemade food." Or you might explain that cream is *lighter* than milk.

Adjectives help you to make such comparisons.

The Comparative

Adjectives have special forms for making comparisons. When you compare one person or thing with another, you use the **comparative** form of an adjective. Here are some examples:

> Evans is a *stronger* pitcher than Richardson.
> This quilt looks *prettier* than that one.
> Loretta is *more patient* than I am.

The comparative is made in two ways:

1. Add *-er* to short adjectives like *big* and *bright*.

> wide + er = wider   young + er = younger
> fancy + er = fancier   dark + er = darker

Notice that the spelling of some adjectives changes in the comparative form.

2. Use *more* for longer adjectives like *unusual*.

> more energetic   more sensitive

Most adjectives ending in *-ful* or *-ous* form the comparative with *more*.

> more powerful   more courageous

The Superlative

When you compare a person or thing with all others in its class, you use the **superlative** form of the adjective. In addition, use the superlative when you compare a person or thing with two or more others.

Here are some examples:

> Kevin has the *smallest* part in the play.
> Carmen is the *friendliest* person I know.
> Football is the *most enjoyable* sport on TV.

The superlative form of an adjective is made by adding -*est* or by using *most*. If an adjective adds -*er* for the comparative, it adds -*est* for the superlative. If an adjective uses *more* for the comparative, it uses *most* for the superlative.

Adjective	Comparative	Superlative
smooth	smoother	smoothest
bright	brighter	brightest
helpful	more helpful	most helpful
difficult	more difficult	most difficult
capable	more capable	most capable

Remember these three points about using adjectives in comparison:

1. To compare two people or things, use the comparative. To compare more than two, use the superlative.

> This old coin is *more valuable* than that one.
> Joe makes the *tastiest* tacos I've ever had.

2. Use the word *other* when you compare something with everything else of its kind.

> Wrong: Tim is faster than any runner.
> (This sentence says that Tim is not a runner.)
> Right: Tim is faster than any *other* runner.
> Wrong: This chair is more solid than any piece of furniture.
> (This sentence says that the chair is not a piece of furniture.)
> Right: This chair is more solid than any *other* piece of furniture.

3. Do not use -*er* with *more*, or -*est* with *most*.

> Wrong: Sue is much more taller than her sister.
> Right: Sue is much *taller* than her sister.
> Wrong: This is the most thickest book in the library.
> Right: This is the *thickest* book in the library.

Irregular Comparisons

Some comparatives and superlatives are formed in unusual ways:

Adjective	Comparative	Superlative
good	better	best
well	better	best
bad	worse	worst
little	less or lesser	least
much	more	most
many	more	most
far	farther	farthest

Exercise A Number your paper from 1 to 10. Two of the following comparisons are correct, but the rest are wrong. If a sentence is correct, write *Correct*. If it is incorrect, write it correctly.

1. Gas mileage has become importanter to car owners.
2. Gasoline is more expensive this month than last.
3. A standard-size car is the bigger size that is made.
4. A mid-size car is more big than a compact.
5. The new cars are made with a lighter frame.
6. Front-wheel drive cars are more better than other cars for getting through snow.
7. Of all the gas stations, Jake's gives the goodest service.
8. This car makes fastest stops than that one.
9. A station wagon is the most roomiest car of all.
10. Of the three cars, this one has the rougher ride.

Exercise B Follow the directions for Exercise A. Three of the comparisons are correct.

1. It's easiest to get parts for American cars than for foreign cars.
2. This car is more expensive than that one.
3. Small cars have a bumpiest ride than big cars.

4. Big cars are often comfortabler.
5. However, big cars get worser gas mileage.
6. Which of these two cars is easiest to handle?
7. Foreign cars often get higher ratings by experts.
8. Which of these two cars sounds quietest?
9. Cars nowadays have more better insulation.
10. The fuel tank is larger in a big car than in a small one.

Part 3   Using Adverbs

An **adverb** is another kind of modifier. Adverbs help you to express yourself clearly and vividly. They tell *how*, *when*, *where*, or *to what extent* about something.

Adverbs are words that modify verbs, adjectives, and other adverbs.

Using Adverbs with Verbs

Adverbs frequently modify verbs. Adverbs tell *how*, *when*, *where*, or *to what extent* something happened.

Adverbs are used with verbs to tell *how*:

Pat *proudly* displayed her sculpture.

This computer works *accurately*.

Adverbs also tell *when* about verbs:

Small car sales have soared *recently*.

The new license plates are required *soon*.

Adverbs can tell *where* about verbs:

A phone booth is located *nearby*.

We sat *there* in the lobby for hours.

In addition, adverbs can tell *to what extent:*

Vanessa *nearly* choked on the soup.

Study the following list of adverbs:

How?	When?	Where?	To What Extent?
quickly	now	here	never
sorrowfully	then	there	often
hurriedly	later	nearby	not
steadily	finally	underground	seldom

Using Adverbs with Adjectives and Other Adverbs

Besides modifying verbs, adverbs also modify adjectives and other adverbs. Look at these sentences:

Some people are *partially* blind.
(*Partially* tells to what extent. It is an adverb modifying the adjective *blind.*)

The assembly line moved *very* quickly.
(*Very* tells to what extent. It is an adverb modifying the adverb *quickly.*)

Here are other adverbs that often modify adjectives or other adverbs:

too	quite	rather	most	more	extremely
just	nearly	so	really	truly	somewhat

The above adverbs tell *to what extent* something is true.

Forming Adverbs

Many adverbs are formed by adding *-ly* to an adjective.

weak + ly = weakly   formal + ly = formally
obvious + ly = obviously   slight + ly = slightly

At times, the addition of *-ly* causes a spelling change in the adjective.

> possible + ly = possibly
> happy + ly = happily
> dull + ly = dully

Some adverbs are not formed from adjectives. *Quite, so, rather,* and *somewhat* are examples.

> The switchboard had never been *so* busy before.

> Job-sharing is a *rather* new idea.

Some words can be either adverbs or adjectives. *Late* and *high* are examples of such words.

> The doctor arrived too *late.*
> (*Late* is an adverb, modifying the verb *arrived.*)

> Tony took a *late* bus.
> (*Late* is an adjective, modifying the noun *bus.*)

> The glider soared *high* above the hills.
> (*High* is an adverb, modifying the verb *soared.*)

> The crew worked on a *high* tower.
> (*High* is an adjective, modifying the noun *tower.*)

Diagraming Adverbs

Adverbs are diagramed like adjectives. An adverb is placed on a slanted line attached to the word it modifies. This diagram shows an adverb modifying a verb:

The fire spread rapidly.

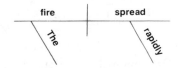

Adverbs that modify adjectives or other adverbs are diagramed like this:

Too many jobs pay very poorly.

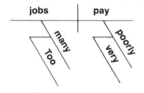

Exercise A Number your paper from 1 to 10. Write the adverbs in these sentences. After each adverb write the word it modifies. Be ready to explain what the adverb tells.

Example: A new family moved here recently.
recently modifies *moved* (tells when)
here modifies *moved* (tells where)

1. The tornado approached slowly.
2. Laura stood dangerously close to the fire.
3. We left early for the ABBA concert.
4. The glider swayed gently from side to side.
5. The pilot immediately controlled the fall.
6. Some spectators had become extremely nervous.
7. Many states have recently lowered their speed limits.
8. Lower speeds are much safer.
9. Our dress rehearsal went quite smoothly.
10. The lead singer moved wildly with the music.

Exercise B Follow the directions for Exercise A.

1. That movie was recently advertised on TV.
2. The movie ads sounded very eerie.
3. The movie itself was less scary.
4. We went to the theater early.
5. The film began slowly but soon improved.
6. Later the action moved very quickly.

7. Stunt people very often replace the real actors.
8. This theater still charges very low prices for tickets.
9. Do movies usually end happily?
10. Adventure films frequently play here.

Exercise C Change the following adjectives into adverbs by adding *-ly*. Check your spelling in a dictionary.

careless	proper	natural	exact
open	joyful	noisy	actual
ready	honest	sincere	real
easy	immediate	serious	safe

Part 4 Adverbs in Comparisons

You can use adverbs to compare actions. For example, you might say, "This team wins often but that team wins *more often.*" Or you might say, "Of all the players, Erica practices *hardest.*" Such comparisons help you to convey ideas clearly. Like adjectives, adverbs have special forms for making comparisons.

The Comparative

The **comparative** form of an adverb compares one action with another. Look at this example:

This storm hit *harder* than the last one.

The comparative is made in two ways:
1. Add *-er* to short adverbs like *long* and *fast.*

A computer does the job *faster* than a person could.

2. Use *more* with most adverbs ending in *-ly.*

Some blockers tackle *more roughly* than is necessary.

The Superlative

The **superlative** form of an adverb compares one action with two or more others. Notice these examples:

> This flight takes off *earliest* of all.
> Of the three boys, Larry spoke the *most bitterly*.

To form the superlative, either add *-est* or use *most*. If an adverb adds *-er* for the comparative, it adds *-est* for the superlative. If an adverb uses *more* for the comparative, it uses *most* for the superlative.

Adverb	Comparative	Superlative
fast	faster	fastest
tightly	more tightly	most tightly

Remember these points about adverbs in comparisons:

1. To compare two actions, use the comparative. To compare more than two actions, use the superlative.

> Air mail will arrive *sooner* than surface mail.
> Special delivery mail will arrive *soonest* of all.

2. Use the word *other* when you compare with every other action of the same kind.

> Wrong: The general lives more comfortably than any officer.
> Right: The general lives more comfortably than any *other* officer.

3. Do not use *-er* with *more*, or *-est* with *most*.

> Wrong: Some tool makers work more faster than others.
> Right: Some tool makers work faster than others.

Irregular Comparisons

Some adverbs change completely in the comparative and superlative forms. These are examples:

Adverb	Comparative	Superlative
well	better	best
much	more	most
little	less	least
far	farther	farthest

This saw works well.
That new saw works better.
A table saw would work best of all.

Exercise A Write the comparative and superlative forms.

1. wildly
2. loosely
3. long
4. gradually
5. deeply
6. soon
7. quickly
8. intelligently
9. generously
10. early

Exercise B If a sentence is correct, write *Correct*. If there is an error in the comparison of adverbs, write the sentence correctly.

1. The gymnasts moved smoothlier after much practice.
2. Foods cook more fast over an open fire.
3. We traveled more frequently when we were younger.
4. Some cars run better on unleaded gas.
5. Of all the machines, this one operates more smoothly.
6. I awaken cheerfulliest on Saturdays.
7. Gardner competes more doggedly than Reese.
8. Apples ripen fastest than pears.
9. Of the four pitchers, James pitches more accurately.
10. Epoxy glue holds bestest of all.

Part 5 Adjective or Adverb?

Read these sentences. Which sentence sounds right to you?

The blast came *sudden*.
The blast came *suddenly*.

If you said the second sentence, you are correct. An adverb (*suddenly*), not an adjective (*sudden*), is needed to modify the verb *came*.

Sometimes you may have trouble deciding whether to use an adjective or an adverb. To decide, ask yourself:

1. What kind of word does the modifier tell about?

   If your answer is an action verb, adjective, or adverb, use the adverb.

   If your answer is a noun or pronoun, use the adjective.

2. What does the modifier tell about the word it goes with?

   If it tells *how*, *when*, *where*, or *to what extent*, use the adverb.

   If it tells *which one*, *what kind*, or *how many*, use the adjective.

An adjective tells	An adverb tells
*Which one *What kind *How many	*How *When *Where *To what extent
About a noun or pronoun	About a verb, adjective, or adverb

Exercise A List each adjective and adverb, together with the word it modifies. Do not list articles.

1. The two motorcycles swerved sharply.
2. Tractors slowly pushed the deep snow aside.
3. Open that window very carefully.

4. Lauren watches television endlessly.

5. Too many shows are reruns.

6. Two favorite programs are "M*A*S*H*" and "Barney Miller."

7. Several series have somewhat similar plots.

8. The screen glows brightly in the dark room.

9. That printer uses heavy machinery.

10. The hikers walked rather quickly.

Exercise B Choose the correct modifier from the two in parentheses. Tell whether it is an adjective or an adverb.

1. We worked (furious, furiously) to halt the flooding.

2. Many houses were destroyed by (heavy, heavily) winds.

3. This battery is (terrible, terribly) weak.

4. You look particularly (nice, nicely) this morning.

5. The truckers drove (slow, slowly) down the steep grade.

6. The new car gleamed (bright, brightly) in the sun.

7. The team felt (awful, awfully) bad about the loss.

8. An (extreme, extremely) hot liquid dripped from the furnace.

9. The two teams battled (fierce, fiercely) at the game.

10. The center turned around so (quick, quickly), she fell.

Adverb or Predicate Adjective?

You have learned that a predicate adjective follows a linking verb and modifies the subject. Besides forms of *be*, other linking verbs are *become*, *seem*, *appear*, *look*, *sound*, *feel*, *taste*, *smell*, and *grow*.

> That lunch smells rotten. (*Rotten* modifies *lunch*.)
>
> The parking lot looks full. (*Full* modifies *lot*.)
>
> The prisoner grew violent. (*Violent* modifies *prisoner*.)

Verbs in the sentences above, *smells*, *looks*, and *grew*, can also be action verbs. So can *sound*, *appear*, *feel*, and *taste*. When these verbs are action verbs, they are followed by adverbs instead of predicate adjectives. Adverbs tell *how*, *when*, *where*, or *to what extent* about the action verbs.

Here are sentences using the same words as linking verbs and as action verbs.

Linking Verbs with Adjectives	Action Verbs with Adverbs
The water *looked* clear.	Dave *looked* carefully.
The team *appeared* eager.	Clouds *appeared* suddenly.
The pizza *smells* delicious.	A bloodhound *smells* keenly.
This music *sounds* peaceful.	The fire alarm *sounds* often.

If you can't decide whether to use an adverb or an adjective in a certain sentence, ask these questions:

1. Can you substitute *is* or *was* for the verb? If so, the modifier is probably an adjective.

2. Does the modifier tell *how*, *when*, *where*, or *to what extent*? If so, the modifier is probably an adverb.

Exercise Choose the right modifier for the following sentences.

1. Adam (angry, angrily) returned the trophy.
2. The rhythm sounded (slow, slowly) and gentle.
3. Stained glass looks (brilliant, brilliantly) in bright light.
4. The operator answered our questions (patient, patiently).
5. During the overtime the crowd grew (tense, tensely).
6. The teller sounded the burglar alarm (immediate, immediately).

7. Heather's carpentry appears so (perfect, perfectly).
8. The new father looked (proud, proudly) at his son.
9. Gravel feels (rough, roughly) on my bare feet.
10. Those big dill pickles taste (sour, sourly).

Part 6 Troublesome Modifiers

Certain modifiers are frequently used incorrectly.

Them and Those

Those can be used as an adjective.

Where are the controls for *those* power saws?

Them is never an adjective. It cannot substitute for *those*.

Wrong: We framed them photos.
Right: We framed *those* photos.
Right: We framed *them*.

Here and There

Sometimes people incorrectly say "this here jacket" or "that there room." "This here" and "that there" repeat ideas. The word *this* includes the idea of *here*. The word *that* includes the idea of *there*. Avoid "this here" and "that there."

Kind and Sort

Kind and *sort* are singular. *Kinds* and *sorts* are plural. No matter what words follow, use *this* or *that* with *kind* and *sort*. Use *these* and *those* with *kinds* and *sorts*.

This kind of boot is made of cowhide. (singular)
Those sorts of food are high in calories. (plural)

Good and Well

Good and well have similar meanings, but the words are not the same. You cannot always substitute one word for the other. Look at the differences in these sentences:

That is a good photo of you. (The adjective good modifies the noun photo.)

You sing well. (The adverb well modifies the verb sing.)

Good is always an adjective, modifying nouns and pronouns. It is never used to describe an action.

Well can be either an adjective or an adverb. In the sentence above, well is used as an adverb modifying an action verb. Well can also be used after a linking verb to mean "in good health."

Tara doesn't look well.
(Well is a predicate adjective modifying Tara.)

Yvonne dances well.
(Well is an adverb modifying the action verb dances.)

If you are describing an action, use well.

The Double Negative

Two negative words used together when only one is necessary is called a **double negative.** Avoid using double negatives.

Wrong: We didn't take no time-outs.
Right: We didn't take any time-outs.

Wrong: My out-of-town friends never write no letters.
Right: My out-of-town friends never write any letters.

Wrong: John couldn't eat nothing all day.
Right: John couldn't eat anything all day.

Contractions like couldn't contain a shortened form of the negative not. Do not use other negative words after them.

Some common negative words are *no, none, not, nothing,* and *never*. Instead of these words, use *any, anything,* or *ever* after negative contractions.

Rod has*n't ever* hit a grand-slam home run.
Michelle could*n't* find *any* bargains.
The new Senator did*n't* change *anything*.

Other negative words are *hardly, scarcely,* and *barely*. Don't use them with negative contractions like *hasn't* and *didn't*.

Wrong: Rick couldn't barely control the machine.
Right: Rick could *barely* control the machine.

Wrong: The movers hadn't scarcely begun.
Right: The movers had *scarcely* begun.

Wrong: Lightning hardly never strikes houses.
Right: Lightning *hardly ever* strikes houses.

Exercise A Choose the correct word from the two in parentheses.

1. Have (them, those) funds run out?
2. Each state collects (that, those) kind of tax.
3. How do you steer (them, those) canoes?
4. (That, That there) phone call was for Debbie.
5. The spacelab brought back (this, these) kinds of pictures.
6. Which radio station plays (them, those) pop hits?
7. Chris Evert Lloyd won (that, that there) title.
8. (This, These) sorts of planes are extremely fast.
9. The airline canceled (this, this here) flight.
10. Is (this, these) sort of convertible still made?

Exercise B Follow the directions for Exercise A.

1. Our coach treats us (good, well).
2. This network has many (good, well) shows.

3. "Lou Grant" did very (good, well) in the ratings.

4. Some gymnasts do not have (good, well) form.

5. Marcy does a (good, well) routine on the balance beam.

6. This coconut cream pie tastes (good, well).

7. Snowplows cleared the streets (good, well).

8. The Colts are doing (good, well) in the standings.

9. Ross understood my worries (good, well).

10. Does Carlotta swim (good, well) enough to make the team?

Exercise C   Number your paper from 1 to 10. Correct the double negatives in the following sentences. If a sentence contains no double negative, write *Correct.*

1. Jason hasn't seen no movies lately.

2. Haven't you never been to a disco?

3. One runner couldn't barely clear the hurdles.

4. During the test Amy couldn't remember nothing.

5. The elevator doesn't ever work.

6. This hot dog doesn't have no mustard on it.

7. Pam hardly knows nobody at work yet.

8. Since their argument Ramon and Todd haven't scarcely talked to each other.

9. Chris doesn't expect any reward for finding the purse.

10. The team doesn't have hardly any returning players.

Additional Exercises

Using Modifiers

A. Recognize adjectives. Write each adjective in these sentences. Tell which word it modifies. Do not include articles.

1. This special exhibit will travel to thirty museums.
2. That Italian sportscar has a deluxe interior.
3. Dense, black smoke poured out of the rusty tailpipe of the car.
4. One candidate received illegal funds.
5. Several artists worked on that huge mural.
6. Two mysterious strangers appeared at the door.
7. No newspaper can print every bit of news.
8. Some Indian food is cooked in clay ovens.
9. The violent storm destroyed many homes.
10. Tiny green buds dotted the branches.

B. Find predicate adjectives. Write the predicate adjective in each sentence. Tell which word it modifies.

1. Rebecca seems quiet today.
2. That tune sounds very familiar.
3. This dead tree is hollow.
4. The bridge might be slippery.
5. Claire is very artistic.
6. That African nation has just become independent.
7. Your jigsaw puzzle looks difficult.
8. The turkey tastes delicious.
9. Many children's shows are educational.
10. This roll-top desk is very old.

C. Use adjectives in comparison. Choose the correct adjective.

1. Jori seems (more cheerful, cheerfuller) than usual.
2. These new shoestrings are (shorter, shortest) than the ones that broke.
3. Of the three stories, which is (more factual, most factual)?
4. The budget for this film was the (most lowest, lowest) of all.
5. The combat forces have become (stronger, more strong) in the past few years.
6. Have you ever tasted (more spicier, spicier) chili?
7. Who was the (younger, youngest) of all the Presidents?
8. This year the business was (more profitable, most profitable) than last year.
9. Jennifer looks (happier, happiest) than her friends.
10. Of all the paperbacks, this one is the (more enjoyable, most enjoyable) to read.

D. Recognize adverbs. Write each adverb and the word it modifies. Sentences may contain more than one adverb.

1. Cindy Nicholas swam the English Channel twice.
2. My grandparents arrived yesterday from Tulsa.
3. A trap door in the floor slowly opened.
4. Carrie is too busy.
5. The photographer carefully focused the camera.
6. Skaters practice here quite frequently.
7. Phil seemed extremely proud of his brother.
8. Currently, Congress is seriously considering other energy sources.
9. That painter usually throws paint wildly at the canvas.
10. Two helicopters hovered loudly overhead.

E. Use adverbs in comparison.   Choose the correct adverb.

1. The sun shines (more intensely, most intensely) in California than in Alaska.
2. You will play (better, more better) if you warm up.
3. Of all the joggers, Al runs (farther, farthest).
4. Charlene read the scene (more dramatically, most dramatically) tonight than last night.
5. Brian eats (littler, less) than anyone else in the family.
6. The storm hit (hardest, most hard) in the tropics.
7. Randy can repair appliances (more skillfully, most skillfully) than his brother.
8. Amanda parked (nearer, nearest) to the curb than Carter did.
9. Washington played (badder, worse, worst) than usual.
10. The flood waters receded (quicklier, more quickly) than expected.

F. Use adjectives and adverbs correctly.   Choose the correct modifier.

1. The clerk smiled (polite, politely).
2. Their coach looks (impatient, impatiently).
3. The winners appeared (proud, proudly).
4. Black clouds appeared (sudden, suddenly).
5. The judges tasted each pie (careful, carefully).
6. Tim's voice sounded (odd, oddly).
7. That African nation has just become (independent, independently).
8. The veterans talked (honest, honestly) about their concerns.
9. The ice-cold watermelon tasted (sweet, sweetly).
10. Nicole looked (eager, eagerly) at the swimming pool.

G. Solve modifier problems. Choose the correct modifier.

1. Are (them, those) twigs for the fire?
2. Take (this, this here) equipment to Brad.
3. You didn't put (any, no) paste on the wallpaper.
4. Kathy couldn't find (any, no) candles for the cake.
5. My brothers scarcely (never, ever) fight.
6. (That, Those) sort of music is called soft rock.
7. Please pass me (them, those) keys.
8. Jeremy dances (good, well).
9. Mr. Viner explained the procedure (good, well).
10. (This, These) kinds of motorbikes use hardly (no, any) gasoline.
11. Phil bought a pair of (them, those) striped socks.
12. The stranded motorist couldn't get (no, any) help.
13. (This, These) sort of fish is good for frying.
14. Lemonade tastes (good, well) on a hot day.
15. The audience (could, couldn't) barely hear the actors.

Section 7

Using Prepositions and Conjunctions

Sometimes you can say what you mean with short sentences like these:

> Beth raced.
> The class uses paints.

Often, though, you will want to provide more information. Modifiers are useful for that purpose.

> Beth raced yesterday.
> The art class uses vivid paints.

At times, what you have to say is even more complicated. Suppose you want to say where Beth raced. Suppose you want to add that the art class also uses clay. Then you will need words to show those relationships.

> Beth raced yesterday along the lake.
> The art class uses vivid paints and clay.

Relationships dealing with people, actions, and things are expressed by words that connect other words. In this section you will learn about two kinds of connecting words: **prepositions** and **conjunctions.**

Part 1 What Are Prepositions?

Words that join other words or word groups are called **connectives.** One important kind of connective is the **preposition.** Prepositions show relationships. Look at the relationships expressed in the following sentences:

> Sare leaped *off* her bike.
> Sara leaped *onto* her bike.
> Sara leaped *over* her bike.

The prepositions *off, onto,* and *over* show the relationship between *bike* and the verb *leaped.* In each of the above sentences, *bike* is the **object of the preposition.** Like all prepositions, *off, onto,* and *over* connect their objects to another part of the sentence.

Prepositions do not show relationships all by themselves. They begin a *phrase,* a group of words that do not have a subject or verb. The **prepositional phrase** makes the relationship clear. In the above sentences, *off her bike, onto her bike,* and *over her bike* are prepositional phrases. Here are some other sentences with prepositional phrases:

> Zack politely asked *for a refund.*
> *In the spring,* Darrell returned *to school.*
> The box *of books* was too heavy.

A preposition is a word used with a noun or pronoun, called its *object,* to show the relationship between the noun or pronoun and some other word in the sentence.

A prepositional phrase consists of a preposition, its object, and any modifiers of the object.

The list below shows words often used as prepositions. Many of them, like *above, over, in,* and *beside,* help to show location. Others, like *until, after,* and *before,* show a relationship of time. Still others show different kinds of relationships. Look at these prepositions and see if you can tell the relationship each one suggests.

Words Often Used as Prepositions

about	behind	during	off	to
above	below	except	on	toward
across	beneath	for	onto	under
after	beside	from	out	until
against	between	in	outside	up
along	beyond	inside	over	upon
among	but *(except)*	into	past	with
around	by	like	since	within
at	concerning	near	through	without
before	down	of	throughout	

Exercise A   Number your paper from 1 to 10. Find the prepositional phrases in the following sentences.

Example: Mac went to the game with Gwen.
to the game, with Gwen

1. Marta works after school.
2. The man slumped against the wall.
3. I waited outside the office for Pam.
4. Rosa vaulted easily over the pole.
5. By all means, talk with Gene about your plans.
6. During this season, Franklin pitched three no-hitters.
7. At first, the bite of a black widow spider may not even be noticed.
8. The designs on totem poles often tell stories.
9. Walter jumped over the fallen halfback.
10. Don't walk through that tunnel after dark.

1. I heard nothing from Ben until today.

2. During the storm, everyone except Dee stayed inside the bus shelter.

3. Beyond a doubt, someone had been there before us.

4. There is no one else like you in the world.

5. Bright crépe paper was strung across the room.

6. There is a fast-food place near the shoe store.

7. Since last week, Anthony has been under pressure.

8. Cecelia walked off the stage with her award.

9. With little trouble, the Cowboys broke through the Bears' defense.

10. For over a month, that rusty old car has been parked in the alley.

Preposition or Adverb?

Many words used as prepositions may also be used as adverbs. How can you tell the difference?

A preposition is never used alone. It is always followed by a noun or pronoun as part of a phrase. If the word is in a phrase, it is probably a preposition. If the word has no object, it is probably an adverb.

The visitors walked *around the courtyard.* (preposition)
The visitors walked *around.* (adverb)

The tuba player lagged *behind the other marchers.* (preposition)
The tuba player lagged *behind.* (adverb)

Exercise A Decide whether the italicized words in these sentences are adverbs or prepositions. Write *Adverb* or *Preposition* for each sentence.

1. Turn the water *on* now.

2. Terry put her mitt *on* the bench.

3. Mindy accidentally knocked the salt *off* the table.
4. Turn the oven *off*.
5. Dolores left last week, and I have not seen her *since*.
6. That was the Pirates' best game *since* last fall.
7. Ed fell *down* and broke his glasses.
8. I have not seen Juanita *around*.
9. James is always looking somewhere *over* the rainbow for happiness.
10. The ball rumbled *down* the alley.

Exercise B   Follow the directions for Exercise A.

1. Suzy does not ride *without* headgear.
2. You forgot to turn your headlights *on*.
3. *Without* a word, Sam handed her the letter.
4. Is that nurse *on* duty now?
5. On weekends, the doctor is rarely *in*.
6. Tony put a quarter *into* the slot.
7. Finally the ball fell *through* the hoop.
8. Finally the ball fell *through*, and the fans breathed again.
9. Do you mind if I go *along?*
10. Caroline inched *along* the narrow ledge.

Part 2   Prepositional Phrases as Modifiers

Single words are often used as modifiers. However, groups of words may also modify. Prepositional phrases may modify various parts of a sentence. They work the same way as single adjectives or adverbs.

An adjective phrase is a prepositional phrase that modifies a noun or pronoun. The phrase always includes the preposition, its object, and any modifiers of the object.

The school needs a new coach *for the track team.*
(*For the track team* is an adjective phrase, modifying the noun *coach.* It tells *what kind* of coach.)

The door *on the left* is the emergency exit.
(*On the left* is an adjective phrase, modifying the noun *door.* It tells *which one.*)

All *of the bank tellers* wear matching uniforms.
(*Of the bank tellers* is an adjective phrase that modifies the pronoun *all.* It tells *what kind.*)

As you can see, adjective phrases, like adjectives, tell *which one* or *what kind.*

Adverbs tell *how, when, where,* and *to what extent* about verbs. Adverb phrases modify verbs in the same way.

Adverb phrases are prepositional phrases that modify verbs

The bottles are sealed *by a huge machine.*
(*By a huge machine* is an adverb phrase telling *how.* It modifies the verb *are sealed.*)

On Saturday the playoffs will begin.
(*On Saturday* is an adverb phrase. It tells *when* about the verb *will begin.*)

Hendricks sat *on the bench.*
(*On the bench* is an adverb phrase. It tells *where* about the verb *sat.*)

Sometimes one prepositional phrase follows another. Frequently, the second phrase is an adjective phrase modifying the object in the first phrase.

Cecily decided *on a name for her new dog.*
(*On a name* is an adverb phrase modifying the verb *decided. For her new dog* is an adjective phrase modifying the noun *name.*)

Jim topped the salad *with bits of cheese.*
(The adverb phrase *with bits* tells *how* about the verb *topped. Of cheese* is an adjective phrase describing the noun *bits.*)

Diagraming Prepositional Phrases

To diagram a prepositional phrase, place it under the word it modifies.

The guests on the show talked about their new movies.

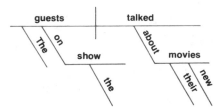

At times a preposition may have two or more nouns or pronouns as objects in the prepositional phrase.

On warm days we fished for trout and bass.

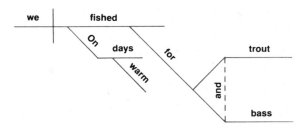

Exercise A Copy these sentences. Circle each prepositional phrase. Draw an arrow from the phrase to the word it modifies. Tell whether the phrase is an adjective phrase or an adverb phrase.

1. Nicole bought a jacket with a hood.
2. The man with a cast on his leg waved to us.
3. Do you work after school?
4. The Navajos and Apaches remained enemies for hundreds of years.
5. Sacramento is the capital of California.
6. We stayed with my aunt from St. Louis.

7. The subways were operating during the blizzard.

8. Did you leave your books at home?

9. We left after lunch and arrived before dinner.

10. During the first half, four of our players fouled out.

Exercise B Follow the directions for Exercise A.

1. Someone is hiding behind the door.

2. The store down the block sells tamales.

3. The autumn trees made a golden arch over the street.

4. Nobody except Vivian knows the answer to that question.

5. The fixture fell from the ceiling and crashed onto the floor.

6. The box under the table contains some sweaters for the clothing drive.

7. With a silly grin, Mick stepped upon the scale.

8. Keith tripped over the rug on the stairs.

9. The tire broke through ice and stuck in a large hole.

10. The girl behind Dana is my sister.

Part 3   Conjunctions

A conjunction is another kind of word that shows relationships.

A conjunction is a word that connects words or groups of words.

Look at the conjunctions in the following sentences:

Jennie *and* Vanessa will replace the broken window.
    (connects nouns)

The sculptor carves either wood *or* stone.
    (connects nouns)

Kent wrote *and* narrated the skits.
    (connects verbs)

My typing is fast *but* sloppy.
(connects adjectives)

We looked *both* in our rooms *and* at school.
(connects prepositional phrases)

Like prepositions, conjunctions show a relationship between the words they connect. Conjunctions differ from prepositions, however, in two ways. Conjunctions link similar kinds of words, like two nouns or two phrases. In addition, conjunctions do not have objects.

Coordinating Conjunctions

Coordinating conjunctions are used to join single words or groups of words of the same kind. *And*, *but*, and *or* are the most common coordinating conjunctions.

The words joined by coordinating conjunctions are compound constructions. Compound constructions include compound subjects, compound direct objects, and compound verbs, for example.

Cars *and* trucks often have different speed limits.
(*And* links *cars* and *trucks*, making them a compound subject of the verb *have*.)

The skater tripped *and* fell.
(*And* connects *tripped* and *fell*, forming a compound verb.)

Sue looked at the engine *but* couldn't locate the problem.
(*But* connects the two predicates.)

The race cars looked low *and* sleek.
(*And* connects two predicate adjectives.)

The candidate spoke realistically *but* hopefully.
(*But* connects two adverbs.)

Kim added fudge, nuts, *and* marshmallows to her sundae.
(*And* connects the three parts of the compound direct object.)

Tell the coach *or* the assistant your idea.

(*Or* connects the compound indirect object.)

On Monday *or* Tuesday, the cleaning will be ready.

(*Or* connects compound objects of a preposition.)

Correlative Conjunctions

Some conjunctions are used in pairs. They are called **correlative conjunctions.** These are correlative conjunctions:

both . . . and	not only . . . but (also)
either . . . or	whether . . . or
neither . . . nor	

Both oak *and* walnut are used for furniture.

You'll need *either* a coat *or* a warm jacket.

Neither cranes *nor* trucks could lift the marble slabs.

The cafeteria serves *not only* lunch *but also* breakfast.

The team discussed *whether* to kick *or* to run.

Exercise A Find the conjunctions in the following sentences. Tell what words or word groups are connected by the conjunction.

Example: The Honda skidded and swerved.

The verbs *skidded* and *swerved* are connected by the conjunction *and*.

1. Pigeons and sparrows are often seen in cities.
2. Alice moved quietly but quickly to the phone.
3. The blueprints were clear and precise.
4. Simon overslept and missed breakfast.
5. Should I use a fork or a spoon for this soup?
6. Either Anita or Joe will win the award.
7. Linda writes slogans for T-shirts and bumper stickers.
8. Todd not only notices but also remembers.
9. I listen to both Barry Manilow and Kenny Rogers.
10. The team had neither an experienced coach nor a good pitcher.

Exercise B Write the kind of compound construction in each sentence. Write the construction with its conjunction.

1. The gymnasts flipped and turned on the uneven bars.
2. Dallas called time-out but couldn't decide on a new strategy.
3. Bobcats and bears prowl the back woods.
4. A piston moves up and down in its cylinder.
5. The wooden walkway was narrow, shaky, and dangerous.
6. I'll telephone either Jane's mother or her brother immediately.
7. Billie has not only a sore throat but also a bad cough.
8. Is Ellis forgetful or rude?
9. Both the length and the width of my skates need adjusting.
10. The vendor sold us hot dogs, Dr. Pepper, and popcorn.

Exercise C Write two sentences using *and*, two sentences using *but*, and two sentences using *or*. After each sentence, write the words or groups of words that are joined by the conjunctions.

Exercise D Write one sentence for each of the following pairs of correlative conjunctions:

both . . . and   either . . . or   neither . . . nor

Additional Exercises

Using Prepositions and Conjunctions

A. Recognize prepositional phrases. Write the prepositional phrase or phrases in each sentence.

1. Miles Davis has played at that club.
2. Mary searched everywhere for the envelope.
3. I enjoy games like Monopoly.
4. Electric cars might be the autos of the future.
5. The cables ran along the roof.
6. I have changed my mind about the party.
7. Have you looked under the chair for your shoes?
8. The plane flew over the clusters of clouds.
9. Ginger woke to the sound of birds outside her window.
10. Bonnie left her bike by the tree near the corner.

B. Recognize prepositions and adverbs. Tell whether the italicized word in each sentence is a *Preposition* or an *Adverb*.

1. Carla heard someone *within* the room.
2. One runner lagged far *behind*.
3. We raced *inside* when the storm began.
4. A long freight train rumbled *past*.
5. Ken has never skated *before*.
6. Ms. Ryan seemed confident *after* her interview.
7. Don't stand *near* the speaker when the music begins.
8. Turn the lights *off* to conserve energy.
9. Did you look *behind* the couch?
10. The restaurant is just *past* that sign.

C. Identify prepositional phrases as modifiers. Write the prepositional phrase in each sentence. Label each phrase *Adjective* or *Adverb* to tell how it is used.

1. Pat threw the line into the river.
2. Are Volkswagens made in Germany?
3. A movie about a baseball player is playing here.
4. Bert hung his hat carefully on the hook.
5. These gloves are lined with fur.
6. The woman with the briefcase is Dr. Sanchez.
7. A crowd of people swarmed the stage.
8. The young man in the green jacket is Jake Houston.
9. The ball landed in the bleachers.
10. Nobody but Rachel understood the question.

D. Recognize conjunctions. For each sentence write the conjunction. Then write the words or groups of words joined by the conjunction.

1. The Pirates and the Steelers are Pittsburgh teams.
2. Father Hildalgo of Mexico was a priest and a political leader.
3. Gilda Radner talked and joked with the audience.
4. The speaker's voice was quiet but firm.
5. Andrew was not only hungry but also thirsty.
6. Can you tell whether a computer or a person made the mistake?
7. Rugs, drapes, and pillows muffle the noises in a room.
8. Somebody called for you but left no message.
9. In gym class, we'll play either volleyball or softball.
10. Neither Kelley nor Rivera caught the grounder to left field.

Section 8

Review of Parts of Speech

Part 1   The Parts of Speech

You have studied nouns, pronouns, verbs, adjectives, adverbs, prepositions, and conjunctions. All of these classes of words are called **parts of speech.** Words are grouped as different parts of speech because of the way they are used in sentences.

There are eight parts of speech. Besides the seven groups listed above, there is one other part of speech. It is called the interjection.

What Is an Interjection?

An interjection is a word or group of words used to express strong feeling.

An interjection may be either a phrase or a word. In any case, the interjection shows strong feeling. Those feelings might be, for example, joy, anger, terror, surprise, disgust, or sadness. Because it conveys strong emotions, an interjection is followed by an exclamation mark.

Notice the following interjections:

> *Wow!* This is fun.
> *Oh!* I didn't see you there.
> *Ugh!* This tastes terrible.

Now you have studied all eight parts of speech:

The Parts of Speech			
nouns	**verbs**	**adverbs**	**conjunctions**
pronouns	**adjectives**	**prepositions**	**interjections**

Exercise A Write each italicized word. Next to it, write what part of speech it is.

1. *Fantastic!* The agent likes Vicky's demonstration record.
2. Phillips *dove* for the end zone.
3. Did *anybody* ever thank the Lone Ranger?
4. Anne hung a poster *inside* her locker.
5. Bonnie *or* Earl will adjust the handlebars for you.
6. I should *probably* wake Roger.
7. Your phone is always *busy*.
8. Paula flashed a *cheerful* smile.
9. The *stories* of O. Henry end with a surprise.
10. Lydia *remembered* the friendliness of her old neighborhood.

Exercise B Follow the directions for Exercise A.

1. The truck swerved and *avoided* a collision.
2. Country music has influenced both rock *and* soul music.
3. Some new homes are heated *by* the sun.
4. *Ugh!* There's a worm in this apple.
5. The steel mills in *Gary* reddened the sky.
6. Angie didn't notice the steps in front of *her*.
7. Leslie cleared the hurdles *easily*.
8. The *polite* bus driver waited for the limping man.
9. Traffic should stop for *pedestrians* with white canes.
10. Margaret Bourke-White *became* famous for her war photographs.

Part 2 Using Words as Different Parts of Speech

Very often the same word can be used as different parts of speech. For example, a word might be a noun in one sentence and an adjective in another.

There is only one way to tell what part of speech any word is. You must see how that word is used in a sentence.

Here are some examples of one word used as two different parts of speech:

The artist folded *paper* into unusual shapes.
   (*Paper* is used as a noun, the direct object of the verb *folded*.)
At the picnic, we ate on *paper* plates.
   (*Paper* is used as an adjective, modifying *plates*.)
The five-dollar *bill* has a picture of Abraham Lincoln.
   (*Bill* is used as a noun, the subject of the sentence.)
The store will *bill* us for our purchases.
   (*Bill* is used as the main verb.)

Carlotta had a *light* snack of carrot sticks.

(*Light* is used as an adjective, modifying the noun *snack*.)

Light the candle, please.

(*Light* is used as a verb.)

Did you park in the *underground* garage?

(*Underground* is used as an adjective, modifying the noun *garage*.)

After seeing its shadow, the groundhog went *underground*.

(*Underground* is used as an adverb, modifying the verb *went*.)

What is your favorite song?

(*What* is used as a pronoun, the subject of the sentence.)

What programs are on TV now?

(*What* is used as an adjective, modifying the noun *programs*.)

A *low* wall surrounded the building.

(*Low* is used as an adjective, modifying the noun *wall*.)

A plane flew *low* over the beach.

(*Low* is used as an adverb, modifying the verb *flew*.)

After her speech, Sally sat *down*.

(*Down* is used as an adverb, modifying the verb *sat*.)

We rowed the boat *down* the river.

(*Down* is used as a preposition.)

Never! I won't try it again.

(*Never* is used as an interjection.)

Mr. Bailey *never* raises his voice.

(*Never* is used as an adverb, modifying the verb *raises*.)

Exercise A Write the italicized word. Next to it, write what part of speech it is in that sentence.

1. *Really!* Do you expect me to believe that?
2. The potato salad was *really* delicious.
3. *Cross* that intersection very carefully.
4. Julie wore a gold *cross* on a chain.

5. The conductor seems *cross* today.
6. *Daydreams* can serve a useful purpose.
7. Paul *daydreams* about sports.
8. Have you ever played *this* game before?
9. *This* is my aunt's house.
10. *Fire* drills are scheduled every month.

Exercise B Follow the directions for Exercise A.

1. Don't turn the television *on* during an electrical storm.
2. Her pay envelope was lying *on* the table.
3. Our mail carrier *growls* back at dogs.
4. The *growls* were getting meaner and deeper.
5 *Park* your bike in those racks.
6. This *park* provides nature walks.
7. The youth center keeps a job *file*.
8. Passengers usually *file* quietly down to the subway.
9, *That* was my idea.
10. Have you already seen *that* movie?

Additional Exercises

Review of Parts of Speech

A. Recognize the parts of speech. Write the italicized word. Tell what part of speech the word is.

1. Did the reporter quote *you* accurately?
2. *Ouch*! That really stings.
3. Most *Canadians* are extremely patriotic.
4. Jim talks too fast *and* too much.
5. The emergency room at Weiss Memorial Hospital is *always* crowded.
6. The art class designed and *sold* calendars.
7. Robert takes his *youngest* sister to a day-care center each day.
8. *Wow*! We got here just in time.
9. Laura dances to any kind *of* music.
10. Here, winter begins *early* and ends late.
11. It rained every evening *for* a week.
12. The detective examined the skid *marks* in an effort to trace the car.
13. *This* is Groundhog Day.
14. Do you feel better *now*?
15. Ghana and Zaire are *African* countries.
16. How did Indian summer get its *name*?
17. Did *anyone* put cool water on the burn?
18. The *leaves* of the ginko tree look like small fans.
19. The California Angels won their first pennant *in* 1979.
20. Frieda *wove* that large rug on the wall.

B. Identify words used as different parts of speech. Write the italicized word. Tell what part of speech it is used as in that sentence.

1. The President tossed out the *game* ball.
2. After the last *game*, the Dodgers were in first place.
3. The police officers looked for *signs* of forced entry.
4. The old man *signs* his name with a flourish.
5. The runner slipped and fell *in* the mud.
6. Please come *in* and stay for a while.
7. *That* shop specializes in repairs for motorcycles.
8. *That* is an Olympic-size swimming pool.
9. That man looks exactly *like* Lou Gossett, Jr.
10. We *like* to visit historic Indian sites.
11. During the *rush* hour, traffic is often at a standstill.
12. We must *rush* to the emergency room!
13. Abby painted a *picture* of the valley.
14. *Picture* yourself swimming in a cool, clear lake.
15. *This* is a great movie.
16. Can anyone read *this* message?
17. Tom trailed *behind* the other hikers.
18. When we moved, we left many good friends *behind*.
19. The hot-air balloon sailed *high* into the sky.
20. At *high* tide, this area is under water.

Section 9

Using
Verbals

You have learned about all eight parts of speech. They are the following:

| nouns | verbs | adverbs | conjunctions |
| pronouns | adjectives | prepositions | interjections |

Besides those parts of speech, our language also contains three other kinds of words. They are **gerunds, participles,** and **infinitives.** All three are similar to verbs. For that reason, they are called **verbals.** A verbal is a word that is formed from a verb but is never used as a verb. In this section you will learn about using the three kinds of verbals.

Part 1 Gerunds

A gerund is a verb form that is used as a noun. A gerund ends in *-ing*. It may be used in any way that a noun is used.

Like a noun, a gerund may be used as a subject.

> *Drawing* is Alissa's hobby.
> (*Drawing* is a gerund, the subject of the verb *is*.)

Like a noun, a gerund may be used as the direct object.

> Debbie tried *surfing.*
> (*Surfing* is a gerund, the object of the verb *tried*.)

Like a noun, a gerund may be used as the object of a preposition.

> The best place for *jogging* is the park.
> (*Jogging* is a gerund, the object of the preposition *for*.)

The Gerund Phrase

A gerund is not always used alone. Often a gerund has a modifier or an object or both. Together, they form a **gerund phrase.** The entire gerund phrase is used like a noun.

Because a gerund is formed from a verb, it can have an object.

> We won by *scoring a touchdown* in the last minute.
> (*Scoring* is a gerund; *touchdown* is the object of *scoring*. The phrase *scoring a touchdown* is the object of the preposition *by*.)

Because a gerund is formed from a verb, it can be modified by adverbs.

> Elliot started *laughing again.*
> (*Laughing* is a gerund; *again* is an adverb modifying *laughing*. The phrase *laughing again* is the object of the verb *started*.)

Because a gerund is used as a noun, it can be modified by adjectives.

> *Quick thinking* saved us.
> (*Thinking* is a gerund; *quick* is an adjective modifying *thinking*. The phrase *quick thinking* is the subject of the verb *saved*.)

Gerunds can also be modified by prepositional phrases.

> *Sitting on these benches* is uncomfortable.
> (*Sitting* is a gerund; *on these benches* is a prepositional phrase modifying *sitting*. The entire gerund phrase is the subject of *is*.)

In all of these examples you can see that gerunds are used as nouns, even though they look like verbs. *Drawing, surfing, jogging, scoring, laughing, thinking,* and *sitting* all look like verbs but are not used as verbs. Because they are used as nouns, they are gerunds. Modifiers and objects that are used with them form gerund phrases.

Diagraming Gerunds

A gerund or gerund phrase used as a subject or direct object is diagramed on a line above the main line. The gerund belongs on a line drawn as a step. Its modifiers are placed on slanted lines below it. Its object is shown on the horizontal line following the gerund.

> Telling jokes will cheer us up.

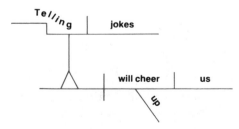

This job requires fast, accurate typing.

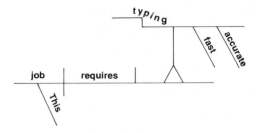

A gerund or gerund phrase used as the object of a preposition is diagramed below the main line. The preposition belongs on a slanted line going down from the word modified. Again, the gerund appears on a stepped line.

We thanked Valerie for helping us.

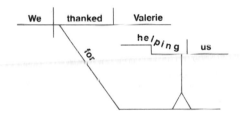

Exercise A Find the gerunds or gerund phrases in these sentences. As your teacher directs, show how each is used.

1. Smiling improves everyone's appearance.
2. Faulty wiring caused the fire.
3. Flooding the engine is usually a beginner's mistake.
4. We were tired from running so far.
5. There is no time for arguing.
6. Washing the windows of skyscrapers is hazardous.
7. Nearly everybody dislikes dieting.
8. Hanging the picture was not easy.
9. Logical thinking can be learned.
10. Colette has always enjoyed singing in the choir.

Exercise B Follow the directions for Exercise A.

1. Sharpening pencils with a knife is tricky.
2. Will hemming the skirt take long?
3. My grandmother enjoys braiding rugs from scraps of cloth.
4. Yawning can be contagious.
5. Painting a dragon on the van was Sonya's idea.
6. Elena practiced skating on one foot.
7. Making the decision was difficult.
8. Scratching mosquito bites only makes them worse.
9. How many calories does an hour of walking burn?
10. The fire department warns against keeping the oven on for warmth.

Part 2 Participles

A participle is a verb form that is used as an adjective.

You learned about the **past participle** as one of the principal parts of a verb. It is formed by adding *-d* or *-ed* to the present tense, as in *dance—danced* or *dress—dressed.* The past participles of irregular verbs are formed differently and must be learned separately: *tear—torn, sing—sung.*

There is another kind of participle besides the past participle. It is called the **present participle.** The present participle is always formed by adding *-ing* to the present tense: *dance—dancing, dress—dressing, tear—tearing, sing—singing.*

Here are more examples of participles:

Verb	Past Participle	Present Participle
look	looked	looking
bring	brought	bringing
cry	cried	crying

As verbals, participles are always used as adjectives. A participle modifies either a noun or a pronoun.

Exhausted, Martina sat down with a sigh.
(*Exhausted* is a past participle modifying the noun *Martina.*)

Whistling, he made his way home through the snow.
(*Whistling* is a present participle modifying the pronoun *he.*)

A *fallen* tree blocked the street.
(*Fallen* is a past participle modifying the noun *tree.*)

The *flying* object had four headlights.
(*Flying* is a present participle modifying the noun *object.*)

The Participial Phrase

A participle is not always used alone. Often a participle has a modifier or an object or both. Together, they form a **participial phrase.** The entire participial phrase is used as an adjective.

Because a participle is formed from a verb, it may have an object.

The person *taking shorthand* is Ms. Baldrini's secretary.
(*Taking shorthand* is a participial phrase modifying *person. Shorthand* is the object of the participle *taking.*)

Because a participle comes from a verb, it may be modified by adverbs.

Racing madly, Carla beat the throw to home plate.
(*Racing madly* is a participial phrase modifying *Carla. Madly* is an adverb modifying the participle *racing.*)

A participle may also be modified by prepositional phrases.

We heard the foghorn *moaning in the distance.*
(*Moaning in the distance* is a participial phrase modifying *foghorn. In the distance* is a prepositional phrase modifying the participle *moaning.*)

In all of these examples you can see that the participles are used as adjectives, even though they look like verbs. *Exhausted, whistling, fallen, taking, racing,* and *moaning* all look like verbs but are not used as verbs. Because they are used as adjectives, they are called participles. Modifiers and objects used with them form participial phrases.

Diagraming Participles

To diagram a participle, place it below the noun or pronoun it modifies. Place the participle on an angled line. Put modifiers of the participle on lines slanted down from it. An object follows the participle on a horizontal line.

Reading carefully, Erin studied the contract.

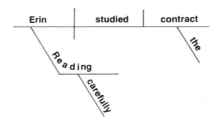

Exercise A Write the participles or participial phrases in these sentences. Show which word the participle or phrase modifies.

Example: Raising her eyebrows, Regina stared at the conductor.
Raising her eyebrows (participial phrase, modifying *Regina*)

1. Working hard, the firefighters controlled the blaze.
2. The glittering snow blinded him for a minute.
3. Fried chicken is a popular food.
4. Cheryl scraped the peeling paint.
5. Frightened, I turned off the horror movie on TV.

6. Harris slipped on the freshly waxed floor.

7. Someone wearing high heels made these footprints.

8. The pie cooling on the table is for dessert.

9. Still snapping her fingers, Lynn left the dance floor.

10. The man with the hat pulled down over his eyes was once a famous boxer.

Exercise B   Follow the directions for Exercise A.

1. Shaking her head, the patient refused the medicine.

2. That is a widely known fact.

3. There was no hope of a seat on the packed bus.

4. Opening the door of the laundromat, Mark accidentally bumped into Mr. Rodriguez.

5. Bits of shattered glass in the street told the story.

6. Take gloves off frostbitten hands slowly and carefully.

7. Falling softly on the roof, the rain sounded peaceful.

8. Most of our scattered relatives got together for the reunion.

9. I was trapped inside the revolving door for an hour.

10. Payton, leaping into the air, caught the ball.

Gerund or Participle?

The two kinds of verbals you have studied, gerunds and participles, often look the same. Gerunds and present participles are both formed by adding *-ing* to the present tense of verbs. How can you avoid confusing them?

To tell whether a word is a gerund or a present participle, look at how it is used. If it is used as a modifier, it is a participle. If it is used as a noun, it is a gerund.

Look at the following sentences.

> *Hiking along the nature trail* takes two hours.
> (The gerund phrase *hiking along the nature trail* is the subject of the verb *takes*.)

Hiking along the nature trail, we saw several deer.
(The participial phrase *hiking along the nature trail* modifies the pronoun *we.*)

Exercise For each sentence, write the gerund or participle and say which each is. Be prepared to explain your answer.

1. Diving from the high board requires control.
2. Diving from the high board, Jeff felt free and happy.
3. Tuning the old piano will improve its sound.
4. Tuning the old piano, Mrs. Arthur listened carefully to each tone.
5. Climbing the hill wore us out.
6. Climbing the hill, Sandy spotted a waterfall.
7. Dusting for fingerprints may give the police clues.
8. Using a newspaper, Lynn chased the bee outside.
9. The people sitting in the front row get the best view.
10. Steve calmed the dog by patting it gently.

Part 3   Infinitives

The third kind of verbal is the **infinitive. An infinitive is a verbal form that usually begins with the word *to.*** *To* is called the **sign of the infinitive.**

to write	to shout	to find	to forget
to say	to like	to join	to remind

Note: You have learned that the word *to* is used as a preposition. *To* is a preposition when it is followed by a noun or pronoun as its object. However, when *to* is followed by a verb, it is the sign of the infinitive. Compare these examples:

Prepositional Phrases	Infinitives
We went to the youth center.	We tried to remember.
Justin listened to the music.	Kristin wants to rollerskate.

The Infinitive Phrase

Like gerunds and participles, infinitives are not always used alone.

An infinitive can have modifiers and objects. The infinitive with its modifiers and objects forms an **infinitive phrase.**

Because an infinitive is formed from a verb, it is like a verb in some ways. Like a verb, an infinitive may have an object.

> Megan planned *to have a party.*
> (*Party* is the direct object of the infinitive *to have.*)
>
> The coach wanted *to give the team a good workout.*
> (*Team* is the indirect object and *workout* is the direct object of the infinitive *to give.*)

Because an infinitive is formed from a verb, it may be modified by adverbs.

> The choir tried *to sing together.*
> (*Together* is an adverb modifying the infinitive *to sing.*)
>
> A tape recording asked me *to call again later.*
> (*Again* and *later* are adverbs modifying the infinitive *to call.*)

Infinitives may also be modified by prepositional phrases.

> One customer demanded *to talk to the manager.*
> (*To the manager* is a prepositional phrase modifying the infinitive *to talk.*)
>
> Many people like *to picnic in the park.*
> (*In the park* is a prepositional phrase modifying the infinitive *to picnic.*)

Uses of the Infinitive Phrase

Unlike gerunds and participles, infinitives can be used as more than one part of speech. An infinitive or infinitive phrase can be used as one of the following: a noun, an adjective, or an adverb.

Infinitives and infinitive phrases can be used in ways that nouns are used. As you know, nouns may be subjects or direct objects.

Subject: *To learn a new language* takes time.
(*To learn a new language* is the subject.)
Direct Object: Diane forgot *to send a birthday card*.
(*To send a birthday card* is the direct object.)

Infinitives and infinitive phrases can also be used as adjectives or adverbs. The infinitive or infinitive phrase is used as an adjective if it modifies a noun or pronoun. It is used as an adverb if it modifies a verb, adjective, or adverb.

Adjective: These are the logs *to burn in the fireplace*.
(*To burn in the fireplace* modifies the noun *logs*.)
Adjective: Shelly needs someone *to advise her*.
(*To advise her* modifies the pronoun *someone*.)
Adverb: Everyone came *to celebrate New Year's Eve*.
(*To celebrate New Year's Eve* modifies the verb *came*.)
Adverb: Greg is afraid *to talk to Jessica*.
(*To talk to Jessica* modifies the adjective *afraid*.)
Adverb: The ball flew too high *to catch*.
(*To catch* modifies the adverb *high*.)

From all of the examples, you can see that infinitives look like verbs but are not used as verbs. Infinitives and their phrases are used as nouns, adjectives, and adverbs.

The Split Infinitive

Sometimes a modifier is placed between the word *to* and the verb of an infinitive. A modifier in that position is said to split the infinitive. Usually, a split infinitive sounds awkward and should be avoided.

Awkward: Marietta tried to *patiently* wait.
Better: Marietta tried to wait *patiently*.

Diagraming Infinitives

To diagram an infinitive or infinitive phrase used as a noun, place it on a bridge above the main line. *To*, the sign of the infinitive, belongs on a slanted line. The infinitive is shown on a horizontal line. Modifiers appear on lines slanted down from the infinitive. An object is shown on a horizontal line following the infinitive.

Dale tried to answer the questions correctly.

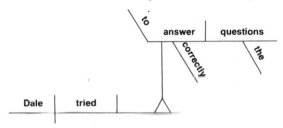

To diagram an infinitive or infinitive phrase used as a modifier, place it below the word modified. Modifiers and objects of the infinitive appear as explained above.

Sandpaper is used to smooth the wood.

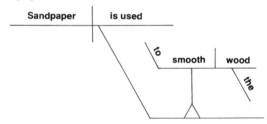

Exercise A   Write each infinitive or infinitive phrase. Be prepared to tell how it is used in the sentence.

> Example: Deborah wants to tell her side of the story.
> *to tell her side of the story* (infinitive phrase, used as direct object)

1. Don neglected to mention a few important facts.
2. The coat was too expensive to buy.

3. Ruth is too intelligent to believe that.

4. Chief Joseph had hoped to lead his people to Canada.

5. To own a Renegade jeep is Sheila's dream.

6. Egypt intends to report the incident to the UN Security Council.

7. All the candidates promised to find people jobs.

8. Has anyone come to check the furnace?

9. Did Cynthia manage to find her way there without a map?

10. To draw better is Carrie's goal in art class.

Exercise B Follow the directions for Exercise A.

1. I never got a chance to thank Quentin.

2. The counselor is the person to ask about a job.

3. Do you want to borrow my eraser?

4. Jeff tried to enter his cat in the dog show.

5. To end the season with an injury is no fun.

6. The pigeons tried to avoid the spray of water from the fountain.

7. A good rock music station is hard to find.

8. To walk to the stadium would take two hours.

9. Bob always tries to please everybody.

10. The potter started to put glaze on the vase.

Part 4   A Review of Verbals

Although verbals are verb forms, they are never used as verbs. They are used as other parts of speech.

The three kinds of verbals are gerunds, participles, and infinitives. All three kinds of verbals may be used alone. At times, though, they are used in phrases. These phrases are called gerund phrases, participial phrases, and infinitive phrases. Because they are like verbs, all three kinds of verbals may take objects or modifiers.

Gerunds are the verb forms used as nouns. Gerunds, which end in *-ing*, may be used in all the ways nouns are used.

> *Marching* tired us out. (subject)
> The troops began *marching along*. (direct object)
> The parade featured *precise marching*. (direct object)
> The band makes designs by *marching in formation*. (object of preposition)

Participles are verb forms used as adjectives. Like adjectives, participles modify nouns and pronouns. Present participles end in *-ing*. Past participles of regular verbs end in *-d* or *ed*.

> *Turning*, Richard skated back to his friends.
> The girl *turning sideways* is Nancy.
> *Turning the car just in time*, Wendy avoided an accident.
> We saw someone *turning somersaults*.

Infinitives are the verbals that begin with the word *to*. Infinitives may be used as three different parts of speech. They may be nouns, adjectives, or adverbs.

> *To say his lines right* was a challenge for Eric. (noun, subject)
> The president asked us *to say our names*. (noun, direct object)
> Ms. Fields has a few words *to say*. (adjective)
> Everyone rose *to say the pledge*. (adverb)
> This tongue-twister is not easy *to say*. (adverb)

Exercise A   Find the verbal in each sentence. Write the verbal or verbal phrase. Tell whether the verbal is a gerund, a participle, or an infinitive.

1. We were invited backstage to meet the cast.
2. The burglar entered through an unlocked basement window.
3. Jeans made in America are popular all over the world.
4. Where did you learn to speak Spanish?

- 5. Rita lugged the broken TV to the repair shop.
6. Keeping secrets is hard for Frank.
7. Lining the coat with flannel will make it warmer.
8. Martin woke to the smell of frying bacon.
9. The nurse is responsible for sterilizing the instruments.
10. It is too early to tell the outcome of the game.

Exercise B Follow the directions for Exercise A.

1. The defeated candidate accused the winner of vote fraud.
2. Try to understand Peggy's position.
3. Talking quietly is impossible for Dan.
4. Turning on the siren, the police officer drove her squad car through the busy intersection.
5. The wastebasket was filled to the brim with crumpled paper.
6. Separating Mexico from the United States, the Rio Grande flows to the Gulf of Mexico.
7. Reading a newspaper every day is a good habit.
8. Martha has saved enough money to buy a ticket to the concert.
9. Diving for the ball, the third baseman brought the fans to their feet.
10. Understanding the rules makes the game more enjoyable.

Additional Exercises

Using Verbals

A. Recognize gerunds. Find each gerund phrase. Tell whether it is used as a subject, direct object, or object of a preposition.

1. Jonas tried pitching with his left hand.
2. Diving through the waves is fun.
3. A pallette is used for mixing oil paints.
4. Twenty sound tracks were used in making this record.
5. Nora suggested returning the carton of sour milk.
6. Rabbits survive by running away from danger.
7. Washing clothes in hot water might shrink them.
8. Gluing the pieces together took several hours.
9. There is an observation deck for viewing the city.
10. Mark tried wrestling in the 130-pound weight class.

B. Recognize participles. Write the participle or participial phrase in each sentence. Tell which word it modifies.

1. Overloaded with cargo, the ship sank.
2. Screaming wildly, fans stormed the court.
3. Sue found the baby fingerpainting on the wall.
4. The hikers found a deserted cabin.
5. We toasted marshmallows over a roaring fire.
6. Hidden rocks could damage the boat.
7. Discouraged, the artist set the sketch aside.
8. Adjusting the wheels, Lee discovered a new problem.
9. The wildflowers growing in the park are goldenrod.
10. Leaping out of the water, the dolphin sailed through the hoop.

C. Recognize Infinitives. Write the infinitive or infinitive phrase in each sentence. Tell whether it is used as a subject, direct object, adjective, or adverb.

1. Kristy planned to take the next flight.
2. Dru has several projects to complete.
3. Each carrier has a certain amount of mail to deliver.
4. Our mayor campaigned to become governor.
5. To admit mistakes takes courage.
6. Julie trained to work as a waitress.
7. I expect to see Mel this afternoon.
8. The government tries to warn us of health hazards.
9. Did you try to talk to Lena first?
10. This copy is difficult to read.

D. Identify verbals. Write the verbal or verbal phrase in each sentence. Label it *Gerund, Participle,* or *Infinitive*.

1. Coral took three hours to sand this cabinet.
2. After baking two dozen cookies, we ate them all.
3. Josh sat on a balcony overlooking Central Park.
4. Refreshed, Al climbed back out of the pool.
5. Skydiving is sometimes called a sport.
6. Moving West was the dream of many Americans in the 1800's.
7. We persuaded Judy to stay for dinner.
8. Forced out of their native country, the refugees sought protection in the United States.
9. The crowd waiting for the bus grew impatient.
10. This is the alarm to ring in case of fire.

Section 10

Making Subjects and Verbs Agree

When two people have similar ideas, they agree. The subject and the verb of a sentence can also be alike in certain ways. Then they are said to agree. In this section you will find out how to make subjects and verbs agree.

Part 1 Making Subjects and Verbs Agree in Number

The **number** of a word refers to whether the word is singular or plural. A word is **singular** when it refers to one thing. A word is **plural** when it refers to more than one thing. If a subject and verb are the same in number, they agree.

A verb must agree in number with its subject.

If a subject is singular, its verb must be singular. If a subject is plural, then its verb must be plural.

Singular	Plural
She *watches*.	They *watch*.
It *rolls*.	They *roll*.
He *dances*.	They *dance*.
Marcy *adds*.	Machines *add*.

You can see that in the examples, the singular of each verb ends in *-s*. In each plural verb, there is no *-s*.

Subject and verb agreement usually seems natural. Problems arise, though, when you are not sure which word is the subject of the sentence. Remember that to find the subject, first find the verb. Then ask *who?* or *what?* before it.

> The papers in this folder are important.
> *Verb:* are
> *What are?* papers
> The subject is *papers*.

The subject of the verb is never found in a prepositional phrase.

When you are trying to make subjects and verbs agree, watch out for phrases. Often a phrase appears between the subject and the verb.

> The *keys* on the dashboard *are* mine.
> That *book* of poems *has* many pictures.
> The *words* to that song *are* catchy.
> *One* of the trains *is* late.

Phrases beginning with the words *with, together with, including, as well as,* and *in addition to* are not part of the subject.

> A fire *truck*, in addition to the police car, *is* here.
> *Honesty*, as well as courage, *is* a virtue.
> The *meal*, including dessert, *costs* two dollars.

Exercise A   Choose the verb that agrees with the subject.

1. Those photographs, including the one of Jake, (is, are) in the album.

2. The radio, as well as the flashlights, (needs, need) batteries.

3. The mission of those pilots (was, were) accomplished.

4. The bag of Fritos (is, are) almost empty.

5. Two of the bones in her foot (is, are) broken.

6. The oil on the waves (was, were) from the tanker.

7. Homes near the river (has, have) to be evacuated.

8. The woman in the red sandals (works, work) at the clinic.

9. The walls, as well as the floor, (has, have) been scrubbed.

10. Even the best players (try, tries) to improve.

Exercise B   Follow the directions for Exercise A.

1. Leslie, as well as many other students, (takes, take) the subway to school.

2. A person with third-degree burns (requires, require) immediate medical help.

3. The dog with brown spots (leads, lead) that pack.

4. That suitcase without handles (belongs, belong) to Jerry.

5. The sounds of summer (includes, include) the music of ice cream trucks.

6. The keys on that piano (is, are) loose.

7. Two theaters in town (shows, show) first-run movies.

8. Hamburgers at that stand (costs, cost) a dollar.

9. All the students in that class (joins, join) in class discussions.

10. The battery, together with the spark plugs, (is, are) new.

Part 2 Compound Subjects

A compound subject is two or more subjects used with the same verb.

A compound subject joined by *and* is plural. Therefore, it requires a plural verb.

The *radio* and the *stereo* **are playing** the same song.
Steve and *Marcella* **write** for the newspaper.

When the parts of a compound subject are joined by *or* or *nor*, the verb should agree with the subject nearer to the verb.

Neither Jan nor her *friends stay* for lunch.
Either cookies or *cake is* a good dessert.

Exercise A   Choose the verb that agrees with the subject.

1. The jacket and the coat (needs, need) to be drycleaned.
2. Janet and Beth (is, are) interested in the job.
3. Ecuador and Colombia (is, are) neighboring countries.
4. Boots and jeans (seems, seem) to be Mike's uniform.
5. Neither the potholes nor the curb (has, have) been repaired.
6. Neither the curb nor the potholes (have, has) been repaired.
7. Either Rhonda or her sister (visits, visit) us often.
8. Either the seat or the handlebars (has, have) to be adjusted.
9. Both Liz and Marilyn (bowls, bowl) at that alley.
10. Neither Joyce nor Pam (bowls, bowl) at that alley.

Exercise B   Follow the directions for Exercise A.

1. Neither the drugstore nor the grocery (opens, open) until 8 A.M.
2. Either Ms. McGee or Mr. Baez (teaches, teach) that math class.

3. Neither noise nor crowds (bothers, bother) Patty.

4. Vicks and Kleenex (sells, sell) better in the winter.

5. The ladder and the paint (is, are) behind the garage.

6. Neither the parade nor the fireworks (was, were) as good as usual this year.

7. Cancer and TB (attacks, attack) people of all ages.

8. Either the piano or the singers (is, are) off-key.

9. Neither the Spencers nor Ms. Davis (is, are) home.

10. Glass windows and a wooden floor (was, were) considered luxuries a few centuries ago.

Part 3   Indefinite Pronouns

To make a verb agree with an indefinite pronoun used as the subject, you must know if the pronoun is singular or plural. As you have learned, some indefinite pronouns are singular, and some are plural. Others may be either singular or plural.

The following indefinite pronouns are **singular:**

another	each	everything	one
anybody	either	neither	somebody
anyone	everybody	nobody	someone
anything	everyone	no one	

Nobody here *knows* the answer.
Someone leads the orchestra.
Each of the rooms *has* a TV.

The following indefinite pronouns are **plural:**

both   few   many   several

Several of the candidates *agree* on the issues.
Both of those countries *have* mild climates.

The following indefinite pronouns are **singular** if they refer to one thing. They are **plural** if they refer to several things.

all   any   most   none   some

All of the equipment *is* clean and new.
All of the representatives *are* in Washington.

Most of the lake *is* shallow.
Most of the beaches *are* open.

Some of the money *is* Linda's.
Some of the boats *are* at the pier.

Exercise A   Choose the verb that agrees with the subject.

1. Most of the batteries (is, are) still good.
2. Each of the coaches (has, have) an even temper.
3. Few of the rumors (seems, seem) likely to be true.
4. (Is, Are) all of the seats taken?
5. Everyone here (has, have) heard that joke before.
6. Somebody upstairs (is, are) playing the piano.
7. Some of Sid's friends (has, have) arrived.
8. Nobody on the block (owns, own) that car.
9. Most of that gossip (is, are) untrue.
10. Some of the spaghetti sauce usually (splatters, splatter).

Exercise B   Follow the directions for Exercise A.

1. Most of the track (needs, need) repair.
2. Most of the roads (needs, need) repair.
3. Neither of the pens (has, have) a fine point.
4. Everybody (believes, believe) her.
5. All of the items (was, were) donated.
6. Most of the raffle tickets (has, have) been sold.
7. Many of us (knows, know) that.
8. One of the twins often (pretends, pretend) to be the other.
9. Everybody in the bleachers (was, were) cheering.
10. Each of the nurses (wears, wear) identification.

Part 4   Other Problems of Agreement

Doesn't and Don't Used with Pronouns

The verb *doesn't* is singular. *Doesn't* is used with the subjects *she*, *he*, and *it*. All other personal pronouns are used with *don't*.

It *doesn't* matter to me.
He *doesn't* live near the city.
She *doesn't* speak Spanish.

They *don't* play fairly.
I *don't* work here.
We *don't* watch much TV.

Sentences Beginning with There

When sentences begin with *there*, *here*, or *where*, the subject comes after the verb. You must look ahead to find the subject of the sentence. Then you must use the verb that agrees with that subject.

There *are* two *versions* of that song.
Here *is* the beach *towel*.
Where *are* the *peaches*?

Exercise A   Choose the verb that agrees with the subject.

1. Michael (doesn't, don't) watch much TV.
2. She (doesn't, don't) often lose her temper.
3. It (doesn't, don't) seem fair to give her both jobs.
4. Where (is, are) the nearest exit?
5. Those names (doesn't, don't) sound familiar to me.
6. (Doesn't, Don't) Lorraine work at Sears?
7. (Doesn't, Don't) the buses run all night?
8. There (is, are) some mail for you on the radiator.
9. There (goes, go) that yellow Thunderbird.
10. There (doesn't, don't) seem to be any soda pop left.

Exercise B Follow the directions for Exercise A.

1. (Doesn't, Don't) Sally and Ken like to dance?
2. Here (is, are) our first customers.
3. (Isn't, Aren't) there any pay phones here?
4. Where (is, are) the outlets?
5. He (doesn't, don't) ever work on weekends.
6. Where (is, are) your new sweatshirt with the hood?
7. Clothes (doesn't, don't) dry as fast in cold weather.
8. Here (is, are) the reference books.
9. I certainly (doesn't, don't) think so.
10. There (is, are) several boxes of powdered milk on the shelf.

·Additional Exercises

Making Subjects and Verbs Agree

A. Make verbs and subjects agree in number. Write the verb that agrees with the subject.

1. The lane for bicycles (is, are) on the west side of the road.
2. A truckload of bananas (has, have) spilled onto the highway.
3. My recipe for brownies (is, are) unbeatable.
4. Two pieces of the puzzle (is, are) left.
5. Several people, including Marion, (has, have) a key to the office.
6. Victor, as well as his co-workers, (goes, go) for a walk at lunchtime.
7. Noises from the street (drifts, drift) up to my room.
8. Our chances of winning (is, are) better than the other team's.
9. The slices of bread in this loaf (isn't, aren't) moldy.
10. Two rooms in addition to this one (is, are) being turned into storage areas.
11. The purpose of these lectures (was, were) to acquaint the audience with different styles of art.
12. Roger, together with his brothers, (works, work) on a ranch each summer.
13. The monkeys in that cage (seems, seem) quieter than they should be.
14. Your collection of old coins (grows, grow) larger each time I see it.
15. The photographs on this page (looks, look) very old.

B. Make verbs agree with compound subjects. Write the verb that agrees with the subject.

1. Peanuts or popcorn (makes, make) a good snack.

2. Warm gloves and a down jacket (is, are) important for skiiers.

3. Either ants or rain (has, have) ruined every picnic I've been on.

4. Privacy and free time (is, are) not always easy to find.

5. The suitcase and the totebag (is, are) both stuffed.

6. In school, neither Thomas Edison nor Albert Einstein (was, were) considered a good student.

7. Neither white rice nor white bread (provides, provide) as much nutrition as brown rice.

8. Mirrors and water (reflects, reflect) images backwards.

9. Farming and ranching (has, have) replaced buffalo hunting for many Plains Indians.

10. Neither Katy nor her sister (looks, look) pleased.

C. Make verbs agree with indefinite pronouns. Write the verb that agrees with the subject.

1. (Has, Have) any of the ice cream bars melted?

2. All of the snow (has, have) been blown into huge drifts.

3. All of the balloons (was, were) released at the rally.

4. Everyone in the stands (cheers, cheer) when the teams enter the stadium.

5. Each of the bikes (has, have) been customized.

6. Both of these books (contains, contain) that story.

7. Some of the injured players (insists, insist) on playing.

8. Some of the fudge (is, are) for the bake sale.

9. Another of those old Westerns (is, are) on tonight.

10. Either the manager or one of her assistants (handles, handle) complaints.

D. Solve other problems of agreement. Write the verb that agrees with the subject.

1. It (doesn't, don't) seem right to exclude Jim.
2. He (doesn't, don't) like these stereo speakers.
3. There (is, are) a lot of Vitamin D in milk.
4. There (is, are) special box seats for famous visitors.
5. Where (is, are) the nearest gas station?
6. Here (is, are) a wood-burning stove.
7. Where (is, are) my running shorts?
8. She (doesn't, don't) want to be on the committee.
9. (Doesn't, Don't) they have the lead roles?
10. Here (is, are) the missing pages from that book

Section 11

Using Compound and Complex Sentences

In preceding sections, you have learned how the parts of a sentence work together. In this section, you will learn about four different kinds of sentences. They can be studied and compared by their different structures. They are called simple sentences, compound sentences, complex sentences, and compound-complex sentences.

Part 1 Review of the Sentence

The sentence is composed of two basic parts. These key parts are the subject and the predicate.

Subject	Predicate
Lights	flash.
Lights	flash a signal.
Blinking lights at the control panel	flash a signal.

The **subject** of a sentence names the person or thing about which something is said. The **predicate** tells something about the subject.

The **simple predicate** is the verb. The subject of the verb is called the **simple subject.**

Within the subject of the sentence are the simple subject and its modifiers. In the predicate of the sentence are the verb, objects, predicate words, and their modifiers.

Compound Parts in a Sentence

You have learned that all of the parts of the sentence may be **compound.** Each one, in other words, may have more than one part.

Compound subject:	Neither sleep nor dreams are fully understood.
Compound verb:	The audience clapped, rooted, and cheered.
Compound predicate:	Derek cleaned the fish and then fried it on an open fire.
Compound object:	Janelle designed the store decorations and window displays.
Compound object of the preposition:	On holidays and weekends, the store is closed.
Compound predicate word:	That TV studio is large and empty.

The Simple Sentence

Even though sentences may have compound parts, they still express only one main idea. Such sentences, like all of those you have been studying, are called **simple sentences.**

A simple sentence is a sentence with only one subject and one predicate. The subject and the predicate, along with any part of the subject or predicate, may be compound.

Now you are ready to distinguish simple sentences from other types of sentences.

Exercise A Copy each of the following simple sentences. Then draw a line between the subject and the predicate.

1. Teresa and Nat have social security cards.
2. Theodore Roosevelt and Franklin D. Roosevelt were Presidents with strong personalities.
3. Dave found the tuxedo and the top hat in a thrift shop.
4. Stevie Wonder and Brenda Lee both began their singing careers as children.
5. China and Russia border Mongolia.
6. The books on that shelf are quite old and fragile.
7. Maria carefully measured the space for the shelf and then sawed the plywood.
8. The electrician was both quick and careful.
9. The orderly on night duty wears a headband and an Apache necklace.
10. Sharon keeps a flashlight and candles on hand for use during power failures.

Exercise B Write the compound subjects, verbs, and objects you find in these simple sentences.

1. The crew cleared and bulldozed ten acres of wilderness.
2. Vince Evans and Doug Williams are both quarterbacks.

3. First peel and then boil the potatoes.

4 Fireflies gathered in the trees and bushes.

5. South American Indians have unique crafts and customs.

6. Scrooge, Tiny Tim, and Oliver Twist are some of Charles Dickens's characters.

7. Early settlers used ashes, water, and grease to make soap.

8. Don wrote, read, and then rewrote the letter to Marsha.

9. Julia and Sandy left an hour ago and have not returned yet.

10. Did you and Martha finish the peanut butter and jam?

Part 2   The Compound Sentence

Sometimes two simple sentences express related ideas, and they are joined to form one sentence. The resulting sentence has more than one subject and more than one predicate. It is called a **compound sentence.**

A compound sentence consists of two or more simple sentences joined together. The parts of the compound sentence may be joined by a coordinating conjunction (*and, or, but*) or by a semicolon (;). Look at the following examples.

> The World Series is over, **and** the football season has begun.
> This hill is small, **but** it's perfect for sledding.
> Return your library books today, **or** you will have to pay a fine.
> Special tags on the clothing can set off an alarm; they help to prevent shoplifting.

Why are compound sentences used? Why don't writers use only simple sentences? This passage will help you to see why.

Young people receive training in many real-life skills. We take driver education. We have practice for sports. We not only have classes in school. We also have training on the job. We can take courses in everything from first aid to disco dancing. Instruction is important. It is not enough. Real-life experience is the final test.

The series of simple sentences one after another becomes dull and tiresome. Notice how much better the same paragraph sounds with compound sentences.

Young people receive training in many real-life skills. We take driver education, and we have practice for sports. We not only have classes in school, but we also have training on the job. We can take courses in everything from first aid to disco dancing. Instruction is important, but it is not enough. Real-life experience is the final test.

Diagraming Compound Sentences

If you can diagram simple sentences, you can diagram compound ones. The diagram simply shows that a compound sentence is two or more simple sentences joined together. The simple sentences are diagramed one under the other. Then the two sentences are connected with a dotted line. The coordinating conjunction sits on a "step" in the line.

The press secretary spoke first, and then the President held a press conference.

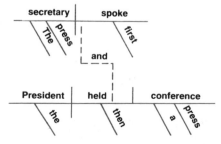

Exercise A   Number your paper from 1 to 10. Label three columns *Subject/Verb, Conjunction,* and *Subject/Verb.* For each sentence, fill in the columns.

Example: Nina sings well, but Angie and Ted sing better.

Subject/Verb	Conjunction	Subject/Verb
Nina/sings	but	Angie, Ted/sing

1. Montana is the Treasure State, and California is the Golden State.

2. The instructions confused me, but the nurse explained them.

3. Max led, and the others followed.

4. The first vehicle with a steam engine worked well for a few hours, but then its engine failed.

5. I have lost my pen, or else somebody has borrowed it.

6. The team is very strong this year, and so we are almost sure to win the city championship.

7. Compact cars get good mileage, but they have little cargo space.

8. Do you have a radio, or should I bring one?

9. The cavalry had ridden into Mexico on the trail of Chief Geronimo, but he evaded them.

10. The disc jockey talks to callers first, and then she plays records.

Exercise B   Follow the directions for Exercise A.

1. Height is important in basketball, and weight helps in football.

2. Marie wrapped the package, and I mailed it.

3. Ted ran all the way, but he missed the bus anyway.

4. The President ordered the strikers back to work, but they would not return.

5. Some plants eat insects, and the sundew plant is one of them.

6. Will you tell the umpire, or shall I talk to him?

7. The hail and rain slammed against the windows, and the wind banged at the door.

8. Sharon and Janet must share the award, or else nobody will receive it.

9. Levi-Strauss designed the first denim jeans in 1853, and the style has been popular ever since.

10. For the past hour Saul has been practicing the same tune on his horn, but he has not improved at all.

Compound Sentence or Compound Predicate?

You need to know the difference between a compound sentence and a simple sentence with a **compound predicate.** A compound predicate is two verbs within one predicate. The parts of a compound predicate, like the parts of a compound sentence, are joined by a coordinating conjunction.

Alana *joined the team* and *made the starting lineup.*
(This compound predicate is joined by *and.*)

How will you know if a sentence is compound or if it has a compound predicate? If each verb has its own subject, then the sentence is compound. If the verbs share the same subject, then only the predicate is compound.

s. v.   v.
Kyle entered a baking contest and *won* first place.

(This simple sentence has a compound predicate. Both verbs, *entered* and *won*, have the same subject, *Kyle.*)

s. v.   s. v.
Kyle entered a baking contest, and his *cheesecake won* first place.

(This is a compound sentence. The verb *entered* has its own subject, *Kyle.* The verb *won* has its own subject, *cheesecake.*)

^{S.}   ^{V.}   ^{V.}

S. V. V.

A *clerk types* letters and *files* information.

(The conjunction *and* joins the compound predicate of this simple sentence. Both verbs, *types* and *files*, have the same subject, *clerk*.)

S. V. S. V.

A *clerk types* letters, and a *computer files* information.

(This compound sentence is actually two simple sentences joined by the conjunction *and*.)

Exercise A Number your paper from 1 to 10. Decide whether the following sentences are compound sentences or simple sentences with compound predicates. Write *Compound Sentence* or *Compound Predicate*.

1. Gloria sits at the table and reads the newspaper after dinner.

2. Margie locked all the windows and then bolted both doors.

3. Mahatma Gandhi used nonviolent protest in India, and Martin Luther King, Jr. used it here.

4. The sand was getting in Rick's eyes, and he had to remove his contact lenses.

5. The lock on our mailbox is broken, but the janitor will fix it.

6. Which one is Mork, and which one is Mindy?

7. Betsy either swims or plays basketball every day.

8. The mail is late today, or maybe we did not get any.

9. I usually walk to school, but sometimes I take the bus.

10. Has Earl found a job, or is he still looking?

Exercise B Follow the directions for Exercise A.

1. Corrie poured salt on the icy sidewalk and then got her shovel.

2. Jeff raised the car's torsion bar and worked on the engine.

3. Dee was hired as a temporary worker but soon was given a permanent job.

4. Mary put some graphite in the old lock, and then the key turned.

5. Several players were cut from the team after the first season, and Barnes was one of them.

6. Network TV is seen across the country, but this station shows only local programs.

7. Did Ginger paint the walls or only wash them?

8. Joni counted the cash and added the checks correctly, but she forgot about the charge purchases.

9. Can you get to the dentist's office by 2:30, or shall I cancel your appointment?

10. Radio, television, and newspapers can change public opinion, but they can also reflect it.

Punctuating Compound Sentences

One of two punctuation marks is used in a compound sentence. Either a **comma** before a coordinating conjunction or a **semicolon** is needed to separate the two parts of a compound sentence. The punctuation keeps the two parts separate. It also shows where to pause in reading the sentence.

In a compound sentence, a comma is used before a coordinating conjunction. Notice how the comma is used in these compound sentences:

> s. v.   s   v
> The subway car was nearly full, **but** all of us piled in anyway.

> s.   v.   s.   v
> Sandra talked to her adviser, **and** he helped her with her schedule.

Instead of a comma and a conjunction, a semicolon may be used in a compound sentence.

           s.   **v.**   **s.**   **v.**
The young boy climbed the palm tree; he returned with a coconut.

       s.   **v.**
Mount McKinley is the highest point in the country;
     s.   **v.**
Death Valley is the lowest.

A semicolon may also be used with a **conjunctive adverb.** A conjunctive adverb is an adverb like *therefore, however, moreover, consequently,* or *otherwise.* It helps to join the two parts of a compound sentence. It also shows the relationship between them.

    s.   **v.**   **s.**   **v.**
We missed our bus; *however,* we caught a later bus.

      s.   **v.**
Heavy rains halted repairs on the highway; therefore, the
     s. **v.**
crew is behind schedule.

As you can see, a conjunctive adverb is used after a semicolon. It is followed by a comma.

The parts of a compound sentence are separated by either a comma or a semicolon. However, no punctuation is used between the two parts of a compound predicate. Notice the difference:

     s.   **v.**   **v.**
Stickball is played like baseball and requires a rubber ball with a stick.

     s.   **v.**   **v.**
The ranchers herded the cattle and branded them.

In addition, commas are not necessary in very short compound sentences.

Alarms rang and everyone awoke.
Either we're early or you're late.

Exercise A Commas and semicolons have been omitted between the parts of the following compound sentences. For each sentence, write the two words between which punctuation belongs. Put in the comma or semicolon. If a sentence needs no punctuation, write *Correct*.

1. You can make delicious pies from Concord grapes however, you must remove their seeds first.

2. Dr. Jekyll was the kind doctor and Mr. Hyde was Jekyll's evil other self.

3. The clouds parted they revealed a full moon.

4. I met Diana last week and I liked her immediately.

5. Sharon writes the newsletter Jerome distributes it.

6. Jay arrived and Cleo left.

7. Vanilla extract and unsweetened chocolate both smell good but they taste bitter.

8. The planet Mars has an average temperature of $-45°$ and Martian winds can blow at 300 miles per hour.

9. Sal and Joy bought season tickets but they attended only the first and the last games.

10. Basketball players must wear appropriate shoes otherwise, they risk injury to their feet and ankles.

Exercise B Follow the directions for Exercise A.

1. Mark did not see the glass door and he ran right into it.

2. Crocuses bloomed and robins returned.

3. Sheila signaled an S.O.S. with her flashlight however, the people on the beach did not know Morse code.

4. Sailors recognize an upside-down flag as an appeal for help and railroad engineers respond to a red flag by the track.

5. Stories about vampires and monsters are popular they have been told for many centuries.

6. Alligators look slow and clumsy nevertheless, they can move very fast.

7. Ms. Gomez manages the buildings Ms. Allweiss maintains them.

8. Quilts and oak furniture were once used in many homes but now they are too expensive to be common.

9. Students in the work-experience program can get jobs with sponsor companies or they can find jobs themselves.

10. Mother Jones was a union organizer and an activist but earlier she had taught in a convent.

Part 3 The Complex Sentence

You have learned about simple sentences and compound sentences. Another kind of sentence, the **complex sentence,** can also help you to express your thoughts.

Before you can understand the structure of a complex sentence, you must know what a clause is.

A clause is a group of words containing a verb and its subject.

According to this definition, a simple sentence is a clause. It contains a verb and its subject.

> s.   v.
> Keith ran in the marathon race.

> s.   v.
> Many stores have clearance sales.

It will be easier to understand sentences, though, if you think of a clause as a *part of a sentence*. Think of a clause as *a group of words within a sentence*.

Compound sentences contain clauses. Compound sentences have two or more groups of words with a subject and verb. Notice these examples.

> s.   v.   s.   v.
> Ms. Jackson demonstrated the loom, and she wove fibers for a rug.

> s.   v.   s. v.
> Sherlock Holmes is a fictional character, but he has a large fan club.

Clause or Phrase?

Clauses differ from phrases. Like a clause, a phrase is part of a sentence. However, a clause has a subject and a verb. A phrase does not.

> Phrases: after the season
> before the gold rush
>
>   **s.**   **v.**
> Clauses: after the Bengals kicked off
>
>   **s.**   **v.**
> before you left

Subordinate Clauses

The clauses of a compound sentence are actually two separate sentences. Each one can stand alone. Each is a **main clause.** A main clause, or **independent clause,** is a clause that can stand by itself as a sentence.

Subordinate clauses, or **dependent clauses,** are clauses that cannot stand alone. A subordinate clause is not a complete sentence. Study these examples:

>   **s.**   **v.**
> *If* you sign the contract
>
>   **s.**   **v.**
> *Before* the gates close

Both of the subordinate clauses above contain subjects and verbs. However, neither of them expresses a complete thought. Neither of them can stand alone. Both leave you wondering *then what?*

The words that begin subordinate clauses have an important function. Without *if* and *before*, the clauses above become sentences. Words like *if* and *before* are called **subordinating conjunctions.** We say that they *subordinate*, or make *dependent*, the words they introduce. Many, though not all, subordinate clauses begin with subordinating conjunctions.

Words often used as subordinating conjunctions are shown here:

Words Often Used as Subordinating Conjunctions			
after	because	so that	when
although	before	than	whenever
as	if	though	where
as if	in order that	till	wherever
as long as	provided	unless	while
as though	since	until	

Note: The words above are subordinating conjunctions only when they begin clauses. Many of them can be used in other ways.

Furthermore, not all subordinate clauses begin with subordinating conjunctions. Some clauses begin with words like these:

that	who, whom, whose
what, whatever	whoever, whomever
which	why
how	

Exercise Using *if, because, when, after,* and *since,* make subordinate clauses out of these sentences.

1. The bus was late.
2. The muffler is loose.
3. Diane enjoys bowling.
4. There is a pinball machine in the back.
5. The juke box played only old songs.
6. Bacon is a salty food.
7. Flies were buzzing around the table.
8. Keith's glasses are broken.
9. Strawberries are in season.
10. Toby worked at Head Start.

Definition of the Complex Sentence

Now that you know the difference between main clauses and subordinate clauses, you can understand the complex sentence.

A complex sentence is a sentence that contains one main clause and one or more subordinate clauses.

Main Clause	Subordinate Clause
We'll be out of the tournament	unless we win this game.
The real fun begins	when Anthony arrives.
King Kong is a fictional ape	that attacks New York.

Exercise A Find the subordinate clause in these complex sentences. Copy it. Underline the subject once and the verb twice.

1. Margaret asked if she could help us.
2. Summer was over before we knew it.
3. These clothes are on sale because they are unusual sizes.
4. The road freezes after the bridge does.
5. Earl stops by whenever he is in the neighborhood.
6. Claudia looks as if she knows the punchline.
7. Mattie steadied the ladder while Dawn replaced the bulb.
8. The ham will spoil unless you refrigerate it.
9. Unless you can think of a better idea, we will use mine.
10. Although Bobbie disliked buckwheat pancakes, she politely finished hers.

Exercise B Follow the directions for Exercise A.

1. Clyde weighs more now than he has ever weighed.
2. Jill climbed onto the top of a truck so that she could see over the crowd.
3. As the Buick was turning left, the light changed.

4. When John is daydreaming, he ignores everything around him.

5. Wherever there are wars, there are refugees.

6. Vanessa works hard at whatever she does.

7. Maria acted as though she had not heard the news.

8. Can't he remember where the bases are?

9. I don't know why she is angry at us.

10. Tina explained how the controls should be set.

Part 4   Adverb Clauses

Complex sentences contain subordinate clauses. The subordinate clause may be one of three kinds. One type is the **adverb clause.** An adverb clause has the same function as an adverb.

An **adverb** modifies a verb, an adjective, or another adverb. It tells *how, when, where,* or *to what extent.*

Adverb: Marissa watched *intently.*

An **adverb phrase** is a prepositional phrase used as an adverb.

Adverb phrase: Marissa watched *on the sidelines.*

An adverb clause is a subordinate clause used as an adverb.

Adverb clause: Marissa watched *while the gymnasts practiced.*

When the voters were polled, Al was leading.

Adverb clauses, like adverbs and adverb phrases, tell *how, when, where,* and *to what extent.* They modify verbs, adjectives, and adverbs.

Remember that a clause, unlike a phrase, has a subject and a verb.

Diagraming Adverb Clauses

To diagram an adverb clause, place it on a separate horizontal line below the main line. A dotted line connects the adverb clause to the word it modifies in the main clause. The subordinating conjunction is shown on the dotted line.

When Carlos was twelve, he moved to New York.

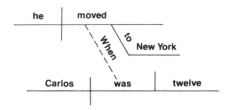

Exercise A   Copy the adverb clause from each sentence.

1. We waited until the street was empty.
2. If the treaty is signed, the two nations will be at peace.
3. Although it was December, the weather was warm.
4. The boss calls us when she needs extra workers.
5. The snow was twelve inches deep before the city managers agreed upon a removal plan.
6. Flies should be kept out because they carry diseases.
7. Helmets flashed in the sun as the bikers roared past.
8. Greg stirred the chili with one hand while he answered the phone with the other.
9. Walt Disney made his cartoon animals act as though they were human.
10. The Greys have needed to call the janitor only once since they moved in.

Exercise B   Follow the directions for Exercise A.

1. Nurses can usually find jobs wherever they go.
2. Although Rita Gomez has not appeared in movies here, she is a popular movie actress in the Philippines.

3. When the President addressed the United Nations, his speech was translated into many languages.

4. The doctor had to reset Linda's broken arm because she fell on it again.

5. Before electricity became available, many people went to sleep right after sundown.

6. If the newsstand is out of papers, try the drug store.

7. Whenever Jeannie makes a winning basket, she seems amazed.

8. As Sam answered the questions, the computer recorded the answers.

9. Matt must work the second shift until Josie can return to the job.

10. Because Gail had taken a first aid class, she knew immediately what to do.

Part 5 Adjective Clauses

The second kind of subordinate clause is the **adjective clause.** An adjective clause has the same function as an adjective.

An **adjective** modifies a noun or pronoun.

Adjective: Melissa wears *big, round* sunglasses.

An **adjective phrase** is a prepositional phrase that modifies a noun or pronoun.

Adjective phrase: We glanced at the list *of sandwiches.*

An adjective clause is a subordinate clause used as an adjective to modify a noun or pronoun.

Adjective clause: A polygraph is a machine *that is used in lie detection.*

Anyone *who tries hard enough* can stay awake.

Adjective clauses, like adjectives and adjective phrases, tell *what kind* or *which one*. They usually come directly after the word they modify. Unlike adjective phrases, adjective clauses have subjects and verbs.

There are several words used to introduce adjective clauses. Two of them are *where* and *when*.

> This is the studio *where recordings are made.*

> This is the time *when the moon is full.*

Relative Pronouns

Besides *when* and *where*, the words *who*, *whom*, and *whose* are also used to begin adjective clauses. *Who*, *whom*, and *whose* are called **relative pronouns.** They relate a clause, called a **relative clause,** to a noun or pronoun in the sentence. Sometimes *that* and *which* are relative pronouns.

Here are the words used as relative pronouns:

> who   whom   whose   that   which

Relative pronouns are special because they have three functions:

1. They introduce adjective clauses.
2. They link the clause to a word in the main clause.
3. They have a function within the clause. They act as subject, object, or predicate pronoun of the verb within the adjective clause. They may also be the object of a preposition in the clause. *Whose* functions as an adjective.

> Students *who work part-time* are dismissed early.
> (*Who* is the subject of *work*.)

> The dentist's office plays music *that is soothing.*
> (*That* is the subject of is.)

> The person *whom we need most* is Anna.
> (*Whom* is the direct object of *need*.)

The girl *with whom I chatted* turned out to be a distant cousin.

(*Whom* is the object of the preposition *with*.)

Children *whose parents work here* may attend the day-care center.

(*Whose* modifies *parents*, the subject of the clause.)

Sometimes you may be confused about whether *who* or *whom* is the correct relative pronoun. To decide, see how the pronoun is used within the clause. Keep in mind that *who* is the subject form. *Whom* is the object form.

Diagraming Adjective Clauses

To diagram an adjective clause, use a separate line beneath the main line. A dotted line runs from the relative pronoun to the word in the main clause that the adjective clause modifies.

The people who run the space program are in Houston.

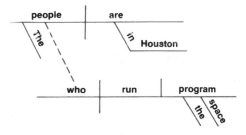

One of the players on whom we depend was injured.

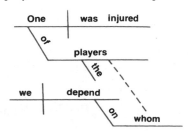

Exercise A Copy the adjective clause from each sentence. Underline the subject once and the verb twice. Before the clause, write the word it modifies.

> Example: She is the teacher who wrote our textbook.
> teacher—who wrote our textbook

1. It had been the coldest winter that New York had ever had.
2. The movie that is playing at the Varsity is a comedy.
3. Staph germs in the body head for tissue that is damaged.
4. Donna is the cheerleader who also plays baseball.
5. One American writer who lived in Paris was James Baldwin.
6. Students who are on the basketball team usually practice after classes.
7. The mayor is the person to whom the petition should be sent.
8. Fireflies, which are really beetles, produce cold lights.
9. The car that Mr. Sardo bought is an old convertible.
10. This is the time of day that I like best.

Exercise B Follow the directions for Exercise A.

1. One of the boxing tournaments that means the most is the Golden Gloves.
2. The mechanic who gave the estimate no longer works here.
3. In almost every family there is someone who cannot throw anything away.
4. Panama, which joins Central America and South America, is a small but important country.
5. The foster home in which the child was placed was near his old neighborhood.
6. The artist and her husband designed their own home, which was made of steel and glass.

7. The manager gave the reporter a list of the players whose contracts had been renewed.

8. The man whose dog bit me drove me to the hospital.

9. Sunday night is the time when television attracts the most viewers.

10. People for whom we have no current address must be crossed from the list.

Part 6   Noun Clauses

The noun clause is the third kind of subordinate clause.

A noun clause is a clause used as a noun in a sentence. Like a noun, a noun clause can be used as a subject, an object of the verb, a predicate word, or an object of a preposition. It can be used in any of the ways that nouns are used. Unlike adverb and adjective clauses, noun clauses do not modify.

Uses of Noun Clauses

Subject:	*Whoever sent the mayday* must need help.
	What concerns everyone is inflation.
Direct object:	Scientists cannot always predict *when an earthquake will occur.*
	The controller radioed *that the runway was clear.*
Object of preposition:	Rod was impressed by *whatever Joyce said.*
	(The clause is the object of the preposition *by*.)
	The signs point to *where the trail begins.*
	(The clause is the object of the preposition *to*.)
Predicate noun:	City life is *what he wants.*
	The fact was *that the car was missing.*

As you can see from these examples, many noun clauses begin with the words *that* and *what*. The words *whatever*, *who*, *whoever*, and *whomever* can also introduce noun clauses. *Where*, *when*, *how*, and *why* are used, too.

Diagraming Noun Clauses

To diagram a noun clause, extend a bridge from the place where the clause is used in the sentence. The word that introduces the clause belongs on a line over the clause.

1. Noun clause used as subject

What you need is a sense of humor.

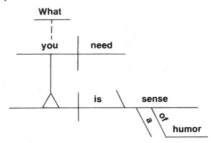

2. Noun clause used as object of the verb

Many people say that good times are ahead.

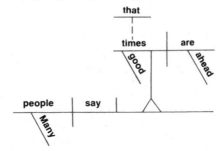

3. Noun clause used as object of a preposition

The candidate talked to whoever would listen.

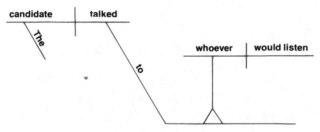

Exercise A Copy the noun clauses in these sentences. Underline the subject once and the verb twice. Tell how the clause is used.

1. Now I understand why you left early.
2. Patrice explained how yogurt is made.
3. Waterloo is where Napoleon was defeated.
4. The reason is that Jake works late.
5. You can make a scarf from whatever fabric is left.
6. Mickie starts a conversation with whoever sits next to her.
7. There will be enough food for whomever you invite.
8. Whoever made that statement does not know the facts.
9. What the audience wanted was another encore.
10. We all worried about where Roland could possibly be.

Exercise B Follow the directions for Exercise A.

1. The manager promised that she would look for my lost roll of film.
2. Hal asked why the game had been delayed.
3. How the pyramids were built is a fascinating story.
4. Alex said that high ozone levels give him headaches.
5. I wonder where the time has gone.
6. When the party is over is up to us.
7. Ken thinks that he has the winning ticket.
8. The only solution is that we raise the funds ourselves.
9. The minister spends her time with whoever needs it.
10. What the neighbors will think bothers him too much.

Part 7 A Review of Subordinate Clauses

You have learned about the three kinds of subordinate clauses. They are the adverb clause, the adjective clause, and the noun clause.

The only way to identify the kind of clause is to look at its use in the sentence. A clause used as a noun is a noun clause. A clause used as a modifier is an adverb or adjective clause, depending on the word modified.

Exercise A Write the subordinate clause in each sentence. If the clause is used as a noun clause, tell how it is used in the sentence. If the clause is used as an adjective or adverb clause, tell what it modifies.

1. Nevada is one state where wild horses still roam.
2. I wonder where I left my backpack.
3. When the movie was over, the audience was silent.
4. Andrew Young, who was once our UN Ambassador, spoke at the assembly.
5. Carol suddenly realized who was on the phone.
6. Tom always worries about what he will say next.
7. The schooldays that were lost during the snowstorm will be made up in June.
8. Ellie remembered that she had a job interview at 3:30.
9. Find a seat wherever you can.
10. Trees that follow day-night cycles may be injured by bright streetlights.

Exercise B Follow the directions for Exercise A.

1. The ring, which had belonged to her grandmother, was Celia's most cherished possession.
2. Call the clinic right away if the pain becomes worse.
3. Neighborhoods that have no parks are rare in Chicago.
4. The census taker who visited our block spoke Spanish.
5. The child could not describe the woman who had left the package.
6. Who will start is the coach's decision.
7. Carl will not answer the phone while he is eating dinner.

8. While Glenda was rehearsing a loud scene from the play, the people next door became worried about her.

9. After Judith wins a game, she sews another tiny smile face on the back of her jacket.

10. The janitor said that he would replace the doorknob tonight.

Part 8   Clauses as Sentence Fragments

You have studied about sentence fragments. You learned about fragments that do not have subjects and verbs.

Alone on the lake.   Played the jukebox.

The subordinate clause can be a sentence fragment, too, even though it does have a subject and verb. It still does not express a complete thought. For that reason, it is a sentence fragment. It is only part of a sentence. It is not meant to stand alone.

Notice the difference between these word groups:

The TV was on
While the TV was on

The first word group is a sentence. The subordinating conjunction *while*, though, makes the second word group a sentence fragment. The subordinate clause should be used as part of a sentence.

A subordinate clause must not be written as a complete sentence. It must always be joined to a main clause.

Fragment: When we have winter.
Sentence: When we have winter, Australia has summer.

Fragment: How the gadget worked.
Sentence: No one understood how the gadget worked.

Exercise A Number your paper from 1 to 10. Decide whether the groups of words below are sentences or fragments. Write *S* for *Sentence* and *F* for *Fragment*. Add words to make each fragment a complete sentence. Punctuate and capitalize where necessary.

1. What did the announcer say
2. When is the playoff game
3. What the instructions said
4. After the rain stops
5. After a while everyone returned
6. That showroom is filled with new cars
7. The book that you needed
8. Before the dance started
9. Why is the flag at half-mast
10. Why the dogs are barking

Exercise B Follow the directions for Exercise A.

1. Why the movie ended that way
2. Winter seems longer than summer
3. Whose notebook is this
4. The team practices after school
5. Before breakfast Julie exercises
6. Before the morning was over
7. Crime increases during a full moon
8. That is the signal
9. Because the building is seventy-five years old
10. If the bicycle tire cannot be patched

Part 9 Compound-Complex Sentences

You have already been introduced to simple, compound, and complex sentences. The fourth and final kind of sentence is the **compound-complex sentence.**

A compound-complex sentence consists of two or more main clauses and one or more subordinate clauses.

It may help you to think of a compound-complex sentence as a compound sentence plus a subordinate clause. Actually, the compound-complex sentence joins two sentences, at least one of which has a subordinate clause. The clause may be an adjective, adverb, or noun clause. The main clauses are joined by either a coordinating conjunction or a semicolon.

These are examples of compound-complex sentences:

Main Clause   Main Clause   Subordinate Clause

Yogurt is nutritious, and some say *that it brings good health*.

Subordinate Clause   Main Clause   Main Clause

When Dan called, he was angry; however, he soon calmed down.

Exercise Identify the two main clauses and the subordinate clause in these compound-complex sentences.

1. A bola is a rope that has weights at the end; it is used to catch cattle.

2. Larry tried the disco steps that we demonstrated, but he couldn't quite master them.

3. The instructor told us how we could revive a heart attack victim, and she demonstrated on a dummy.

4. Blair House is located across the street from the White House, and foreign leaders who visit Washington often stay there.

5. Hiawatha was the hero of a poem; moreover, he was a Mohawk chief who organized tribes into the Five Nations.

6. The election judges distribute the ballots, and then they count them after the polls close.

7. In earlier times, infants were wrapped with strips of cloth; people thought that the bindings made babies feel secure.

8. Al drives a snow-removal truck, and whenever a heavy snow falls, he is called to work.

9. Some television sets have tubes; however, newer models, which are usually smaller, are solid state.

10. I've just learned that Congress has set a new minimum wage; consequently, my pay will increase.

Part 10   A Review of Sentences

There are four basic kinds of sentences.

A **simple sentence** contains one subject and one predicate. Parts of the simple sentence, however, may be compound. A simple sentence tells one idea.

> s.　　　v.
> The tower transmits radio signals.

> s.　　v.　　　　　　　　v.
> Alexis was born in Alaska but grew up in Texas.

A **compound sentence** is made up of two simple sentences. These simple sentences are connected by a comma and coordinating conjunction or by a semicolon. Sometimes a conjunctive adverb follow the semicolon. A compound sentence expresses two related ideas.

> s.　v.　　　　　　　　　s.　　v.
> The tower is 300 feet tall, and it transmits radio signals.

> s.　　v.　　　　　　　　s.　　v.
> Alexis was born in Alaska; however, she grew up in Texas.

A **complex sentence** contains one main clause and one or more subordinate clauses. The subordinate clauses may be used as adverbs, adjectives, or nouns. A complex sentence expresses one main idea and one or more dependent ideas.

> s.　v.　　　　　　　　　　　　s.　v.
> *Because the tower is the tallest structure in the city*, it is used to transmit radio signals.

> s.　　v.　　　　　　　　s.　　v.
> *Although Alexis was born in Alaska*, she grew up in Texas.

A **compound-complex sentence** contains two main clauses and one or more subordinate clauses. The subordinate clauses may be adverb, adjective, or noun clauses. A compound-complex sentence expresses two main ideas, as well as one dependent idea.

         s.   **v.**   **s.**   **v.**

The tower is the tallest structure in the city, and it transmits

         s.   **v.**

radio signals *that are heard throughout the Midwest.*

       s.   **v.**   **s.**   **v.**

Although Alexis was born in Alaska, she grew up in Texas;

       s.   **v.**

now she is living in New York.

Exercise A Number your paper from 1 to 10. For each sentence, write *Simple, Compound, Complex,* or *Compound-Complex* to show what kind it is.

1. Why did the governor veto that bill?

2. Ron asked why everyone was laughing, and Sylvia explained.

3. The helicopter can carry thirty-three armed soldiers, a truck, and supplies.

4. The members of the Drama Club not only produce plays but also write them.

5. When Cortez arrived in Mexico, the Aztecs mistook him for the god of the morning star.

6. What a costly mistake that was!

7. Juanita hopes that one day she will become a chef.

8. Deep in space is a cloud of comets that are made of dust, rock fragments, and frozen gases.

9. Because the planet Pluto is very small and very far away, it was not discovered until 1930.

10. How does the discovery of a new planet influence astrology?

Exercise B Follow the directions for Exercise A.

1. Tracy sings while she plays.

2. Tim ran to the field as fast as he could, but the coach had already left.

3. The planner interviewed the neighborhood residents, and then she wrote her recommendations.

4. After I wrote the report, I proofread it.

5. After this exercise you should flex your shoulders and stretch.

6. The man in the pinstriped, three-piece suit looked odd with the wet dog in his arms.

7. Did you invite Vanessa, or did she just stop by?

8. Do you drink diet drinks, which might contain a harmful substance, or do you drink sugared drinks, which are fattening?

9. General MacArthur said that he would return.

10. The airlines know that some passengers will not show up; therefore, extra tickets are sold for each flight.

Additional Exercises

Using Compound and Complex Sentences

A. Analyze simple and compound sentences. Write *Simple* or *Compound* to show what kind each sentence is.

1. At this airport, a plane departs or lands every minute.
2. Jan borrowed money from me and never paid it back.
3. The map is old, but it will serve as a general guide.
4. The hubcap fell off and clattered down the road.
5. Debra applied for a job at the stables, and she got it.
6. Batman and Robin have amazed children for years.
7. Some Islamic women wear veils, but others do not.
8. This beanbag chair is comfortable, I fell asleep in it.
9. Ernie is on vacation but he will be home on Monday.
10. This restaurant is always open and always full.

B. Analyze and punctuate compound sentences. Copy these compound sentences. Underline each subject once, and each verb twice. Punctuate correctly.

1. Marshmallows are candy marsh mallows are plants.
2. Many players dislike artificial turf nevertheless, they must play on it.
3. We must catch that train it is the last one today.
4. The fare increased and service improved.
5. Ron's dive was superb but he didn't win the contest.
6. Will you choose an album or shall I pick one?
7. The snow has melted and soon the trees will bud.
8. The truck weighs three tons it cannot stop very fast.
9. The factory shut down however it will reopen soon.
10. Rachel is shy but she has a good sense of humor.

C. Distinguish clauses and phrases. Tell whether the italicized words in each sentence are a *Clause* or a *Phrase*.

1. The pool doesn't open *until Memorial Day*.
2. The passenger was nervous *until the plane landed*.
3. *As Jerry made a basket*, the backboard shattered.
4. As *a special reward*, John received twenty dollars.
5. The coach gave us a pep talk *before the second half*.
6. *Before she became editor*, Marla was a features writer.
7. We have been awake *since 5:00 A.M.*
8. *Since Joshua lives close to school*, we often stop at his house.
9. *After the alarm rang*, firefighters dashed to their trucks.
10. *After the concert*, fans waited by the stage door.

D. Recognize adverb clauses. Write each adverb clause. Underline its subject once and its verb twice. Then write the word modified by the clause.

1. Although we came to Boston for a weekend, we stayed there for two weeks.
2. Carolyn spilled the paint as she reached for the brush.
3. Because Ed has practice every day, he values his free time.
4. Since Ian had been benched, Cal got a chance to play.
5. Danny helped with the dishwashing after the other guests had left.
6. Our radio doesn't play well unless it is facing south.
7. The editor spliced the film after she cut a scene.
8. The courtroom artist sketched as the witness talked.
9. Dennis needs braces because his front teeth aren't straight.
10. After her defeat, Natalie trained harder than she ever had before.

E. Recognize adjective clauses. Write each adjective clause. Underline its subject once and its verb twice. Then write the word modified by the clause.

1. One of the courses that start next semester is Science Fiction 100.
2. February 2 is the day when the groundhog looks for its shadow.
3. One artist whom I admire is Georgia O'Keeffe.
4. The candidate who earns the most electoral votes wins the nomination.
5. Ms. Simmons is the only choir member who can do justice to that spiritual.
6. The cabinet where the supplies are kept is in here.
7. The coach, who had once played professional basketball, brought the team to first place.
8. Where did Karen put the card that I brought?
9. The priest calmed the people who had been hurt.
10. Here is the saw that I borrowed.

F. Recognize noun clauses. Write each noun clause. Underline the subject once and the verb twice. Tell whether the clause is used as a subject, direct object, object of a preposition, or predicate noun.

1. Nicole explained how an electric car operates.
2. Whatever the child asked for was given to him.
3. In the fog, Liz could hardly see where she was going.
4. Your problem is that you never listen.
5. A trophy was made for whoever won the contest.
6. The newspapers told how the crime was committed.
7. The sportscaster commented that the Steelers had a strong defense.
8. Whoever answered the phone has a high voice.
9. Everybody listened to what the coach said.
10. David told us only what we wanted to hear.

G. Identify sentences. For each sentence, write *Simple, Compound, Complex*, or *Compound-Complex*.

1. Pauline and Laura gathered the pages together, and Matt stapled them.

2. Until midnight Jerome rehearsed his speech.

3. Jane steered the jeep down the muddy road to the river, and then she discovered that the bridge had collapsed.

4. The callouses on her hands are not from work; they are from climbing the rope in gym.

5. Long ago, soldiers bit on bullets while they were having surgery.

6. The young recruits lined up and listened for their orders.

7. If you place the avocado pit in water, it will soon sprout.

8. When there is a snowstorm, cars are towed away.

9. Eric Heiden won five Olympic gold medals, and his sister Beth won a bronze medal.

10. Our van holds more people than a station wagon does.

Section 12

The Right Word

You have studied how to use the sentence and its parts correctly. In this section you will learn to use specific problem words correctly.

Part 1 Standard and Nonstandard English

The language that is presented in this textbook is appropriate at all times and in all places. It is called **standard English.** Standard English is the language of educated people. It is the language that would be judged correct by people in all situations.

In many situations, if you do not use standard English, some people may think of you as less careful or less intelligent. **Nonstandard English** is language that is not generally accepted by all people in all situations.

Here are some examples of standard and nonstandard English:

Nonstandard	Standard
Al should of brung the wood hisself.	Al should have brought the wood himself.
Me and Jody set in the shade.	Jody and I sat in the shade.
He don't know there ain't no difference.	He doesn't know there isn't any difference.

Part 2 Formal and Informal English

Even if you always use standard English, you will use different kinds of language at different times. You wouldn't use the same words, for example, in a letter asking for a job as you would on the phone to a friend. Some situations are more formal than others. In the same way, the language is either formal or informal. Read the following examples:

Formal: During the past five years, the rate of migration from the city to rural areas has increased sharply.

Informal: It's time for a change. Let's move out of the city. We'll find a little farm somewhere and raise chickens.

Formal English is marked by longer sentences, longer words, fewer contractions, and a less personal approach. It is used in the writing of some papers, books, and articles. Informal English, on the other hand, is better for speaking and for using in less important writing situations.

Part 3 Other Types of Language

There are other kinds of English, too. **Slang,** for example, includes expressions that are acceptable only in very casual speech. Some slang phrases are "going bananas," "off the wall," and "uptight." Words from the past that are outdated are called **archaic** or **obsolete.** In addition, language relating to sports, music, science, law, and the military often has a special meaning.

Each kind of language is appropriate at certain times. Legal phrases, for example, belong in the courts, and poetic phrases belong in poetry. At the dinner table, you wouldn't say, "Ere we begin, 'tis the sugar I shall request." In the same way, you wouldn't write in a job application, "Hey, man, how's about givin' me a job?"

Using any of these kinds of language in the wrong situation would be inappropriate. Someone wearing a winter coat during a heat wave would seem odd. In the same way, using slang in a report or using formal English in the locker room would stand out. As you gain more and more skill with English, you will learn to gear your language to the appropriate time and place.

The next part of this section will help you to sharpen your skills in using standard English.

Part 4 Words Often Confused

The words listed in this section are often misused. The pairs of words may look alike or have similar meanings. However, they are not alike. One word cannot be used in place of the other. Study the lists of words often confused. Try to use the right word at the right time.

These words are often confused because they look alike. Notice, however, that their meanings differ.

capital means "most important." It also names the city or town that is the official center of government for a state or country.

capitol refers to the building where a state legislature meets.

the Capitol is the building in Washington, D.C., where the United States Congress meets.

> The *capital* of New York is Albany.
> The state *capitol* dome can be seen for miles.
> Farmers protested outside the *Capitol* in Washington.

des′ ert means "a dry, barren region."

de sert′ means "to abandon."

des sert′ (note the difference in spelling) is a sweet food at the end of a meal.

> The explorers were stranded in the *desert*.
> Did the soldier *desert* his company?
> Our *dessert* tonight is banana cake.

hear means "to listen to or to receive sound by the ear."

here refers to this place.

> Did you *hear* the screeching brakes?
> A new record store will open *here*.

its is a possessive, meaning belonging to *it*.

it's is the contraction for *it is* or *it has*.

> The band has *its* own sound system.
> *It's* almost midnight.

loose means either "not tight" or "free and untied."

lose means "to be unable to find or keep." It is also the opposite of *win*.

> Several snakes from the zoo are *loose*.
> I *lose* my balance when I spin on skates.
> Did the wrestlers *lose* the meet?

principal means "leading, chief, or highest in importance."

principle refers to a basic truth, rule, or law.

The *principal* industry here is steel-making.
The basic *principle* of this country is democracy.

stationary means "not moving, fixed."
stationery refers to writing materials like paper and envelopes.

The trailer can move, but right now it's *stationary*.
The drugstore sells boxes of *stationery*.

their shows possession by *them*.
there means "in that place."
they're is the contraction for *they are*.

The steelworkers have *their* own union.
The bus route ends *there*.
They're losing their courage.

to means "toward or as far as."
too means "also or extremely."

Tracy slid *to* home plate.
I read the book, and I saw the movie *too*.

weather refers to the condition of the atmosphere, such as its heat or cold, wetness or dryness.
whether indicates a choice between two things.

The *weather* in Florida is usually pleasant.
Ask Stacy *whether* she is going or staying.

who's is the contraction for *who is* or *who has*.
whose is the possessive form of *who*.

Who's running the duplicating machine?
Whose sandwich is this?

your shows possession by *you*.
you're is the contraction for *you are* or *you were*.

When is *your* birthday?
You're on the team, aren't you?

459

Exercise A Choose the right word from the words given.

1. From the top of the Washington Monument, we looked down at the white dome of the nation's (capital, capitol, Capitol).

2. The (deserted, desserted) building was a dangerous place to play.

3. Sand dunes in the (desert, dessert) are always shifting due to wind and rain.

4. We could (hear, here) the alarm four blocks away.

5. The computer can correct some of (its, it's) own mistakes.

6. (Its, It's) always cold in the supermarket.

7. Ballet slippers should be tight, not (loose, lose).

8. I don't want to (loose, lose) my place in line.

9. The (principals, principles) stated in the Hippocratic Oath are still important to doctors.

10. The letter was typed on official (stationary, stationery).

Exercise B Follow the directions for Exercise A.

1. Holly arrived at the meeting early, but Hank got (their, there, they're) late.

2. Sometimes the players get careless when (their, there, they're) ahead.

3. All the students in the speech class have heard (their, there, they're) own voices on tape.

4. The bowling ball veered (to, too) far to the left.

5. Josh yielded (to, too) the school bus making a turn.

6. Are you getting off at this stop, (to, too)?

7. I wonder (weather, whether) I should call her or write her a letter.

8. (Who's, Whose) that leaning against the stop sign?

9. (Who's, Whose) story do you believe?

10. (Your, You're) certainly in fine form today.

Part 5   Troublesome Verbs

These pairs of verbs are often confused. Notice how they differ.

Bring and Take

Bring refers to movement toward the person speaking. Example: The pipeline *brings* water here to the desert.

Take refers to motion away from the speaker. Example: Did you *take* those books back to the library?

Here are the principal parts of these verbs:

bring, brought, brought

Present: *Bring* that hammer to me, please.
Past: We *brought* Janet with us.
Past Participle: No one *has brought* enough money.

take, took, taken

Present: When you leave, *take* some cake.
Past: I *took* my cycle there to be fixed.
Past Participle: Someone *has taken* my keys.

Learn and Teach

Learn means "to gain knowledge or skill." Example: Did you *learn* the words to that song?

Teach means "to help someone learn." Example: Will you *teach* me to dribble?

Here are the principal parts of these verbs:

learn, learned, learned

Present: *Learn* the metric system.
Past: Cal *learned* karate.
Past Participle: We *have learned* Spanish.

teach, taught, taught

Present: Mrs. Rivera *teaches* music.
Past: Kelly *taught* me about photography.
Past Participle: This course *has taught* us about carpentry.

Let and Leave

Let means "to allow or permit." Example: *Let* her go.

Leave means "to go away from" or "to allow something to remain." Example: *Leave* us alone.

The principal parts of these verbs are as follows:

let, let, let

Present: *Let* the motor run for a minute.
Past: Dad *let* the dog out.
Past Participle: The landlord *has let* us stay.

leave, left, left

Present: *Leave* your jacket on.
Past: Jennifer *left* in a hurry.
Past Participle: The robbers *had left* with the cash.

Lie and Lay

Lie means "to rest in a flat position" or "to be in a certain place." Example: *Lie* still.

Lay means "to place." Example: *Lay* the wreath here.

Here are the principal parts of these verbs:

lie, lay, lain

Present: *Lie* down on this mat.
Past: Jason *lay* in bed all day.
Past Participle: The patient *has lain* very still.

lay, laid, laid

Present: *Lay* the baby in her crib.
Past: The nurse *laid* a bandage on the wound.
Past Participle: Workers *have laid* the foundation.

May and Can

May refers to permission. *May* also refers to something that is possible. *Might* is another form of the word.

May we *have* dessert?   I *might be* wrong.

Can refers to ability. *Can* means being physically or mentally able to do something. *Could* is another form.

> *Can* you *do* a push-up?   We *could* not *remember*.

May and *might* and *can* and *could* have no principal parts. They are used as helping verbs.

Rise and Raise

Rise means "to go upward." Example: The sun rises.
Raise means "to lift or to make something go up." Example: *Raise* your right hand.
The principal parts of these verbs are as follows:

rise, rose, risen

Present: The steam *rises* and disappears.
Past: The choir *rose* from their seats.
Past Participle: The drawbridge *has risen*.

raise, raised, raised

Present: Please *raise* the window shade.
Past: Kim *raised* the ladder to reach the roof.
Past Participle: Inflation *has raised* the cost of living.

Sit and Set

Sit means "to occupy a seat." Example: *Sit* on this bench.
Set means "to place." Example: *Set* the tools there.
The principal parts of these verbs are as follows:

sit, sat, sat

Present: *Sit* near me, please.
Past: We *sat* in the waiting room.
Past Participle: All of the passengers *have sat* down.

set, set, set

Present: *Set* your toothbrush on the sink.
Past: John *set* the books in his new bookcase.
Past Participle: We *have set* the costumes backstage.

Exercise A   Choose the right verb from the two given.

1. We (sat, set) aside some money in a savings account.
2. The sales tax has (raised, risen) to 6 percent.
3. Litter (lay, laid) all over the park.
4. Stranded passengers (sat, set) in the airport.
5. I'll (bring, take) my glasses here to be repaired.
6. The dog (learned, taught) to obey simple commands.
7. Someone (let, left) the blueprints on the table.
8. (May, Can) we use the employees' elevator, please?
9. The photographer (sat, set) the film in a jar to develop.
10. Marlene's boss (raised, rose) her pay.

Exercise B   Follow the directions for Exercise A.

1. Many people (may not, cannot) change a flat tire.
2. (Take, Bring) those books to the library, please.
3. The players (lay, laid) their cards on the table.
4. Who (learned, taught) you about self-defense?
5. When (may, can) students (let, leave) the campus?
6. The gymsuit has (lain, laid) in that locker all year.
7. The manager would not (let, leave) the boys in.
8. Ms. Rawls said we (may, can) park in her driveway.
9. As a plumber's aide, Mike (learned, taught) a trade.
10. The factory (raised, rose) its level of production.

Part 6   Usage Problems

The words in this section are often used incorrectly. Notice the standard usages for these problem words.

accept means "to agree to something or to receive something willingly."

except means "to leave out." *Except* also means "not including."

"I *accept* the blame," Todd said.

"We'll *except* you from this rule," the counselor said.

We bought all the supplies *except* glue.

agree on means "to come to an understanding." You and others agree *on* a plan.

agree to means "to consent to." You agree *to* something, such as a plan.

agree with means "to have the same opinion as someone else." You agree *with* somebody. *Agree with* may also refer to something being suitable, as when foods don't *agree with* you.

The Democrats *agreed on* a candidate.

The team *agreed to* stiff training rules.

Mr. Jackson likes people who always *agree with* him.

Chocolate doesn't *agree with* me.

all right is the correct spelling. *Alright* is nonstandard. There are two words.

All right, I'll turn off the TV.

Ariel felt *all right* after her tonsils were removed.

among refers to a group of more than two people or things.

between refers to two people or things.

We divided the food *among* the four of us.

There is a treaty *between* the two countries.

anywhere, nowhere, somewhere, and **anyway** are standard usages. The words *anywheres, nowheres, somewheres,* and *anyways* are nonstandard. The final *s* should be dropped.

Nonstandard: She wasn't anywheres in sight.
Standard: She wasn't *anywhere* in sight.

Nonstandard: I know that clip is here somewheres.
Standard: I know that clip is here *somewhere*.

between each, followed by a singular noun, is incorrect. *Between* should not be used with a singular noun.

Nonstandard: Between each game, the Bears practiced hard.
Standard: *Between games*, the Bears practiced hard.

Nonstandard: The elevator stopped
between every floor.
Standard: The elevator stopped
between floors.

borrow means "to receive something on loan." Don't confuse it with *lend*, meaning "to give out temporarily."

Nonstandard: Will you borrow me your pen?
Standard: Will you *lend* me your pen?
Standard: May I *borrow* your pen?

Exercise A Look for sentences with nonstandard usage. Rewrite those sentences, using the right words. If a sentence is correct, write *Correct* after that number.

1. Between each quarter of the game, the band plays.
2. Every block accept ours has sidewalks.
3. Will you borrow me your scissors?
4. Scott couldn't find his sister anywheres.
5. We divided the tips among the three of us.
6. Did you agree on what that columnist wrote?
7. Do you feel all right?
8. The jury agreed on a verdict.
9. My purse has to be around here somewheres.
10. Jane would not except my gift.

Exercise B Follow the directions for Exercise A.

1. Bill borrowed me his radio.
2. The shoe store has every size accept the one I need.
3. Did Jessica and David agree with the best route to take?
4. Alright, tell me what's bothering you.
5. Deena had to choose among the two jobs.
6. The teacher walked between each row of desks.

7. Rachel agrees with me that playing softball is fun.
8. Anyways, I'm heading for home.
9. Ken borrowed my hat for the costume party.
10. The President excepted the resignation of his aide.

fewer refers to numbers or things that can be counted.
less refers to amount or quantity.

> Tom makes *fewer* typing errors than Rona.
> We hear *less* noise at night.

in means "inside something."
into tells of motion from the outside to the inside of something.

> Nonstandard: The performers went in the studio.
> Standard: The performers went *into* the studio.

> Nonstandard: Joe hit the hockey puck in the goal.
> Standard: Joe hit the hockey puck *into* the goal.

kind of a and **sort of a** are nonstandard. The *a* is not necessary.

> Nonstandard: What kind of a jacket do you have?
> Standard: What *kind of* jacket do you have?

> Nonstandard: There is some sort of a problem here.
> Standard: There is some *sort of* problem here.

like is a preposition. Using *like* as a conjunction before a clause is not fully accepted. Especially in writing, it is better to use *as* or *as if*.

> Nonstandard: *Like* I said, you can depend on Sara.
> Standard: *As* I said, you can depend on Sara.

> Nonstandard: Ramon talked *like* he had a cold.
> Standard: Ramon talked *as if* he had a cold.

of is sometimes incorrectly used in phrases like *could of*, *shouldn't of*, and *must of*. The correct word is *have* or its contraction: *could have, could've, shouldn't have, must have, might have, might've.*

> Nonstandard: Darryl should of locked his bike.
> Standard: Darryl *should have* locked his bike.

ways does not refer to distance. *Way* is correct.

> Nonstandard: We drove a short ways down the road.
> Standard: We drove a short *way* down the road.

Exercise A Correct the sentences with nonstandard usage. If a sentence is correct, write *Correct.*

1. Chris acted like the world was ending.
2. This car needs less repairs than I thought.
3. I will have less trouble with this car than with that one.
4. Carolyn stuffed her change in her pocket.
5. Like the President says, we must conserve energy.
6. There are less new TV programs this season.
7. The center should of practiced her lay-up shots.
8. What kind of a penalty did the ref call?
9. The stadium is a ways farther south.
10. The coach sent the players on the bench in the game.

Exercise B Follow the directions for Exercise A.

1. Kate has less lines to memorize in this play.
2. The council must of held some sort of a meeting.
3. The movie ended just like I thought it would.
4. Lauren slipped a message in our mailbox.
5. Fewer radio stations are playing the top ten songs now.
6. The parking garage is quite a ways from here.
7. Less people go to the later show.
8. Jim looks as if he needs more time.
9. What kind of peg goes in this hole?
10. We should of stopped at the park for our picnic.

Additional Exercises

The Right Word

A. Use confusing pairs of words correctly. Choose the correct word from the two given.

1. Did you (loose, lose) your ticket stub?
2. Have you cashed (your, you're) check yet?
3. The fish had jumped out of (it's, its) bowl.
4. Please (bring, take) me a glass of water.
5. (May, Can) we make a U-turn on this street, officer?
6. A trainer (learned, taught) the boxer proper footwork.
7. A tug-of-war ends when one team (lets, leaves) go of the rope.
8. The test pilot (sat, set) at the controls.
9. Meredith (lay, laid) awake and couldn't sleep.
10. The oil has (raised, risen) to the surface of the sea.

B. Use problem words correctly. Choose the correct word or phrase.

1. Denver is a long (way, ways) from here.
2. What (kind of a, kind of) truck is this?
3. Tim dove (in, into) the lake.
4. (All right, Alright), we'll agree (with, on, to) a rematch.
5. Will you (borrow, lend) me some warmer gloves?
6. Divide the work (among, between) the five of us.
7. Yes, operator, we'll (accept, except) the charges.
8. Trisha looked (as if, like) she didn't feel well.
9. There is a curb (between, between each) parking spaces.
10. I should (have, of) eaten (fewer, less) pretzels.

C. Use standard English. Rewrite these sentences. Correct all nonstandard usage.

1. The art league hear announced it's annual contest.
2. I don't know weather the conductor will except the ticket.
3. Do you get homesick when your a long ways from home?
4. You should of waited until the train was stationery.
5. Raise the cage door and leave the dog run lose.
6. In England, the driver of a car sets on the right side.
7. Can I please bring a friend here too the new swimming pool?
8. Alright, I'll meet you somewheres if we can agree on a place.
9. My sister always carries less books than I do, but she goes to her locker between each class.
10. Before they're events, the swimmers laid on the pool deck.

Capitalization

Capital letters make your writing easier to read. They call attention to certain special words and to words that begin sentences.

There are specific rules for capitalizing words. This section will show you the rules. You can refer to this section at any time if you have questions about capitalization.

Proper Nouns and Adjectives

Capitalize proper nouns and proper adjectives.

A **proper noun** is the name of a particular person, place, or thing. In contrast, a **common noun** is the name of a whole group of people, places, or things. A **proper adjective** is an adjective formed from a proper noun.

Common Noun	Proper Noun	Proper Adjective
queen	Victoria	Victorian
country	Ireland	Irish
government	Congress	Congressional

There are many kinds of proper nouns. The following rules will help you to decide whether or not a noun is a proper noun.

Names of People

Capitalize people's names. Also capitalize the initials or abbreviations that stand for names.

> **F. D. R**oosevelt   Franklin **D**elano **R**oosevelt
> **S**usan **B. A**nthony   **S**usan **B**rownell **A**nthony

Capitalize the titles used with people's names. Also capitalize the initials or abbreviations that stand for those titles.

The titles *Miss, Ms., Mrs.,* and *Mr.* are always capitalized.

> **G**ov. R. T. Alberg   **M**ajor Edward J. Brooks
> **M**s. Susan Manzano   **D**r. Evelyn Santucci
> **J**udge Ellen O'Brien   **R**ev. L. K. Jenkins

Do not capitalize a title that is used without a name. It is a common noun.

> Barbara Sloan is president of the bank.
> The judge in this courtroom is Justice Black.

Capitalize titles of very high importance, even when they are used without names.

> the **P**resident of the United States
> the **C**hief **J**ustice of the Supreme Court
> the **P**rime **M**inister of Canada
> a **C**ongresswoman
> the **P**ope

Family Relationships

Capitalize such family words as *mother, father, aunt,* and *uncle* when they are used as names. If the noun is preceded by a possessive word or by *a* or *the,* it is not capitalized.

What was **D**ad like when he was sixteen, **G**randma?
Jessica's mother is here, **M**om.
We call our aunt and uncle **U**ncle Hy and **A**unt Lo.
My **m**om's car needs a new battery.

The Pronoun *I*

Capitalize the pronoun *I*.

He and **I** saw a movie.   **I** work after school

The Supreme Being
and Sacred Writings

Capitalize all words referring to God, to the Holy Family, and to religious scriptures.

the **A**lmighty	the **B**ible	the **S**on of **G**od
the **L**ord	the **T**almud	the **N**ew Testament
the **B**lessed **V**irgin	**A**llah	the **B**ook of **J**ob

Capitalize personal pronouns referring to God.

They asked the Lord for **H**is blessing.

Exercise A   Copy the following sentences. Change small letters to capital letters wherever necessary.

1. A hurricane hit the town that dad and i were visiting.

2. My mother's doctor is dr. herrera.

3. If you enjoy being scared, read the horror stories of h. p. lovecraft.

4. The minister read from the new testament.

5. Yesterday ms. turner told me that i could now call her sgt. turner.

6. The pope visited this country in 1979.

7. The director of the hospital is rowine hayes brown.

8. Some religions honor god by not speaking his name.

9. In her lecture, professor bailey explained how laws are made.

10. State sen. dawn clark netsch sponsored the bill.

Exercise B   Follow the directions for Exercise A.

1. Can nate tell mr. banzali the best route to memphis?

2. The best-known leader of the dakota tribes was chief sitting bull.

3. Last week reverend williams read to us from the book of job.

4. Did lorene help with the work on your brother's bike?

5. Few people who write to the president of the united states receive a personal answer.

6. Ms. eppie lederer gives advice under the name of ann landers.

7. My cousin dale and i work at mr. j. j. vernon's downtown office.

8. Did dad make an appointment with dr. case?

9. According to the bible, adam and eve disobeyed god.

10. Will the president meet with governor ray?

Geographical Names

In a geographical name, capitalize the first letter of each word except articles and prepositions.

If the article *the* appears before a place name, it is not part of the name and is therefore not capitalized.

Continents:	Africa, North America, Europe, Asia
Bodies of Water:	the Atlantic Ocean, the Ohio River, the Gulf of Mexico, the South China Sea, Hudson Bay, the Panama Canal, Lake Michigan
Land Forms:	Mount McKinley, Aleutian Islands, Death Valley, Cadillac Mountain, Black Hills, Cape Lookout
Political Units:	Florida, Denver, Province of Ontario, Republic of Kenya, State of Israel, Thirteenth Congressional District
Public Areas:	Glacier National Park, Fort Sumter, Badlands National Monument, Ford Theater, Dunes State Park, Fallen Timbers Battlefield
Roads and Highways:	Route 66, Interstate Highway 610, Hampton Road, Thornwood Avenue, Main Street

Directions and Sections

Capitalize names of sections of the country.

The West has several old trading posts.
The South is sometimes called "Dixie."
The Sorensons moved from New England to the West Coast.

Capitalize proper adjectives that come from names of sections of the country.

a Midwestern town	Western saddle
Southern food	East Coast company

Do not capitalize directions of the compass.

Barrow, Alaska, is north of all other United States cities.
Drive east on Interstate 80 to New York.

Do not capitalize adjectives that come from words showing direction.

> The parking lot is on the north side of the building.
> The southerly breeze turned into a fierce wind.

Exercise A Number your paper from 1 to 10. Find the words in the following sentences that should be capitalized. Write the words after the proper number, using the necessary capital letters.

1. The tenth congressional district is north of chicago.
2. There is an extinct volcano called mount shasta in california.
3. The yucatan channel connects the gulf of mexico with the caribbean sea.
4. The andes mountains are in south america.
5. The district of columbia's biggest park is rock creek park.
6. Some southern foods are now popular in the north.
7. Hurricanes attacked the southeast, and the tornadoes hit the southwest.
8. Both interstate 90 and route 20 run from albany to buffalo.
9. The north defeated the south in a key battle at gettysburg, pennsylvania.
10. In japan, the cities are extremely crowded.

Exercise B Follow the directions for Exercise A.

1. We live north of daytona beach, florida.
2. Mrs. evans works by her east window in the morning and by her west window in the afternoon.
3. Actually, the trucker bought her western boots in boston.
4. Please meet me on the southeast corner of pearl street and archer road.
5. This new england cookbook has many recipes for fish.

6. The typhoon swept across the bay of bengal.

7. On the frozen midwestern plains, south winds are welcome.

8. How does an eastern accent differ from a southern one?

9. Mount desert island is part of acadia national park in maine.

10. The yukon territory is north of british columbia.

Names of Organizations and Institutions

Capitalize the names of organizations and institutions, including political parties, governmental bodies or agencies, schools, colleges, churches, hospitals, clubs, businesses, and abbreviations of these names.

Republican Party	Children's Memorial Hospital
Federal Trade Commission	American Medical Association
Stevenson High School	National Urban League
St. Joseph's Church	A.F.L.-C.I.O.

Do not capitalize such words as *school, company, church,* and *hospital* when they are not used as parts of names.

Several people from our church work at the hospital.

Names of Events, Documents, and Periods of Time

Capitalize the names of historical events, documents, and periods of time.

Battle of Concord	Panama Canal Treaty
Vietnam War	the Middle Ages
United States Constitution	the Reformation

Months, Days, and Holidays

Capitalize names of months, days, and holidays, but not the names of seasons.

July	Thursday	winter
Halloween	Thanksgiving	summer

Races, Languages, Nationalities, Religions

Capitalize the names of races, languages, nationalities, and religions. Also capitalize any adjectives that come from these names.

Greek	Oriental	Catholicism	Protestant
German	Hinduism	Puerto Rican	Polish

School Subjects

Do not capitalize the names of school subjects, except course titles followed by a number.

history	Reading Workshop I
industrial arts	Math 300

Remember that the names of languages are always capitalized.

French	Spanish	Japanese	English

Ships, Trains, Airplanes, Automobiles

Capitalize the names of ships, trains, airplanes, and automobiles.

U.S.S. *Constellation*	Concorde	Buick Skyhawk

B.C., A.D.

Capitalize the abbreviations B.C. and A.D.

The Pyramids of Egypt were begun about 300 **B.C.**
The Middle Ages were from **A.D.** 500 to about 1500.
Mohammed was born in **A.D.** 570.

Exercise A Write the words in each sentence that should be capitalized. Use the necessary capital letters.

1. The national basketball association will hold its playoffs in march.

2. Every june, elizabeth seton high school holds a carnival.

3. The high school is across the street from lakeview hospital.

4. There are many different protestant religions.

5. In the middle ages, people believed that a woman would dream of her future husband on st. agnes' eve, january 20.

6. The battle of antietam was one of the fiercest in the american civil war.

7. Montezuma II, the last aztec ruler of mexico, died in a.d. 1520.

8. Amtrak's *southwest limited* travels over eighty miles per hour on some runs.

9. King tut, the egyptian ruler, was buried in 1344 b.c.

10. Last saturday ms. marzo bought new tires for her plymouth horizon.

Exercise B Follow the directions for Exercise A.

1. The second monday in october is celebrated as columbus day.

2. Both the french and the americans celebrate their independence in july.

3. The democratic party received contributions from many unions.

4. The united mineworkers' union is a member of the a.f.l.-c.i.o.

5. We are reading the declaration of independence in my history class.

6. Cheryl could not sign up for family living 101 because it conflicted with her math class.

7. The national language of the israelis is hebrew.

8. The alaskans make the most of their short summer.

9. After graduating from howard university, judy received job offers from the fbi and general foods corporation.

10. The powells bought a new datsun.

First Words

Sentences and Poetry

Capitalize the first word of every sentence and the first word of most lines of poetry.

>The disc jockey began her program. She played a new album.

>Tiger, tiger, burning bright
>In the forests of the night, . . .
>—"The Tiger," William Blake

Sometimes, especially in modern poetry, the lines of a poem do not begin with capital letters.

Quotations

Capitalize the first word of a direct quotation.

A **direct quotation** tells the exact words of a speaker or writer.

>Emerson said, "The only way to have a friend is to be one."

In a **divided quotation,** a direct quotation is broken into two parts by words like *he said* or *she explained*. Do not capitalize the first word of the second part unless it starts a new sentence.

"I agree," Tim said, "that a good friend is rare."
"I agree," Tim said. "A good friend is rare."

Letter Parts

Capitalize the first word in the greeting of a letter. Also capitalize the name of the person addressed, or words like *Sir* and *Madam* that stand for names.

Dear Ms. Valdez   Dear Mr. Nash   Dear Sir:

In the complimentary close, capitalize only the first word.

Very truly yours,   Sincerely yours,

Outlines

Capitalize the first word of each item in an outline. Also capitalize the letters before each line.

I. Holidays
   A. Chief legal holidays
      1. National
      2. State or local
   B. Religious holidays

Titles

Capitalize the first word and all important words in the titles of chapters, magazine articles, short stories, essays, poems, television programs, radio programs, and songs or short pieces of music.

Chapter title:	Chapter 3, "Food and Health"
Magazine article:	"Today's Changing Family"
Short story:	"To Build a Fire"
Essay:	"Friendship"
Poem:	"The Base Stealer"
Television program:	"The Muppet Show"
Song:	"Oh, What a Beautiful Morning!"

Capitalize the first word and all important words in titles of books, newspapers, magazines, plays, movies, works of art, and long musical compositions.

Book title:	*Where the Lilies Bloom*
Newspaper:	*Los Angeles Times*
Magazine:	*Ebony*
Play:	*You Can't Take It with You*
Movie:	*Star Trek*
Work of art:	*The Sunflowers*
Long musical composition:	*Carmen*

Exercise A   Number your paper from 1 to 10. Write the words that should be capitalized. Use the correct capital letter.

1. dear ms. kruger:
    your two tickets to our preview showing of *the empire strikes back* are enclosed. thank you for your order.
                    sincerely yours,
2. television shows about hospitals, such as "general hospital," always attract some viewers.
3. the action photography in *sports illustrated* is excellent.
4. I. finding a cure for the common cold
    A. difficulties
        1. more than 200 cold viruses
5. our school library has back issues of several newspapers, including *the washington post.*
6. rachel chose the poem "a dream deferred" to memorize.

7. "dave," joyce called, "how do you like this new fender?"

8. "i keep forgetting my locker combination," said adam. "maybe i should write it down."

9. mary cassatt's painting *the letter* shows a sad woman sealing an envelope.

10. john p. davis and the russian author gogol both wrote stories titled "the overcoat."

Exercise B Follow the directions for Exercise A.

1. all the radios at the beach were playing "summertime."

2. it was many and many a year ago,
    in a kingdom by the sea,
    that a maiden there lived whom you may know
      by the name of annabel lee;
              —Edgar Allan Poe, "Annabel Lee"

3. we discussed the chapter called "two images of the future" from the book *this endangered planet*.

4. "i'm not sure," said gerard, "what we should do now."

5. i read the article "new research in dental care" in *prevention* magazine.

6. megan asked, "have you seen the latest issue of *time*?"

7. george lucas directed *american graffiti* before he made *star wars*.

8. my little sister insisted that i turn to "the muppet show."

9. the song "some enchanted evening" is from the musical *south pacific*.

10. dear sir:
    i would like two tickets to monday night's
    performance of *the messiah*.
                yours truly,

Additional Exercises

Capitalization

A. Use capital letters with proper nouns and adjectives.
Copy these sentences, adding capitals where necessary.

1. Reg dwight changed his name to elton john.
2. My brother saw carol burnett at the airport.
3. Margaret thatcher became prime minister in 1979.
4. This new testament passage comes from st. luke.
5. Rabbi levy and father kraus teach courses in ethics.
6. How can uncle gene convert that old junkheap into a racecar?
7. When he was rescued, capt. john smith thanked god.
8. Last year my mother and i took an auto repair course.
9. State's attorney mary m. newton made her closing statement.
10. Who was vice-president during president ford's term?

B. Use capital letters correctly. Copy these sentences, adding capitals where necessary. Some sentences may already be correct.

1. The okefenokee swamp is in georgia and florida.
2. We drove south through brown county into kentucky.
3. The southwest is very hot in the summer.
4. The coast of poland is on the baltic sea.
5. Motocross races are held on the south side of town.
6. Palm trees grow in the south and on the west coast.
7. The grand canyon is a major attraction in the west.
8. The largest lake in the united states is lake superior.
9. Sanibel island is west of fort myers.
10. Lake geneva is located in southern wisconsin.

C. Use capital letters correctly. Copy these sentences, adding capitals where necessary.

1. Next saturday the anti-cruelty society will move to a new building.
2. Aren't volkswagens german cars?
3. The republican candidate was a pilot during world war II.
4. Students in spanish III have lab sessions on thursdays.
5. Will revell industries be closed on december 24?
6. The scanners at many food stores are made by i.b.m.
7. My cousin graduated from roberto clemente high school.
8. Our history class toured the united nations.
9. Most catholic schools are closed on good friday.
10. When is the jewish holiday of yom kippur celebrated?

D. Capitalize first words corrctly. Write the words that should be capitalized. Use the correct letter.

1. my sister auditioned for a part in *annie*.
2. the comedy "benson" was a spinoff from "soap."
3. naomi said, "this is ridiculous!"
4. tom wolfe's book *the right stuff* is about astronauts.
5. hazlitt said, "no really great man ever thought himself so."
6. "hold the ladder," said mark. "it's not too steady."
7. "hopes," pindar said, "are but the dreams of those who are awake."
8. dear mr. ortega:
   your order will be shipped immediately.
   very truly yours,
9. tammy asked, "do you subscribe to *sports illustrated*?"
10. dogs display reluctance and wrath
    if you try to give them a bath.
    —ogden nash

Section 14

Punctuation

Road signs and traffic lights guide a driver. Likewise, punctuation marks guide a reader. **Punctuation marks** show readers where to stop or slow down or change direction.

When you write, your punctuation signals your reader. It marks groups of words that belong together. It tells how a sentence should be read. All in all, punctuation helps your reader to understand your meaning.

End Marks

End marks are the punctuation marks that indicate the end of a sentence. The three kinds of end marks are the **period,** the **question mark,** and the **exclamation point.**

The Period

Use a period at the end of a declarative sentence.

A **declarative sentence** is a sentence that makes a statement. You use declarative sentences when you tell something.

The streets are covered with ice.

Use a period at the end of most imperative sentences.

An **imperative sentence** is a sentence that orders or requests someone to do something.

Use the revolving door, please.

At times, imperative sentences express strong excitement or emotion. Then an exclamation point, rather than a period, is used at the end of the sentence.

Get away!   Hurry up!

Use a period at the end of an indirect question.

An **indirect question** tells that someone asked a question. However, it does not give the exact words of the question.

The captain asked whether the ship was on course.

Notice how a **direct question** differs:

The captain asked, "Is the ship on course?"

A direct question shows the exact words of the person asking the question. A direct question ends with a question mark.

Use a period at the end of an abbreviation or an initial. An **abbreviation** is a shortened form of a word. An **initial** is a first letter that stands for a word.

Gov. James R. Thomas   4 P.M. on Aug. 4

Lt. Margaret B. Hill   6 lb., 12 oz.

Certain abbreviations do not use periods. To check

whether or not to use a period with an abbreviation, look up the abbreviation in your dictionary.

CIA (*Central Intelligence Agency*)
CB (*Citizens' Band*)
UN (*United Nations*)

Use a period after each number or letter for an item in an outline or a list.

(An Outline)	(A List)
I. Sports	1. nails
A. Contact	2. hammer
1. Football	3. putty

Use a period between dollars and cents and before a decimal.

$13.64   3.14

The Question Mark

Use a question mark at the end of an interrogative sentence.

An **interrogative sentence** is a sentence that asks a question.

What do you want for dinner?

The Exclamation Point

Use an exclamation point at the end of an exclamatory sentence.

An **exclamatory sentence** expresses excitement or other strong emotion.

You're terrific!   How nice you look!

Use an exclamation point after an interjection.

An **interjection** is one or more words that show strong feeling. Sometimes the interjection is a sound.

Nice!   Ouch!   Not again!   Super!

Exercise A   Copy the following sentences, adding the necessary punctuation. Be prepared to tell what punctuation marks you used and why you used them.

1. Where is Lt Moseley stationed
2. Vince asked why the car had a fiberglass hood
3. Fantastic Those twenty-dollar shirts have been marked down to $999
4. Did she want me to call at 8:15 A M or P M
5. Say Where have you been
6. I Foods containing calcium
       A Dairy products
           1 Milk
7. The initials WHO stand for the World Health Organization
8. Is your appointment with Dr Sam Williams, Jr or with Dr Sam Williams, Sr
9. Gena's new address is PO Box 12, Altoona, Pennsylvania
10 The USS *Pueblo* was captured by North Korea

Exercise B   Follow the directions for Exercise A.

1. Aaron asked if China bordered the USSR
2. Please send all complaints to Brown, Brooks, and Co in New York
3. Is that an AM radio
4. Darryl Fields, RN, helps his patients to keep smiling
5. Oh, no Why did you do that
6. Should I make the check out to Dr Sara Bosco or to Sara Bosco, MD
7. If the amount is $991 or more, round it off to ten dollars
8. The NEA is an educational organization
9. Does the winter sun really set by 3 PM in Alaska
10. Halt Who's there

The Comma

A comma is used to separate words that do not go together. When you are speaking, you can pause. When you are writing, you use commas for breaks in thought. In this way, commas help you to communicate clearly.

Using Commas in a Series

Use a comma after every item in a series except the last one.

A series is three or more items of the same kind. Your writing may contain a series of words, of phrases, or of clauses.

Words: Mel Brooks is a writer, an actor, and a director.

Phrases: We searched under beds, inside drawers, and in closets.

Clauses: The doctor explained how the blood test is made, what it tells, and why it is necessary.

Use commas after *first, second, third,* and so on, when these adverbs introduce a series.

There are four steps to any house-painting job: first, scraping; second, sanding; third, priming; and fourth, painting.

When there are two or more adjectives before a noun, use commas between them.

The vet treated the cold, wet, sick dog.

Exercise A Number your paper from 1 to 10. Copy the following sentences and add commas where necessary.

1. January February and March are cold bitter months here.

2. Football basketball and baseball are all televised in the fall.

3. Nan wanted to know three things about the car: first its gas mileage; second its cruising speed; and third its price.

4. The workers picked grapes in the hot dusty fields.

5. Ron groped for the alarm shut it off and went back to sleep.

6. Mae's radio woke her with news of a fire an airplane crash and a bus strike.

7. Kerry lifted the phonograph needle removed the dust and set the needle back down.

8. Seth has had three part-time jobs: first as a newspaper carrier; second as a cook; and third as an usher.

9. His eyes widened brightened and seemed to smile.

10. Maureen told the class where Libya is when it was founded and how it is governed.

Exercise B   Follow the directions for Exercise A.

1. The building inspector listed these problems: first falling plaster; second cracked windows; third peeling paint.

2. Lightning black clouds and blowing leaves streaked across the sky.

3. To make a soda, mix syrup ice cream and soda water.

4. Baking soda and water make a cheap effective toothpaste.

5. Betty climbed the wall gripped the ledge and threw the rope.

6. Tall thin gray lockers lined the halls.

7. Hondas Yamahas Suzukis and Harley-Davidsons glittered in the lot.

8. Denny looked for work at supermarkets theaters restaurants and amusement parks.

9. First I checked the plug; second I looked at the fuse box; third I fiddled with the antennas; fourth I gave up and called the repair shop.

10. The plumber stood up stretched and flexed her fingers.

Using Commas with Introductory Words

Use a comma to separate an introductory word, long phrase, or clause from the rest of the sentence.

No, I'm not leaving yet. (introductory word)

After four rounds with the champ, Diaz was knocked down. (prepositional phrases)

Laughing wildly, Lauren walked offstage. (verbal phrase)

When you pay the toll, the gate goes up. (adverb clause)

As you can see, commas are used after introductory words like *yes* and *no*. They are also used after prepositional phrases, verbal phrases, and adverb clauses that begin sentences.

Sometimes the comma may be left out. When there would be little pause in speaking, no comma is used.

At noon the auction will begin.

Using Commas with Interrupters

Use commas to set off one or more words that interrupt the flow of thought in a sentence.

The judge, in any event, sentenced the man.

William, moreover, made the all-state squad.

The bus lines, I think, have increased the fare.

The cost of some foods, however, has gone down.

The following words are additional examples of interrupters. Set them off with commas.

therefore	I believe	of course
for example	by the way	furthermore
I suppose	in fact	nevertheless

Exercise A Number your paper from 1 to 10. Copy the following sentences. Add commas where necessary.

1. No the Marvin Gaye album is not on sale.
2. After dialing Tony's number Rita had second thoughts.
3. Waiting for her coffee the reporter overheard a startling conversation.
4. Carlos I believe deserves our support.
5. Dazed from lack of sleep the swimmer finally reached the beach.
6. Yes the plane is on schedule.
7. You will be at the party I suppose.
8. To tell the truth this pie could have used more time in the oven.
9. After he talked with the coach Glenn felt better.
10. As other nations get more industry they will share our pollution problems.

Exercise B Follow the directions for Exercise A.

1. Campbell's interception was I think the high point of the game.
2. Brenda on the other hand enjoys her math class.
3. Yes that is the quickest route.
4. The British however do not like iced tea.
5. On the way home from the dentist's office Fran chipped her tooth.
6. Although the street is noisy it is safe.
7. Delighted at the prospect of a summer on the beach Carmen took the job.
8. Whenever a new mail carrier delivers the mail we get somebody else's letters.
9. The rust I am afraid has eaten through the floor of the car.
10. Because the public pool was closed we had no place to swim.

Using Commas with Nouns of Direct Address

Use commas to set off nouns of direct address.

Sometimes when you speak or write to someone, you use the person's name. The name of someone directly spoken to is a **noun of direct address.**

> Marsha, call a time-out!
>
> In the hallway, Mark, is a package for you.
>
> Did anybody call, Cynthia?
>
> After you leave, boys, lock the garage.

As in the last example, nouns of direct address may be common nouns.

Using Commas with Appositives

Use commas to set off most appositives.

An **appositive** is one or more words that explain or identify another word. The appositive directly follows the word it explains.

> Art Buchwald, a humorous writer, has a column in this newspaper.
>
> Our assistant coach, Mr. Wagner, played with the Jets.
>
> The Superbowl, the biggest game of the year, is Sunday.

As in the final example, an appositive may contain a prepositional phrase.

Nouns used as appositives are called **nouns in apposition.** When the noun in apposition is a single name, it is not usually set off by commas.

> My sister Jennifer works here.

Using Commas with Quotations

Use commas to set off the explanatory words of a direct quotation.

The explanatory words are the statements like *he said*, *Greg replied*, or *Sheila asked*. They are not part of the quotation.

Explanatory words often come before the quotation. Use a comma after the explanatory words.

Rich said, "Take the expressway to the third exit."

Now look at this quotation:

"Take the expressway to the third exit," Rich said

In the sentence above, the explanatory words come after the quotation. Notice that the comma belongs at the end of the quotation inside the quotation marks.

Sometimes a quotation is broken into two parts. The explanatory words separate the two parts. Here is an example of a *divided quotation*:

"Take the expressway," Rich said, "to the third exit."

In a divided quotation, a comma is used within the quotation marks at the end of the first part of the sentence. A comma is also used after the explanatory words.

Indirect quotations do not tell the speaker's exact words. No commas are used.

Rich said that we should take the expressway to the third exit.

Using Commas in Compound Sentences

Use a comma before the conjunction between the two main clauses of a compound sentence.

The Dodgers won the pennant, but they lost the World Series.

The comma is not necessary when the main clauses are very short and are joined by *and*.

We worked and then we relaxed.

Sometimes very short main clauses are joined by *but* or *or*. A comma is used since the words *but* and *or* mark a change in the flow of thought.

Ken works, but he isn't paid much.

Don't confuse compound sentences with compound subjects or compound predicates. There is no comma before the *and* that joins a compound subject or predicate.

Beth dove into the pool *and* retrieved her wallet.

Exercise A Copy these sentences. Add commas as needed.

1. Lincoln Logs the building blocks for children were designed by a famous architect's son.

2. The dentist a kind woman always puts her patients at ease.

3. Ms. Calder this is my cousin James.

4. Use your imagination Cory.

5. Don's sketch a realistic drawing of the park was displayed at the library.

6. Please submit your application to Dr. Vasquez the director of the project.

7. Shawn said "The breakfast will be held in the church."

8. "I was at that show myself" said Vic.

9. "The sun" said the pitcher "was in my eyes."

10. Martin called several times but Nathan's line was busy for hours.

Exercise B Follow the directions for Exercise A.

1. Is Molly still working at Burger King or did she find a new job?

2. Coleman chrome-plated his motorcycle and then he painted a dragon on the fender.

3. Captain William Kidd a well-known pirate buried treasure in New York.

4. Melissa found her information at the library and Ben got his from City Hall.

5. Jackie said "I am in the work-study program."

6. "The tornado broke windows and tore off roofs Cindy" explained Travis.

7. "These recruits already act like professionals" said Sergeant Willis.

8. Gary likes knockwurst a sausage with lots of seasoning.

9. "Your engine" said the mechanic "needs a lot of work."

10. The coach said "Keep up the good work girls."

Using Commas in Dates

In dates, use a comma between the day of the month and the year.

February 22, 1976   May 8, 1945

When a date is part of a sentence, a comma follows the year.

The first talking picture was shown on July 6, 1928, in New York.

Using Commas in Place Names

Use a comma between the name of a city or town and the name of its state or country.

Detroit, Michigan   Santiago, Chile

Athens, Greece   Houston, Texas

When an address is part of a sentence, use a comma after each item.

> For more information, write to the National Wildlife Federation, 1412 Sixteenth Street, Washington, D.C. 20005.

Note that you do not put a comma between the state name and the ZIP code.

Using Commas in Letters

Use a comma after the salutation of a friendly letter. Use a comma after the complimentary close of a friendly letter or a business letter.

> Dear Gretchen,   Yours truly,

Using Commas with Nonrestrictive Clauses

Use commas to set off nonrestrictive clauses.

A **nonrestrictive clause** is a clause that merely adds an idea to the sentence. The sentence would be complete without it. The meaning would be definite without it.

A **restrictive clause** is a clause that is essential to the meaning of a sentence. The clause is needed for the sense of the sentence. If a restrictive clause is dropped out of a sentence, the meaning changes.

Nonrestrictive clause: Terry Reese, *who is the center for the Wildcats,* scored the most points.

Terry Reese scored the most points. (The clause can be dropped from the sentence.)

Restrictive clause: Terry Reese is the player *who scored the most points.*

Terry Reese is the player. (The clause cannot be dropped.)

To see if a clause is nonrestrictive, read the sentence without it. If the meaning doesn't change, the clause is nonrestrictive. Use commas before and after it.

Restrictive clauses are often used to identify or to point out the person or thing they modify. Without this identification, the meaning of the sentence would not be clear. Nonrestrictive clauses, on the other hand, add no essential meaning to the sentence.

Restrictive clause:	Janice is the girl *who found the money.* (The clause tells which girl.)
Nonrestrictive clause:	Janice, *who is very alert,* found the money.
	Janice found the money. (The clause is not needed.)
Restrictive clause:	This is the book *that has the map.* (The clause tells which book.)
Nonrestrictive clause:	This book, *which has pictures,* is my choice.
	This book is my choice. (The clause is not needed.)

Using Commas To Avoid Confusion

Use a comma whenever the reader might otherwise be confused. Sometimes no rule applies, but a sentence might be misread without commas.

Without commas, the following sentences could be misunderstood:

Inside everything was a mess.
Whoever called called twice.

With commas, the sentences are clearer.

Inside, everything was a mess.

Whoever called, called twice.

Exercise A   Copy the following sentences. Add commas where necessary.

1. The walking catfish was first reported near Clearwater Florida on May 25 1968.

2. Dear Nicole
   My summer address will be 205 Linden Street Ladysmith Wisconsin 54848.
   I hope to hear from you.
                                   With best wishes
                                   Katy

3. On May 24 1844 the first telegraph message was sent.

4. Duluth Minnesota is one city that produces much iron and steel.

5. The album was made in Nashville a city with many recording studios.

6. On November 1 1835 Texas declared its independence from Mexico.

7. Coins are made in Denver Colorado and Philadelphia Pennsylvania.

8. John Brown's raid on Harper's Ferry West Virginia began on October 16 1859 and was crushed on October 18.

9. Write to Lynn Brown at 665 California Avenue Ames Iowa 50010.

10. Outside the wind blew fiercely.

Exercise B   Follow the directions for Exercise A.

1. On December 3 1967 a doctor successfully transplanted a human heart.

2. Dear Caroline
   My Aunt Betsy's new address is Rural Route 3 Ridgeway Virginia 62321.
                                   Sincerely
                                   Michael

3. On August 27 1859 Edwin Drake struck oil near Titusville Pennsylvania.

4. The intruder you saw saw you.

5. Martin Luther King, Jr. was assassinated on April 4 1968 in Memphis Tennessee.

6. The school is located at 6900 South Stewart Avenue Chicago Illinois.

7. Do you come from Barcelona Venezuela or Barcelona Spain?

8. He seems to believe the saying, "Whatever is is right."

9. The first American automobile which was called a "gasoline buggy" by some was completed on April 19 1892.

10. Mary's grandmother who lives downstairs left Warsaw Poland in 1935.

The Semicolon

Use a semicolon to join the parts of a compound sentence if no coordinating conjunction is used.

The operator interrupted the call; our time was up.

When there are several commas in the parts of a compound sentence, separate the clauses with a semicolon.

On this diet I can eat bread, fruits, and vegetables; but candy, soft drinks, and desserts are forbidden.

When there are commas within parts of a series, use semicolons to separate the parts.

In the Olympics the winner in first place gets a gold medal; second place, a silver medal; and third place, a bronze medal.

Use a semicolon before a conjunctive adverb that joins the clauses of a compound sentence.

You have learned that the parts of a compound sentence are sometimes joined by such words as *therefore, however, so,*

consequently, besides, nevertheless, then, yet, and *moreover.*
These words, called **conjunctive adverbs,** follow a semicolon.

> The Rams have a fine offense; however, their defense is weak.

The Colon

Use a colon after the greeting of a business letter.

Dear Ms. Nolan: Dear Sir or Madam:

Use a colon between numerals indicating hours and minutes.

4:30 P.M.   8:15 A.M.

Use a colon to introduce a list of items. The colon indicates a pause before the items that follow.

> The FBI investigates the following federal crimes: spying, treason, kidnaping, and counterfeiting.

If there would be no pause in speaking, a colon is not used before a list.

> The term "mass media" refers to television, radio, newspapers, magazines, and books.

Exercise A Copy the word before and after each missing semicolon or colon. Add the correct punctuation mark.

1. The fullback outran the ball the fans went wild.

2. Some people object to the following clothes made from animal skins leopard furs, sealskin coats, and alligator shoes.

3. Dear Madam
      The item that you ordered is out of stock.

4. Skaters, cyclists, and joggers crowded the path it was not a good place to stroll.

5. From the road, the ocean looked blue however, it was dull brown at the shore.

6. The Community Center requests the following foods dry milk, canned meat, canned soup, and cereals.

7. The flight was scheduled to depart at 7 30 however, we did not even board until 8 15.

8. There were many cars on the road consequently, the smog was thick.

9. The following cities are growing quickly Calcutta, India San Juan, Puerto Rico and Mexico City, Mexico.

10. Willie Nelson was not a typical country and western singer nevertheless, he became quite popular.

Exercise B   Follow the directions for Exercise A.

1. The two sides could not reach an agreement therefore, a third party was called in.

2. The picnic tables held bowls of thick, tangy barbecue sauce platters of warm, crisp, fried chicken and big, shiny loaves of fresh-baked bread.

3. Karen built a large, roaring fire and we toasted hot dogs, corn, and marshmallows.

4. Barbara works after school therefore, she will not be home until 6 30.

5. Some popular home remedies for colds include the following fruit juices, chicken soup, garlic cloves, and aspirin.

6. Dear Resident
   Would you like to win $500 a week for life?

7. Rafael Septien has an amazing kick besides, he thinks quickly.

8. On Labor Day at 7 30 P.M., the lifeguard closes the pool.

9. Spices are used in cooking for the following reasons they preserve food, they add variety to meals, and they are flavorful.

10. This year, a serious flu is widespread flu shots are being given at the clinic.

The Dash

Using Dashes with Interrupters

You have learned about using commas with words or short phrases, like *however* and *I think*, that interrupt a sentence. A dash is used with a long explanation that interrupts the thought.

> An electric car—its battery must be recharged every 1,000 miles—was introduced by one auto maker.
>
> A TV crew—a noise truck, huge cameras, complex sound equipment, and eager reporters—arrived at the scene.

Using the Dash Before a Summary

Use a dash after a series to indicate that a summary statement will follow.

> Edsels, Packards, Studebakers, Hudsons—these cars are no longer made.
>
> Chocolate milkshakes, hamburgers, and potato chips—this is the diet of some teen-agers.

Exercise   Copy these sentences. Insert dashes as needed.

1. Layoffs a nearby factory cut 100 workers are one way to lower costs.

2. Taxi fares, school busing, and a new shopping district these issues were decided by the city council.

3. The Chicago Hustle what a great season they're having will play here next week.

4. That magazine the new one I told you about is in the library.

5. The coach talked about team work, timing, concentration the keys to any victory.

6. Trains, cars, buses, planes all of them were halted by the snowstorm.

7. The winter of 1978 there were not enough trucks to remove the snow set records for snowfall.

8 We can take the elevator unless it is broken again to the tenth floor.

9. Parks, beaches, shops, interesting sights Toronto has them all.

10. Trumpets, drums, saxophones, trombones the band has all these instruments.

The Hyphen

Use a hyphen if part of a word must be carried over from one line to the next. Words are separated by hyphens only between syllables.

> The FBI has about 195,000,000 finger
> prints on file.

Only words having two or more syllables can be broken by a hyphen. Never divide one-syllable words, like *growl* or *weight,* at the end of a line. Check your dictionary to learn the syllables of a word.

A single letter should not be left at the end of a line. For instance, this division of *election* would be wrong: *e- lection.* A single letter should not begin a line either. This division of *ordinary* would be incorrect: *ordinar- y.*

Use a hyphen in compound numbers from twenty-one to ninety-nine.

> forty-six chairs   sixty-five lockers

Use a hyphen in fractions.

> a two-thirds majority   one-fourth of the votes.

Use a hyphen in certain compound nouns, such as *brother-in-law, drive-in,* and *great-grandmother.*

> The *editor-in-chief* of the local paper is my *sister-in-law.*

Use a hyphen or hyphens between words that make up a compound adjective used before a noun.

> The radio announcer gives a play-by-play account of the game.
>
> *but:* The radio announcer describes the game play by play.

When compound adjectives are used after a noun, they are not usually hyphenated.

A dictionary will tell you if a word needs a hyphen. These are some examples of compound adjectives:

five-year-old boy	well-oiled machine
beat-up truck	best-selling book
little-used street	long-legged spider
double-edged sword	half-hearted attempt

Exercise Number your paper from 1 to 15. After the proper number, write the word or words that should be hyphenated. Add the necessary hyphens. Use your dictionary if you need to.

1. This out of date map is no help.
2. Have you ever heard a twenty one gun salute?
3. That is a half baked idea.
4. Turn of the century houses lined the street.
5. The old library had built in bookcases.
6. My great grandmother sent me twenty five dollars for my birthday.
7. Only one third of the students at that school have up to date health records.
8. The used paperbacks are forty five cents each, or three for one dollar and twenty five cents.
9. About fifty one out of every 100 babies born each year are boys.
10. Carl prefers his make believe world to the real one.
11. One half of those surveyed were younger than twenty two.

12. Three fourths of the students walk to school.

13. Most of my friends headed for the drive in.

14. The patient had a wild eyed look.

15. The editor in chief of that newspaper writes the editorials himself.

The Apostrophe

The apostrophe is frequently used to form the possessive of nouns. To use the apostrophe correctly, you should know whether a noun is singular or plural.

To form the possessive of a singular noun, add an apostrophe and an s.

student + 's = student's Les + 's = Les's
baby + 's = baby's   Vanessa + 's = Vanessa's

To form the possessive of a plural noun that does not end in s, add an apostrophe and an s.

women + 's = women's   frogmen + 's = frogmen's

To form the possessive of a plural noun that ends in s, add only an apostrophe.

racers + ' = racers'   players + ' = players'
Reeses + ' = Reeses'   sponsors + ' = sponsors'

To form the possessive of indefinite pronouns, use an apostrophe and an s.

everybody + 's = everybody's   someone + 's = someone's

Do not use an apostrophe with a personal pronoun to show possession.

hers   ours   yours   its   theirs

The team changed *its* attitude.

Use an apostrophe in a contraction.

In contractions words are joined and letters are left out. An apostrophe replaces one or more letters that are left out.

she's = she is	hasn't = has not
we'll = we will	won't = will not
they're = they are	I'm = I am
it's = it is	shouldn't = should not

Use an apostrophe to show the omission of numbers in a date.

the spring of '79 (the spring of 1979)
a '71 Ford (a 1971 Ford)

Use an apostrophe and s to form the plurals of letters, figures, and words used as words.

ABC's   two *n*'s   three 4's   *yes*'s and *no*'s

Exercise A   Number your paper from 1 to 10. Write the words that need apostrophes. Insert apostrophes where they are needed.

1. Experts cannot tell the difference between a mans handwriting and a womans.
2. Ive already met Russs sister.
3. Its going to rain before we reach the Carlsons porch.
4. The class of 70 is holding its reunion in the gym.
5. Thats Sandras favorite team.
6. Im sure the brakes of most cars are lined with asbestos.
7. Anybodys guess is as good as mine.
8. Theyve admitted that the fault is theirs.
9. DeeAnnes name is spelled with three *es*.
10. He didnt notice the childrens absence.

Exercise B   Follow the directions for Exercise A.

1. Is that Suzys book youre reading?
2. How would you describe the 1970s?

3. His *maybes* arent the same as *yess*.

4. The coachs jacket was a gift from her team.

5. Dont the Reeses dogs ever stop barking?

6. The band lost some of its best musicians when the class of 80 graduated.

7. Arent the clinics hours from 2:00 until 8:00?

8. The two scientists conclusions were the same.

9. This is everyones park, not just yours.

10. The young children havent learned to tell the *d*s from the *b*s.

Quotation Marks

Use quotation marks at the beginning and at the end of a direct quotation.

Quotation marks tell your reader that a speaker's exact words are being given. Here is an example:

Linda said, "Someone is following me."

Quotation marks are *not* used with indirect quotations. An indirect quotation does not tell the speaker's exact words.

Linda said that someone was following her.

At the beginning of a sentence there are often explanatory words. Use a comma directly after these words. Then begin the quotation with quotation marks. A period at the end of a sentence belongs *inside* the quotation marks.

The pilot said, "Fasten your seat belts."

Sometimes explanatory words end the sentence. Then the quoted statement at the beginning of the sentence is followed by a comma. The comma belongs inside the quotation marks.

"Fasten your seat belts," the pilot said.

Using Divided Quotations

Sometimes a quotation is divided into two parts by explanatory words. In that case, each part is enclosed by quotation marks.

"One very healthful food," Pamela said, "is granola."

When the divided quotation is a single sentence, the second part begins with a small letter. Look at the example above. At times, however, the second part begins a new sentence. Then a capital letter is used at the beginning of the second part.

> "There is entertainment at halftime," Toby noted. "The band will play."

The first part of a divided quotation is followed by a comma. Commas always appear inside quotation marks.

> "On the way," Derek said, "we will pick up Kelly."

The explanatory words in the middle of a divided quotation are followed by either a period or a comma. A period is used if the first part completes a sentence. A comma is used if the sentence continues after the explanatory words.

> "At the plant," Eric said, "we work in shifts."

> "First, we spread paste on the wallpaper," Ginger explained. "Then we hang the paper and cut it to size."

Exercise Write each of the following sentences three ways as a direct quotation.

> Example: I need an honest answer.
> > a. "I need an honest answer," she said.
> > b. She said, "I need an honest answer."
> > c. "I need," she said, "an honest answer."

1. Don't talk to me while I'm working.
2. Yes, Stevie Wonder writes many of his own songs.

3. I'm sorry that I forgot to call you.
4. In the last two minutes, the Cowboys took the lead.
5. Finally, a wrecking crew attacked the vacant building.

Using Punctuation with Quotation Marks

Place question marks and exclamation points inside the quotation marks if they belong to the quotation itself.

> Andrew asked, "Who sent you a telegram?"
> Andrea screamed, "Move fast!"

Place question marks and exclamation points outside the quotation marks if they do not belong to the quotation.

> Did Keith say, "Meet me at school"?
> What a surprise it was when the manager said, "You're hired"!

Commas and periods, as you have seen, always appear within quotation marks.

Exercise A Copy the following sentences. Punctuate them correctly with quotation marks, end marks, and commas. (There are three indirect quotations that need only end punctuation.)

1. Go away yelled Pat
2. Do you like that yellow Chevette asked Mindy
3. Oh well said Angie a little glue will fix that
4. Ms. Pappas explained why copper wiring is used
5. I have finally learned to use the brakes on my skates Tisha said
6. Terry announced proudly I knocked down all ten pins
7. Adam said that he was on a diet
8. We locked this door when we left said Harris nervously Why is it open now
9. Did Dr. Korshak say that you should tape your ankle?
10. Did the dentist say I think your tooth must be pulled

Exercise B Write each of the following sentences as a direct quotation. In some examples, put the quotation first. In others, put the quotation last. Also, for variety, divide some quotations.

1. Is Costa Rica part of Central America?
2. Don't say that!
3. I called the fire department from a neighbor's house.
4. There's a restaurant by the bowling alley.
5. I never know what Merle will say next.
6. By next June, I should have my driver's license.
7. We swam in the quarry.
8. Stand back!
9. Was that snake a copperhead?
10. This weekend I have to help my cousin.

Using Long Quotations

You may wonder how to use quotation marks for quoting two or more sentences by the same speaker. Look at the following example:

> "When you keep accounts, there are credits and debits," Stacy explained. "Debits are amounts that you owe. Credits are amounts that are paid to you."

Using Quotation Marks for Dialogue

Dialogue is conversation between two or more people. It is punctuated in a special way. Begin a new paragraph each time the speaker changes.

> "What are your favorite TV commercials?" Christy asked.
> "I like the commercials for Coca-Cola," replied Ted.
> "My favorites are Dr. Pepper and Pepsi commercials," Delia said. "I also like the new ones for Hubba Bubba. Which ones do you like, Christy?"
> "I like most of them," Christy answered. "Some of them are better than the TV programs that come in between."

Exercise   Rewrite the following conversation. Make correct paragraph divisions, and use the right punctuation.

What kind of job do you want after you graduate Ms. Morales asked. Well answered Shirley I haven't thought much about it. I do know that I'm good at keeping calm in a crisis. James said I know what kind of job I *don't* want. I would hate a job that kept me in one room all day. Marva looked sympathetic. I feel that way, too she said. I want a job that will keep me on the go.

Punctuating Titles

Use quotation marks to enclose the titles of magazine articles, chapters, short stories, essays, poems, television and radio programs, songs, and short pieces of music.

Magazine article:	"On-the-Job Training for You"
Chapter title:	Chapter 7, "The New World"
Short story:	"Clothes Make the Man"
Essay:	"The Dog That Bit People"
Poem:	"The Raven"
Television program:	"Eight Is Enough"
Song:	"Jingle Bells"

Underline the titles of books, newspapers, magazines, plays, movies, works of art, and long musical compositions.

In writing or typing, such titles are underlined, like this: <u>The Chocolate War</u>.

In print, these titles appear in italics instead.

Book title:	*The Pigman*
Newspaper:	*New Haven Register*
Magazine:	*Motor Trend*
Play:	*Annie*
Movie:	*Rocky II*
Work of art:	*Mona Lisa*
Long musical composition:	*Porgy and Bess*

Exercise A Copy the following sentences, adding quotation marks around titles or underlining titles where necessary.

1. The story Requiem was published in Ms. magazine.
2. Old Abe Lincoln Came Out of the Wilderness was a popular marching song during the Civil War.
3. I reported on Althea Gibson's article, I Always Wanted To Be Someone.
4. The article appeared in the book Out of the Bleachers.
5. Our city was featured on the TV show 60 Minutes.
6. Of all the Frankenstein movies, I like Young Frankenstein most.
7. The Daily Defender is a Chicago newspaper.
8. The musical West Side Story is a modern version of Shakespeare's play Romeo and Juliet.
9. Monet's painting Waterlilies has now been reproduced on bedsheets.
10. Many people recognize the eerie notes of the ballet music The Firebird.

Exercise B Follow the directions for Exercise A.

1. Surely you can think of a better title for your essay than What I Did During My Summer Vacation.
2. I like Langston Hughes's poem Dreams.
3. Julia Ward Howe wrote the song The Battle Hymn of the Republic.
4. Please read Chapter 10, The Last Frontier.
5. John Tenniel, who illustrated the book Alice in Wonderland, also drew cartoons for the magazine Punch.
6. The Time Machine was first a novel and then a movie.
7. The Searchers was a famous Western.
8. The first New York newspaper was called the Gazette.
9. The Devil's Dictionary is a book of humorous definitions.
10. Our school play last year was A Raisin in the Sun.

514

Additional Exercises

Punctuation

A. Use end marks and commas. Rewrite the following sentences, adding the missing punctuation.

1. Skates are becoming more popular and skateboards have almost been forgotten

2. How thin you are

3. How thin are you

4. Should Carol bring her own pliers wrench and wire

5. Joan of Arc the French heroine was declared a saint in 1920

6. Ms Doyle Dr Antonelli and Mr McCoy are holding a meeting at 8:00 P M on Saturday September 3

7. On March 13 1852 the first newspaper cartoon of Uncle Sam appeared

8. Robin bought the tickets but then she lost them

9. Yes Mel I remembered to buy Doritos and ginger ale

10. Georgia looked in her address book rummaged through a stack of old mail and finally found this address: 215 Main Street Carthage Illinois 62321

11. When the bubble popped Rick's face was covered with gum

12. On Tuesday by the way you'll meet Ann Archer the co-captain of the team

13. "Are you done Ron" Mike asked "We want to leave"

14. Dear Tommy
    Here is the clipping that you asked for
                              Sincerely

15. Renee who lived in France for two years can speak French fluently

B. Use semicolons, colons, dashes, and hyphens. Add semicolons, colons, dashes, and hyphens as you rewrite these sentences.

1. Racquetball, tennis, squash, and badminton Mark can play them all well.

2. The Cougars will need the following players pitchers, infielders, and left handed batters.

3. At eighty six, my great grandmother still has a happy go lucky view of life.

4. Deidre can remember everything she reads furthermore, she understands the material.

5. The commander in chief, the general, and the prime minister these people will arrive at 7 15 P.M.

6. Three fourths of the students listed these long term goals more education, an interesting job, and a happy family life.

7. Dear Madam
We have received your letter, it will be published in next week's column.

8. This weekend I can hardly wait we'll be leaving for the lake.

9. Seventy five people have entered the five mile race.

10. Margie had only a four week course in self defense however, she is already very good at it.

C. Use apostrophes, quotation marks, and underlining. Write each sentence, putting in necessary apostrophes, quotation marks, and underlining.

1. Rachel said, I like the TR-7s that were made in the early 1970s.

2. The students theme for their dance will be from the movie Grease.

3. The song Fire Lake reminds me of the spring of 80.

4. Did the teacher say that we would discuss Tillie Olsens story, I Stand Here Ironing?

5. Get out of the way! yelled Lee.

6. Is it true, asked Glorias brother, that the injured player is my sister?

7. Its somebodys problem, but not yours, said Ms. Kane.

8. Little Chriss laces are always flapping because he cant tie his shoes.

9. All three teachers classes are reading the novel Ordinary People.

10. I dont see Cheryl Tiegss picture in this copy of People, said Beth. Maybe its in last weeks issue.

D. Use apostrophes, quotation marks, and underlining.
Write each sentence, putting in necessary apostrophes, quotation marks, and underlining.

1. Walt Disneys feature cartoon films, like Cinderella and Bambi, are shown every seven years.

2. Most American families have two or more TVs, Mr. Lloyd said.

3. The freshmens lockers are on the first floor.

4. John Ciardis poem Beagles in the book Introduction Poetry is one of my favorites.

5. Jenny asked, Isn't Jasons dog much older than yours?

6. Jodys grandpa recalls the stock market crash of 29.

7. Ken shouted, Somebodys car just hit ours!

8. Didnt you see this weeks 60 Minutes?

9. Eubie, Bonnie explained, is a musical about ragtime musician Eubie Blake.

10. Do most students parents help them with homework? Ms. Richardson asked.

Section 15

Spelling

Good spelling is a skill that is valuable throughout a lifetime. It is a skill that is important in all writing, ranging from school reports to messages, letters, and job applications. On the job, too, you will often need to write. Good spelling is noticed and admired.

Becoming a good speller is not an easy task, though. The spelling of many English words does not seem to make sense. Many words are not spelled the way they sound.

Learning to spell well is not hopeless, however. There are certain patterns of spelling that English words follow. There are general rules that make spelling easier. In addition, there are methods for attacking spelling problems. With such tools, you can avoid many problems and improve spelling. This section will show you some solutions.

How To Improve Your Spelling

1. Locate and conquer your own specific spelling problems. What spelling errors do you make over and over? Study your past written assignments. Make a list of words you misspelled on them. Work on mastering those words.

2. Pronounce words carefully. Are you misspelling words because you aren't pronouncing them right? If you are writing *famly* for *family*, for instance, you are probably mispronouncing the word. Try to pronounce your words more precisely.

3. Try to remember the letters in new words. Do you really look at the spelling of new or difficult words? That habit can help you to remember how to spell words. Write the correct spelling of a new word several times.

4. Always proofread your writing. Are some of your misspellings careless mistakes? By examining your writing, you may catch such errors. Read over your work slowly, word by word.

5. Look up difficult words in a dictionary. Do you reach for the dictionary when you're unsure of a spelling? Get into the habit of letting the dictionary help you to spell well.

6. Learn the few important spelling rules explained in this section.

How To Spell a Particular Word Correctly

1. Look at the word and say it to yourself. Make sure to pronounce it correctly. Say it twice, looking at the syllables as you say them.

2. Look at the letters and say each one. Sound out the word from its spelling. Divide the word into syllables and pronounce each syllable.

3. Write the word without looking at your book or list.

4. Check to see if you spelled the word correctly. Look back at your book or list. If you spelled the word correctly, repeat the process.

5. If you made an error, note what it was. Then repeat steps 3 and 4 until you have written the word correctly three times.

Spelling Rules

Adding Prefixes

When a prefix is added to a word, the spelling of the word remains the same.

im- + perfect = imperfect   ir- + rational = irrational
re- + entry = reentry   mis- + use = misuse
inter- + action = interaction   de- + face = deface
dis- + agree = disagree   il- + legal = illegal

Suffixes with Silent e

When a suffix beginning with a vowel is added to a word ending in a silent e, the e is usually dropped.

save + ing = saving   value + able = valuable
style + ish = stylish   rate + ing = rating
grace + ious = gracious   imagine + ation = imagination

When a suffix beginning with a consonant is added to a word ending in a silent e, the e is usually retained.

time + less = timeless   strange + ly = strangely
like + ly = likely   amaze + ment = amazement
same + ness = sameness   hope + ful = hopeful

The following words are **exceptions.** Study them.

truly   argument   ninth   wholly

Exercise A Find the misspelled words. Spell them correctly.

1. Dorothy was gazeing at the graceful skaters.
2. She is leaveing that missmanaged company.
3. The driver of the handsomly painted car made an illegal turn.
4. These arguements are not solveing the problem.
5. We were dissappointed that the sportscaster mistated the facts.
6. That penalty was wholly unecessary.
7. Our district relected that insincere politician.
8. Tim has trouble wakeing up on these freezeing days.
9. A fameous surgeon performed the operatcion.
10. Leaving everything to chance is imature.

Exercise B Add the prefixes and suffixes as shown and write the new word.

1. like + ing
2. mis + understand
3. im + mobile
4. note + able
5. ir + regular
6. separate + ion
7. tape + ing
8. un + needed
9. un + wanted
10. mis + spent
11. re + apply
12. dance + ing
13. re + examine
14. place + ment
15. place + ing
16. amuse + ing
17. amuse + ment
18. love + able
19. dis + similar
20. dis + prove

Suffixes and Final *y*

When a suffix is added to a word ending in *y* preceded by a consonant, the *y* is usually changed to *i*.

carry + er = carrier   fury + ous = furious
worry + ed = worried   thirty + eth = thirtieth
silly + est = silliest   holy + ness = holiness

Note the following exception: When -*ing* is added, the *y* does not change:

hurry + ing = hurrying   study + ing = studying
rally + ing = rallying   cry + ing = crying

When a suffix is added to a word ending in *y* **preceded by a vowel, the** *y* **usually does not change.**

play + ing = playing   destroy + er = destroyer
decay + ed = decayed   annoy + ing = annoying

Exercise   Add the suffixes as shown and write the new word.

1. dizzy + ness
2. carry + ing
3. ready + ness
4. heavy + er
5. witty + est
6. marry + ing
7. marry + age
8. fifty + eth
9. employ + able
10. stay + ed
11. terrify + ing
12. creepy + est
13. relay + ed
14. glory + ous
15. cozy + er
16. history + an
17. joy + ful
18. enjoy + able
19. tiny + ness
20. fry + ed

Adding the Suffixes -*ness* and -*ly*

When the suffix -*ly* **is added to a word ending in** *l*, **both** *l*'s **are kept. When** -*ness* **is added to a word ending in** *n*, **both** *n*'s **are kept.**

cruel + ly = cruelly   even + ness = evenness
general + ly = generally   lean + ness = leanness

Doubling the Final Consonant

In words of one syllable that end in one consonant preceded by one vowel, double the final consonant before adding -*ing*, -*ed*, **or** -*er*.

beg + ing = begging   scar + ed = scarred
flap + ed = flapped   grab + ing = grabbing
thin + er = thinner   tap + ed = tapped

In words of one syllable that end in one consonant preceded by two vowels, the final consonant is not doubled.

steer + ing = steering lead + er = leader
join + ed = joined fool + ing = fooling

Exercise A Find the misspelled words. Spell them correctly.

1. Lana foolled everyone by speaking truthfuly.
2. Chris spoted the actress and beged for her autograph.
3. I finaly stopped the driping of the water faucet.
4. Something is cloging the exhaust.
5. Dot is hoping on one foot because she stepped on a bee.
6. Reservations are not usualy booked a month in advance.
7. The miser Scrooge is gencraly known for his meaness.
8. The days are geting cooler now.
9. The openess of this building makes it especialy comfortable.
10. Are you realy digging a new trench?

Exercise B Add the suffixes as shown and write the new word.

1. green + ness
2. tip + ed
3. boom + ed
4. lag + ed
5. top + ed
6. awful + ly
7. grim + est
8. playful + ly
9. brag + ing
10. plain + ness
11. cook + ed
12. sob + ed
13. run + ing
14. clip + ed
15. stern + ness
16. cheerful + ly
17. groan + ing
18. pat + ed
19. stop + ing
20. stoop + ing

Words with the "Seed" Sound

There is only one English word ending in *sede: supersede.* Three words end in *ceed: exceed, proceed, succeed.* All other words ending with the sound of *seed* are spelled *cede:*

recede   precede   concede   secede

Words with *ie* and *ei*

There is a general rule for words with the long *e* (*ē*) sound. The word is spelled *ie* except after *c*.

I before E

piece	fierce	field	grief	chief
believe	relief	niece	reprieve	retrieve

Except after C

perceive	deceit	ceiling	receipt
conceive	conceit	receive	deceive

The following words are exceptions to the rule. Study them.

either	weird	leisure
species	seize	neither

Exercise   Find the misspelled words in these sentences and spell them correctly.

1. This new law superceeds the old one.

2. South Carolina seceded from the Union in 1860 and siezed Fort Sumter in 1861.

3. My neice Meredith received a wierd surprise.

4. Sally beleives that she can clear that field in her liesure time.

5. The warden conceeded that the prisoner should get a reprieve.

6. Erin succeded in tying the boat to the pier.

7. Niether peice of land is big enough for an apartment building.

8. The forged reciept did not deceive the sales clerk, who proceded to call the detective.

9. In some cultures the period of grieving excedes two years.

10. That species of owl has a peircing shriek.

Additional Exercises

Spelling

A. Add prefixes and suffixes. Add the prefix or suffix as shown. Write the new word.

1. thin + ness
2. hot + ter
3. dis + satisfied
4. shop + ing
5. rusty + est
6. engage + ment
7. true + ly
8. spine + less
9. stage + ing
10. move + ment
11. un + necessary
12. excite + able
13. angry + er
14. destroy + ing
15. stain + ed
16. continual + ly
17. luxury + ous
18. merry + ment
19. un + attractive
20. ninety + eth

B. Add prefixes and suffixes. Add the prefix or suffix as shown. Write the new word.

1. join + ed
2. natural + ly
3. slim + est
4. include + ing
5. early + er
6. dis + appoint
7. happy + ly
8. regulate + ory
9. copy + ing
10. like + ness
11. in + voluntary
12. hope + less
13. forty + eth
14. even + ness
15. grin + ed
16. usual + ly
17. employ + er
18. carry + ing
19. argue + ment
20. mis + judge

C. Spell words with _ie_, _ei_, or the _seed_ sound. Find the misspelled words. Write them correctly on your paper.

1. Feirce winds knocked the pier into the lake.
2. The doctor conceeded that there was only one way to releive the pain.
3. In the preceeding weeks we enjoyed our leisure time.
4. "Procede with your weird tale," Gail said.
5. She defended her cheif loyally, I beleive.
6. Niether of the advertisements is meant to decieve us.
7. Unbeleivable! Martin has finally succeeded in making that radio work.
8. Sam hurried over to his crying neice.
9. We recieved directions to the new baseball field.
10. Gus has succeded in putting the peices together.

D. Spell Words Correctly. Find the misspelled words in each sentence. Write them correctly on your paper.

1. The feirce cougar dissappeared into the cave.
2. Marcy's horse gracefully steped and trotted around the ring.
3. Annie is planning to send out the inviteations today.
4. The wide reciever was completly unnaware of the new plan.
5. David shouted angryly at his friends but immediatly was sorry.
6. Some taxpayers worryed that the money was mispent.
7. The uneveness of the slope makes skiing unusualy hard.
8. Police cars generaly preceed the President's car in a parade.
9. In all of the excitment we accidentaly misplaced our tickets.
10. The weight of the ship's cargo excedes ten tons.

A List of Commonly Misspelled Words

abbreviate
accidentally
achievement
across
address
all right
altogether
always
amateur
analyze
anonymous
answer
apologize
appearance
appreciate
appropriate
argument
arrangement
associate
awkward
balance
bargain
beginning
believe
bicycle
bookkeeper
bulletin
bureau
business
cafeteria
calendar
campaign
candidate
certain
changeable
characteristic
column

committee
courageous
courteous
criticize
curiosity
cylinder
dealt
decision
definitely
despair
desperate
dictionary
dependent
description
desirable
different
disagree
disappear
disappoint
discipline
dissatisfied
efficient
eighth
eligible
eliminate
embarrass
emphasize
environment
enthusiastic
equipped
especially
exaggerate
excellent
exhaust
expense
experience
familiar

fascinating
February
financial
foreign
fourth
fragile
generally
government
grammar
guarantee
guard
gymnasium
handkerchief
height
humorous
imaginary
immediately
incredible
influence
intelligence
interesting
knowledge
laboratory
lightning
literature
loneliness
maintenance
marriage
mathematics
medicine
minimum
mischievous
missile
misspell
mortgage
municipal
necessary

nickel
ninety
noticeable
nuclear
nuisance
obstacle
occasionally
occur
opinion
opportunity
original
outrageous
parallel
particularly
permanent
permissible
persuade
picnicking
pleasant
pneumonia
politics
possess
possibility
practice
prejudice
preparation
privilege
probably
professor
pronunciation
propeller
psychology
quantity
realize
recognize
recommend
reference

referred	separate	syllable	transferred
rehearse	sergeant	sympathy	truly
repetition	similar	symptom	Tuesday
representative	sincerely	temperament	twelfth
restaurant	sophomore	temperature	undoubtedly
rhythm	souvenir	thorough	unnecessary
ridiculous	specifically	throughout	vacuum
sandwich	strategy	together	vicinity
schedule	strictly	tomorrow	village
scissors	success	traffic	weird
secretary	surprise	tragedy	writing

Section 16

The Correct Form for Writing

Anyone who reads your papers notices the content. What you say is important. You may not realize, though, that a reader also notices the form of your papers. Your writing is judged not only on its content, but also on its form.

Good form is careful, neat, and consistent. Such form will impress any reader. Some schools set their own specific rules for the correct form for written work. In this section you will learn about the kind of form that is accepted by many schools.

Guidelines for Clear Writing

Neatness

A neat, legible paper can be read easily. Neatness also suggests that the writer cares about what he or she is writing. There are several ways to give your papers a neat appearance.

Legible Writing

Typewritten papers are usually more legible than handwritten ones. However, many students do not have typewriters, and few schools require typed papers.

Handwritten papers can be clear and legible, too. They should always be written in ink. Blue or black is easiest to read. Make sure that letters are distinct, since some letters look similar. For example, *a*'s and *o*'s can be confused unless they are formed carefully. So can *e*'s and *i*'s.

The First Draft and the Final Copy

You cannot expect the first draft of a paper to be in perfect form. You write a first draft from your pre-writing notes or an outline. Then you need to correct or revise the first draft. You may need to change words and sentences or rearrange whole sections.

Afterward, you can make your final copy. Proofread this new copy. You may find errors or words left out. To insert a word, write it above the line. Use a caret (∧) to show where the word belongs. To change a word, draw a line through it and write the correction above it. If you have made more than about three corrections on a page, you should recopy the page.

Acceptable Form

The correct form for writing means more than a neat appearance. In a paper with acceptable form, the various parts are positioned correctly. Headings, titles, margins, and spacing should be in the correct form.

The Heading

A heading identifies your paper. It is usually placed in the upper right-hand corner of the first page. Place your name on the first line. Write the name of your class on the second line. Write the date on the third line. In a paper with a title page, the heading is placed in the upper right corner of that page.

Each page, except for page one, should be numbered. Beginning with page two, place the page number in the upper right hand corner. To identify all pages, you might want to put your name under the page number.

Some teachers may require a different form for labeling your paper. Follow any special instructions you are given.

The Title

The title of a paper should appear near the top of the first page. In general, place the title two lines down from the last line of the heading. Begin the first line of your paper two lines below the title.

Correct form for a title also means proper capitalization. The first word and all important words in the title should be capitalized. Use capitals for only the first letters of words, not for every letter. Do not underline your title or place it in quotation marks.

When a paper is more than three pages long, sometimes a title page is used. This page precedes the paper.

Margins and Spacing

Use correct margins and spacing to achieve an attractive appearance. Margins of one inch at the top, bottom, and left side of the paper look pleasing.

Try to keep the right-hand margin fairly even. Do not break too many words with hyphens, though, in order to keep the margin straight. A safe rule is to avoid hyphens in more than two lines in a row.

Double-spacing makes typed papers look neat. Paragraphs are usually indented five spaces. Skip two spaces after the punctuation mark at the end of a sentence.

Writing Numbers

The form for writing numbers should be consistent. Numbers that can be expressed in fewer than four words are usually spelled out. Larger numbers are written in figures.

> I got a raise of *twenty-four* dollars a month.
> The National League consists of *twelve* teams.
> Ticket sales amounted to *$2,125*.
> Over *170* players have made the Baseball Hall of Fame.

A number at the beginning of a sentence is always spelled out.

> *Thirty thousand* people attended the game.
> *One thousand* millimeters make up one meter.
> *Four hundred dollars* was stolen.

Figures rather than spelled-out words are used for these numbers: dates, street and room numbers, telephone numbers, temperatures, page numbers, decimals, and percentages.

> The Battle of Concord took place on April 19, 1775.
> The clinic is at 66 West Schiller.

Our typing class meets in Room 35 today.
Matthew's phone number is 328-6610.
Last night the temperature went down to 10 degrees.
Did you see that article about vans on page 16?
Ann ran the hurdles in 15.8 seconds.
The new sales tax is 4 percent.

In large sums of money or expressions of large quantities, commas are used to separate the figures. Commas are not used in dates, serial numbers, page numbers, addresses, or telephone numbers.

Correct: The Statue of Liberty cost $500,000.
Correct: The Milky Way has 200,000,000,000 stars.
Incorrect. The first World Series was in 1,903.
Correct: The first World Series was in 1903.

Exercise Copy these sentences, correcting any errors in the writing of numbers.

1. A movie shows fourteen hundred and thirty-five frames of film per minute.

2. The serial number of the typewriter is 20,002.

3. 1st prize is one thousand two hundred and fifty dollars.

4. About ninety percent of the patients who have this operation recover fully within 6 months.

5. Although the temperature was actually 30 degrees, the wind chill factor lowered it to two degrees.

6. The profit of twelve thousand two hundred and five dollars is ten percent higher than last year's.

7. 3 years ago the Chandlers moved to 1,682 Garfield Street.

8. 1 barrel of oil is equal to 31 gallons.

9. 1000 grams equals a little more than three pounds.

10. On March eighteenth, 1,959, Hawaii became our 50th state.

Using Abbreviations

Abbreviations are shortened forms of words. In formal writing, abbreviations are usually not acceptable.

Abbreviations, however, may be used for most titles before and after names. Abbreviations may also be used for government agencies and for time.

Titles before proper names:	Mrs., Mr., Ms., Gen., Dr., Rev., Sgt., Fr., Sen.
Titles after proper names:	Jr., M.D., D.D.S., Ph.D.
Government agencies:	FBI, VA, EPA, FTC
Dates and times:	A.M., P.M., B.C., A.D.

Notice that periods are not used in the abbreviations of government agencies.

A title is abbreviated only when it is used with a person's name, as in *Dr. Lauren Sherwood*. The following, for example, would not be acceptable: The dr. found a cure for the disease.

Abbreviations are not used for certain titles. *Honorable* and *Reverend* are not abbreviated when preceded by *the: the Reverend Lee Withers*. Abbreviations are not used for the titles of the President and Vice-President of the United States.

In most writing, abbreviations are not acceptable for the following: names of countries and states, months and days of the week, addresses, and firm names.

Incorrect:	The Mayans built pyramids in Mex.
Correct:	The Mayans built pyramids in Mexico.
Incorrect:	Detroit, Mich., is called "Motor City."
Correct:	Detroit, Michigan, is called "Motor City."
Incorrect:	Tues., Nov. 2, is Election Day.
Correct:	Tuesday, November 2, is Election Day.

Incorrect: The Coca-Cola Co. has a plant on Oak Ave.
Correct: The Coca-Cola Company has a plant on Oak Avenue.

In ordinary writing, abbreviations are not acceptable for the following: names of school courses, and the words *page*, *chapter*, and *Christmas*. Abbreviations for measurements, like *ft.*, *in.*, *min.*, *hr.*, *oz.*, *qt.*, *mi.*, are also unacceptable.

Exercise   Correct the errors in abbreviation in these sentences.

1. The secy. of H.E.W. is usually not a medical dr.
2. The Pres. met with the Secy. of Defense at Camp David, Md.
3. The Rev. Amelia Gleason gave a sermon about the true meaning of Xmas.
4. McDonald's Corp. has its headquarters on Twenty-second Ave. in Oakbrook, Ill.
5. Mr. Frank Ransom, Jr. is applying for a govt. grant to start a center for sr. citizens.
6. Benito Juarez, a nineteenth-century pres. of Mexico, is described in Ch. 10.
7. Last Fri., our home ec. class visited Mercy Hosp.
8. I lost two lbs. in forty-eight hrs. on the diet Dr. Rossi gave me.
9. Cleopatra ruled Egypt in the first cent. B.C.
10. Pres. Roosevelt closed all banks in the U.S. on Mar. 6, 1933.

Acknowledgments

International Paper Company: for "How to Read Faster" on page 173. For a reprint of the entire advertisement from which the selection has been adapted, write to "Power of the Printed Word," International Paper Company, Department 4, P.O. Box 900, Elmsford, New York 10523.

William Collins Publishers, Inc., for entries from *Webster's New World Dictionary of the American Language, Student's Edition;* appearing on page 14, 17, and 19. Harcourt Brace Jovanovich, Inc., for poem "To Look at Any Thing" from *The Living Seed* by John Moffitt, copyright © 1961 by John Moffitt. Camels Coming Magazine, for "For Poets" from *The Song Turning Back into Itself* by Al Young. The New York Times Company, Inc., for "November Afternoon." E. P. Dutton & Company, Inc., for a selection from *Rascal* by Sterling North, copyright © 1963 by Sterling North.

Editor-in-Chief: Joseph F. Littell
Editorial Director, English Programs: Joy Littell
Managing Editor: Kathleen Laya
Assistant Editors: Bonnie Dobkin, Joseph L. Page

Cover design: Sandra Gelak
Art production and handwritten art: Kenneth Izzi
Diagrams: Amy Palmer

Index

a, an, the. See Articles.
Abbreviations
   capitalization of, 472,479
   in dates, 190
   period with, 487–488
   in reference works, 219
   in writing, 534–535
   ZIP code, 184
Action verbs, 326, 343, 363
Active verbs, 341–342, 345
Addresses
   comma with, 184, 497–498,
      500–501, 515
   on envelopes, 182 185
   inside, 194–196
   return, 183
Adjective clause, 137–111, 447–
      450, 453
Adjective phrase, 376–379, 384,
      437
Adjectives, 347–354, 360–371,
      385–391, 437
   adverbs or, 360–364, 383
   articles, 348–349, 473–474
   comma with, 490
   comparative forms of, 350–354,
      369
   in comparisons, 350–354, 369
   compound, 506–507, 516
   in descriptions, 27–51
   modifying gerunds, 394
   infinitives used as, 401–406,
      408
   participles used as, 396–400,
      404–408
   predicate, 265–267, 269–270,
      348–350, 368, 370

compound, 269, 349, 380–
      382, 421
proper, 347, 349–350, 471–480,
      484
in sentence patterns, 274
subordinate clauses used as,
      437–441, 443–450, 453
superlative forms of, 351–354,
      369
Adverb clause, 435–437, 443–445,
      447–450, 452
Adverb phrase, 377–379, 384, 435
Adverbs, 354–367, 369–371, 385–
      391, 435
   adjectives or, 360–362
   forming from adjectives, 355–
      356
   comparative forms of, 358–360,
      370
   in comparisons, 358–360, 370
   in compound constructions,
      380–382
   conjunctive, 429–431, 451,
      501–502
   first, second, third, 490
   modifying gerunds, 393
   infinitives used as, 401–406, 408
   modifying infinitives, 401
   modifying participles, 397
   predicate adjectives or, 362–
      364
   prepositions or, 375–376, 383
   subordinate clauses used as,
      435–437, 443–445, 447–450,
      452
   superlative forms of, 359–360,
      370

varying sentences with, 68
Agreement of pronouns and antecedents, 311
Agreement of subjects and verbs, 409–419
Almanacs, 222
Alphabetical order
  of books in library, 210, 212
  of cards in card catalog, 213–215, 217
  of encyclopedia articles, 221
  in *Readers' Guide to Periodical Literature*, 224–225
and, but, or, nor. See Coordinating conjunctions.
Anecdote, to develop paragraph, 105–106, 131
Announcements, making, 231–232
Antecedents of pronouns, 310–312, 323
Antonyms, 19–22
Apostrophe, 507–509, 516–517
  in contractions, 508–509, 516–517
  in shortened dates, 508–509, 516–517
  to form plurals of letters and numbers, 508–509, 516–517
  to form possessive indefinite pronouns, 507–509, 516–517
  to form possessive nouns, 296–297, 299, 507–509, 516–517
Appositives, 494, 496–497, 515
  as context clue, 3
Archaic words, 457
Articles (*a, an, the*), 348–349
  definite, 348
  before geographical names, 474
  indefinite, 348
  in titles, 481–482, 485

Atlases, 224
Audience for compositions, 144–145, 165
Author card, 213–216, 218–219
Authors, books about, 223
Auxiliary verbs. *See* Helping verbs.

be, forms of, 264–265
  to form passive verbs, 341–342, 345
Biographical references, 222–223
Biographies in library, 212
Body of business letter, 194–199, 201–206
Body of composition, 134, 151–152, 155–162, 165, 168–172, 174–175, 178
Body of formal talk, 241–242
Body of friendly letter, 191–193
Body of informal note, 187
Books in library. *See* Library.
Business letters, 193–206

Call numbers, 213–219
Capitalization, 471–485
  of abbreviations, 472–474, 479, 484–485
  of directions of the compass, 475–476
  of first words, 480–483, 485
  in letter parts, 187, 191, 196, 481, 485
  in outlines, 481–483, 485
  of poetry lines, 480, 482–483, 485
  of proper nouns and adjectives, 288, 347, 471–480, 484–485
  in quotations, 480–483, 485
  in titles
    of school papers, 531

of persons, 472–474, 484
of written works, 481–483, 485
Card catalog, 213–219
Case of words used as nouns
  nominative. *See* Subject of the verb entries.
  objective. *See* Object of the preposition, Object of the verb entries.
  possessive. *See* Possessive noun, Possessive pronouns entries.
Cause and effect relationship as basis for inference, 11
Characters in compositions, 176, 178
Chronological order, 122, 127–128, 131, 150, 169–171, 173, 175, 178
Clauses 431–454
  adjective, 437–441, 443–450, 453
  adverb, 435–437, 443–445, 447–450, 452
  main (independent), 432, 434, 445, 447–449, 496
  nonrestrictive, 498–501, 515
    simplifying in writing, 59–61
  noun, 441–445, 447–450, 453
  in padded sentences, 59–61
  phrases or, 432
  relative, 438–441, 453
  restrictive, 498–501, 515
  subordinate (dependent), 432–450, 452–454
    beginning sentences, 70
    as sentence fragments, 445–446
Climax in formal talk, 242
Closing (complimentary close)

in business letter, 194–196, 481, 498
in friendly letter, 190–191, 481, 498
in informal note, 187
Coherence in compositions, 169–173, 175, 178
Colon, 502–503, 516
  in salutation, 196, 502
Comma, 490–501, 515
  in addresses, 184, 497–498, 500–501, 515
  to separate adjectives, 490–491
  to set off appositives, 494, 496–497, 515
  to set off clauses, 118, 492–493, 498–501, 515
  in compound sentences, 428–431, 451, 495–497, 515
  to avoid confusion, 499–501, 515
  after conjunctive adverbs, 429, 431, 451
  in dates, 497, 500–501, 515
  after *first*, *second*, *third*, 490–491
  with interrupters, 492–493, 515
  after introductory words, 492–493, 515
  in letter parts, 187, 191, 498, 500
  with nonrestrictive clauses, 498–501, 515
  with nouns of direct address, 494, 496–497, 515
  with numbers, 533
  with quotations, 495–497, 509–510, 515
  in run-on sentences, 282, 283
  in a series, 490–491, 501, 515
Commands (imperative sentences), 258–259, 271–272, 278

Commercials, doing, 234
Common nouns, 287–288, 298, 471–472
Comparative forms
    of adjectives, 350–354, 369
    of adverbs, 358–360, 370
Comparison
    adjectives in, 350–354, 369
    adverbs in, 358–360, 370
    as context clue, 5, 7–9
    to develop composition, 172
    to develop paragraph, 106–109
    avoiding faulty, 65, 67
    implied, as basis for inference, 11–13
Complaint, letter of, 201–206
Complete predicate, 249–251, 272–273, 275, 421
Complete sentence, 248–251, 275, 279–285
Complete subject, 249–251, 272–273, 275, 421
Complex sentences, 431–446, 448–450, 452–454
Complimentary close. *See* Closing.
Compositions, 133–165
    audience for, 144–145, 165
    body in, 134, 151–152, 155–162, 165, 168–172, 174–175, 178
    characters in, 176–178
    checklist for writing, 165
    chronological order in, 150, 169–171, 173, 175, 178
    coherence in, 169–173, 175, 178
    comparison in, 172
    conclusion in, 134–136, 151–152, 162–163, 165, 172, 174
    conflict in, 176–178
    contrast in, 172

descriptive, 167–172
details in, 168–171, 173, 175, 178
developing, 133–165
emphasis in, 167, 170–173, 175, 178
example(s) in, 172
explanatory, 172–175
facts or statistics in, 172
first draft of, 152–163, 530
based on first-hand experience, 136–137, 141–142
form for writing, 529–535
ideas for, 146–149
based on imagination, 139–140
indentation in, 157, 532
introductory paragraph in, 135, 151–155, 157, 165, 171–172, 174
based on learned information, 138–139, 142
logical order in, 150–152, 165, 168–169, 171, 173, 175
main idea in, 134–136, 152–157, 162, 165
mental point of view in, 168–169, 171
narrative, 176–179
outline for, 150–152
order of familiarity in, 150
order of importance in, 150
parts of, 134–136, 151
physical point of view in, 168–169, 171
planning, 146–152
pre-writing steps for, 146–152
process of writing, 75–81
proofreading, 164, 530
purpose for, 144–146, 165
rewriting, 163–165
setting in, 176–178

spatial order in, 150–151
statement of purpose for, 144–146
subjects for, 136–143, 165
synonyms in, 159, 171
time words in, 157–158
title for, 163, 165, 531
topic sentences in, 156–157, 165, 169, 174
transitional devices in, 157–162, 165, 169, 173, 175, 178
types of, 167–179
unity in, 157–162, 165, 167, 169, 171–175, 178
Compound adjectives, 506–507, 516
Compound-complex sentences, 446–450, 454
Compound direct objects, 269–270, 309, 380–382, 421–423
Compound indirect objects, 269, 309–310, 381–382
Compound nouns, 505–507, 516
Compound numbers, 505–507, 516
Compound objects of preposi tions, 309–310, 381–382, 421
Compound personal pronouns, 312–313
Compound predicate adjectives, 269–270, 349, 380–382, 421
Compound predicate nouns, 269–270
Compound predicate pronouns, 269–270, 309–310
Compound predicates, 380–382, 421–423, 426–428, 496
Compound sentences, 420, 423–431, 448–451, 454
    compound predicate or, 426–428, 496

punctuation with, 428–431, 451, 495–497, 501–502, 515–516
Compound subjects, 268, 270, 309–310, 380–382, 412–413, 418, 421–423
Compound verbs, 268, 270, 380–382, 421–423
Conclusion in compositions, 134–136, 151–152, 162–163, 165, 172, 174
Conclusion in formal talks, 242
Conflict in compositions, 176–178
Conjunctions, 372–373, 379–382
    coordinating, 380–382, 418, 423 426, 428–431, 496
    correlative, 381–382
    in overloaded sentences, 62–63
    subordinating, 432–433, 436
Conjunctive adverbs, 429–431, 451, 501–503
Connectives. See Conjunctions, Prepositions.
Context, 2–15, 22–25
    inferring meaning from, 9–12, 22–24
Context clues to word meanings, 2–9, 22–24
Contractions
    apostrophe in, 317, 508–509, 516–517
    negative, 365–367, 371
    possessive pronouns or, 317–319, 324
Contrast
    as context clue, 5–9
    to develop compositions, 172
    to develop paragraphs, 106–109
    implied, as basis for inference, 11–12

Conversation, writing. *See* Dialogue.
Coordinating conjunctions, 380–382, 423, 426
Correlative conjunctions, 381–382
Cross reference cards, 216–217

Dash, 504–505, 516
Dates
  apostrophe in, 508–509, 516–517
  comma in, 497, 500–501, 515
  in headings of letters, 190, 195
  in school papers, 531
Declarative sentences, 271–272, 278, 487
Definite articles, 348
Definition as context clue, 2–3, 6–9, 22–24
Delivery of formal talk, 243
Demonstration talk, 233
Demonstrative pronouns, 313–314, 323
Dependent clauses. *See* Subordinate clauses.
Descriptive compositions, 167–172
Descriptive paragraphs, 111–112, 131
Details in writing. *See* Compositions, Paragraphs, Sentences.
Dewey Decimal System, 210–213
Diagraming the sentence
  adjectives, 349
  adverbs, 356–357
  clauses, 436, 439, 442
  compound parts, 268–269, 349
  compound sentences, 424
  direct objects, 263
  gerunds and gerund phrases, 394–395

indirect objects, 263
infinitives and infinitive phrases, 403
participles and participial phrases, 398
predicate words, 265–266, 269, 349
prepositional phrases, 378
simple sentences, 252–253
with unusual word order, 256, 258–259
Dialogue, writing, 512–513
Dictionaries, 219–221
Directions, giving, 232–233
Directions of the compass, capitalizing, 475–476
Direct objects of verbs, 260–264, 273, 327, 341–342
  compound, 269–270, 309, 380–382, 421–423
  gerunds as, 393–396, 404–408
  infinitives as, 402–406, 408
  noun clauses as, 441–445, 453
  nouns as, 290–292, 299
  predicate word or, 266–267
  pronouns as, 306–310, 322, 438–439
  in sentence patterns, 273
  before the subject, 68–69
Direct questions, 487
Direct quotations, 480, 495–497, 509–512, 516–517
Divided quotations, 481, 495–497, 510–512, 515
doesn't, don't, 415–416
Double negatives, 365–367, 371
Doubling the final consonant, 522–523

Emphasis in compositions, 167, 170–173, 175, 178

Empty sentences, 54–58, 72–73
Encyclopedias, 221–222
End marks, 486 489, 515
  See also Exclamation point,
  Period, Question mark.
English
  standard and nonstandard,
    455–470
  usual sentence order in, 68
  vocabulary, 1–25
  See also Words.
Envelopes, addressing, 182–185
Example(s)
  as context clue, 4, 6–9
  to develop composition, 172
  to develop paragraph, 103–104
Exclamation point (or mark)
  in exclamatory sentences, 271–
    272, 278, 488–489, 515
  in imperative sentences, 487
  after interjections, 386, 488
  with quotation marks, 511
Exclamatory sentences, 271–272,
  278, 488
Explanatory compositions, 172–
  175
Explanatory paragraphs, 121–126,
  131

Facts or statistics in writing. See
  Compositions, Paragraphs.
Fiction books in library, 210
First draft
  of compositions, 152–163
  of school papers, 530
  of paragraphs, 78, 81
First-hand experience
  in compositions, 136–137, 141–
    142
  in formal talks, 239
First-person, paragraphs written

in, 126
Formal and informal English, 456
Formal talks, 235–243
Fractions, hyphen in, 505–507, 516
Fragments of sentences, 248–
  249, 275, 279–282, 284–285,
  445–446
Friendly letters, 189–193
Future perfect tense of verbs,
  331–333, 344
Future tense of verbs, 330–333, 344

Gerund phrases, 393–396, 399–
  400, 404–408
Gerunds, 392–396, 399–400, 404–
  408
  as direct objects, 393–396, 400,
    404–408
  modifiers of, 394
  objects of, 393–396, 404
  as objects of prepositions, 393–
    396, 404–408
  participles or, 399–400
  as subjects, 393–396, 399–400,
    405–408
good, well, 365–367
Greeting in letters. See
  Salutation.
Guide cards, 217
Guide letters and words in
  encyclopedia, 221

Handwriting, 530
Heading in letters, 190, 194–195
Heading in school papers, 531
"Hearing" words, 35–39, 117,
  119–120
Helping verbs, 254–255, 329–330,
  344
Hyphen, 505–507, 516

I, capitalization of, 473
Imagination
  in compositions, 139–141
  in paragraphs, 126
Imperative sentences (commands), 271–272, 278, 487
Indefinite articles, 348
Indefinite pronouns, 315–317, 323–324, 413–414, 418
  agreement with verbs, 413–414, 418
  plural, 315–316, 413–414, 418
  possessive, 507–509, 516–517
  singular, 315–316, 413–414, 418
Indenting
  in compositions, 157
  in dialogue, 512–513
  in letters, 193–195
  in school papers, 532
Independent clauses. *See* Clauses, main.
Indirect objects of verbs, 262–264, 306–310
  compound, 269, 309–310, 381–382
  nouns as, 291–292, 299
  pronouns as, 306–310
  in sentence patterns, 273
Indirect quotations, 495, 509, 511–512
Inference, 9–13, 22–24
Infinitive phrases, 401–406, 408
  beginning sentences, 69–71
Infinitives, 392, 400–406, 408
  as direct objects, 402–406, 408
  as modifiers, 401–406, 408
  modifiers of, 401
  objects of, 401–402
  split, 402
  as subjects, 402–406, 408
  to, as sign of, 400

Informal English, 456
Informal notes, 186–189
Informal talks, 229–235
Information
  for compositions, 138–139, 141–142
  in reference works, 219–227
Initials
  capitalization of, 472, 479
  period with, 487
Inside address, 194–196
Instructions, writing, 121–122, 124–126, 131
Interjections, 386–391, 488–489
Interrogative pronouns, 314–315, 323
Interrogative sentences (questions), 258, 271–272, 278, 488
Intransitive verbs, 261–262, 327–328, 343
Introduction
  in composition, 134–135, 151–155, 157, 165, 171–172, 174–175
  in formal talk, 240–241
Introductions, making, 234–235
Invitations, 187–189
Irregular verbs, 334–340
Italics, underlining for, 513–514, 516–517
its, it's, 317–318, 458

kind, sort, 364

Language. *See* Words.
Letters, 181–206
  business, 193–206
    capitalization in, 196, 481
    carbon copy of, 197
    of complaint, 201–206

forms for, 193–198
  inside address in, 194–196
  of order, 200–201
  parts of, 194–196
  punctuation in, 196
  of request, 201–202
  types of, 201–206
envelopes, addressing, 182–185
  ZIP code, 182, 184
friendly, 189–193
  capitalization, 191, 481
  parts of, 190
  punctuation, 191, 498
informal notes, 186–189
  capitalization in, 187
  parts of, 187
  punctuation in, 187
  R.S.V.P., 187–189
  invitations, 187–188
  thank-you notes, 186–187, 189
Library, 209–227
  call numbers, 213–219
  card catalog, 213–219
  classification and arrangement
    of books, 210–213
  Dewey Decimal System, 210–
    213
  encyclopedias, 221–222, 226
  fiction books, 210–213
  nonfiction books, 210–213
  Readers' Guide to Periodical
    Literature, 224–225, 227
  reference works, 212, 219–227
Linking verbs, 264–267, 326–328,
  343, 363
  in sentence patterns, 273–274
Listening skills
  training in, 35–39
Literary reference books, 223–224,
  227
Logical order

in compositions, 150–152, 165,
  168–169, 171, 173, 175
in formal talks, 242
in paragraphs, 112–115, 122,
  131

Magazines in library, 224
Main idea. See Compositions,
  Formal talks, Paragraphs,
  Sentences.
Main verbs, 254–255, 329–330,
  344
Margins and spacing for school
  papers, 532
Mental point of view in com-
  positions, 168–169, 171
Modifiers, 346–371
  See also Adjectives, Adverbs,
    Infinitives, Participles,
    Prepositions.
more, most
  with adjectives, 350–354, 369
  with adverbs, 358–360, 370

Narrative compositions, 176–179
Narrative paragraphs, 126–131
Negative words, 365–366
  double negatives, 365–367, 371
Nominative case. See Subject of
  the verb entries.
Nonfiction books in library, 210–
  213
Nonrestrictive clauses, 498–501,
  515
Nonstandard English, 455–470
not and n't, 254
Note cards for formal talks, 240
Notes, informal, 186–189
Notes, prewriting, 76–77, 146–152
Noun clauses, 441–450, 453

Nouns, 286–300, 385–391
  in apposition, 494
  common, 287–288, 298, 471–472
  compound, 505–507, 516
  compound predicate, 269–270
  of direct address, 494, 496–497, 515
  as direct objects of verbs, 290–291, 299
  gerunds used as, 393–396, 399–400, 404–408
  as indirect objects of verbs, 291–292
  infinitives used as, 402–406
  as objects of prepositions, 373, 373–379
  plural forms of, 294–296, 299
  possessive, 296–297, 299
  predicate, 265–267, 270, 293–294, 299
    noun clause as, 441
  proper, 287–288, 298, 471–480, 484
  in sentence patterns, 272–274
  singular forms of, 294–296, 299
  as subjects of verbs, 289–290, 299
number of words, 409–410
Numbers
  compound, 505–507, 516
  in writing, 532–533

Object form of pronouns, 306–310, 322
Objective case. *See* Object of the preposition, Object of the verb entries.
Objects of gerunds, 393–394
Objects of infinitives, 401, 403
Objects of participles, 397–398

Objects of prepositions, 306–307, 309–310, 373, 376–378, 393–396, 400
  compound, 309–310, 381–382, 421
  gerunds as, 393–396, 400, 404–408
  noun clauses as, 441–442, 453
  nouns as, 373, 376–379
  pronouns as, 306–307, 309–310, 438–439
Objects of verbs. *See* Direct objects of verbs, Indirect objects of verbs.
Oral reports, 235
Order, letter of, 201
Order of familiarity in compositions, 150
Order of importance in compositions, 150
Outlines
  capitalization in, 481–482
  for compositions, 150–152
  for formal talks, 242
  period in, 488
Overloaded sentences, 62–63, 72–73

Padded sentences, 58–61, 72–73
Papers, form for writing, 529–535
Paragraphs, 83–109, 111–131
  anecdote in, 105–106, 122
  checklist for writing, 131
  chronological order in, 122, 127–128, 131
  comparison in, 106–109, 124, 131
  contrast in, 106–109, 124, 131
  descriptive, 111–121, 131
  details in, 76–77, 93–98, 111–112, 115–121, 131

developing, 100–109, 122–124, 126–131

in dialogue, 512–513

example(s) in, 103–104, 123, 131

explanatory, 121–126, 131

facts or statistics in, 100–103, 122–123, 131

first draft of, 78, 81

written in the first person, 126

imagination in, 126

incident in, 105–106, 123, 131

logical order in, 112–115, 122, 131

main idea in, 83–100

narrative, 126–131

narrowing a topic for, 76–77, 81

pre writing steps for, 76–77, 81

process of writing, 75–81, 131

proofreading, 80

rewriting, 78–79, 81

appealing to the senses in, 111–112, 117–121

space words and phrases in, 112–115

specific details in, 93–98

specific examples in, 103–104

written in the third person, 126

time words and phrases in, 127–128, 131

topic sentence in, 83–100, 128–131

types of, 111–131

unity in, 89–92

Participial phrases, 396–400, 404–408

beginning a sentence, 69

Participles, 396–400, 404–408

gerund or, 399–400

as modifiers, 396–400, 405–408

modifiers of, 397

objects of, 397–398

Parts of speech, 385–391

using words as different, 387–391

See also Adjectives, Adverbs, Conjunctions, Interjections, Nouns, Prepositions, Pronouns, Verbs.

Passive verbs, 341–342, 345

Past participles of verbs, 333–342, 344

forming passive verbs, 341–342, 344

used as verbals, 396–399, 405–408

Past perfect tense of verbs, 331–333, 344

Past tense of verbs, 331–340, 344

Perfect tenses of verbs, 331–333

Period, 486–489, 509–510, 515

in abbreviations, 487–488

after initials, 487

with numerals, 488

in outlines, 488

with quotation marks, 509–510, 516–517

at the end of sentences, 271–272, 278, 487, 489, 515

Personal pronouns, 302–312

Phrases

adjectives, 376–379, 384

adverb, 377–379, 384

clauses or, 432

gerund, 392–396, 399–400, 404–408

infinitive, 69–70, 401–406, 408

participial, 69, 396–400, 404–408

prepositional, 69–70, 373–379, 383–384

beginning sentences, 69–70

not part of subject, 410–411

Physical point of view in compositions, 168–169, 171

Plagiarism, avoiding, in formal talks, 240

Plural forms of letters and numbers, 508–509, 516–517

Plural forms of words. *See* Nouns, Pronouns, Verbs.

Poetry lines, capitalization of, 480

Point of view in compositions, 167–169, 171

Possessive case. *See* Possessive nouns, Possessive pronouns.

Possessive nouns, 296–297, 299, 507–509, 516–517

Possessive pronouns, 303–305, 307–308, 317–319, 322, 507–509, 516–517

   contractions or, 317–319, 324

Predicate adjectives, 265–267, 269–270, 348–350, 368, 370

   adverbs or, 362–364

   compound, 269–270, 349, 380–382, 421

   in sentence patterns, 274

Predicate nouns, 265–267, 270, 293–294, 299

   compound, 269–270

   noun clauses as, 441

   in sentence patterns, 273

Predicate pronouns, 265–267, 269–270, 305–308

   compound, 269–270, 309–310

   in sentence patterns, 273

Predicate of the sentence

   complete, 249–251, 272–273, 275

   compound, 380–382, 421–423, 426–428

   simple (the verb), 251–278

See also Verbs.

Prefixes, 520, 525

Prepositional phrases, 373–379, 383–384

   in appositives, 494

   as modifiers, 376–379, 384, 394, 397, 401

   beginning the sentence, 69

   avoiding misuse as subject, 65, 410

Prepositions, 372–379, 383–384, 385–391

   adverbs or, 375–376, 383

   objects of, 306–307, 309–310, 373, 376–378, 393–396, 400, 404–408, 438–442, 453

     compound, 309–310, 381–382, 421

Present participle used as verbal, 396–400, 405–408

Present perfect tense of verbs, 331–333, 344

Present tense of verbs, 331–340, 344

Pre-writing steps

   for compositions, 146–152

   for paragraphs, 76–77, 81

Principal parts of verbs

   irregular verbs, 334–340

   regular verbs, 333–334

Process of writing, 75–81

Pronouns, 301–324, 385–391

   antecedents of, 310–312, 323

     agreement in number, 311

   compound personal, 312–313

   as compound sentence parts, 269, 309–310

   demonstrative, 313–314, 323

   as direct objects of verbs, 306–310, 322, 438–439

   forms of, 303–308, 322

indefinite, 315–317, 323–324, 413–414, 418
possessive, 507–509, 516–517
as indirect objects of verbs, 306–310, 322
interrogative, 314–315, 323
object forms of, 303–310, 322, 439
as objects of prepositions, 306–307, 309–310, 438–439
personal, 302–303
plural, 302, 315–316
possessive forms of, 303–305, 307–308, 322, 507–509, 516–517
contractions or, 317–319, 324
predicate, 265–267, 269–270, 305–307, 438
compound, 269
relative, 438–441, 453
in sentence patterns, 272–274
singular, 302, 315–316
subject forms of, 303–306, 309–310, 322
them, those, 320–321, 324
as transitional device in writing, 159–160
we, us, 320–321, 324
who, whom, 319–320, 324
Proofreading, 80–81, 164, 530
Proper adjectives, 347, 349–350, 471–480, 484
Proper nouns, 287–288, 298, 471–480, 484
Punctuation, 281–282, 486–517
See also Apostrophe, Colon, Comma, Dash, End marks, Exclamation point, Hyphen, Period, Question mark, Quotation marks, Semicolon, Underlining.

Question mark, 271–272, 278, 487–489
with quotation marks, 511
Questions (interrogative sentences), 258, 271–272, 278, 488
direct, 487
indirect, 487
subject in, 258
Quotation marks, 509–517
with certain titles, 513–517
Quotations
capitalization in, 480–483, 485
in dialogue, 512–513
direct, 480, 495, 509–512, 516–517
divided, 481, 510–512, 516–517
indirect, 495
punctuation with, 495–497, 509–517

Readers' Guide to Periodical Literature, 224–225, 240
Reference works in library, 212, 219–227, 240
Regular verbs, 333–334
Relative clause, 438–441, 453
Relative pronouns, 438–441, 453
Request, letter of, 201–202
Restatement as context clue, 2–3, 6–9, 22–24
Restrictive clause, 498–501, 515
Return address, 182–183
Rewriting
compositions, 163–165
paragraphs, 78–79
sentences that don't make sense, 64–67
R.S.V.P., 187–188
Run-on sentences, 279, 282–285

Salutation (greeting)

in business letter, 194–196, 481
in friendly letter, 191, 481, 498
in informal notes, 187
"See" and "See also" cards, 216–217
Semicolon
in compound sentences, 423, 428–431, 451, 501–502, 516
in compound-complex sentences, 447
before conjunctive adverbs, 429–431, 451, 502
Senses, using in writing, 27–51, 111–121, 131
Sensory words, 27–51
Sentence fragments, 248–249, 275, 279–282, 284–285
subordinate clauses as, 445–446
Sentence order, usual, 68
Sentence patterns, 272–274
Sentences, 247–285, 420–454
agreement of subject and verb in, 409–419
beginning of, varying, 68–71
capitalization in, 480
clauses in, 431–454
commands (imperative sentences), 258–259, 271–272, 278
complete, 248–251, 275, 279–285
complete predicate in, 249–251, 272–273, 275, 421
complete subject in, 249–251, 272–273, 275, 421
complex, 431–446, 448–450, 452–454
compound, 420, 423–431, 448–451, 454, 495–497, 515
compound-complex, 446–450, 454

compound predicate in, 380–382, 421–423, 426–427
compound subject in, 268, 270, 309–310, 380–382, 418, 421–423
compound verb in, 268, 270, 380–382, 421–423
declarative, 271–272, 278, 487
empty, 54–58, 72–73
exclamatory, 271–272, 278, 488
fragments of, 248–249, 275, 279–282, 284–285, 445–446
imperative (commands), 258–259, 271–272, 278, 487
interrogative (questions), 258, 271–272, 278, 488
kinds of (purpose), 271–272, 278, 487–488
kinds of (structure), 420–454
overloaded, 62–63, 72–73
padded, 58–61, 72–73
parts of, 249–251
phrases in, 258
punctuation in, 271–272, 278, 281–283, 285
questions (interrogative sentences), 258, 271–272, 278, 488
run-on, 279, 282–285
sensory words in, 27–51
simple, 247–275, 422, 448–451, 454
simple predicate (the verb) in, 251–270, 272–274, 276–278, 421
simple subject in, 251–253, 255–259, 268, 276–278, 421
beginning with *there* and *here*, 256–257, 415–416, 419
thesis, in formal talks, 238–239
topic, 83–106, 128–131, 156–157, 165, 169, 174

understood subject in, 258–259
unsupported statements, 56–58
with unusual word order, 255–259
the verb in, 251–270, 272–274, 276–278, 421
writing, 53–73
Setting in compositions, 176–178
"Sight" words, 28–35, 112–117
Signature in letters, 190, 194–197
Sign of the infinitive, 400
Simple predicate, 251–270, 272–274, 276–278, 421
See also Verbs.
Simple sentences, 247–275, 422, 448–451, 454
Simple subject, 251–253, 255–259, 268, 276–278, 421
Simple tenses of verbs, 331–333, 344
Slang, 457
"Smell" words, 47–49, 118, 120
Social notes. See Informal notes.
Sound, sense of, in writing, 117
Space words and phrases, 112–115
Spatial order in compositions, 150–151
Speaking skills. See Talks.
Speeches. See Talks.
Spelling, 518–528
how to improve, 519
list of commonly misspelled words, 527–528
mastering a particular word, 519–520
adding prefixes, 520, 525
rules for, 520–524
adding suffixes, 520–523, 525
words with "seed" sound, 523, 526
words with ie or ei, 524, 526

Split infinitives, 402
Standard and nonstandard English, 455–470
Statement of purpose of composition, 144–146
State of being verbs. See Linking verbs.
Stories, writing. See Compositions.
Subject card, 213–219
Subject pronouns, 303–306, 309–310, 322, 413–416, 418
Subject of the sentence
complete, 249–251, 275, 279–285
simple. See Subject of the verb.
Subject of the verb, 251–253, 255–259, 268, 272–278
agreement with verb, 409–419
in clauses, 431–454
in commands (imperative sentences), 258–259
compound, 268, 270, 309–310, 380–382, 412–413, 418, 421–423
gerunds and gerund phrases as, 393–396, 399–400, 405–408
infinitives and infinitive phrases as, 402–406, 408
noun clause as, 441–450, 443–445
nouns as, 289–290, 299
phrases not part of, 410
pronouns as, 303–306, 309–310, 322, 413–416, 418
in questions (interrogative sentences), 258
in sentence patterns, 272–274
understood (you), 258–259
in unusual positions, 255–259
Subjects for compositions, 136–

143, 165
Subordinate (dependent) clauses,
    432–450, 452–454
  beginning sentences, 70
Subordinating conjunctions,
    432–433, 436, 445
Suffixes, 520–523, 525
Superlative forms
  of adjectives, 351–354, 369
  of adverbs, 359–360, 370
Synonyms, 16–22, 24–25
  in compositions, 159, 171
synonymy in dictionary, 17–18

Talks, giving, 229–243
  formal, 235–243
    body in, 241–242
    conclusion in, 242
    delivery of, 243
    introduction in, 240–241
    material for, 239–240
    purpose of, 237–238
    thesis of, 238–239
    topic for, 235–237
  informal, 229–235
    announcements, 231–232
    commercials, 234
    demonstrations, 233
    directions, 232–233
    introductions, 234–235
    preparing, 230
    presenting, 230
    types of, 231–235
"Taste" words, 44–46, 118–119
Tenses of verbs, 330–340, 344
Thank-you notes, 186–187, 189
them, those, 320–321, 324, 364,
  366
there, here, 256–257, 364, 415
  416, 419
Thesaurus, 18

Thesis of formal talk, 238–239
Third-person, paragraphs written
  in, 126
Time words and phrases
  in compositions, 157–158
  in paragraphs, 127–128, 131
Title card, 213–219
Title page for papers, 531
Titles
  of books in library, 210–213
  capitalization of, 472–474, 481–
    483, 485
  for compositions, 163, 165
  for school papers, 531
  of persons, 472–474, 534
  of written works, 481–483, 485
    quotation marks with, 513–
     517
    underlining for italics, 513–
     517
to, as the sign of the infinitive,
  400
Topics for formal talks, 236–237
Topics for writing. *See* Compositions, Paragraphs, Sentences.
Topic sentences
  in compositions, 156–157, 165,
    169, 174
  in paragraphs, 83–100, 128–131
"Touch" words, 39–43, 118–119
Transitional devices in compositions, 157–162, 165, 169, 173,
  175, 178
Transitive verbs, 261–262, 327–
  328, 343
Troublesome verbs, 461–464, 469

Underlining for italics, 513–514,
  516–517
Understood subject (you), 258–
  259

Unity
  in compositions, 157–162, 165,
    167, 169, 171, 175, 178
  in paragraphs, 89–92
Unsupported statements in writing, 56–59

Verb, the (simple predicate),
  251–278
  See also Verbs.
Verbals, 392–408
  gerunds and gerund phrases,
    392–396, 399–400, 404–408
  infinitives and infinitive
    phrases, 392, 400–406, 408
  participles and participial
    phrases, 396–400, 404–408
Verbs, 251–278, 325–345, 385–391
  action, 326, 343, 363
  active, 341–342, 345
  agreement with subjects, 409–419
  be, forms of, 264–265
  compound, 268, 270, 380–382,
    421–423
  in contractions, 254
  direct objects of, 260–264, 269,
    273, 290–292, 299, 306–310,
    327, 341–342, 393–396, 402–408, 438–445
    compound, 269–270, 309,
      380–382, 421–423
  future perfect tense of, 331–333, 344
  future tense of, 331–333, 344
  helping, 254–255, 329–330, 344
  indirect objects of, 262–264,
    306–310
    compound, 269, 309–310,
      381–382

intransitive, 261–262, 327–328, 343
irregular, 334–340
linking, 264–267, 326–328, 343,
  363
main, 254–255, 329–330, 344
number of, 409–410
parts of, 254–255, 329–330
passive, 341–342, 345
past participles of, 333–342,
  344, 396–399, 405–408
past perfect tense of, 331–333,
  344
past tense of, 331–340, 344
perfect tense of, 331–333
present participles of, 396–400,
  405–408
present perfect tense of, 331–333, 344
present tense of, 331–340, 344
principal parts of, 333–340
regular, 333–334
in sentence patterns, 272–274
separated parts of, 254–255,
  329–330
simple tenses of, 331–333, 344
before the subject, 68
subject of, 251–253, 255–259,
  268, 272–278
  See also Subject of the verb.
tenses of, 330–340, 344
transitive, 261–262, 327–328, 343
troublesome, 461–464, 469
Vertical file in library, 224
Vocabulary
  building, 1–25
  of the senses, 27–51
  See also Words.

we, us, 320–321, 324
who, whom, 319–320, 324, 438–441, 453

Word parts
  prefixes, 520, 525
  suffixes, 520–523, 525
Words, 455–470
  antonyms, 19–22
  archaic (obsolete, outdated),
    457
  often confused, 457–460, 469
  context clues to meanings of,
    2–9, 22–24
  formal standard English, 456
  "hearing," 35–39, 117, 119
  inferring meaning of, 9–13,
    22–24
  informal standard English, 456
  commonly misspelled, 527–528
  multiple meanings of, 13–15,
    22, 24
  nonstandard English, 456–470
  as different parts of speech,
    387–391
  sensory, 27–51, 111–121, 131
  "sight," 28–35, 112–117
  slang, 457
  "smell," 47–49, 118, 120
  space, 112–115, 131
  spelling, 518–528
  standard English, 455–470
  synonyms, 16–22, 24–25, 159
  synonymy in dictionary, 17–18

"taste," 44–46, 118–119
time, 127–128, 131, 157–158
"touch," 39–43, 118–119
transitional, 157–162
troublesome verbs, 461–464
usage problems, 464–469
Writing
  abbreviations in, 534–535
  compositions, 133–165, 167–
    179
  correct form for, 529–535
  handwriting, 530
  letters, 181–206
  numbers in, 532–533
  papers, form for, 529–535
  paragraphs, 75–81, 83–109
    checklist for writing, 131
  process of, 75–81
  using the senses in, 27–51, 111–
    121, 131
  sentences, 53–73
    that don't make sense, 64–67

Yearbooks, 222
you, as understood subject, 258–
  259

ZIP code, 182, 184, 190
  list of state abbreviations, 184